Henry Steele Commager

The Story of the Second World War

BARNES
&NOBLE
BOOKS
NEW YORK

First published in 1945 by Little, Brown and Company

Copyright © 1991 by Henry Steele Commager

This edition published by Barnes & Noble, Inc.,
by arrangement with Brassey's, Inc.

"A Lou Reda Book"

1998 Barnes & Noble Books

ISBN 0-7607-0962-9

Printed and bound in the United States of America

98 99 00 01 02 M 9 8 7 6 5 4 3 2 1

FG

TABLE OF CONTENTS

PREFACE

THIS BOOK DOES not purport to be a history of the Second World War in any formal sense. It claims neither comprehensiveness nor authoritativeness. It is altogether too soon to write a systematic history of the war: even our own records are not now, and will not be for years, available to the student; records from our Allies are for the most part unavailable, and enemy records are either entirely inaccessible or destroyed. What this book does present is a series of stories, episodes, vignettes, descriptions, analyses, and historic statements by the men and women who participated in or observed or analyzed the war, all bound together with a very general, and by any rigorous scholarly standards, uncritical running narrative.

The material is drawn from a wide variety of sources. War correspondents loom large, for no other war was ever so fully covered. The radio and the newspaper contribute. Official statements, usually trustworthy enough, inevitably intrude. Here and there an historian or critic, convulsively attempting some degree of objectivity, is allowed his say.

I have not inquired too closely into the credentials of the contributors, nor attempted to correct errors, or what seem to be errors, of fact or of opinion. To do so at this state would be not only presumption but folly. Some day the official histories will be written, in scores and hundreds of volumes. Some day enemy sources will be available. Some day the great figures, political and military, who contrived victory or were responsible for defeat, will write their memoirs. We will never know the whole truth about this war, any more than we know the whole truth about the American Revolution or the Civil War, or World War I. It is some satisfaction to think that our children will know more of the causes and conduct of the war than it is permitted us to know.

But war is not only a matter of information and statistics. It is felt experience, and no later generation can quite recapture that experience. Here is the story of the war as it came to the American and the British people—as it looked and felt while the fighting was going on to those whose business or good fortune it was to be articulate about it.

The task of an editor is always a painful one. Limitations of space have required the exclusion of a great deal of material that ought to be in, the neglect of many major battles, campaigns and even theatres of the war. What is even more deplorable—reprehensible if you will—is that considerations of space required major surgical operations upon most of the source material. I hope the authors represented here will understand, and forgive me for not including their chapters and articles in whole rather than in part.

I am deeply grateful to those who assisted me in collecting the material for this book and seeing it through the press: to my wife, first of all, whose judgment is unerringly sound, and whose unflagging aid made enchanting what would otherwise have been drudgery; to Donald Porter Geddes, who played the role of Simon Legree but did not spare himself; to James Mitchell Clarke, Helen D. Livingston, Mary E. Marquette, Arnold Mitchell, Thelma Sargent, and Ernst Reichl; to the gracious librarians of the Rye Free Reading Room and the Columbia University Library who bore with me patiently.

This book is dedicated to my son.

HENRY STEELE COMMAGER

1

HOW WAR CAME

Collective Insecurity

BEFORE DAWN OF September 1, 1939, clouds of bombers and fighters flew eastward into the skies over Poland, raining death and destruction on helpless towns and villages, on airfields, railroads, bridges, and factories. From East Prussia, Pomerania, Silesia, and Slovakia mighty gray-clad armies poured across the frontiers into the doomed country. The greatest of wars was on, a war which was, in the end, to involve the whole world in one vast conflagration.

How did it happen that a generation still healing the desperate wounds of the War of 1914–18 permitted this second and more terrible war to come?

The explanation was to be found in the breakdown of the system of collective security and the growth of international anarchy, moral and political, in the post-war years.

For the emergence of moral anarchy the democracies were unprepared. The breakdown of collective security, however, was neither sudden nor unexpected. Its causes were inherent in the First World War and in the political and economic rearrangements that followed. There had indeed been little real security in the immediate post-war years, but there had been peace, of a sort, and a general acknowledgment of the sanctity of treaties and the necessity of preserving peace and maintaining international law. During the nineteen thirties international law was repudiated and peace shattered.

The democratic powers, victors in the last war, might have enforced the treaty settlements and maintained peace. They could have done this only by a positive policy of cooperation and by applying to the problems of peace the same zealous attention and energetic action that they displayed in the war. Instead each sought its own security and permitted the only effective instrument of international security—the League of Nations—to sink into futility and contempt. They lulled themselves into the belief that trouble could be avoided by the abandonment of the instruments of force and embarked upon the policy which became known by the name of appeasement.

1

The Rise of Dictators

If the democracies were thus willing to let treaties and international law go by default, the non-democracies were prepared to repudiate and flout them. Across the seas, unappreciated by the average American or Englishman, there had arisen a new threat to peace, to law, and, ultimately, to American security. This was totalitarianism, as expressed in the political organization of Italy, Germany, and Japan. The essence of totalitarianism was the subordination of all individual or social interests to the interests of the "master race" as represented in the State; its object, the division of the world into spheres of influence, each sphere to be controlled by a master nation; its method, the ruthless use of force. Italy, under Benito Mussolini, had inaugurated the first totalitarian state in 1922; Adolf Hitler, who became Chancellor of Germany in 1933, improved vastly on the Italian model; Japan, long inured to despotism, borrowed methods and techniques rather than philosophy from these European powers who were shortly to become allies.

Totalitarianism had developed in those states that had suffered defeat in the First World War or in the subsequent treaty arrangements, or that had experienced economic collapse and social demoralization in the postwar years. To the discontented leaders of these states, democratic processes seemed too slow and ineffectual for the accomplishment of domestic reforms, while the observation of international law and the maintenance of peace implied an acquiescence in the alleged injustices and inequalities of the *status quo*. Totalitarianism promised the articulation of every phase of economy and the regimentation of all activities of society to the service of the State, the suppression of protest and dissent, and the concentration of the whole energy of the nation on expansion and aggrandizement. It promised a solution of domestic difficulties, an escape from embarrassing international obligations, and, ultimately, power and prosperity in a new world order. That regimentation was to be achieved at the cost of liberty and democracy was no deterrent to those who thought liberty dangerous and democracy decadent; that the policy of expansion would usher in a new era of lawlessness and war did not discourage those who regarded law as an instrument for their oppression and who held war to be a positive good. Not for years did the democratic peoples appreciate the fact that this totalitarian philosophy was a threat to world peace and a challenge to the values of Christian civilization and to the inherent dignity of man.

The Bell Tolls

Early in the thirties the first of these totalitarian nations felt strong enough to strike. Japan, long restless under the limitations of the Open Door policy and the Nine Power Treaty, and determined to establish her hegemony in the Far East, invaded Manchuria in September 1931, crushed Chinese resistance, and, a year later, set up the puppet state of Manchukuo. The United States protested and the League of Nations condemned the aggression, but Japan ignored the American protest, withdrew from the League, and prepared to extend her conquests.

The moral was not lost on other discontented nations. Throughout the

twenties Germany had wrestled with the economic disorganization and
social demoralization that followed her defeat, and although Britain and
the United States had co-operated to ameliorate her condition, the crisis
was, by 1930, acute. German democracy seemed unable to cope with this
crisis, but Adolf Hitler and his national Socialist party promised relief
from economic ills, escape from the "bondage" of the Versailles Treaty,
and the union of the entire German race under one strong government. In
1933 the aged President von Hindenburg was persuaded to appoint Hitler
to the chancellorship, and within a few months all opposition leaders were
in jail and the national Socialist party had a firm grip on the entire political
and military machinery of the country. Hitler moved swiftly to consolidate
his position and implement his promises. Determined to make Germany
the greatest military power in the world, he contemptuously withdrew
from both the Geneva Disarmament Conference and the League of Nations and embarked upon a full-scale program of rearmament. And, as if
to dramatize his dissociation from the moral standards of the Western
world, he invoked the discredited doctrine of Aryan superiority to justify
a reign of terror against the Jews.

By 1935 Hitler felt sufficiently strong and sufficiently confident of democratic weakness openly to take the aggressive. In January of that year a
plebiscite, provided for in the Versailles Treaty, returned the Saar to Germany; having used the Treaty Hitler denounced it two months later, admitted that Germany had illegally created an air force, and openly
reintroduced compulsory military service. Faced with these *faits accomplis*,
distrustful of one another, and fearful of communist Russia, the European
signatories of the Versailles Treaty meekly acquiesced, while Britain rati-
fied the new arrangements by a formal agreement permitting Germany to
build her navy up to thirty-five percent of the total British tonnage, with an
even more generous allotment for submarines.

As early as 1927 Benito Mussolini had declared that 1935 would be the
turning point in European history and had promised the Italians that
when that time came "we shall be in a position to make our voice felt and
to see our rights recognized." Mussolini thought the time was now ripe to
re-establish the Roman Empire of ancient days. Ethiopia, which blocked
the way from Italian Libya to Italian Somaliland and which was reputed to
be rich in raw materials and weak in military power, seemed an easy victim
to start on. Early in 1935 Mussolini persuaded the slippery French Premier, Pierre Laval, to consent to an Italian conquest of Ethiopia, and
during the winter of 1935–36 that conquest was consummated. Haile Selassie, the Negus of Ethiopia, appealed to the League of Nations, which,
after tedious wrangling, denounced Italy as an aggressor nation and invoked against her the sanctions of arms, credits, and trade embargoes.
Italy had arms enough, however, and the exemption of iron, steel, copper,
and oil from the trade embargo made a joke of sanctions. It was inescapably clear that the League was impotent and that both France and Great
Britain preferred the dubious course of appeasement to the more honor-
able one of resistance. On March 7, when the conquest of Ethiopia was all
but complete, Mussolini agreed to arbitration "in principle"; that same day
Hitler denounced the Locarno Treaty, which he had expressly promised
to observe, and ordered his army into the demilitarized Rhineland.

It was clear that similar philosophies produced similar consequences in the realm of power politics. Both Germany and Italy were on record as indifferent to the obligations of treaties and of international law, and contemptuous alike of the League of Nations and of the democracies who so feebly supported it. The identity of interest of these two totalitarian states was shortly dramatized in one of the great crises in the history of modern Europe and of modern democracy—the Spanish Civil War. Restless under an incompetent and oppressive dictatorship the Spanish people, in 1931, had overthrown their decrepit monarchy and proclaimed a republic. The following years were troubled by the conflict of extreme conservative and extreme radical groups. The indecisive election of 1936 placed a Popular Front coalition government in uneasy control of the nation, but reactionary groups still commanded the support of the Church, the great landowners, and—above all—the army. Emboldened by promises of support from Italy and Germany, the Nationalists, as these reactionary groups came to be known, raised the standard of rebellion, and in mid-summer 1936 Spain was plunged into a devastating civil war that had much the same relation to the Second World War that the Kansas struggle of the 1850s had to the American Civil War.

Although the Republican regime was not a democratic one in the American sense, and although it had failed conspicuously to maintain order and safeguard liberty and property, it was clear that its defeat would constitute a severe setback for democracy and a signal triumph for the forces of reaction and of lawlessness. Nazi Germany and Fascist Italy saw this readily enough, and promptly made the cause of the Nationalists their own. The governments of Great Britain and France failed to appreciate the implications of this war, or feared that intervention might lead to a widening of the conflict which would involve all Europe. Russia alone actively supported the Loyalists, but was in no position to extend much assistance; and her support, raising as it did the bogey of Communism, further discouraged the timid governments of the democracies. So while Germany and Italy hurried hundreds of planes and tens of thousands of "volunteers" and enormous quantities of war material into the nationalist camp, Britain and France adopted the short-sighted and unheroic policy of nonintervention, and the United States Congress clamped an embargo on the shipment of munitions to either side. These divergent policies ultimately decided the outcome of the war, and a Nationalist dictatorship was set up under General Franco. The democracies condemned Republican Spain to defeat and dissolution; the totalitarian powers saw to it that their side won, and so gained an ally and enormous prestige.

Once more it was Japan's turn. That nation had followed up her early successes in Manchukuo with an invasion of Jehol and persistent efforts to wrest all the North China provinces from China proper. Those efforts proved unavailing, and in July 1937 Japan deliberately precipitated the "China incident" which was to plunge the Far East into a prolonged war. A hastily summoned international conference formally adjudged Japan an "aggressor" nation, but the pronouncement was unaccompanied by any positive acts, and both England and the United States continued to ship such war materials as oil and scrap iron to the guilty nation. Immensely superior in armaments, the Japanese swept from victory to victory, over-running most of northern China and all the important seaports, and placing themselves in a position to strike through Indo-China or Siam whenever that seemed politically desirable. The Chinese, under the leadership of the undaunted Chiang Kai-shek, retired to the interior, whence they fought a series of delaying actions against the invaders. From the United States and Great Britain they got sympathy, a driblet of supplies, and some small loans; but only Russia gave them any substantial aid in their fight for survival.

The pattern and the menace of totalitarian conquest were becoming clear enough, yet the democracies, unprepared to risk war, continued to follow a policy of appeasement. Nazi Germany, taking advantage of their military weakness, their mutual fears and suspicions, and their spiritual timidity, moved swiftly and boldly to the creation of the "new order" in which she should be the dominant world power and the German people the "master race." From the beginning of his political career Hitler had been committed to three major objectives: the reincorporation into a greater Germany of all German peoples, the control by Germany of Middle Europe and the road to the Middle East, and the erection of a totalitarian barrier against Communism. Already in 1936 he had called into existence the "Rome-Berlin" Axis, and an anti-Communist alliance which shortly embraced Japan, Italy, Spain, and Hungary, and which was designed quite as much to give respectability to totalitarianism as to frighten Russia. Secure in his new system of alliances, confident of the strength of the mighty military machine which he was creating, and emboldened by the ineptitude and demoralization of the governments of France and Britain and the isolation of Russia, Hitler inaugurated a policy of territorial aggrandizement.

Austria was the logical place to begin: she was small and defenseless, her population was largely German, she occupied a strategic position on the road to Italy and on the flank of Czechoslovakia, and her seizure would serve as a laboratory for further aggrandizements. Late in 1937 Hitler decided that union now with Austria was imperative, and in February of the following year he boasted of German power and promised the return to the Reich of ten million Germans beyond her frontiers. The next month the blow fell. While Britain and France held futile conferences, and Mussolini hid away, a Nazi fifth column in Austria took control of the army and the police. The plucky Austrian Chancellor, Schuschnigg, who had resisted Nazi aggression to the last, abdicated, and on the night of March 11 the German mechanized army pounded across the border and took over the helpless country. Two days later the union of Austria and Germany was formally announced. Without firing a gun Germany had added seven million people to her strength, had established her boundary at the Bremer pass, had flanked Czechoslovakia and interposed an effective barrier between Russia and France, and had vindicated her "strategy of terror."

Before the democracies had recovered from this shock, Hitler was ready for the next stroke. This time the prize was an even greater one. Czechoslovakia lay athwart German access to the Danubian Valley; she was rich in natural resources and in industry; her army and air force were powerful enough to be valuable prize but not sufficiently powerful to resist German might; she was thoroughly democratic and therefore a standing rebuke to totalitarian pretensions. In the Sudetenland, along the German border, lived some three million Germans. Hitler was ready to demand the cession of the Sudeten, yet the demand was not unaccompanied by risks. For little Czechoslovakia, it was thought, had powerful friends and allies. France was bound to her by the most solemn obligations; Russia was prepared to support her; Great Britain and the United States—which had been largely instrumental in her establishment—regarded her with affection. Throughout the spring and summer of 1938 Hitler stormed at the hapless Czechs while he alternately threatened and cajoled Britain and France. His tactics were successful. When, early in September, he demanded the immediate cession of the Sudeten, the English Government admonished the Czechs to yield. Abandoned by her friends Czechoslovakia capitulated, and the crisis seemed past. But apparently Hitler did not want so undramatic a victory, for he refused to await the outcome of a plebiscite or the slow processes of arbitration, and insisted on immediate and complete surrender. Determined to avoid war at all costs the British Prime Minister, Neville Chamberlain, flew to Hitler's mountain retreat at Berchtesgaden to plead for delay. The appeal seemed successful, but when the Czech Premier Beneš promised to resist invasion a new crisis arose. This time both Chamberlain and Daladier, Premier of France, made the pilgrimage to Hitler's Canossa. At the Munich Conference of September 29–30, Britain and France abandoned the little democracy to her fate. "I bring you peace with honor," said Chamberlain on his return to London. "I believe it is peace in our time." But Winston Churchill said, "Britain and France had to choose between war and dishonor. They chose dishonor. They will have war." The diagnosis was correct, the prophecy true.

Thus by 1938 the system of collective security had completely disintegrated. The Versailles territorial settlements of 1919, which had followed racial lines and popular will as closely as possible, had been repudiated, international law flouted, promises broken, the League of Nations reduced to impotence, and the doctrine that might makes for success triumphantly vindicated. Ruthlessness, treachery, and violence had proved stronger than the armor of a righteous cause. Ethiopia, Spain, China, Austria, Czechoslovakia, each in turn had been sacrificed by the democracies to the principle of appeasement, until it was clear that that principle was bankrupt. "If we have to fight," Chamberlain had said fatuously of the Czech crisis, "it must be on larger issues than this," and in America as in England and France millions echoed the sentiment. But three centuries ago an English preacher-poet, John Donne, had pointed out that mankind is a unit and that injury to any part of it hurts the whole. Alluding to the custom of churches tolling a "passing bell" when a parishioner died, he wrote:

> Who bends not his ears to any bell, which upon any occasion rings? but who can remove it from that bell, which is passing a peece of himselfe out of this world? No man is an Iland, intire of it selfe; every man is a peece of the Continent, a part of the maine; if a Clod bee washed away by the Sea, Europe is the lesse, as well as if a Promontorie were, as well as if a Mannor of thy friends or of thine owne were; any mans death diminishes me, because I am involved in Mankinde; And therefore never send to know for whom the bell tolls; *it tolls for thee.*

The bell tolled for Britain and France, for Holland and Belgium, for Denmark and Norway, even for the United States, when Ethiopia, Spain, Austria, and Czechoslovakia passed, but its somber notes were muffled and dim.

War

For Hitler Munich was not only a diplomatic triumph; it was a moral one. The democracies had been brought to the verge of war and on an issue which would have justified war in the eyes of the world; they had looked into the abyss and reeled back in dismay. Munich had revealed not only the unwillingness of Britain and France to stand by their commitments and fight for their principles; it had uncovered, too, the hollowness of the Franco-Russian agreement and the inability—or unwillingness—of the democracies to co-operate with the one European power that might have saved them. Emboldened by this spectacle of timidity and dissension, confident that his tactics were both sure and safe, Hitler drove implacably ahead. In March 1939 he sent his army into Czechoslovakia, and, while Britain and France looked helplessly on, dismembered that hapless country. Back in the United States, Senator Borah explained to a bemused Congress that this was not a violation of the Pact of Paris, and as if to confound him Mussolini three days later seized little Albania. In May the two totalitarian leaders concluded a formal military alliance, directed against France and Britain. When Franklin Delano Roosevelt, in a message of April 14, asked for specific guarantees that Germany would not attack some twenty little countries, Hitler replied with a masterpiece of evasion, defiance, and chicanery which revealed not so much his ingenuity as his contempt for American concepts of international morality. Then, drunk with success, the German Feuhrer turned on Poland, demanding the return of the Free City of Danzig and a wide zone across the Polish Corridor. Edified by the fate of Czechoslovakia when she had yielded to the first demands for the Sudeten, Poland refused to cave in, but agreed to arbitrate. Hitler promptly inaugurated that war of nerves which had so often been a prelude to surrender—or to the war of weapons.

Thoroughly frightened now, England and France attempted to repair the damage of prolonged appeasement. But the diplomatic humpty-dumpty had had so great a fall that it was quite impossible to put it together again. France distrusted Britain and Britain, France—and both with some reason; Russia had lost confidence in both of them; the smaller nations could not fail to read the moral of Munich and of Prague. Yet Britain and France pushed doggedly ahead. They offered to guarantee Poland against aggression—though they failed conspicuously to indicate how they proposed to do this. They gratuitously presented guarantees against attack to Greece and Rumania, and Britain concluded a hasty alliance with Turkey. These tardy gestures heartened the democracies as little as they frightened the totalitarian states. As if to test the realism of the British, Russia proposed an alliance on the understanding that she be permitted to march troops into Poland and to take the Baltic states of Latvia, Lithuania, and Estonia into "protective custody." Acquiescence in this proposal might have exposed the British government to the charge of insincerity in its zeal for the welfare of the non-aggressor nations, and the proposal was rejected. Of necessity, perhaps, Russia turned to Germany, and on August 23 the world was startled to learn that the two great antagonists had concluded a non-aggression pact.

This was nothing less than a disaster, but though there was a strong faction in both Britain and France that advocated further appeasement, this time the two governments did not back down. Hitler promptly renewed his demands on Poland, but when he offered to "guarantee" the British Empire in return for a free hand in Poland, the British reply was firm: "His Majesty's government have obligations to Poland by which they are bound and which they intend to honour." Perhaps Hitler did not take seriously this display of firmness; perhaps he was sufficiently confident of his military power to discount any aid which Britain and France might be able to give Poland or any damage they might inflict on Germany.

On August 25 Roosevelt sent a final plea to Hitler: "Countless human lives can be yet saved and hope may still be restored that the nations of the modern world may even now construct a foundation for a peaceful and happier relationship if you . . . will agree to the pacific means of settlement accepted by the Government of Poland."

On the afternoon of September first, twelve hours after he had attacked Poland, Hitler replied that he had "left nothing untried for the purpose of settling the dispute in a friendly manner."[1]

2

JUGGERNAUT OVER EUROPE

The Belligerents

ON SEPTEMBER 3 millions of people all over the civilized world, their radios alert to every step in the unfolding tragedy of the European war, heard the grave but firm voice of Neville Chamberlain announcing that Britain, in fulfillment of her commitments, was at war with Germany. "Now," he concluded, "may God bless you all. May He defend the right. It is the evil things we shall be fighting against—brute force, bad faith, injustice, oppression, and persecution—and against these I am certain that the right will prevail."

That same day, reluctantly, as we now know, France too went to war. And, with the single exception of Eire, the British Commonwealth of nations rallied to the support of the mother country and of the good cause.

Thus the war, which Hitler had hoped to confine to a series of episodes, was under way; thus the great combination against Hitler was already beginning to be formed.

Superficially, the belligerents seemed not unevenly matched. As the historians Grove Haines and Ross Hoffman put it:

From the strictly military point of view, the initial advantage lay with the Germans, despite the greater reservoirs of manpower on the Franco-Polish-British side. Although Germany's standing army numbered approximately 850,000 and was capable of expansion to 10,000,000, the combined armies of France (750,000), Great Britain (250,000), and Poland (450,000) were numerically greater at the moment and potentially greater in the future. But sheer numbers were relatively unimportant. What counted most was the will and determination to fight, tactical and strategical ingenuity, and, especially, superiority in mechanized equipment. In these respects, Germany held the advantage. When hostilities began, she had five fully equipped panzer divisions and an industrial establishment organized to supply others when needed. The Allies had no comparable forces, having confided chiefly in implements of defense that had proved their use-

9

fulness a quarter of a century earlier. Germany enjoyed also a heavy preponderance of air power. It is likely that she had as many as 12,000 planes of all categories, half of which were first line and the remainder reserve. Moreover, German factories were producing as many as 1,200 planes a month. In contrast, the Allies probably had no more than 8,000 planes and a capacity production which did not exceed 700 or 800 per month. Of even greater significance was the fact that Germany had integrated the air force with the other fighting services and had developed it as an offensive instrument, whereas the Allies continued to regard the air arm as of secondary importance.

If Germany held the edge in military equipment and organization, it was the Allies who enjoyed preponderance on the seas. The British and French fleets together totalled nearly 2,000,000 tons, as against approximately 235,000 tons for the German. Allied strength in capital ships alone was more than three times that of the enemy. And yet the disparity between the belligerents was hardly as great as these figures would indicate, for while the Nazis could limit their naval operations principally to the North Sea and the Baltic the Allies were required to disperse their strength to patrol the seven seas. Moreover, Germany relied upon the submarine, and in this instrument she enjoyed more than equality with the enemy.

The larger and better equipped army or navy may win the first battles, but unless they can be perpetually reinforced and strengthened, their losses repaired, and their instruments refurbished, they may not be capable of winning the war. In the long run, it is the industrial machine behind the lines, geared to the peak of efficiency and with available materials, which may decide the issue.

Germany began the war with an industrial machine second only to that of the United States and already keyed to the pitch of war-time needs. Toward this end all German economic planning had been pointed during the preceding six years. On the other hand, Britain and France had done little preliminary planning and had preserved their essentially peace-time economies until the end. This was not considered, however, to be an insurmountable obstacle, for their combined shipping and credits would enable them to outdistance their enemy, if given sufficient time.[1]

Poland

But Germany did not intend to give any of her victims sufficient time, and soon the melancholy phrase "too little and too late" was to sound like a dirge over Allied military operations.

Poland, certainly, did not have sufficient time to organize her defense, nor was time vouchsafed the Allies to come to her aid. Czechoslovakia, with her vast armament industry and her modern army, might have helped, but Czechoslovakia was dismembered and prostrate. Russia might have helped, but Russia had a non-aggression pact with Germany and she was, in any event, unprepared to challenge Nazi might. So Poland fought alone.

The conquest of Poland was swift, violent, and overwhelming, a stunning revelation of the potentialities of mechanized warfare, a dress rehearsal for action in the west. Within a week the Nazis had broken through to the defenses of Warsaw; within a month the Poles had capitulated, and the fighting was over. Yet we must remember that, notwithstanding all the might hurled against her, Poland held out as long as France did the following spring.

For the invasion the Nazis had massed 73 divisions—14 of them armored—some 4,000 planes, and thousands of tanks and motorized vehicles. Against this tremendous array the Poles were able to mobilize only some 22 infantry divisions, 8 cavalry brigades, and a single motorized brigade, and perhaps 1,000 planes, most of them antiquated. Time did not permit the mobilization of the whole of the Polish army, and the destruction of bridges and railroads made it impossible for the Poles to bring into combat a substantial part of their reserves west of the Bug.

The German campaign was planned with masterly skill. Three great armies converged on Warsaw—one from East Prussia, one from Pomerania, and one, under Von Rundstedt, who was to be heard from later, from the south. Western Poland offered no natural barriers to an advancing enemy, no convenient defense line. Hopelessly outnumbered, without planes or armor, the Polish defenses cracked. Otto Tolischus, who saw the campaign, describes what happened the first week:

With the German Armies in Poland, September 11—Having hurled against Poland their mighty military machine, the Germans are today crushing Poland like a soft-boiled egg.

After having broken through the shell of Polish border defenses, the Germans found inside, in comparison with their own forces, little more than a soft yolk, and they have penetrated that in many directions without really determined general resistance by the Polish Army.

That is the explanation of the apparent Polish military collapse in so short a time as it was gathered on a tour of the Polish battlefields made by this correspondent in the wake of the German Army and, sometimes, in the backwash of a day's battle while scattered Polish troops and snipers were still taking potshots at motor vehicles on the theory that they must be Germans. But such is the firm confidence of the Germans that a cocked pistol in front of the army driver is held to be sufficient protection for the foreign correspondents in their charge.

Even a casual glance at the battlefields, gnarled by trenches, barbed-wire entanglements, shell holes, blown-up roads and bridges and shelled and gutted towns, indicates that the Poles made determined resistance at the border. But even these border defenses seem weak, and beyond them there is nothing.

It is a mystery to both Germans and neutral military experts on the tour with the writer that the Poles made no provisions for second or third lines and that in retreat they did not attempt to throw up earthworks or dig trenches such as helped the Germans stop the Allies after the Marne retreat in 1914.

In fact, the only tactics the Poles seemed to have pursued in the retreat were to fall back on towns from which, later, they were either easily driven out by artillery fire or just as easily flanked. But presumably neither their number nor their equipment, which, judging from the remnants thrown along the road of retreat, was pitifully light as compared with the Germans', permitted them to do anything else in view of the enormous length of the border they had to defend.

Again God has been with the bigger battalions, for the beautiful, dry weather, while converting Polish roads into choking dust clouds on the passage of motor vehicles, has kept them from turning into mud as would be normal at this time of year; this has permitted the German motorized divisions to display the speed they have.

But the Germans have proceeded not only with might and speed, but with method, and this bids fair to be the first war to be decided not by infantry, "the queen of all arms," but by fast motorized divisions and, especially, by the air force.

The first effort of the Germans was concentrated on defeating the hostile air fleet, which they did not so much by air battle but by consistent bombing of airfields and destruction of the enemy's ground organization. Having accomplished this, they had obtained domination of the air, which in turn enabled them, first, to move their own vast transports ahead without danger from the air and, second, to bomb the Poles' communications to smithereens, thereby reducing their mobility to a minimum.

Today the German rule of the air is so complete that, although individual Polish planes may still be seen flying at a high altitude, the German army has actually abandoned the blackout in Poland. It is a strange sensation to come from a Germany thrown into Stygian darkness at night to a battlefront town like Lodz, as this correspondent did the night after the Germans announced its occupation, and find it illuminated although the enemy is only a few miles from the city.

With control of the air, the Germans moved forward not infantry but their tanks, armored cars and motorized artillery, which smashed any Polish resistance in the back. This is easy to understand when one has seen the methods of open warfare attempted by the Poles and an almost amateurish attempt at digging earthworks for machine-gun nests.

To German and neutral experts the Poles seem to have clung to eighteenth-century war methods, which, in view of modern firing volume and weight, are not only odd but also futile. This does not mean that the Poles have not put up a brave fight. They have, and the Germans themselves freely admit it.

As a purely military matter, the German army is the height of efficiency. It moves like clockwork, without hurry and apparently almost in a leisurely manner. Yet that army moves with inexorable exactitude. The roads into Poland are jammed but not choked with heavy vans and motor trucks carrying food and munitions, while the Poles have to depend mainly on their smashed railroads or on horse carts. Bombed bridges are soon passable for the Germans and they move forward quickly. Communication lines follow them almost automatically.[2]

By September 8 von Rundstedt was hammering at the outer defenses of Warsaw. Another week and the two armies from the north had encircled 170,000 Poles at Kutno, one hundred miles west of Warsaw, and annihilated them. The Polish corridor was cut; the great Polish port of Gdynia assaulted and captured.

Meantime other German armies were slicing in to the rear of Warsaw from north and south. Von Kuechler, advancing from East Prussia, had tried to force the heavily fortified Narew River line only to meet with a severe check. Once again armor and new techniques of warfare overcame mere courage.

Warsaw, invested on the ninth, was by now completely encircled, and battered day and night by heavy artillery and bombers. Food was low; water, gas, and electricity gone; on the 26th ammunition ran out. Two days later came the formal surrender. Resistance continued, in isolated spots, for a few more days—in Lublin and Lwow to the south, in the Carpathians, on the Hel Peninsula. An officer who participated in that last fight has left a record of it.

"Hel was really a mathematical trap for us," the Commander once said. "Thirty-five kilometres of peninsula produced in numbers seventy kilometres of coast line. But what did that amount to, since the peninsula in its widest spot extended only two kilometres and its narrowest point covered only 150 metres. That's good for statistics, but not for living. In addition to Hel we had only sixty-five kilometres of coast line. Just compare now our poverty with these thousands which surround us here and tell me what we were to do with our love."

It may have been that the consciousness of this disproportion and in-commensurability with the world was one of the incentives of Polish ambition and in time of war a spur to increased resistance. In any case Hel was defended as fiercely as one defends a most ardent love.

When Colonel Dabek's last shot rang out in the ravine on Oksywie, Polish resistance was transferred to the peninsula. Cut off from the mainland on the fourteenth of September, Hel had not much more than two thousand soldiers for its defense and from the first day of the war had been subjected to most trying ordeals. First came the air attacks which set fire to the pine forests made dry by the continued hot weather. Into this conflagration whose smoke the wind would not blow away fell bombs and artillery shells. Two German cruisers, obsolete but equipped with new guns, the *Schlesien* and the *Schleswig-Holstein*—the latter known to the Poles from the battle on Westerplatte—shelled Hel with 280 millimetre guns. Two 150 millimetre batteries mounted on mobile platforms, an armored train coming up from Puck, and the artillery of the attacking infantry kept up a constant barrage from the conquered coast.

In this rain of fire one did not know where to take cover or whom to fight. Day after day news came of another ship sunk, of another fierce attack. At one time thirty-five bombs were dropped on the submarine *Sep* and fifty-three on the *Rys*. The crews of the rescued boats came out only half conscious.

But the fearful nervous tension and the fury of destruction did not overcome the defenders. The hopeless position, being surrounded by the sea and being fired at from all sides, did not keep them from returning a constant fire.

Hel did not have an air field and was forced to defend itself from the ground. The anti-aircraft gunners performed wonders. Their companions looked upon this duel of gunners bound to the peninsula-raft with swarms of planes circling overhead as the only possible means of retaliation. Every plane shot down was rewarded by loud shouts from all the units. Not a day passed in which the almost deafened garrison did not raise such a cheer.

The guns of the ships which had been damaged in battle and which had returned only to sink were demounted and set up in new positions; the sailors became infantrymen and gunners. Those trawlers which had not yet been sunk went out each night on unbelievably difficult missions among the German ships to lay mines in the Bay of Danzig which seemed to be completely occupied by the enemy. At the tip of the peninsula the commander of the battery stood wrapped in bandages beside his guns, having willfully escaped from the hospital. One Polish salvo landed accurately on the cruiser *Schleswig-Holstein*, disabled one of its gun turrets, and silenced its biggest guns.

By land, however, the foe was slowly entering upon the Polish dam. He was repulsed by counterattacks one of which, made by sailors, annihilated the intruders and reached as far as Swarzew. But the Germans returned a second and a third time, with fresh forces. The main attack was entrusted to a crack regiment, the famous Klehm-Regiment, named after its commander.

After being painfully mauled in these frontal assaults by the desperate men on Hel they adopted tactics to which there seemed to be no answer. They massed an enormous amount of artillery and began shelling the earth of the narrow peninsula metre by metre, with a fire which nothing could withstand. The attacking infantry came upon a veritable debris of terrain which had once demanded so much toil and labor in order to exist and maintain itself in the sea. Hel, attacked in this way at its base, under artillery fire along its entire length, and shattered by the strongest concentration of fire at its tip, was being engulfed by an irresistible force.

Headquarters was forced to try its last chance. It was decided to blow up the narrowest portion of the peninsula and thus cut themselves off from the attacking Germans, at least for some time.

"In place of the peninsula we were to create an island," the Commander said, "I was commanded to carry out the order."

As commander of the submarine fleet he had under his control the supplies of torpedoes used by the submarines. Because these ships had all been damaged there was no further point in keeping the torpedoes. They were designated for another task now, for ground defense. The Commander planned to use them for mine fields.

The torpedo heads were used for this purpose. They are the forward parts, filled with explosives. Their strength was great; they weighed 660-700 pounds apiece.

The Commander decided to lay down three mine fields. One was to be located a kilometre beyond the locality Chalupy; the second three kilometres behind the first; and the third before Kuznice, approximately in the middle of the peninsula where there were previously erected concrete reinforcements.

The torpedo heads were arranged in chessboard fashion at intervals of ten meters. They were connected by a detonating fuse. A firing post was built in a special trench behind the mine field from which one motion of a hand was to blow the isthmus into the air. The post was also connected with the underground explosive system of the field by means of a detonating fuse and in addition to that by means of double electric wires. This gave a maximum certainty that the explosion would not fail. Immediately behind the mine field there was a forest. A belt running parallel to the field was cut down and an abatis constructed from it. The first line was completed on the twentieth of September. Hel was mined. The Commander began the construction of the second and third fields.

Meanwhile the battle was continuing as usual beyond the field. The Germans after each attack brought their artillery up closer and set up barbed wire defenses. On the twentieth a Polish counterattack was still able to penetrate their defenses and drive back the invaders from conquered ground. But five days later Hel was to become an island.

As always the Germans began their action with a fierce artillery barrage. An hour long hurricane of fire flooded the small area with exploding lava. Then the infantry moved in for attack. Signalmen ran along the beaches in the first line. They signalled to observers how far the infantry had reached and where to throw the artillery fire forward. Our units kept withdrawing until they were behind the mine field. A mining patrol with a naval officer, Lieutenant J., remained in the firing post.

"I talked with him afterwards," the Commander said. "You can easily guess how curious I was about every detail. Night and day I couldn't rest, not knowing whether my work would be of any use. My part was the preparation; one second alone was to decide the matter without me. The lieutenant told me that he had a moment of anxious suspense. He saw the Germans coming into the open terrain and the artillery throwing its fire forward metre by metre. They passed the ruined houses in Chalupy, entered finally on the mine field, and reached the clearing where we had built the abatis. The deciding moment was approaching, my lone second. Lieutenant J. threw the electric switch—we call it a lighter. Would there be an explosion or not? The artillery might have disrupted the connection with the firing post. But the torpedoes apparently felt secure in their hiding places. Ten tons exploded under ground. Separate craters joined swiftly; the water rushed in from both sides and covered the breach almost instantly. The German attack was halted in that chasm. Hel became an island. That was my apogee," he concluded.

While telling me about this the Commander did not vary his controlled voice. He never commented on the related facts. Now he limited himself to a few words.

"That second gave me a foretaste of victory, something that fate denied us in this war. Despair is not the natural substance of life, even though one can live on narcotics. For a while only, but one can do it."

Hel lived through in this fashion to the first of October. It obstinately defended the remaining shred of Polish earth. The battles diminished the new island, unknown on any map, even more. Withdrawing forces blew up the second line and took cover behind the last. Further defense became impossible, however; provisions and ammunition were exhausted.

On the first of October at two in the afternoon all military activity ceased according to the conditions of surrender. Five minutes before that, at 1:55, Polish artillery brought down one more plane. It repulsed the last very fierce air attack made by the Germans which seemed to have no intelligible cause except a wild desire to kill Poles.

It was the fifty-third plane shot down in defense of the sea. Afterwards Hel was silent.[3]

The fall of Warsaw, even the forcing of the Narew River, would not necessarily have spelled the end of Poland. But in the midst of the fight against the Nazi invader, a new situation arose. On September 17 the Russians, anxious now for their own defense, marched in from the east. Confronted with the *Wehrmacht* on the west, the Red Army on the east, resistance collapsed. On September 28, as the battered remnants of Warsaw were surrendered, Germany and Russia arranged the partition of Poland. The boundary ran roughly along the old Curzon Line of 1919. To Russia went the larger territory, but only one-third the population and few of the industrial resources in which western Poland was so rich. But what Russia wanted was space in which to erect a barrier against possible German attack. For this even eastern Poland was not enough. Soon came a demand for military and naval bases in the Baltic Republics of Estonia, Latvia, and Lithuania, which were perforce conceded. The following June, when the collapse of France had freed the Germans for further ventures, Russia took over these three states as well as Bessarabia and Bukowina from Rumania.

One other frontier gave the Russians concern, and to that, having secured themselves along the Baltic Sea, they now turned their attention.

Finland

From 1809 to 1917 Finland had been part of Czarist Russia. In the general collapse of the Russian Revolution she achieved—with some outside aid—her independence. The loss was not serious, nor was an independent Finland any threat to the Soviet Union. But a Finland controlled by a hostile power was a different matter. From the Karelian Peninsula such a power might attack Leningrad; from Petsamo she might threaten the supply port of Murmansk on the Arctic.

There was not, to be sure, any reason, in the fall of 1939, to suppose that Finland might lend herself to any such designs or fall prey to any hostile power. But the Nazi conquest of Poland had made Russia nervous. She was successful in building up a defense barrier from the Baltic to Rumania. She wanted to protect herself similarly in the north. On October 5 went the first request to Finald for a conference to discuss "certain questions of a concrete political nature." What these questions were soon emerged: Russia wanted a rectification of the Russo-Finnish frontier on the Karelian and to the north, and a lease on the strategically important island of Hangoe in the Gulf of Finland. Finland yielded on everything but Hangoe. On November 13 negotiations were broken off; on the 30th

Russian planes bombed Viipuri and Helsinki. The League of Nations, at its last gasp, expelled Russia!

The world, which had expected an easy conquest, was shortly astonished at the skill and tenacity of the Finnish defence. The Russians launched five heavy attacks: on the Mannerheim Line along the Karelian Isthmus, north of Lake Ladoga, in central Finland at Suomussalmi, still farther north at Salla, and from Murmansk towards Petsamo. This latter town was captured, but elsewhere the Russians, unprepared for winter fighting, unfamiliar with the terrain, and—it would seem—badly led, suffered costly defeats. North of Lake Ladoga the Finns cut three Russian divisions to pieces; at Suomussalmi two more divisions were wiped out. Virginia Cowles describes this battlefield of ice and snow, white forests and glassy lakes, shortly after the Russian defeat:

Kajaani served as G.H.Q. for the Central Command. There in the slender waistline of Finland, some of the fiercest battles of the war were taking place. During the previous seven weeks, over a hundred thousand Russian troops had crossed the frontier, in repeated attempts to cut Finland in two. But the Finns had repulsed the onslaughts with some of the most spectacular fighting in history; they had annihilated entire divisions and hurled back others thirty and forty miles to the border from where they started.

To understand how they did it, you must picture a country of thick snow-covered forests and ice-bound roads. You must visualize heavily-armed ski patrols sliding like ghosts through the woods; creeping behind the enemy lines and cutting their communications until entire battalions were isolated, then falling on them in furious surprise attacks. In this part of Finland skis out-manœuvred tanks, sleds competed with lorries, and knives even challenged rifles.

We approached the village of Suomussalmi just as dawn was breaking, and here I witnessed the most ghastly spectacle I have ever seen. It was in this sector that the Finns, a few weeks previously had annihilated two Russian divisions of approximately 30,000 men. The road along which we drove was still littered with frozen Russian corpses, and the forests on either side had become known as "Dead Man's Land." Perhaps it was the beauty of the morning that made the terrible Russian *débâcle* all the more ghastly when we came upon it. The rising sun had drenched the snow-covered forests, with trees like lace valentines, with a strange pink light that seemed to glow for miles. The landscape was marred only by the charred framework of a house; then an overturned truck and two battered tanks. Then we turned a bend in the road and came upon the full horror of the scene. For four miles the road and forests were strewn with the bodies of men and horses; with wrecked tanks, field kitchens, trucks, gun-carriages, maps, books, and articles of clothing. The corpses were frozen as hard as petrified wood and the colour of the skin was mahogany. Some of the bodies were piled on top of each other like a heap of rubbish, covered only by a merciful blanket of snow; others were sprawled against the trees in grotesque attitudes.

All were frozen in the positions in which they had died. I saw one with his hands clasped to a wound in his stomach; another struggling to open the collar of his coat; and a third pathetically clasping a cheap landscape drawing, done in bright, childish colours, which had probably been a prized possession that he had tried to save when he fled into the woods. They were everywhere, hundreds and hundreds of grotesque wooden corpses; in the ditches, under the trees, and even in dugouts beneath the snow where they had tried to escape from the fury of the attack. I learned, with a shock, that they had been members of the 44th Division—the same division that just a year ago I had been swinging along the country roads in the Ukraine.

What these troops must have suffered from the cold was not difficult to imagine. They were wearing only ordinary knitted hoods with steel helmets over them, and none of them had gloves on. This was accounted for by the fact that the Russians didn't wear "trigger finger" mittens as the Finns did; they wore only ordinary mittens which they had to take off to fire their rifles. And how they must have suffered from hunger; the horses had even eaten the bark off the trees.

I was staggered by the amount of equipment they had brought with them. Although the Finns had hauled away all the usable stuff the ditches were still gutted with battered lorries, machine-guns, bayonets, helmets—even an amphibian tank which seemed pretty useless in a country of frozen lakes. Our Finnish officer told us for at least a week after the battle it was impossible to drive down the road at all. As it was, our chauffeur had to thread his way along the four-mile stretch slowly. Near the end of it, we passed a group of Finnish boys playing in the roadside, curiously prodding the corpses. They had taken one of the bodies and stuck it head down in the snow; all we could see was two brown stems with boots at the end. . . .

From a military point of view, the Russian onslaught will be studied as one of the most fantastic campaigns in history. All through the north the Russian High Command ignored the elementary necessity of keeping open its lines of communications. Thousands of Russian soldiers were sent into the wilds of Finland to be isolated from their bases and swallowed up by the forests. This extraordinary stupidity was hard to understand. The only explanation was that Russia had reckoned on a blitzkrieg lasting only a few days and had organized the campaign accordingly. The first divisions had been equipped with an enormous amount of propaganda, banners and pennants, which they had expected to distribute among a vanquished people; and in the north, a Division entered with a brass band, actually expecting to be welcomed by the people it had been sent to "liberate." The reason the Kremlin was so greatly misinformed as to the political stamina of Finland may have been due to the fact that Soviet observers were afraid to reveal the true state of affairs for fear of being shot as saboteurs.[4]

After these costly defeats the Russians abandoned the effort to drive through snow-bound wilderness and began a direct attack upon the Mannerheim Line. Here Russian superiority in man-power, artillery, and planes could make itself felt and here, after two months of the hardest kind of fighting, a breakthrough was achieved.

On March 11 the Russians occupied Viipuri; the next day Finland surrendered. Russia obtained what she asked for, and the new boundary line west of Viipuri and Lake Ladoga may well have saved Leningrad two years later. The cost in lives was high, the cost in moral support from the democracies higher still, but from the Russian point of view the balance was clearly on the credit side of the ledger.

The Phony War

What were France and Britain doing while the German armies were fighting in Poland? If they were unable to bring direct aid to Poland, they might at least have furnished a distraction in the west. But there was no attack. There was war at sea, to be sure, but on land the British contented themselves with dropping leaflets, the French with nibbling at the German frontier. Even this was not meant to be taken seriously, and after a short time the French pulled back. High Command directed that all but outposts be withdrawn. The Germans promptly attacked and rewon the strategically important strip of ground. Strategicus has pointed the moral of this story:

This, of course, by itself was no great matter. It is true that the French had abandoned all the ground they had gained at some cost; but ground in the final analysis means little, as a rule. But something else had been abandoned with the lost ground, though it is difficult to think it was intended or even realized at the time. The positions commanding the territory over which any advance must take place had been abandoned; and that was of importance, since the fact signified the abandonment of the idea of an offensive. There is a mind in events whatever the causes that produce them. This event now took charge of the French strategy and the French outlook. It dominated every future development, so that the initiative was left to the Germans, even for the most part in the raiding activity; and the French came to regard their role as purely defensive. It was almost inevitable; but it was fatal. The conviction spread and drew increasing strength that the Germans would never attack the Maginot Line, since it was to all intents and purposes impregnable. Men were demobilized and sent back to their homes; and France settled down to allow the war to take its course.

In the long and bitter winter the French came to think that they had only to sit tight behind their fortress wall, putting up with the hardships as best they could; and somehow the war would be won.[5]

Clearly the French were unready for war, and their unreadiness was more psychological than military. They had been bled white in the last war, and they hoped to confine this one to proper limits. During the previous years they had built the great Maginot Line—though failing, curiously, to extend it to the sea—and the Maginot, or defensive, psychology possessed them. The Germans, too, had their line—the Siegfried or West Wall, even more modern, even more formidable, but they did not allow it to dominate their strategy. During the first six months of the war French and Germans established themselves along their respective lines, and permitted few untoward incidents to mar their harmonious relations. Edmond Taylor reminds us what things were like at the front during this period of "phony war":

The real front was three or four miles farther into Germany. From the window of the officers' mess in a villa on the hillside, where a friendly captain led us for lunch, pending determination of our fate, we looked out across the Saar Valley at the front as passengers on a ship look at the equator. What we saw was a green and pleasant land, rising to gently curving, wooded heights, dotted here and there with toylike Teutonic villages: Hitlerdorf, held by the French; Bubingen, in the Saar, still German. Somewhere between in the landscape was the front. Nothing marked it. In fact later on, after another trip, I wrote, "You know when you are at the front when the landscape, which has been military, becomes simply pastoral and empty."

There were no shell-holes, no bomb craters, no blasted tree-trunks, no ruined houses or broken windows. After the sordid battlefields of Spain which had given me the same idea of war that a brutal sexual initiation gives to a young girl of love, this seemed miraculous and a comfort. It did not seem terrible to me that men should be dying in these green fields; moreover, I knew that not many were dying or the fields would not be so green. (A few days later a semi-official agency declared that the French army had suffered more casualties in automobile accidents than at the front. . . .)

In Sarreguemines, while we were awaiting the examination of our papers in the hallway of the local high school, which was then the headquarters of a French division, the war came to us in greeting. Whistles blew and a droning sound began and guns started going off. There was a stampede of bodies as soldiers rushed, not to get under cover but out in the courtyard to see. Out of sight to us—but the soldiers' eyes saw them—two German planes were passing almost directly overhead and the anti-aircraft batteries were sowing mushroom beds of white and black puffs in the warm sky.

The little soldiers wanted to crane and point, excited, but the officers reminded them about cover and they rearranged themselves obediently in the shade of things.

"You see they are getting to be quite prudent," said an officer in kind approval.

I thought what a strange war where imprudence is discouraged, but remembered that it is in courting, too, and this war was at the stage of courtship. . . .

Correspondents in Luxembourg who from neutral soil were able to study the effects of both German and French fire were convinced that the gunners on both sides deliberately tried not only to avoid damaging civilian property but to avoid inflicting serious losses. The uncanny accuracy with which shells framed objectives where infantry were certain to be sheltered, dropping all around but almost never directly upon the target, was too frequent to be accidental, the observers in Luxembourg thought. Whether that is true or not, I saw myself some striking demonstrations of the live-and-let-live principle.[6]

"Hitler," said Neville Chamberlain—and it was perhaps his most fatuous remark—"has missed the bus." But moral dry rot was preparing the way for the collapse of France. And Hitler was massing his most powerful weapons for a renewal of the blitz.

Denmark and Norway

On February 25 that astute observer William L. Shirer confided to his journal that:

X told me a fantastic story today. He claims a plot is afoot to hide S.S. shock troops in the bottom of a lot of freighters, have them put in at ports in Scandinavia, Belgium, and Africa, and seize the places. I don't get the point. Even if they got into the ports, which is doubtful, how could they hold them?

And a month later:

I hope I didn't put myself out on a limb, but from what I've heard this week I wrote tonight in my broadcast: "Some people here believe the war may spread to Scandinavia yet. It was reported in Berlin today that last week a squadron of at least nine British destroyers was concentrated off the Norwegian coast and that in several instances German freighters carrying iron received warning shots. . . . From here it looks as if the neutrals, especially the Scandinavians, may be drawn into the conflict after all."[7]

Mr. Shirer was not out on a limb. At four o'clock in the morning of April 9 German armies rolled across the unfortified frontier of Denmark, with whom the Germans had recently concluded a non-aggression pact. An hour later the Danish government was presented with an ultimatum. There was nothing to do but accept it. Denmark, however, was not to be "conquered." It was to be a model protectorate, a laboratory of the New Order. But even when on their good behavior the Nazis were unable to conciliate the people of an occupied country. Soon the usual process of exploitation and looting began, and soon, too, the Danish resistance movement was organized and began its long and heroic campaign of sabotage.

As German troops were marching across the Danish frontier at Flensburg, powerful elements of the German navy, with numerous transport and supply ships, were steaming into every important Norwegian port: Oslo, Kristiansand, Stavanger, Bergen, Trondheim, and Narvik. The Norwegians were caught unprepared: whether general treachery was responsible for some of that unpreparedness is still to be determined. Yet everywhere but at Narvik they put up a stout resistance, inflicting heavy losses on the invaders. A. D. Divine tells what happened in Oslofjord:

In Oslofjord, the great indentation which continues the inverted "V" of the Skagerrak and the Kattegat and thrusts seventy miles into the very heart of Norway, there was a handful of ships. In Horten harbour the *Harald Haarfagre* and the *Tordenskjold*, lying at their quaysides without steam up and incapable of combat, were the largest units. With them, but lying at a buoy in the roadstead of Horten, was the *Olav Tryggvason*, and elsewhere in Oslofjord were four submarines. . . .

With the exception of the *Olav Tryggvason* there was not a single combat vessel of a thousand tons. And against them Germany flung the pocket battleship *Deutschland*, the 10,000-ton armoured cruiser *Blücher*, the light cruiser *Emden* of 5,600 tons, the *Brummer*, a modern gunnery training ship of 2,140 tons, and a screen of minesweepers, torpedo-boats and motor craft.

There could have been no sea battle in the Oslofjord even had Norway time to organise her whole defences. There could have been only a sea massacre.

Already the guns of the lower fjord had opened on the enemy. At 11:40 the German line, with the *Blücher* leading, had reached the vicinity of the Rauóy fortress, in the outer defences of Oslo. The mist was heavy over the fjord, but in a brief instant of clarity the garrison of the fortress sighted the German ships and got off four rounds before the mist swirled down on them again. The second fortress of the outer defences was the island of Bolaerne; but Bolaerne, blinded by the darkness of the mist, saw nothing of the enemy, and the *Blücher* and the *Deutschland* went past in safety.

In Oslo over the tense telephones the messages came winging in as look-outs and watchers on the shore reported the progress of the enemy. There came a message that told of foreign warships steaming in past the outer defences of Bergen. A little after two, through an extraordinary call to the Swedish Legation, came a report of a German torpedo-boat lying outside Stavanger.

The Government had been re-summoned at 1:30 A.M. At 3:30 it was reported that two battleships had raced by the Agdenes forts and had thrust into the fjord of Trondheim. In an atmosphere of disaster, in the knowledge that they were surrounded on the sea north, west and south, the Norwegian Government, preserving always courage and dignity, gave the orders for mobilisation. There was no need yet for loss of hope. The main German force directed on the capital itself had still to pass the inner fortress of Oscarsborg.

And at 3:30 A.M. the inner battle began. The story of the Oscarsborg defences has in it every element of drama. That was the last line—beyond was nothing but an open city. That was the last hope of a proud and independent nation.

At 3:30 A.M., at a distance of 2,000 metres, the look-outs of Oscarsborg sighted the leaders of the German line, the cruiser *Blücher* towering above the little vessels of the screen. Swiftly the range fell, the head of the line coming on every moment closer and closer to the old 11-inch guns of the fort. At 1,400 metres—less than a mile—the commander of the Oscarsborg fortress gave the order to open fire. For 11-inch guns the range was point-blank. The first salvo hit *Blücher* on "A" turret, putting the turret out of action: the second hit on "B," the super-imposed turret just below the bridge. Vast streamers of flame roared into the night, and blazing, the great ship went by.

In a matter of moments she came into the line of the fixed torpedo defences of the narrows. Two torpedoes struck her in rapid succession, and, blazing still more fiercely, she heeled over and sank. And where she had gone down a vast lake of flaming oil made the dark night brilliant.

And with her went eight hundred members of her crew, and fifteen hundred men of the military landing party that was to have taken the surrender of the capital of Norway, the staff of the General in command of the landing, Gestapo units that were to have policed the new territory. Two hundred men came out of that inferno to the shore.

Almost at point-blank range *Brummer*, the 2,400-ton gunnery training ship, was sunk by the Oscarsborg guns. The *Deutschland* and the *Emden* were hit and damaged. Swinging at once with their escort of minesweepers and torpedo-boats, they turned for the safety of the night beyond the narrows. The battle of Oscarsborg was over. It had broken the main German thrust on Oslo. It had caused grievous loss to the German Navy—the first of the loss that was to cripple the German surface Fleet for the rest of the war.

But it was not enough.[8]

The British fleet, too, inflicted losses upon the invaders. Without adequate air protection it was unable to operate freely in the North Sea or the Skagerrak, but to the far north, at Narvik, it gave a good account of itself. Here, on April 10 and 13, took place two naval battles which, if properly followed up, might have changed the course of the Norwegian campaign. But an isolated victory at Narvik was not enough; the Germans could bring up forces from the south and make that port untenable. In southern Norway things were going badly. The government had fled to Harmar and then to Elverum, near the Swedish frontier, and the Nazis had established a new government under the leadership of Vidkun Quisling whose name was soon to be a synonym throughout the world for traitor. German armies pushing rapidly northward from Oslo quickly brushed aside the fierce but unorganized resistance which they encountered. Within a week the British had landed reinforcements—British, French, and Polish—at the ports of Aandalsnes and Namsos, flanking Trondheim. These reinforcements were too little and too late. The enemy controlled the sea lanes and the air, and by the end of April the Allied forces, outnumbered and outpowered, were forced to withdraw. Only at Narvik did the Allies hang on. But the *Luftwaffe*, based on Trondheim, battered the Allied forces and threatened their supply lines, and on June 9 they abandoned their last foothold in Norway, taking with them King Haakon and his government who continued to wage war from London.

In just two months Hitler had conquered Denmark and Norway and isolated Sweden. From Denmark he obtained bacon and butter and oils and control of the Skagerrak and Kattegat, gateway to the Baltic. From Norway he obtained a supply route for Swedish iron ore, timber, wood pulp, and fish—and, what was equally important—denied these things to Britain. From deep Norwegian fjords submarines could swim out to destroy British shipping and warships attack the supply route to Murmansk, soon to be so important.

Against this the Allies could mark up very little on the credit side of the ledger. Some of the Danish and a large part of the Norwegian merchant marine, fourth largest in the world, had escaped to Britain. So, too, had thousands of Norwegian seamen, soldiers, and airmen. But that the Allies had lost this round was beyond dispute. As Clement Attlee said, "The people of this country . . . are not satisfied that the war is being waged with sufficient energy, capacity, drive, and resolution. The Norwegian campaign is the culmination of other discontents." As a result of these discontents, Chamberlain was forced to retire, and on May 10 a new government was formed under the leadership of Winston Churchill. He inspired the British people, and free peoples everywhere, with an implacable resolution to endure the worst that the Nazis could hurl against them and fight through to ultimate victory. It was entirely fitting that on the very day that Hitler launched his attack on the Low Countries, France, and ultimately Britain, he should be confronted by that indomitable and valiant man who, more than any other, was to be responsible for frustrating his wicked designs and destroying those evil forces which he represented.

The Low Countries

"The hour has come for the decisive battle for the future of the German nation. For 300 years the rulers of England and France have made it their aim to prevent any real consolidation of Europe and above all to keep Germany weak and helpless. With this your hour has come. The fight which begins today will decide the destiny of the German people for 1,000 years. Now do your duty."

Thus Hitler to his army on the eve of the assault against the west. The army's duty was to conquer Holland, Belgium, and Luxembourg, overrun France, and bring Britain to her knees. It did not seem too difficult. The attack had all been planned with meticulous care and, in its early stages, it was carried through with consummate skill. Holland, Belgium, and Luxembourg seemed assured. It was one of the most skillfully conceived and competently conducted campaigns in military history.

As with the Polish and Scandinavian campaigns, surprise, treachery, and ruthlessness added to the advantage which the Nazis already possessed in numerical superiority and equipment. Had time and circumstances permitted Britain, France, and the Low Countries to consolidate all their forces and organize a co-ordinated defense, the invasion might have been repulsed. But Holland and Belgium, mortally afraid of giving Germany any excuse to attack, had failed to mobilize their armies or co-ordinate their defenses with those of France. The French had dispersed their forces in the north, in the Maginot Line, and along the Italian frontier. The British were still frantically building up their army and air force and were as yet unprepared to make a contribution comparable to that which they had made in 1914–15.

At early dawn, May 10, the Germans struck, all along the western front from the North Sea to Luxembourg. One spearhead drove along the Frisian coast, another thrust at the Yssel towards Utrecht, a third smashed at Maastricht and the fortress of Eben Emael commanding the Albert Canal, a fourth—the major attack—rolled through the rugged Ardennes towards the Meuse. Planes bombed helpless cities, parachutists seized airfields and bridges, fifth columnists spread confusion and terror behind the lines.

The Dutch put up a stout resistance, but were speedily overwhelmed. parachutists had captured the Rotterdam airfields, and held them. A German column, pushing through Brabant, seized the strategic Moerdijl bridge leading to the great city, cutting off Allied reinforcements. Within four days most of Holland was in German hands. Then, while negotiations for the surrender were under way, the Germans subjected Rotterdam—which was an open city—to a hideous air bombardment in which from 30,000 to 60,000 civilians were killed. Under the threat to subject every Dutch city to similar treatment, resistance ceased. But Queen Wilhelmina and the Dutch government—as well as most of the Dutch fleet—had escaped to England and there carried on the fight.

The conquest of Belgium was even more spectacular. Holland had managed to maintain its neutrality in the last war, but Belgium had been a battleground, and the Belgians were better prepared for war than most of the small countries of Europe. They had massed their army along the Albert Canal and the Meuse River, and their great fortress of Eben Emael, the pivot of these defense lines, was thought to be impregnable. The Germans took it in thirty-six hours. Theodore Draper explains how this was accomplished:

The capture of Eben-Emael and the Albert Canal bridges was long one of the great mysteries of the war and for some time gave Dr. Goebbels one of his most powerful psychological weapons, the propaganda about Germany's "secret weapons." It is now perfectly clear from both German and Belgian sources that these weapons were nothing else than a willingness to take infinite pains, to adopt other people's ideas, and to gamble on easy victories before trying the hard way.

In the winter of 1939–40 the Germans went to the trouble of building a full-scale model of Eben-Emael. A chosen battalion of engineers and a platoon of parachutists were familiarized with every feature of the fort and trained to perfection under the most realistic conditions. According to the

Belgians, German espionage agents had gathered the necessary information during the construction of the Albert Canal. The willingness to imitate
was shown in the employment of parachutists, first introduced by the
Russians. The selection of Eben-Emael as the main objective was typical of
German strategy when a rapid decision was sought. . . .

While it was still dark, about ten gliders, each carrying a dozen troops
besides explosives, guns, and ammunition, commanded by a Lieutenant
Witzing, landed on the superstructure of the fort. The gliders were suddenly released from their towing planes while still over German territory.
Obviously the architects of Eben-Emael had never imagined that human
cargoes of destruction would some day be dropped from the sky, because
Eben-Emael, unlike some of the other forts, had no men available and
armed for sorties to deal with them. The intruders went to work so quickly
and skillfully that their training was evidently not wasted. Hiding behind
a smokescreen, they immediately struck out for the cupolas which they
began to destroy with explosives. Detonating charges, inserted into the
barrels of guns, put them out of action. Observation posts, exits, and
ventilating shafts were dynamited. The cupola with the two 120-mm. guns
was knocked out but the southern cupola armed with 75-mm. guns was still
firing and the northern cupola with 75s was only damaged. The entire fort
had 36 guns of 60-mm. and 75-mm. caliber, 45-mm. anti-aircraft guns,
and 36 machine guns, so that it could not be silenced at once. Each cupola
was a separate job. A single German soldier would edge his way carefully
to a cupola, climb on the roof, lower a charge of explosives close to the
porthole, light the fuse, and slip away, all the while unnoticed by the men
inside the cupola. Hand grenades were thrown into the muzzles of the
guns. The ammunition elevators were put out of action by similar methods. Thus Eben-Emael's guns were unable to keep the captured bridges
under fire.

The predicament of the Eben-Emael garrison was quite fantastic. It was
virtually imprisoned in its own fortress, the single strongest fortified position in the world, by a few men. Salvation could only come from the
outside. On May 10, when the glider troops were relatively isolated on the
superstructure of the fort, the situation might still have been saved. Major
Jottrand, the commander of Eben-Emael, appealed to the nearest forts,
Pontisse and Neufchâteau, for help. They responded, ironically enough,
by bombarding the superstructure of Eben-Emael with shrapnel. The spectacle of one Belgian fort firing on another was the ultimate satire on
immobile defense.

At this point the German dive-bombers went into action, adding to the
din. Word was received from the forts at Pontisse and Barchon that dive-
bombers were active there too. Several casemates were hit at Eben-Emael;
the other two forts reported that some of their guns were out of action.
After an intense bombardment, the Stukas suddenly departed. Major Jottrand made use of the results to take stock of the situation in the fort and
receive further reports from his outposts. He learned that German parachutists were landing in force all around and that the enemy was crossing
the Albert Canal in force. The bridges at Vroenhoven and Veldwezelt
were completely unheard from. It seems that he concluded that the situ-

ation was "grave but not desperate." At the same time the glider troops were sitting on the cupolas, waiting for a Belgian counterattack which never materialized. They had crippled Eben-Emael, but they were too few to capture it and had to wait for reinforcements.

Meanwhile German forces outside the fort were not sleeping. While the glider troops were planting their explosives, a force consisting of 4 companies of engineers and 2 infantry companies, commanded by a Lieutenant-Colonel Mikosch, was trying to cross the Albert Canal on rubber boats. At about noon, using an anti-aircraft battery as artillery support, they started across near the tiny village of Canne, a little more than a mile north of the fort. The passage was extremely costly and difficult because some of the fort's guns and machine-gun outposts blasted at the rubber boats. All afternoon was wasted getting one company across, but the successful one attacked and captured Canne. Lieutenant-Colonel Mikosch assumed that the road to Eben-Emael was clear.

The colonel was disappointed. As the battalion moved southward toward Eben-Emael, it ran into a branch canal which the Belgians had flooded. It was impossible and the colonel decided to wait for nightfall before attempting to cross. Meanwhile, his force took cover. . . .

By nightfall both sides were reaching a crisis. The fort was badly crippled, but some portions were more badly hurt than others. The psychological damage was almost as great as the material. The men were cooped up inside, almost powerless to fight back while the explosive charges were bursting around them through the ventilating and munition shafts, generating an unbearable air pressure in all the rooms. In the evening the morale was definitely sinking. As for the attackers, they were also under great pressure. The parachutists' havoc was immense, but they were still isolated from the main body of engineers outside and just able to hang on for the night. Their arms were probably giving out and the danger of Belgian relief forces was great. . . . By 10 A.M. the preliminaries were over.

Now was unleashed a full-scale attack on all the surviving cupolas and other works. From the other side of the canal, anti-tank and anti-aircraft batteries went into action, scoring direct hits almost at will. Small groups of engineers crawled from cupola to cupola, planting their explosive charges and scrambling away for safety. The work was not particularly dangerous because the men in the cupolas were unable to see the crawling attackers, who had all the advantage as long as their nerves were strong.

As Major Jottrand gave up hope that relief forces would come from the outside and as deep gashes were torn in the fort's superstructure by the explosives and incessant bombardment, the garrison retreated into the interior of the fort and the attackers began to enter the openings after it. The last telephonic message from Eben-Emael to the outside came at 11 A.M.: "Accept no more messages from Eben-Emael." At 12:30 the entire fort surrendered. The total casualties were only 60 dead, 40 wounded. This left 1,100 men and the hulk of the greatest fort in the world. The German casualties were probably less. The action from beginning to end took less than thirty-six hours.[9]

From Maastricht the Germans smashed through to Louvain, forced the river Dyle, and threatened Brussels and Antwerp, which fell on the 18th. The Allies fell back on the Scheldt and Lys.

Meantime, von Rundstedt had broken through the Ardennes. This rugged forest-covered country, criss-crossed by winding roads and swift rivers, was thought to be wholly unsuitable to mechanized warfare and was therefore lightly defended. It was assumed that it would take weeks for the Nazis to fight their way through here, and in that time the French could bring up the whole of their Ninth Army. But the *Wehrmacht* broke through in two days, and on the 13th crossed the Meuse barrier.

It was a catastrophe of the first order. At one stroke the Germans were in position to flank the Maginot Line, strike westward to Paris, or swing northward to cut off the Belgian and British armies along the coast. On May 21 the Germans reached the sea at Abbeville, and the encirclement of the Belgians and the British Expeditionary Force was complete. The French, to the south, were unable to break through to their relief. On May 26, Lord Gort, commanding the B.E.F., was authorized to re-embark his army to Britain, and began to concentrate his forces on the only remaining port, Dunkirk. At this juncture, the whole situation was altered, the whole B.E.F. Threatened, by the surrender of the Belgian army. Theodore Draper analyzes King Leopold's action:

Half-dazed, bled white, overwhelmingly outnumbered in men and arms, its soldiers virtually paralyzed by the hordes of demoralized refugees in their midst, its leaders on the verge of capitulation, the Belgian Army was never in any shape to cover any Franco-British offensive, as Weygand had vainly hoped. But it was in no better shape to cover a retreat either. It was stretched thin along a wide arc which started at Zeebrugge on the North Sea and followed the Lys Canal and Lys River as far as Menin where it connected with the B.E.F. The enemy had only to choose the spot to break through. The B.E.F., which had its hands full trying to stave off the enemy in the south, would be hopelessly exposed in the north. . . .

Leopold's last defiance of his ministers was a cruel experience for all. Four of them, Premier Pierlot, Foreign Minister Spaak, War Minister General Denis, and Interior Minister Vanderpoorten, representing the whole cabinet, came to see him, after a mutual boycott of three days, in the early morning hours at the huge dim castle of Wynendael in the midst of woods south of Bruges. It was still dark. The discussion was long and futile. Leopold flatly declared that the Belgian Army was bearing the brunt of the German attack and should withdraw from the war. They begged him to leave the active command to the Belgian General Staff and go to France or England. He refused. He said that he would never leave Belgian soil and invited them to remain with him, waiting for the Germans to arrive. Spaak related: "In the face of the King's formal declaration, we told him frankly that we did not share his views on surrender and we begged him to leave with us immediately." Nothing could move Leopold. When daylight came, the four ministers departed for Dunkerque. That day Leopold issued an Order of the Day to the Army in which he said: "Whatever may happen, I shall share your fate." The die was cast. . . .

Leopold called on Gort to launch a counterattack between the Lys and the Escaut on the enemy's flank. To Gort, such an operation was "out of the question." Although Leopold did not yet know it, Gort had already received authorization to withdraw to the coast, and his problem was how to disengage the B.E.F., not how to get tangled up in a futile offensive in a hopeless cause. Gort's advice to Leopold and Leopold's advice to Gort were never taken seriously by either. All the partners of the coalition were thinking primarily of themselves—to Gort, it was the "safety of the B.E.F." as Eden had put it; to Leopold, how to end at all cost the slaughter of the Belgian Army and the destruction of its cities and fields; to Blanchard, how to hold out to give the southern French armies a chance to establish a stronger line in front of Paris behind the Somme. They made impossible demands on each other and found additional reasons for going their own ways when the demands were ignored or rejected.

At noon on the 26th the Belgian command handed the following note to the head of the French Mission, General Champon: "The Belgian Command asks you to inform the Commander-in-Chief of the Allied Armies that the Belgian Army is in a serious situation and that the Commander-in-Chief intends to carry on the fight as long as his resources permit. The enemy is at present attacking from Eecloo to Menin; the Army has nearly reached the limits of its endurance. . . ."

Leopold sent Gort this message at about 12:30 on the 27th: "The Belgian Army is losing heart. It has been fighting without a break for the past four days under a heavy bombardment which the R.A.F. has been unable to prevent. Having heard that the Allied group is surrounded and aware of the great superiority of the enemy, the troops have concluded that the situation is desperate. The time is rapidly approaching when they will be unable to continue the fight. The King will be forced to capitulate to avoid a collapse. . . ."

And at 5 P.M. Leopold decided to send an envoy to ask for an armistice between the German Army and the Belgian Army. . . .

If Leopold had waited a few days before surrendering, he would have saved himself a good deal of misunderstanding and recrimination. But after delaying for a week and muttering dark threats, Leopold acted abruptly. He did not make sure that the Allied Commanders in the field were forewarned in plenty of time to take the necessary measures of security. Undoubtedly he saved a number of Belgian lives by not waiting another hour, but he jeopardized as many British and French. Above all he jeopardized future relations with the Allies.[10]

Dunkirk

The B.E.F., as well as remnants of the French and Polish armies, along the Channel—a total of some 400,000 men—seemed doomed. The Germans confidently announced that "the ring around the British, French, and Belgian armies has been definitely closed." It had, indeed, as far as they could close it. But the sea was still open, and Britain still ruled the waves. With a valor that aroused the admiration even of the enemy, the French fought rearguard actions at Lille, Cassel, and in Dunkirk itself. A small British force of perhaps 4,000 held out with fanatical courage at Calais.

Then came Operation Dynamo or, as John Masefield has called it, the Nine Days' Wonder. The task was one that might well appall even the hardiest. The Germans pressed on Dunkirk from all sides. Their artillery subjected it to ceaseless pounding, their planes smashed at piers and docks and at the embarkation fleet. The town itself was aflame, the water supply gone, the docks a shambles.

The Admiralty had already anticipated the task of re-embarking the army from France. When it became clear that the withdrawal could not longer be delayed, the word went out for the gathering of the ships. The most fantastic armada in history—numbering 665 civilian craft and 222 naval units—assembled in the British ports nearest Dunkirk.

For nine days the evacuation went on, from May 26 to June 3, and even on the 4th and 5th a few stragglers and last-ditch fighters were brought out. Arthur D. Divine, who took part in the whole operation, has described it:

I am still amazed about the whole Dunkirk affair. There was from first to last a queer, medieval sense of miracle about it. You remember the old quotation about the miracle that crushed the Spanish Armada, "God sent a wind." This time "God withheld the wind." Had we one onshore breeze of any strength at all, in the first days, we would have lost a hundred thousand men.

The pier at Dunkirk was the unceasing target of bombs and shell-fire throughout, yet it never was hit. Two hundred and fifty thousand men embarked from that pier. Had it been blasted. . . .

The whole thing from first to last was covered with that same strange feeling of something supernatural. We muddled, we quarreled, everybody swore and was bad-tempered and made the wildest accusations of inefficiency and worse in high places. Boats were badly handled and broke down, arrangements went wrong.

And yet out of all that mess we beat the experts, we defied the law and the prophets, and where the Government and the Board of Admiralty had hoped to bring away 30,000 men, we brought away 335,000. If that was not a miracle, there are no miracles left.

When I heard that small boats of all sorts were to be used at Dunkirk I volunteered at once, . . . and within two hours of my first telephone call I was on my way to Sheerness. From Sheerness I acted as navigator for a party of small boats round to Ramsgate, and at Ramsgate we started work. The evacuation went on for something over a week, but to me the most exciting time was the night before the last.

I was given a motorboat about as long as my drawing room at home, 30 feet. She had one cabin forward and the rest was open, but she had twin engines and was fairly fast. For crew we had one sub-lieutenant, one stoker and one gunner. For armament we had two Bren guns—one my own particular pet which I had stolen—and rifles. In command of our boat we had a real live Admiral—Taylor, Admiral in charge of small boats.

We first went out to French fishing boats gathered off Ramsgate, boats from Caen and Le Havre, bright little vessels with lovely names—*Ciel de France, Ave Maria, Gratia Plena, Jeanne Antoine*. They had helped at Calais and Boulogne and in the preceding days at Dunkirk, and the men were very tired, but when we passed them new orders they set out again for Dunkirk.

They went as the leaders of the procession, for they were slow. With them went a handful of Dutch *schouts*, stumpy little coasting vessels commandeered at the collapse of Holland, each flying the white ensign of the Royal Navy, sparkling new, and each fitted out with a Lewis gun. Next went coasters, colliers, paddle steamers that in time of peace had taken trippers around the harbor for a shilling, tugs towing mud scows with brave names like *Galleon's Reach* and *Queen's Channel*.

There was a car ferry, surely on its first trip in the open sea. There were yachts; one the *Skylark*—what a name for such a mission! There were dockyard tugs, towing barges. There were sloops, mine sweepers, trawlers, destroyers. There were Thames fire floats, Belgian drifters, lifeboats from all around the coast, lifeboats from sunken ships. I saw the boats of the old *Dunbar Castle*, sunk eight months before. Rolling and pitching in a cloud of spray were open speedboats, wholly unsuited for the Channel chop.

There was the old *Brighton Belle* that carried holiday crowds in the days before the Boer War. She swept mines in the Great War, and she swept mines in this war through all the fury of last winter. . . .

There was never such a fleet went to war before, I think. As I went round the western arm of the harbor near sunset, passing out orders, it brought my heart into my throat to watch them leave. They were so small! Little boats like those you see in the bight of Sandy Hook fishing on a fine afternoon. Some were frowsy, with old motorcar tires for fenders, and some of them were bright with paint and chromium—little white boats that were soon lost to view across the ruffled water. And as they went there came round from the foreland a line of fishing boats—shrimp catchers and what not, from the east coast—to join the parade.

When this armada of oddments was under way, we followed with the faster boats—Royal Air Force rescue launches, picket boats and the like—and with us went an X-lighter, a flatboat, a kerosene-powered, built for landing troops at Gallipoli and a veteran of *that* evacuation more than 20 years ago.

It was the queerest, most nondescript flotilla that ever was, and it was manned by every kind of Englishman, never more than two men, often only one, to each small boat. There were bankers and dentists, taxi drivers and yachtsmen, longshoremen, boys, engineers, fishermen and civil servants. There were bright-faced Sea Scouts and old men whose skins looked fiery red against their white hair. Many were poor; they had no coats, but made out with old jerseys and sweaters. They wore cracked rubber boots. They were wet, chilled to the bone, hungry; they were unarmed and unprotected, and they sailed toward the pillars of smoke and fire and the thunder of the guns, into waters already slick with the oil of sunken boats, knowing perfectly well the special kind of hell ahead. Still, they went, plugging gamely along.

I had a feeling, then and after, that this was something bigger than organization, something bigger than the mere requisitioning of boats. In a sense it was the naval spirit that has always been the foundation of England's greatness, flowering again and flowering superbly. I believe 887 was the official figure for the total of boats that took part over the ten days of the evacuation. But I think there were more than a thousand craft in all. I myself know of fishermen who never registered, waited for no orders, but, all unofficial, went and brought back soldiers. Quietly, like that.

It was dark before we were well clear of the English coast. It wasn't rough, but there was a little chop on, sufficient to make it very wet, and we soaked the Admiral to the skin. Soon, in the dark, the big boats began to overtake us. We were in a sort of dark traffic lane, full of strange ghosts and weird, unaccountable waves from the wash of the larger vessels. When destroyers went by, full tilt, the wash was a serious matter to us little fellows. We could only spin the wheel to try to head into the waves, hang on, and hope for the best.

Mere navigation was dangerous in the dark. Clouds hung low and blotted out the stars. We carried no lights, we had no signals, no means of recognition of friend or foe. Before we were halfway across we began to meet the first of the returning stream. We dodged white, glimmering bow waves of vessels that had passed astern, only to fall into the way of half-seen shapes ahead. There were shouts in the darkness, but only occasionally the indignant stutter of a horn. We went "by guess and by God."

From the halfway mark, too, there were destroyers on patrol crossing our line of passage, weaving a fantastic warp of foam through the web of our progress. There were collisions, of course. Dover for days was full of destroyers with bows stove in, coasting vessels with great gashes amidships, ships battered, scraped and scarred. The miracle is that there were not ten for every one that happened.

Even before it was fully dark we had picked up the glow of the Dunkirk flames, and now as we drew nearer the sailing got better, for we could steer by them and see silhouetted the shapes of other ships, of boats coming home already loaded, and of low dark shadows that might be enemy motor torpedo boats.

Then aircraft started dropping parachute flares. We saw them hanging all about us in the night, like young moons. The sound of the firing and the bombing was with us always, growing steadily louder as we got nearer and nearer. The flames grew, too. From a glow they rose up to enormous plumes of fire that roared high into the everlasting pall of smoke. As we approached Dunkirk there was an air attack on the destroyers and for a little the night was brilliant with bursting bombs and the fountain sprays of tracer bullets.

The beach, black with men, illumined by the fires, seemed a perfect target, but no doubt the thick clouds of smoke were a useful screen.

When we got to the neighborhood of the mole there was a lull. The aircraft had dispersed and apparently had done no damage, for there was nothing sinking. They had been there before, however, and the place was a shambles of old wrecks, British and French, and all kinds of odds and ends. The breakwaters and lighthouse were magnificently silhouetted against the flames of burning oil tanks—enormous flames that licked high above the town. Further inshore and to the east of the docks the town itself was burning furiously, but down near the beach where we were going there was no fire and we could see rows of houses standing silent and apparently empty.

We had just got to the eastward of the pier when shelling started up. There was one battery of 5.9's down between La Panne and Nieuport that our people simply could not find and its shooting was uncannily accurate. Our place was in the corner of the beach at the mole and as they were shelling the mole, the firing was right over our heads. Nothing, however, came near us in the first spell.

The picture will always remain sharp-etched in my memory—the lines of men wearily and sleepily staggering across the beach from the dunes to the shallows, falling into little boats, great columns of men thrust out into the water among bomb and shell splashes. The foremost ranks were shoulder deep, moving forward under the command of young subalterns, themselves with their heads just above the little waves that rode in to the sand. As the front ranks were dragged aboard the boats, the rear ranks moved up, from ankle deep to knee deep, from knee deep to waist deep, until they, too, came to shoulder depth and their turn.

Some of the big boats pushed in until they were almost aground, taking appalling risks with the falling tide. The men scrambled up the sides on rope nets, or climbed hundreds of ladders, made God knows where out of new, raw wood and hurried aboard the ships in England.

The little boats that ferried from the beach to the big ships in deep water listed drunkenly with the weight of men. The big ships slowly took on lists of their own with the enormous numbers crowded aboard. And always down the dunes and across the beach came new hordes of men, new columns, new lines.

On the beach was a destroyer, bombed and burned. At the water's edge were ambulances, abandoned when their last load had been discharged.

There was always the red background, the red of Dunkirk burning. There was no water to check the fires and there were no men to be spared to fight them. Red, too, were the shell bursts, the flash of guns, the fountains of tracer bullets.

The din was infernal. The 5.9 batteries shelled ceaselessly and brilliantly. To the whistle of shells overhead was added the scream of falling bombs. Even the sky was full of noise—anti-aircraft shells, machine-gun fire, the snarl of falling planes, the angry hornet noise of dive bombers. One could not speak normally at any time against the roar of it and the noise of our own engines. We all developed "Dunkirk throat," a sore hoarseness that was the hallmark of those who had been there.

Yet through all the noise I will always remember the voices of the young subalterns as they sent their men aboard, and I will remember, too, the astonishing discipline of the men. They had fought through three weeks of retreat, always falling back without orders, often without support. Transport had failed. They had gone sleepless. They had been without food and water. Yet they kept ranks as they came down the beaches, and they obeyed commands.

Veterans of Gallipoli and of Mons agreed this was the hottest spot they had ever been in, yet morale held. I was told stories of French troops that rushed the boats at first so that stern measures had to be taken, but I saw nothing like that. The Frenchmen I brought off were of the rear guard, fine soldiers, still fighting fit.

Having the Admiral on board, we were not actually working the beaches but were in control of operations. We moved about as necessary, and after we had spent some time putting small boats in touch with their towing boats, the 5.9 battery off Nieuport way began to drop shells on us. It seemed pure spite. The nearest salvo was about 20 yards astern, which was close enough.

We stayed there until everybody else had been sent back, and then went pottering about looking for stragglers. While we were doing that, a salvo of shells got one of our troopships alongside the mole. She was hit clean in the boilers and exploded in one terrific crash. There were then, I suppose, about 1000 Frenchmen on the mole. We had seen them crowding along its narrow crest, outlined against the flames. They had gone out under shell-fire to board the boat, and now they had to go back again, still being shelled. It was quite the most tragic thing I ever have seen in my life. We could do nothing with our little park dinghy.

While they were still filing back to the beach and the dawn was breaking with uncomfortable brilliance, we found one of our stragglers—a navy whaler. We told her people to come aboard, but they said that there was a motorboat aground and they would have to fetch off her crew. They went in and we waited. It was my longest wait, ever. For various reasons they were terribly slow. When they found the captain of the motorboat, they stood up and argued with him and he wouldn't come off anyway. Damned plucky chap. He and his men lay quiet until the tide floated them later in the day. Then they made a dash for it, and got away.

We waited for them until the sun was up before we got clear of the mole. By then, the fighting was heavy inshore, on the outskirts of the town, and actually in some of the streets.

Going home, the Jerry dive bombers came over us five times, but some-how left us alone though three times they took up an attacking position. A little down the coast, towards Gravelines, we picked up a boatload of Frenchmen rowing off. We took them aboard. They were very much both-ered as to where our "ship" was, said quite flatly that it was impossible to go to England in a thing like ours. Too, too horribly dangerous.[11]

All the equipment mobilized for the battle of France was left behind on the beaches. But altogether 335,000 British and Allied fighting men had been rescued to fight another day.

The Fall of France

Even while the remnants of the B.E.F. were being evacuated the Germans began the final campaign of the Battle of France. In a few days they had crossed the Somme and by the tenth of June were hammering the Marne, scene of some of the most famous battles of the last war. Other armies were driving into Brittany, across the Loire toward Nantes, down along the Maginot Line towards Lyon. At this juncture, while France was reeling from thunderous blows, Mussolini decided that it was safe to enter the war. Herbert Matthews gives us a word-picture which shows how the Italians felt about this fateful decision:

At 4:30 in the afternoon of June 10, Ciano received the French ambassador at the Chigi Palace and told him that "His Majesty the King Emperor declares that Italy considers herself in a state of war against France, beginning tomorrow, June 11." Fifteen minutes later he communicated the same message to the British ambassador. . . .

It was taken for granted that Mussolini knew what he was doing, and a more or less bloodless victory would bring to Italy some benefits. . . .

The attitude was clear enough on the fateful day June 10, 1940. There was an immense demonstration in front of the Piazza Venezia for the Duce, and later for the King, but it was entirely organized. The local Fasci had their orders to collect members, meet at a certain time, and proceed to the square. Fascists went around telling shopkeepers that they had to close at 5 o'clock. The radio kept announcing throughout the day that Mussolini was going to speak, and everywhere in Italy the citizens had to gather around loud-speakers to listen. There was not the slightest spontaneous feeling, and the only cheering came from those, especially the students, who had been brought into the center of the mob, under the balcony. Outside of that relatively tiny group of organized applauders, there was a lighthearted indifference which was really appalling, considering what was happening. I saw troops marching through nearby streets while the passersby did not even turn their heads to look at them.[12]

By this time France was in a state of panic. The government had fled to Tours, and from there moved on to Bordeaux. The armies, still large, and potentially powerful, but demoralized, were in headlong retreat. Their progress was impeded by the hundreds of thousands of refugees jamming all the roads to the south. Virginia Cowles, who was in the retreat, tells us what happened:

Try to think in terms of millions. Try to think of noise and confusion, of the thick smell of petrol, of the scraping of automobile gears, of shouts, wails, curses, tears. Try to think of a hot sun and underneath it an unbroken stream of humanity flowing southwards from Paris, and you have a picture of the gigantic civilian exodus that presaged the German advance.

I had seen refugees before. I had seen them wending their way along the roads of Spain and Czechoslovakia; straggling across the Polish-Roumanian frontier, trudging down the icy paths of Finland. But I had never seen anything like this. This was the first *mechanized* evacuation in history. There were some people in carts, some on foot and some on bicycles. But for the most part everyone was in a car.

Those cars, lurching, groaning, backfiring, represented a Noah's Ark of vehicles. Anything that had four wheels and an engine was pressed into service, no matter what the state of decrepitude; there were taxi-cabs, ice trucks, bakery vans, perfume wagons, sports roadsters and Paris buses, all of them packed with human beings. I even saw a hearse loaded with children. They crawled along the roads two and three abreast, sometimes cutting across the fields and straddling the ditches. Tom and I caught up with the stream a mile or so outside Paris on the Paris-Dourdan-Chartres road and in the next three hours covered only nine miles.

We saw terrible sights. All along the way cars that had run out of petrol or broken down, were pushed into the fields. Old people, too tired or ill to walk any farther, were lying on the ground under the merciless glare of the sun. We saw one old woman propped up in the ditch with the family clustered around trying to pour some wine down her throat. Often the stream of traffic was held up by cars that stalled and refused to move again. One car ran out of petrol halfway up a hill. It was a bakery van, driven by a woman. Everyone shouted and honked their horns while she stood in the middle of the road with her four children around her begging someone to give her some petrol. No one had any to spare. Finally, three men climbed out of a truck and in spite of her agonied protests, shoved the car into the ditch. It fell with a crash. The rear axle broke and the household possessions piled on top sprawled across the field. She screamed out a frenzy of abuse, then flung herself on the ground and sobbed. Once again the procession moved on.

In that world of terror, panic and confusion, it was difficult to believe that these were the citizens of Paris, citizens whose forefathers had fought for their freedom like tigers and stormed the Bastille with their bare hands. For the first time, I began to understand what had happened to France. Morale was a question of faith; faith in your cause, faith in your goal, but above all else, faith in your leaders. How could these people have faith in leaders who had abandoned them? Leaders who had given them no directions, no information, no reassurances; who neither had arranged for their evacuation nor called on them to stay at their places and fight for Paris until the last? If this was an example of French leadership, no wonder France was doomed. Everywhere the machinery seemed to have broken down. The dam had begun to crumble and hysteria, a trickle at first, had grown into a torrent.

Even the military roads were overrun with panic-stricken civilians. Tom was an officially accredited war correspondent, so he swung off on to one of them. Although the entrance was patrolled by gendarmes, who demanded our credentials, there was no one to keep traffic from streaming in at the intersections and a mile or so father on we once again found civilian cars moving along two or three abreast. At one point an artillery unit on its way up to the new front southeast of Paris was blocked by a furniture truck stalled across the road. The driver, with perspiration pouring down his face was trying to crank the car while the soldiers yelled and cursed at him. One of them paced angrily up and down, saying "Filthy civilians. Filthy, filthy civilians." At last, the truck got started again and the unit moved past. Another time, a procession of ambulances, with gongs clanging frantically, were held up by congestion on the outskirts of a village for over an hour. The drivers swore loudly but it had little effect; I wondered what was happening to the poor devils inside.

The only military units that succeeded in getting a clear berth were the tanks. Once we looked back to see two powerful fifteen-ton monsters thundering up behind us. They were traveling about forty miles an hour and the effect was remarkable. People gave one look and pulled in to the ditches. They went rolling by, the great treads tearing up the earth and throwing pieces of dirt into the air like fountain. After them came a number of fast-moving lorries and a string of soldiers on motor-cycles with machine-guns attached to the side-cars. They all seemed in excellent spirits: one of the tanks was gaily marked in chalk *"La Petite Marie,"* and the trucks and guns were draped with flowers. Two of the motor-cyclists shouted at us, asking if we had any cigarettes. Tom told me to throw them a couple of packages. They were so pleased they signalled us to follow them, escorted us past the long string of civilian cars to the middle of the convoy and placed us firmly between the two tanks. For the next ten or fifteen minutes we roared along at forty miles an hour. Unfortunately, eight or nine miles down the road they turned off, the motor-cyclists waved good-bye and blew us kisses, and once again we found ourselves caught up in the slow-moving procession of evacuees.[13]

On the 14th the Germans entered Paris, one of the few "open cities" which they had seen fit to spare. Reynaud's appeal to Roosevelt for "clouds of planes" was futile. By a vote—so it was said—of 13–11 the French cabinet decided to ask for an armistice; Renaud resigned, and President Lebrun asked the aged Marshal Pétain to form a government. Pétain promptly threw in the sponge. "Too few children," he said, "too few arms, too few allies" were the cause of France's debacle. His own responsibility was clear enough, even at the time: five years later a French jury was to find him guilty of treason to the Republic.

On June 21 came the formal surrender in the railroad carriage at Compiègne, where Marshal Foch had dictated terms to the Germans in November 1918. William Shirer has given us a memorable picture of the scene:

PARIS, June 21—On the exact spot in the little clearing in the Forest of Compiègne where at five a.m. on November 11, 1918, the armistice which ended the World War was signed, Adolf Hitler today handed *his* armistice terms to France. To make German revenge complete, the meeting of the German and French plenipotentiaries took place in Marshal Foch's private car, in which Foch laid down the armistice terms to German twenty-two years ago. Even the same table in the rickety old *wagon-lit* car was used. And through the windows we saw Hitler occupying the very seat on which Foch had sat at that table when he dictated the other armistice.

The humiliation of France, of the French, was complete. And yet in the preamble to the armistice terms Hitler told the French that he had not chosen this spot at Compiègne out of revenge; merely to right an old wrong. From the demeanour of the French delegates I gathered that they did not appreciate the difference. . . .

The armistice negotiations began at three fifteen p.m. A warm June sun beat down on the great elm and pine trees, and cast pleasant shadows on the wooded avenues as Hitler, with the German plenipotentiaries at his side, appeared. He alighted from his car in front of the French monument to Alsace-Lorraine which stands at the end of an avenue about two hundred yards from the clearing where the armistice car waits on exactly the same spot it occupied twenty-two years ago.

The Alsace-Lorraine statue, I noted, was covered with German war flags so that you could not see its sculptured work nor read its inscription. But I had seen it some years before—the large sword representing the sword of the Allies, and its point sticking into a large, limp eagle, representing the old Empire of the Kaiser. And the inscription underneath in French saying: "TO THE HEROIC SOLDIERS OF FRANCE . . . DEFENDERS OF THE COUNTRY AND OF RIGHT . . . GLORIOUS LIBERATORS OF ALSACE-LORRAINE."

Through my glasses I saw the Führer stop, glance at the monument, observe the Reich flags with their big Swastikas in the centre. Then he strode slowly towards us, towards the little clearing in the woods. I observed his face. It was grave, solemn, yet brimming with revenge. There was also in it, as in his springy step, a note of the triumphant conqueror, the defier of the world. There was something else, difficult to describe, in his expression, a sort of scornful, inner joy at being present at this great reversal of fate—a reversal he himself had wrought.

Now he reaches the little opening in the woods. He pauses and looks slowly around. The clearing is in the form of a circle some two hundred yards in diameter and laid out like a park. Cypress trees line it all round— and behind them, the great elms and oaks of the forest. This has been one of France's national shrines for twenty-two years. From a discreet position on the perimeter of the circle we watch.

Hitler pauses, and gazes slowly around. In a group just behind him are the other German plenipotentiaries: Göring, grasping his field-marshal's baton in one hand. He wears the sky-blue uniform of the air force. All the Germans are in uniform, Hitler in a double-breasted grey uniform, with the Iron Cross hanging from his left breast pocket. Next to Göring are the two German army chiefs—General Keitel, chief of the Supreme Command, and General von Brauchitsch, commander-in-chief of the German army. Both are just approaching sixty, but look younger, especially Keitel, who had a dapper appearance with his cap slightly cocked on one side.

Then there is Erich Raeder, Grand Admiral of the German Fleet, in his blue naval uniform and the invariable upturned collar which German naval officers usually wear. There are two non-military men in Hitler's suite—his Foreign Minister, Joachim von Ribbentrop, in the field-grey uniform of the Foreign Office; and Rudolf Hess, Hitler's deputy, in a grey party uniform.

The time is now three eighteen p.m. Hitler's personal flag is run up on a small standard in the centre of the opening.

Also in the centre is a great granite block which stands some three feet above the ground. Hitler, followed by the others, walks slowly over to it, steps up, and reads the inscription engraved in great high letters on that block. It says: "HERE ON THE ELEVENTH OF NOVEMBER 1918 SUCCUMBED THE CRIMINAL PRIDE OF THE GERMAN EMPIRE . . . VANQUISHED BY THE FREE PEOPLES WHICH IT TRIED TO ENSLAVE."

Hitler reads it and Göring reads it. They all read it, standing there in the June sun and the silence. I look for the expression on Hitler's face. I am but fifty yards from him and see him through my glasses as though he were directly in front of me. I have seen that face many times at the great moments of his life. But today! It is afire with scorn, anger, hate, revenge, triumph. He steps off the monument and contrives to make even this gesture a masterpiece of contempt. He glances back at it, contemptuous, angry—angry, you almost feel, because he cannot wipe out the awful, provoking lettering with one sweep of his high Prussian boot. He glances slowly around the clearing, and now, as his eyes meet ours, you grasp the depth of his hatred. But there is triumph there too—revengeful, triumphant hate. Suddenly, as though his face were not giving quite complete expression to his feelings, he throws his whole body into harmony with his mood. He swiftly snaps his hands on his hips, arches his shoulders, plants his feet wide apart. It is a magnificent gesture of defiance, of burning contempt for this place now and all that it has stood for in the twenty-two years since it witnessed the humbling of the German Empire. . . .

It is now three twenty-three p.m. and the Germans stride over to the armistice car. For a moment or two they stand in the sunlight outside the car, chatting. Then Hitler steps up into the car, followed by the others. We can see nicely through the car windows. Hitler takes the place occupied by Marshal Foch when the 1918 armistice terms were signed. The others spread themselves around him. Four chairs on the opposite side of the table from Hitler remain empty. The French have not yet appeared. But we do not wait long. Exactly at three thirty p.m. they alight from a car. They have flown up from Bordeaux to a near-by landing field. They too glance at the Alsace-Lorraine memorial, but it's a swift glance. Then they walk down the avenue flanked by three German officers. We see them now as they come into the sunlight of the clearing.

General Huntziger, wearing a bleached khaki uniform, Air General Bergeret and Vice-Admiral Le Luc, both in dark blue uniforms, and then, almost buried in the uniforms, M. Noël, French Ambassador to Poland. The German guard of honour, drawn up at the entrance to the clearing, snaps to attention for the French as they pass, but it does not present arms.

It is a grave hour in the life of France. The Frenchmen keep their eyes straight ahead. Their faces are solemn, drawn. They are the picture of tragic dignity.

They walk stiffly to the car, where they are met by two German officers, Lieutenant-General Tippelskirch, Quartermaster General, and Colonel Thomas, chief of the Führer's headquarters. The Germans salute. The French salute. The atmosphere is what Europeans call "correct." There are salutes, but no handshakes.

Now we get our picture through the dusty windows of that old *wagon-lit* car. Hitler and the other German leaders rise as the French enter the drawing-room. Hitler gives the Nazi salute, the arm raised. Ribbentrop and Hess do the same. I cannot see M. Noël to notice whether he salutes or not.

Hitler, as far as we can see through the windows, does not say a word to the French or to anybody else. He nods to General Keitel at his side. We see General Keitel adjusting his papers. Then he starts to read. He is reading the preamble to the German armistice terms. The French sit there with marble-like faces and listen intently. Hitler and Göring glance at the green table-top.

The reading of the preamble lasts but a few minutes. Hitler, we soon observe, has no intention of remaining very long, of listening to the reading of the armistice terms themselves. At three forty-two p.m., twelve minutes after the French arrive, we see Hitler stand up, salute stiffly, and then stride out of the drawing-room, followed by Göring, Brauchitsch, Raeder, Hess, and Ribbentrop. The French, like figures of stone, remain at the green-topped table. General Keitel remains with them. He starts to read them the detailed conditions of the armistice.

Hitler and his aides stride down the avenue towards the Alsace-Lorraine monument, where their cars are waiting. As they pass the guard of honour, the German band strikes up the two national anthems, *Deutschland, Deutschland über Alles* and the *Horst Wessel* song. The whole ceremony in which Hitler has reached a new pinnacle in his meteoric career and Germany avenged the 1918 defeat is over in a quarter of an hour.[14]

Thus the French government took the road to Vichy. But not all the French followed the aged Marshal. General Charles de Gaulle, who had fought courageously through the bitter campaign, made his way to London and from there rallied the forces of free France:

France has lost a battle. But France has not lost the war. A makeshift government may have capitulated, giving way to panic, forgetting honor, delivering their country into slavery. Yet nothing is lost! Nothing is lost because this war is a world war. In the free universe, immense forces have not yet been brought into play. Some day these forces will crush the enemy. On that day France must be present at the victory. She will then regain her liberty and her greatness. That is why I ask all Frenchmen, wherever they may be, to unite with me in action, in sacrifice, and in hope. Our country is in danger of death. Let us fight to save it.

And under the banner of the red cross of Lorraine, which Joan of Arc carried when she freed France at Orléans, the Free French fought on.

3

BRITAIN STANDS ALONE

The Blitz

DUNKIRK WAS A catastrophic defeat which the British turned, miraculously, into a moral victory. Most of the British forces and over one hundred thousand of the French had been evacuated to England, but they had left all of their equipment behind, and in this crisis Britain was all but defenceless. But the British spirit was unbroken and unterrified, and in this hour of mortal peril Britain had found new and inspiring leadership. For with the failure of the Norwegian expedition the reins of government had passed from the faltering hands of Chamberlain to the iron grip of Winston Churchill, who was to prove the greatest war leader since the elder Pitt. When, on June 4, 1940, the "nine days' wonder" was complete the last troops evacuated from Dunkirk, Churchill hurled defiance at the enemy hosts crowding the French channel ports.

I, myself, have full confidence that if all do their duty, if nothing is neglected, and if the best arrangements are made, as they are being made, we shall prove ourselves once again able to defend our Island home, to ride out the storm of war, and to outlive the menace of tyranny, if necessary for years, if necessary alone. At any rate, that is what we are going to try to do. That is the resolve of His Majesty's Government—every man of them. That is the will of Parliament and the nation. The British Empire and the French Republic, linked together in their cause and in their need, will defend to the death their native soil, aiding each other like good comrades to the utmost of their strength. Even though large tracts of Europe and many old and famous States have fallen or may fall into the grip of the Gestapo and all the odious apparatus of Nazi rule, we shall not flag or fail. We shall go on to the end, we shall fight in France, we shall fight on the seas and oceans, we shall fight with growing confidence and growing strength in the air, we shall defend our Island, whatever the cost may be, we shall fight on the beaches, we shall fight on the landing grounds, we shall fight in the fields and in the streets, we shall fight in the hills; we shall never surrender, and even if, which I do not for a moment believe, this Island or a large part of it were subjugated and starving, then our Empire beyond the seas, armed and guarded by the British fleet would carry on the struggle, until, in God's good time the New World, with all its power and might, steps forth to the rescue and liberation of the old.[1]

Had Hitler invaded at once, he might indeed have driven the British from their "ancient and famous island." Yet invasion would have been a risky business. The RAF, as the summer was to show, still commanded the skies over Britain; the Royal Navy still swept the seas; the British army and the home guard were fired by determination to resist any assault. British scientists, working at fever pitch, had prepared a warm welcome for invasion barges: vast walls of flame from gasoline piped far out into the sea, other walls of flame on land. All that summer the Nazi soldiers sang "Wir fahren gegen England," but they never did more than sing about it. Instead Hitler turned south, Paris was occupied on June 14, and on the 17th the feeble, and probably traitorous, government of the aged Marshal Pètain capitulated. But neither Pètain, nor Quisling, nor any of the collaborators could bring about the docile co-operation that the Nazis hoped for.

The freedom-loving people of Europe rallied to Britain. From Norway, Belgium, Holland, France, Poland, Czechoslovakia, exile governments fled to London, while remnants of their armies, navies, and air forces trained in Britain for the counter-offensive that would some day come.

But first Britain would have to defend herself from invasion by sea or by air. Upon her ability to do this successfully rested the fate of civilization itself.

. . . The battle of France is over. I expect that the Battle of Britain is about to begin. Upon this battle depends the survival of Christian civilization. Upon it depends our British life, and the long continuity of our institutions and our Empire. The whole fury and might of the enemy must very soon be turned on us. Hitler knows that he will have to break us in this Island or lose the war. If we can stand up to him, all Europe may be free and the life of the world may move forward into broad, sunlit uplands. But if we fail, then the whole world, including the United States, including all that we have known and cared for, will sink into the abyss of a new Dark Age made more sinister, and perhaps more protracted, by the lights of perverted science. Let us therefore brace ourselves to our duties, and so bear ourselves that, if the British Empire and its Commonwealth last for a thousand years, men will still say, "This was their finest hour."[2]

Hitler was confident that invasion was not necessary: the all-powerful *Luftwaffe* would itself reduce Britain to rubble, while the U-boats, launched from new bases in Norway and France, would cut the precious life line of the Atlantic. On July 19 Hitler, flushed with such success as no other conqueror had known since Napoleon, gave the British a last chance:

Mr. Churchill ought, perhaps, for once to believe me when I prophesy that a great empire will be destroyed—an empire which it was never my intention to destroy or even to harm. I do, however, realize that this struggle if it continues can end only with the complete annihilation of one or the other of the two adversaries. Mr. Churchill may believe that this will be Germany. I know that it will be Britain.

In this hour I feel it my duty before my own conscience to appeal once more to reason and common sense to Great Britain as much as elsewhere. I consider myself in a position to make this appeal since I am not the vanquished seeking favors but the victor speaking in the name of reason. I can see no reason why this war must go on. I am grieved to think of the sacrifices which it will claim. I should like to avert them also for my own people.[3]

This overture was treated with the contempt which it deserved. The blow, long anticipated, came soon thereafter. All through May and June and July the British and the Germans had bombed each other, somewhat ineffectually, even half-heartedly. Now Göering prepared to launch the *Luftwaffe* in a full-scale attack on what he thought the helpless island. First came an effort to destroy the ports and the airfields; then a blow at London; then attacks on all the major industrial cities. This was the Battle of Britain—the first great air battle of history. Beginning in August, it reached its crescendo in October and November, exacting a terrible toll of life and destruction. But the RAF fought back with superb courage; AA gunners put a roof of flak over the island; fire fighters, wardens, ambulance drivers, home guard and all the other agencies of defense performed miracles of courage and endurance. In the end, to the astonishment of most of the world, the proud lines of *King John* were once more vindicated:

Come three corners of the world in arms
And we shall shock them. Nought shall make us rue
If England to itself do rest but true.

Their Finest Hour

The RAF, outnumbered four to one, proved itself plane for plane and man for man better than the *Luftwaffe*. The British, not the Germans, came out master of the skies above Britain. It was the skill and heroism of the RAF pilots—pilots recruited not only from Britain itself but from Canada, Ireland, and the United States—that won the Battle for Britain and thereby, perhaps, the war itself. No tribute was ever more deserved than that which Churchill paid to these intrepid men: "Never before in human history was so much owed by so many to so few."

Accounts of individual feats of heroism by RAF pilots are numberless. Here is the story of twenty-one-year-old Pilot Officer John Maurice Bentley Beard, D.F.M., as he himself told it:

I was supposed to be away on a day's leave but dropped back to the airdrome to see if there was a letter from my wife. When I found out that *all* the squadrons had gone off into action, I decided to stand by, because obviously something big was happening. While I was climbing into my flying kit, our Hurricanes came slipping back out of the sky to refuel, reload ammunition, and take off again. The returning pilots were full of talk about flocks of enemy bombers and fighters which were trying to break through along the Thames Estuary. You couldn't miss hitting them, they said. Off to the east I could hear the steady roll of anti-aircraft fire. It was a brilliant afternoon with a flawless blue sky. I was crazy to be off.

An instant later an aircraftsman rushed up with orders for me to make up a flight with some of the machines then reloading. My own Hurricane was a nice old kite, though it had a habit of flying left wing low at the slightest provocation. But since it had already accounted for fourteen German aircraft before I inherited it, I thought it had some luck, and I was glad when I squeezed myself into the same old seat again and grabbed the "stick."

We took off in two flights (six fighters), and as we started to gain height over the station we were told over the R.T. (radiotelephone) to keep circling for a while until we were made up to a stronger force. That didn't take long, and soon there was a complete squadron including a couple of Spitfires which had wandered in from somewhere.

Then came the big thrilling moment: ACTION ORDERS. Distantly I heard the hum of the generator in my R.T. earphones and then the voice of the ground controller crackling through with the call signs. Then the order: "Fifty plus bombers, one hundred plus fighters over Canterbury at 15,000 heading northeast. Your vector (steering course to intercept) nine zero degrees. Over!"

We were flying in four V formations of three. I was flying No. 3 in Red flight, which was the squadron leader's and thus the leading flight. On we went, wing tips to left and right slowly rising and falling, the roar of our twelve Merlins drowning all other sound. We crossed over London, which, at 20,000 feet, seemed just a haze of smoke from its countless chimneys, with nothing visible except the faint glint of the barrage balloons and the wriggly silver line of the Thames.

I had too much to do watching the instruments and keeping formation to do much thinking. But once I caught a reflected glimpse of myself in the windscreen—a goggled, bloated, fat thing with the tube of my oxygen supply protruding gruesomely sideways from the mask which hid my mouth. Suddenly I was back at school again, on a hot afternoon when the Headmaster was taking the Sixth and droning on and on about the later Roman Emperors. The boy on my right was showing me surreptitiously some illustrations which he had pinched out of his father's medical books during the last holidays. I looked like one of those pictures.

It was an amazingly vivid memory, as if school was only yesterday. And half my mind was thinking what wouldn't I then have given to be sitting in a Hurricane belting along at 350 miles an hour and out for a kill. *Me* defending London! I grinned at my old self at the thought.

Minutes went by. Green fields and roads were now beneath us. I scanned the sky and the horizon for the first glimpse of the Germans. A new vector came through on the R.T. And we swung round with the sun behind us. Swift on the heels of this I heard Yellow flight leader call through the earphones. I looked quickly toward Yellow's position, and there *they* were!

It was really a terrific sight and quite beautiful. First they seemed just a cloud of light as the sun caught the many glistening chromium parts of their engines, their windshields, and the spin of their airscrew discs. Then, as our squadron hurtled nearer, the details stood out. I could see the bright-yellow noses of Messerschmitt fighters sandwiching the bombers, and could even pick out some of the types. The sky seemed full of them, packed in layers thousands of feet deep. They came on steadily, wavering up and down along the horizon. "Oh, golly," I thought, "golly, golly . . . "

And then any tension I had felt on the way suddenly left me. I was elated but very calm. I leaned over and switched on my reflector sight, flicked the catch on the gun button from "Safe" to "Fire," and lowered my seat till the circle and dot on the reflector sight shone darkly red in front of my eyes.

The squadron leader's voice came through the earphones, giving tactical orders. We swung round in a great circle to attack on their beam—into the thick of them. Then, on the order, down we went. I took my hand from the throttle lever so as to get both hands on the stick, and my thumb played neatly across the gun button. You have to steady a fighter just as you have to steady a rifle before you fire it.

My Merlin screamed as I went down in a steeply banked dive on to the tail of a forward line of Heinkels. I knew the air was full of aircraft flinging themselves about in all directions, but, hunched and snuggled down behind my sight, I was conscious only of the Heinkel I had picked out. As the angle of my dive increased, the enemy machine loomed larger in the sight field, heaved toward the red dot, and then he was there!

I had an instant's flash of amazement at the Heinkel proceedingly so regularly on its way with a fighter on its tail. "Why doesn't the fool *move?*" I thought, and actually caught myself flexing my muscles into the action *I* would have taken had I been he.

When he was square across the sight I pressed the button. There was a smooth trembling of my Hurricane as the eight-gun squirt shot out. I gave him a two-second burst and then another. Cordite fumes blew back into the cockpit, making an acrid mixture with the smell of hot oil and the air-compressors.

I saw my first burst go in and, just as I was on top of him and turning away, I noticed a red glow inside the bomber. I turned tightly into position again and now saw several short tongues of flame lick out along the fuselage. Then he went down in a spin, blanketed with smoke and with pieces flying off.

I left him plummeting down and, horsing back on my stick, climbed up again for more. The sky was clearing, but ahead toward London I saw a small, tight formation of bombers completely encircled by a ring of Messerschmitts. They were still heading north. As I raced forward, three flights of Spitfires came zooming up from beneath them in a sort of Prince-of-Wales's-feathers maneuver. They burst through upward and outward, their guns going all the time. They must have each got one, for an instant later I saw the most extraordinary sight of eight German bombers and fighters diving earthward together in flames.

I turned away again and streaked after some distant specks ahead. Diving down, I noticed that the running progress of the battle had brought me over London again. I could see the network of streets with the green space of Kensington Gardens, and I had an instant's glimpse of the Round Pond, where I sailed boats when I was a child. In that moment, and as I was rapidly overhauling the Germans ahead, a Dornier 17 sped right across my line of flight, closely pursued by a Hurricane. And behind the Hurricane came two Messerschmitts. He was too intent to have seen them and they had not seen me! They were coming slightly toward me. It was perfect. A kick at the rudder and I swung in toward them, thumbed the gun button, and let them have it. The first burst was placed just the right distance ahead of the leading Messerschmitt. He ran slap into it and he simply came to pieces in the air. His companion, with one of the speediest and most brilliant "getouts" I have ever seen, went right away in a half Immelmann turn. I missed him completely. He must almost have been hit by the pieces of the leader but he got away. I hand it to him.

At that moment some instinct made me glance up at my rear-view mirror and spot two Messerschmitts closing in on my tail. Instantly I hauled back on the stick and streaked upward. And just in time. For as I flicked into the climb, I saw the tracer streaks pass beneath me. As I turned I had a quick look round the "office" (cockpit). My fuel reserve was running out and I had only about a second's supply of ammunition left. I was certainly in no condition to take on two Messerschmitts. But they seemed no more eager than I was. Perhaps they were in the same position, for they turned away for home. I put my nose down and did likewise.

Only on the way back did I realize how hot I was. I had forgotten to adjust the ventilator apparatus in all the stress of the fighting, and hadn't noticed the thermometer. With the sun on the windows all the time, the inside of the "office" was like an oven. Inside my flying suit I was in a bath of perspiration, and sweat was cascading down my face. I was dead tired and my neck ached from constantly turning my head on the lookout when going in and out of dog-fights. Over east the sky was flecked with A.A. Puffs, but I did not bother to investigate. Down I went, home.

At the station there was only time for a few minutes' stretch, a hurried report to the Intelligence Officer, and a brief comparing of notes with the other pilots. So far my squadron seemed to be intact, in spite of a terrific two hours in which we had accounted for at least thirty enemy aircraft.

But there was more to come. It was now about 4 P.M., and I gulped down some tea while the ground crews checked my Hurricane. Then, with about three flights collected, we took off again. We seemed to be rather longer this time circling and gaining height above the station before the orders came through on the R.T. It was to patrol an area along the Thames Estuary at 20,000 feet. But we never got there.

We had no sooner got above the docks than we ran into the first lot of enemy bombers. They were coming up in line about 5,000 feet below us. The line stretched on and on across the horizon. Above, on our level, were assorted groups of enemy fighters. Some were already in action, with our fellows spinning and twirling among them. Again I got that tightening feeling at the throat, for it really was a sight to make you gasp.

But we all knew what to do. We went for the bombers. Kicking her over, I went down after the first of them, a Heinkel 111. He turned away as I approached, chiefly because some of our fellows had already broken into the line and had scattered it. Before I got up he had been joined by two more. They were forming a V and heading south across the river.

I went after them. Closing in on the tail of the left one, I ran into a stream of cross fire from all three. How it missed me I don't know. For a second the whole air in front was thick with tracer trails. It seemed to be coming straight at me, only to curl away by the windows and go lazily past. I felt one slight bank, however, and glancing quickly, saw a small hole at the end of my starboard wing. Then, as the Heinkel drifted across my sights, I pressed the button—once—twice . . . Nothing happened.

I panicked for a moment till I looked down and saw that I had forgotten to turn the safety-catch knob to the "Fire" position. I flicked it over at once and in that instant saw that three bombers, to hasten their getaway, had jettisoned all their bombs. They seemed to peel off in a steady stream. We were over the southern outskirts of London now and I remember hoping that most of them would miss the little houses and plunge into fields.

But dropping the bombs did not help my Heinkel. I let him have a long burst at close range, which got him right in the "office." I saw him turn slowly over and go down, and followed to give him another squirt. Just then there was a terrific crash in front of me. Something flew past my window, and the whole aircraft shook as the engine raced itself to pieces. I had been hit by A.A. fire aimed at the bombers, my airscrew had been blown off, and I was going down in a spin.

The next few seconds were a bit wild and confused. I remember switching off and flinging back the sliding roof almost in one gesture. Then I tried to vault out through the roof. But I had forgotten to release my safety belt. As I fumbled at the pin the falling aircraft gave a twist which shot me through the open cover. Before I was free, the air stream hit me like a solid blow and knocked me sideways. I felt my arm hit something, and then I was falling over and over with fields and streets and sky gyrating madly past my eyes.

I grabbed at the rip cord on my chute. Missed it. Grabbed again. Missed it. That was no fun. Then I remember saying to myself, "This won't do. Take it easy, take it slowly." I tried again and found the rip cord grip and pulled. There was a terrific wrench at my thighs and then I was floating still and peacefully with my "brolly" canopy billowing above my head.

The rest was lovely. I sat at my ease just floating gradually down, breathing deep, and looking around. I was drifting across London again at about 2,000 feet.[4]

August saw large scale attacks on the ports—Portsmouth, Bourne-mouth, Dover—and on the southern airdromes, including Croydon. In the two great attacks of August 16 and 18 the *Luftwaffe* lost some 250 planes; in the fist ten days after they had launched their blitz they lost 697 planes to RAF losses of 153. Nor were the gains anywhere commensurate with these intolerable losses.

What did the enemy succeed in accomplishing in just under a month of heavy fighting during which he flung in squadron after squadron of the *Luftwaffe* without regard to the cost? His object, be it remembered, was to "ground" the fighters of the Royal Air Force and to destroy so large a number of pilots and aircraft as to put it, temporarily at least, out of action. . . . The Germans, after their opening heavy attacks on convoys and on Portsmouth and Portland, concentrated on fighter aerodromes, first on, or near the coast, and then on those farther inland. Though they had done damage to aerodromes both near the coast and inland and thus put the fighting efficiency of the Fighter Squadrons to considerable strain, they failed entirely to put them out of action. The staff and ground services worked day and night and the operations of our Fighting Squadrons were not in fact interrupted. By the 6th of September the Germans either be-lieved that they had achieved success and that it only remained for them to bomb a defenceless London until it surrendered, or, following their pre-arranged plan, they automatically switched their attack against the capital because the moment had come to do so.[5]

The first great blow came on September 7, when 375 bombers—a small number by 1945 standards but stupendous for that day—unloaded their bombs on the capital in full daylight. "This is the historic hour," said Göering, "when our air force for the first time delivered its stroke right into the enemy's heart." Next day they were over London again, and the next, and the next, day after day, trying to knock out the world's greatest city, break British morale, and bring Britain to her knees.

At first London was stunned—stunned but defiant. With astonishing rapidity and efficiency the whole complex organization of anti-aircraft warfare and fire-fighting was brought into play. The RAF rose to chal-lenge the invaders, and on one memorable day, September 15, shot down 185 Nazi aircraft. Fire-fighters worked day and night to cope with the flames which raged through the capital. Intrepid ambulance drivers—many of them mere girls—rescued the trapped and the wounded; wardens and other relief workers provided temporary food and shelter. And the anti-aircraft gunners threw a "roof" over the city, forcing the enemy higher and higher into the skies.

By the end of October the Nazis were forced, by mounting losses, to give up daylight bombing and shift to night attacks—less accurate but no less murderous. An American newspaperman in London described the effect of one such night attack:

It was a night when London was ringed and stabbed with fire.

They came just after dark, and somehow you could sense from the quick, bitter firing of the guns that there was to be no monkey business this night.

Shortly after the sirens wailed you could hear the Germans grinding overhead. In my room, with its black curtains drawn across the windows, you could feel the shake from the guns. You could hear the boom, crump, crump, crump, of heavy bombs at their work of tearing buildings apart. They were not too far away.

Half an hour after the firing started I gathered a couple of friends and went to a high, darkened balcony that gave us a view of a third of the entire circle of London. As we stepped out onto the balcony a vast inner excitement came over all of us—an excitement that had neither fear nor horror in it,because it was too full of awe.

You have all seen big fires, but I doubt if you have ever seen the whole horizon of a city lined with great fires—scores of them, perhaps hundreds.

There was something inspiring just in the awful savagery of it.

The closest fires were near enough for us to hear the crackling flames and the yells of firemen. Little fires grew into big ones even as we watched. Big ones died down under the firemen's valor, only to break out again later.

About every two minutes a new wave of planes would be over. The motors seemed to grind rather than roar, and to have an angry pulsation, like a bee buzzing in blind fury.

The guns did not make a constant overwhelming din as in those terrible days of September. They were intermittent—sometimes a few seconds apart, sometimes a minute or more. Their sound was sharp, near by; and soft and muffled, far away. They were everywhere over London.

Into the dark shadowed spaces below us, while we watched, whole batches of incendiary bombs fell. We saw two dozen go off in two seconds. They flashed terrifically, then quickly simmered down to pin points of dazzling white, burning ferociously. These white pin points would go out one by one, as the unseen heroes of the moment smothered them with sand. But also, while we watched, other pin points would burn on, and soon a yellow flame would leap up from the white center. They had done their work—another building was on fire.

The greatest of all the fires was directly in front of us. Flames seemed to whip hundreds of feet into the air. Pinkish-white smoke ballooned upward in a great cloud, and out of this cloud there gradually took shape—so faintly at first that we weren't sure we saw correctly—the gigantic dome of St. Paul's Cathedral.

St. Paul's was surrounded by fire, but it came through. It stood there in its enormous proportions—growing slowly clearer and clearer, the way objects take shape at dawn. It was like a picture of some miraculous figure that appears before peace-hungry soldiers on a battlefield.

The streets below us were semi-illuminated from the glow. Immediately above the fires the sky was red and angry, and overhead, making a ceiling in the vast heavens, there was a cloud of smoke all in pink. Up in that pink shrouding there were tiny, brilliant specks of flashing light—antiaircraft shells bursting. After the flash you could hear the sound.

Up there, too, the barrage balloons were standing out as clearly as if it were daytime, but now they were pink instead of silver. And now and then through a hole in that pink shroud there twinkled incongruously a permanent, genuine star—the old-fashioned kind that has always been there.

Below us the Thames grew lighter, and all around below were the shadows—the dark shadows of buildings and bridges that formed the base of this dreadful masterpiece.

Later on I borrowed a tin hat and went out among the fires. That was exciting too; but the thing I shall always remember above all the other things in my life is the monstrous loveliness of that one single view of London on a holiday night—London stabbed with great fires, shaken by explosions, its dark regions along the Thames sparkling with the pin points of white-hot bombs, all of it roofed over with a ceiling of pink that held bursting shells, balloons, flares and the grind of vicious engines. And in yourself the excitement and anticipation and wonder in your soul that this could be happening at all.

These things all went together to make the most hateful, most beautiful single scene I have ever known.[6]

Winston Churchill said:

These cruel, wanton, indiscriminate bombings of London are, of course, part of Hitler's invasion plans. He hopes, by killing large numbers of civilians, and women and children, that he will terrorize and cow the people of this mighty imperial city, and make them a burden and an anxiety to the Government and thus distract our attention unduly from the ferocious onslaught he is preparing. Little does he know the spirit of the British nation, or the tough fiber of the Londoners, whose forebears played a leading part in the establishment of Parliamentary institutions and who have been bred to value freedom far above their lives. This wicked man, the repository and embodiment of many forms of soul-destroying hatred, this monstrous product of former wrongs and shame, has now resolved to try to break our famous Island race by a process of indiscriminate slaughter and destruction. What he has done is to kindle a fire in British hearts, here and all over the world, which will glow long after all traces of the conflagration he has caused in London have been removed. He has lighted a fire which will burn with a steady and consuming flame until the last vestiges of Nazi tyranny have been burnt out of Europe, and until the Old World—and the New—can join hands to rebuild the temples of man's freedom and man's honor, upon foundations which will not soon or easily be overthrown.[7]

An Englishwoman, Mollie Panter-Downes, describes how it was for the people on whom the rain of fire and destruction fell.

For Londoners, there are no longer such things as good nights; there are only bad nights, worse nights, and better nights. Hardly anyone has slept at all in the past week. The sirens go off at approximately the same time every evening, and in the poorer districts, the queues of people carrying blankets, thermos flasks, and babies begin to form quite early outside the air-raid shelters. The air *Blitzkrieg* continues to be directed against such military objectives as the tired shop-girl, the red-eyed clerk, and the thousands of dazed and weary families patiently trundling their few belongings in perambulators away from the wreckage of their homes. After a few of these nights, sleep of a kind comes from complete exhaustion. The amazing part of it is the cheerfulness and fortitude with which ordinary individuals are doing their job under nerve-racking conditions. Girls who have taken twice the usual time to get to work look worn when they arrive, but their faces are nicely made up and they bring you a cup of tea or sell you a hat as chirpily as ever. Little shopkeepers whose windows have been blown out paste up "Business as usual" stickers and exchange cracks with their customers.

On all sides, one hears the grim phrase: "We shall get used to it." Everyone takes it for granted that the program of wanton destruction, far from letting up, will be intensified when bad weather sets in and makes anything like accuracy in bombing impossible. Although people imagined early in the war that vicious bombardments would be followed by the panic-stricken departure of everybody who could leave the city, outward-going traffic on one of the major roads from London was only normal on the day after the worst of the raids so far. The government, however, has announced new details concerning the evacuation of children who were not sent away under former schemes of removing them to the country or whose mothers last week had the unhappy inspiration to bring them back to town for a holiday at home.

The East End suffered most in the night raids this week. Social workers who may have piously wished that slum areas could be razed to the ground had their wish horribly fulfilled when rows of mean dwellings were turned into shambles overnight. The Nazi attack bore down heaviest on badly nourished, poorly clothed people—the worst equipped of any to stand the appalling physical strain, if it were not for the stoutness of their cockney hearts. Relief workers sorted them out in schools and other centres to be fed, rested, and provided with billets. Subsequent raids killed many of the homeless as they waited.

The bombers, however, made no discrimination between the lowest and the highest homes in the city. The Queen was photographed against much the same sort of tangle of splintered wreckage that faced hundreds of humbler, anonymous housewives in this week's bitter dawns. The crowd that gathered outside Buckingham Palace the morning after the picture was published had come, it appeared on closer inspection, less to gape at boarded windows than to listen to the cheering notes of the band, which tootled away imperturbably at the cherished ceremony of the Changing of the Guard. This was before the deliberate second try for the Palace, which has made people furious, but has also cheered them with the idea that the King and Queen are facing risks that are now common to all.

Broken windows are no longer a novelty in the West End, though the damage there so far has been slight. In getting about, one first learns that a bomb has fallen near at hand by coming upon barriers across roads and encountering policemen who point to yellow tin signs which read simply "Diversion," as though the blockage had been caused by workmen peacefully taking up drains ahead. The "diversion" in Regent Street, where a bomb fell just outside the Café Royal and remained for hours before exploding, cut off the surrounding streets and made the neighborhood as quiet as a hamlet. Crowds collected behind the ropes to gaze respectfully at the experts, who stood looking down into the crater and chatting as nonchalantly as plumbers discussing the best way of stopping a leaking tap. Police went around getting occupants out of the buildings in the vicinity and warning them to leave their windows open, but even with this precaution, when the bomb finally went off that evening there were not many panes of glass left.

The scene next morning was quite extraordinarily eerie. The great sweep of Regent Street, deserted by everyone except police and salvage workers, stared gauntly like a thoroughfare in a dead city. It would have been no surprise to see grass growing up out of the pavements, which were covered instead with a fine, frosty glitter of powdered glass. The noise of glass being hammered out of upper windows, swept into piles at street corners, and shovelled into municipal dust vans made a curious grinding tinkle which went on most of the day. The happiest people there were two little boys who had discovered a sweet shop where most of the window display had been blown into the gutter, and who were doing a fine looting job among the débris. Around the corner, the florid façade of Burlington Arcade had been hit at one end, and an anxious jeweller was helping in the work of salvaging his precious stock from the heap of junk that a short while before had been a double row of luxury shops. Scenes like these are new enough to seem both shocking and unreal; to come across a wrecked filling station with a couple of riddled cars standing dejectedly by its smashed pumps makes one feel that one must have strayed on to a Hollywood set, and it's good to get back to normality among the still snug houses in the next street.

Wednesday night's terrific, new-style anti-aircraft barrage reassured people, after scaring them badly. A.R.P. Workers, who have been heroic all the week, were told to warn as many as possible that something special and noisy was going to be tried out that evening, but all over town persons who hadn't been tipped off thought that the really terrifying din was a particularly fierce bombardment. Houses shuddered unceasingly until the all-clear sounded in the dawn, when everyone felt better because, although Londoners had had a bad night, the raiders must have had a worse one. The behavior of all classes is so magnificent that no observer here on the spot could ever imagine these people following the French into captivity. From the point of view of breaking civilian morale, the high explosives that rained death and destruction on the capital this week were futile.[8]

London proved that she could take it. Frustrated, the *Luftwaffe* turned to the industrial midlands and the North, and November and December witnessed the "ordeal of the provinces." Not the largest, but perhaps the most murderous of all the attacks on industrial centers was the great night-long bombing of Coventry on November 14.

Other midland cities suffered just as cruelly—and rose just as heroically to the challenge. Birmingham, Manchester, Liverpool, Sheffield, one after another were subjected to devastating raids. The toll of civilian dead mounted to over 40,000; hundreds of thousands of houses were wrecked or damaged; essential services—gas and electricity and water and transport—were paralyzed; factories were laid in ruins. But somehow Britain survived—survived and grew miraculously stronger with each week.

The Atlantic Life Line

The fight against the *Luftwaffe* was only part of the titanic contest which Britain waged throughout the world. Cut off from her former continental Allies, Britain depended more and more upon her Dominions and Empire—and, increasingly, upon the United States. Above all it was essential to her survival to guard the Atlantic and Mediterranean life lines: if either of them were cut the consequences might be fatal. Upon the British navy and its air arm, then, was placed the almost intolerable burden of patrolling the waterlanes of the world, hunting down maurauding cruisers, destroyers and pocketbattleships, protecting convoys against packs of U-boats, sweeping mines from her harbors, getting supplies through not only to Britain but from the mother country to Gibraltar, Malta, Egypt, Russia, India, and the Far East.

In the beginning the combined British and French navies, though comparatively weaker than in World War I, had unchallenged superiority over the German. But with the fall of France the balance shifted. Not only was the French navy immobilized—soon the British went in to destroy it—but Italy brought to the Axis a powerful modern surface fleet and perhaps a hundred submarines. Germany, too, though weak in surface ships, could boast two giant battleships, the *Bismarck* and the *Tirpitz*, and three fast pocketbattleships, in addition to several older battleships like the *Scharnhorst* and the *Gneisenau*. From nearby airfields her planes could bomb convoys approaching the British Isles and sow mines in British harbors. And she had close to one hundred submarines which could operate from pens all along the Atlantic from Norway to the Spanish border.

How serious was the U-boat menace was speedily dramatized when, within two weeks of the outbreak of war, a submarine sank the aircraft carrier *Courageous*. The following month another U-boat penetrated the great naval base at Scapa Flow and sank the battleship *Royal Oak*. British submarines retaliated, the *Salmon* torpedoing the cruisers *Leipzig* and *Bluecher*. Far more satisfactory to the British public was the first major surface engagement which took place, significantly enough, in the distant waters of the South Atlantic. In this Battle of the Plate three British cruisers, the *Ajax*, *Achilles*, and *Cumberland* ran down the German pocketbattleship *Graf Spee*, damaged it severely, and drove it into Montevideo harbor where its commander scuttled it.

Other German warships roamed the Atlantic preying upon convoys from the United States and Canada. In November, 1940, the *Deutschland* caught a convoy out of Halifax including H.M.S. *Jervis Bay*, which tried to give the rest of the convoy time to escape by taking the full fire of the Germans on herself. F. Tennyson Jesse has told this gallant story:

Up on the deck one of the most awe-inspiring actions of the war had been watched by men who still can hardly describe it, so overcome are they with the horror and grandeur of what they saw.

Directly the attack began, *Jervis Bay* turned to port—towards the enemy battleship—and a shell caught her amidships.

"They've got her," cried one man on board *San Demetrio*. "She's hit!"

"She's on fire," said another, "but she's making for the raider."

Jervis Bay was indeed on fire amidships, and she hadn't, as the Chief expressed it afterwards, a hope in hell of saving herself. Few of her men and none of her officers were picked up after the engagement. But she steamed straight on into the range of the enemy's gunfire for several miles, blazing like a bonfire, riddled by shells the whole time. For some fifteen minutes the men of board *San Demetrio* watched this terrific fight, this uttermost expression of the human will.

When *Jervis Bay* came within her own range, her bridge had gone, she was alight from stem to stern, and the enemy must have thought she was finished, but suddenly she let off all her guns that could bear.

She had held her fire until she could be sure of hitting the pocket-battleship; she had drawn the enemy's fire upon herself, and given the convoy of which she was in charge all the time she could in which to scatter and get up speed. And only four vessels out of a convoy of thirty-nine were lost.

Thus *Jervis Bay* steamed on to death and immortality.

She went down blazing, her colors shot away, but a new ensign lashed in her rigging; her bridge shot away, but her master still in command, though mortally wounded.

And who shall say that, in the haven where gallant ships drop anchor, Drake and Raleigh, Grenville, Frobisher and a goodly company, led by a little man with only one arm and a patch over his eye, did not come forward to greet the one-armed Fegan and his battle-scarred men?[9]

The German surface raiders and battleships did not have things their own way. In May, 1941, the superdreadnaught *Bismarck*, of 45,000 tons, together with the *Prinz Eugen*, slipped out of their hiding place in a fjord near Bergen to harry British convoys. Reconnaisance planes of the Coastal Command spotted the battleships almost at once, and the hunt was on. The raiders were intercepted on the morning of Saturday, May 24th, off the coast of Greenland. The *Hood* received her fatal hit soon after the engagement opened. One who saw the *Hood* go down described it as "an unbelievable nightmare." The British chased a "thick squat ghost of a ship"—the *Bismarck*—through the ice floes, caught her and sank her with torpedoes from planes and destroyers and salvos from 14- and 16-inch guns that "bored their way through the Krupp armour belt like cheese."

The *Prinz Eugen* got away, to join her sister battleships, the *Gneisenau* and *Scharnhorst* at Brest. Bombed again and again these ships nevertheless managed to escape and, under cover of fog, make a spectacular dash around Brittany and up the Channel to their home ports. Fully repaired, the *Scharnhorst*, lurking in the fjords of northern Norway, preyed upon the convoys to Russia. Finally on December 26, 1943, the incessant efforts of the Royal navy to lure her into a fight were rewarded, and the *Scharnhorst* was sunk. C. S. Forester's account of this battle is one of the most dramatic in our literature:

Maybe the Nazis knew about the presence of that convoy, making its way to Murmansk round the most northerly point of Norway. Maybe the *Scharnhorst* was sent out into the arctic night on the mere chance of striking against something. At any rate, out she went from her Norwegian Fiord, wearing at her masthead the flag of Rear Admiral Bey.

For the purposes of raid this 26,000-ton battle cruiser had all the desirable qualities. Designed for a speed of 29 knots, she was faster than any British battleship. With nine 11-inch guns she was more powerful than any British cruiser. And her enormous secondary armament would insure that if she once got into a convoy she would sink ships faster than a fox killing chickens in a hen roost.

She left on the afternoon of Christmas Day, and at precisely the right time, just when the gloomy northern sea was beginning to be faintly illumined by the next dawn, made her contact with the convoy. There was up to half a million tons of shipping there. It was possible for her, in the next hour, to do as much damage as the whole U-boat navy could achieve in six months.

The British convoy was heading east some 150 miles north of North Cape. It was guarded against submarine attack by a ring of corvettes and destroyers, small craft. To guard against attack by surface vessels, Admiral Burnett had three cruisers, *Belfast*, *Norfolk* and *Sheffield*. He had stationed his squadron to the southeast of the convoy, and it was from the southeast that Bey arrived.

The *Scharnhorst* and the British escorted sighted each other at six miles. Aboard the British ships, the unsleeping eye which all United Nations ships carry—the eye that can see in the dark, can see through the arctic night, through fog or snowstorm—had been watching over their safety. It had given the first alarm, and now was reporting just where this intruder, this almost certain enemy, was to be found and whither she was headed. The guns were training in accordance with its observations, and the gunnery officers awaiting the moment to open fire. In obedience to the commodore's orders, the convoy turned itself about while the *Norfolk*, the *Sheffield* and the *Belfast* went dashing forward to meet the enemy.

In a broadside the *Scharnhorst* could fire rather more than the weight of shells that could be fired by the three cruisers all put together. It would be a fortunate light cruiser that could sustain a hit from one of her 11-inch shells and live through it, while the armor over her own vitals would keep out the cruisers' shells at all but the closest range. Mathematically, the approaching conflict was unfair. Yet the three cruisers flung themselves upon the *Scharnhorst*.

In the twilight of that arctic morning—the sun would not all day long come above the horizon—the glittering white bow wave flung up by the speeding *Scharnhorst* could be seen even when her gray upper works were invisible. A gun was fired in the British squadron and a star shell traced a lovely curve of white light before it burst fairly over the battle cruiser, lighting up the sea for a mile around her. As it hung in the sky from its parachute the cruisers' guns opened fire.

The shells went screaming on their mission, and the spotting officer of the *Norfolk*, through his glasses, saw, just at that very second when the *Norfolk*'s shells should land, a vivid green flash from the *Scharnhorst*'s black hull. The *Norfolk* carried 8-inch guns, the other cruisers only 6-inch. There was a chance that the *Scharnhorst* had been hurt.

The *Scharnhorst* spun about rapidly, so that the next salvo missed. Then she dashed out of the illuminated circle, and vanished into the twilight. Bey is dead now. We never shall know what were the motives that induced him to turn away. It is not likely that a man could rise to admiral's rank in the German Navy if he were of the stuff that flinches. Bey probably was acting on a plan he had devised long beforehand. It was the convoy he was after. He knew now where were the main defenses of the convoy, and could guess with some accuracy where the merchant ships themselves were to be found. He could circle away, losing himself in the gloom, and make a fresh stab.

Admiral Burnett, aboard the *Belfast*, had to guess what Bey would do next, where and when he would attack the convoy. A 30-knot battleship could circle the whole convoy in an hour. It might dash in from any direction, and in ten minutes sink many merchant vessels. So there was no margin whatever for miscalculation on the part of Burnett, standing there on the crowded and exposed bridge of the *Belfast*, with the spray flying aft as the cruiser steamed at top speed over the heaving sea.

At 12:30—three hours after the first contact from the southeast—the *Scharnhorst* reappeared from the northeast. She found Burnett and his cruisers right in her path. It was an extraordinary achievement on Burnett's part. What Bey thought of this apparition of three indomitable cruisers, when by all the laws of chance they should have been 20 miles away, can be guessed from his actions. There was a sudden flurry of salvos, during which a shell burst on the *Norfolk*'s stern, and then Bey turned and ran for home.

He could not doubt that three hours ago hurried messages had been broadcast to the British Admiralty and to the main British fleet; nor could he doubt that the British were straining every nerve to send ships and aircraft to attack a ship as valuable as the *Scharnhorst*.

As a matter of fact there was far more risk than he knew. Some 150 miles to the southwest of him and steaming fast to cut him off, was a force which could make scrap iron of his ship. This was the *Duke of York* with her attendant cruiser, the *Jamaica*, and her screen of four destroyers. From her masthead flew the St. George's cross of a full admiral—no less a person that Sir Bruce Fraser, commander of the Home Fleet.

Nobody outside a few favored persons knows how many times the Royal Navy had set that trap, how many times a battleship force had plodded along to Russia on a course parallel to, but well away from, that of the convoy, in the hope of intercepting any Nazi force sent out from Norway. This was the first time that patience and resolution were to be rewarded.

The *Duke of York* had been about 200 miles away when Burnett's first message came. The enemy had an advantage in speed of several knots. Fraser had to be sure of being able to interpose between the *Scharnhorst* and her base; any mere pursuit was doomed to failure before it started. He headed toward the strategical center of gravity—the nearest point of a straight line between the *Scharnhorst*'s last known position and the German base.

When the next news came from Burnett, after the *Scharnhorst* had made her second appearance, Fraser knew her exact position again. She was still 150 miles away.

It was time for Burnett to distinguish himself once more. The *Scharnhorst*, after scoring her hit on the *Norfolk*, had headed south through the twilight. Burnett swung his ships in pursuit. It was of the utmost importance that Fraser should be kept informed of the German's course. So Burnett had to keep in touch with the *Scharnhorst*, but to keep in touch with a ship that mounts 11-inch guns is more easily asked than done. Those guns were capable of hitting a target clean over the horizon, and it needed only one salvo, landing square, to sink any of Burnett's cruisers.

All during that anxious afternoon Fraser did nothing to reveal his position. One whisper from his radio and the *Scharnhorst* would know of the presence of another British force to the southward. Then at 4:30 all doubts were suddenly resolved. The *Duke of York* broke her wireless silence with an order from Fraser to Burnett to "illuminate the enemy with star shell." Then they knew that Fraser was very close—the *Duke of York*'s navigating officers had done a neat professional job. Counting every turn of their ship's propellers, making allowance for current and wind, deducing the *Scharnhorst*'s position and course from Burnett's reports, they had accurately tracked down their quarry.

It was quite dark. The *Scharnhorst* was on Fraser's port bow, and the *Belfast* was eight miles astern of the Nazi ship. A streak of white fire shot from one of the *Belfast*'s guns and soared against the black sky. The shell burst high up, and then the tremendous white flare blazed out.

Right in the center of that blaze of light was the *Scharnhorst*, and the lookouts and spotters and gunnery officers in Fraser's force saw her upper works standing out boldly against the horizon. Five 14-inch guns roared out with the incredible loud din of their kind and sent three and a half tons of hot steel and high explosive at their mark. For a score of seconds the shells rumbled through the air; one of the destroyers in the *Duke of York*'s screen under the arch of their trajectory heard them pass overhead like maddened express trains.

Then they landed, flinging up 200-foot splashes, and so closely had the range been estimated that this first salvo was registered as a "straddle." The next, half a minute later recorded a hit. Bey turned his ship sharply to port, and sent her wildly seeking safety in the eastward darkness. After her plunged the *Duke of York*. The *Scharnhorst* was hit and hit again, but was not wounded sufficiently to make any immediate difference to her speed. Before half past six she was out of range, battered, on fire, but safe for the moment from the *Duke of York*.

But hardly had the *Duke of York* ceased fire when a new blaze of gunfire lit the horizon far ahead. The *Scharnhorst* was having to defend herself against other enemies. The four destroyers of the *Duke of York*'s screen, with their superior speed, had overhauled her—the *Savage* and *Suamarez* on the starboard side, the *Scorpion* and *Stord* (the last a vessel of the Norwegian Navy) on the portside. They were dashing in, two on either bow, and just in the nick of time to prevent Bey's escape.

The *Scharnhorst* opened fire with all the guns of her secondary battery. From a spectacular point of view her defense was dramatic enough. She was one vast glow from the orange-red flames of her guns, and from this central nucleus radiated the innumerable streaks of tracer shells. But destroyers charging in at 40 knots are hard to stop. Moreover, the *Scharnhorst* had been hard hit, with almost certain damage to her guns and communications system. Her fire was singularly ineffective. Only the *Saumarez* was hit. The destroyers pressed home their attack to the uttermost limit. They did not loose their torpedoes at 10,000 yards, nor at 6000 yards, which is the nearest a destroyer can hope to approach a well-defended capital ship. They pressed in to 2000 yards and less, launched their torpedoes, and then sheered away from the doomed battleship.

Several of the torpedoes struck home, but the *Scharnhorst* survived these underwater blows and maintained a tremendous volume of fire, comparatively ill-directed but impressive. One singular advantage which the German Navy has always possessed was clearly demonstrated at this crisis. As the weaker naval power, she has never had to design her ships for ability to keep the sea for long periods of time; swift and sudden blows were all she expected of them, with the result that habitability is not considered a necessity. They can lie in harbor with their crews on shore in barracks most of their time, so that they can be compartmented in a fashion impossible to British or American ships.

The *Scharnhorst*, however, had lost speed, and now the *Duke of York* came up in range again, and the 14-inch guns began to smash her to pieces. The *Duke of York*'s attendant cruiser, *Jamaica*, closed to point-blank range. At the same time there arrived on the scene Burnett's three cruisers and four destroyers from the convoy escort. In the pitch darkness no fewer than eight destroyers, four cruisers and a battleship were tearing about at their highest speed round the *Scharnhorst*. It was time for the master hand to take control again. The signal sent out by the commander in chief was in plain English: "Clear the area of the target except for those ships with torpedoes and one destroyer with searchlight."

All the ships but two sheered away. One destroyer trained her searchlights on the wreck—long, long pencils of intense white light reaching through the darkness—and the *Jamaica* came in for the kill. She swung round and a salvo of torpedoes leaped from her deck. There were tremendous explosions when they hit the mark. When the smoke cleared away, the *Scharnhorst* was revealed for the last time, on her side, with the flames of her ammunition fires still spouting from her. Then the smoke closed round her again and she went to the bottom, while the British cruisers raced in to try to pick up survivors. There is on record the comment made by one of the British sailors who went into that smoke, but it is not well to repeat it. More than 1000 men had burned in those flames.

It is hard to criticize the Nazi tactics or strategy. Yet the fact remains that the *Scharnhorst* came out and was destroyed. In the months to come, the Nazi sailor who is ordered out will remember the *Spee* and the *Bismarck* and the *Scharnhorst*, and will go with a reluctance that will not increase his efficiency.[10]

As early as summer 1941 the Royal Navy had won unquestioned command of the surface seas, but the menace from mines and from submarines remained. The magnetic mine was, indeed, Hitler's first great secret weapon—potentially more dangerous even than the V-bombs of 1944—and it almost worked. How British scientists cracked its secret in a week is told by one of the anonymous historians of the British navy.

The first ship to be mined in the present war was the British steamer *Magdepur*, which blew up and sank off the East Coast on 10th September, 1939. Six days later the *City of Paris* struck a mine but escaped with little damage. As the weeks passed losses became more serious, and statements made by a prisoner of war revealed that the enemy was discharging magnetic mines from submarines. This evidence appeared to be confirmed by a number of unexplained explosions and sinkings off the coast.

Hitler had boasted of his "secret weapon" and it seemed that this might be the magnetic mine. It was not, however, a new invention, for the Royal Navy had used magnetic mines off the Belgian coast during the previous war, and, so far from its being a secret, an American citizen, Mr. Cæsar Marshall, had been granted a British patent for such a device in 1918. Other inventors had experimented with mines of similar type, and the Mine Experimental Department of H.M.S. *Vernon* was well aware of their existence; indeed, its own magnetic mines were in an advanced state of development. . . .

Against this weapon neither the existing sweeps nor the paravane availed. But counter-measures were taken, first with the "Bo'sun's Nightmare," which was still in the experimental stage. This was a wire sweep to which a number of magnetized bars were attached and towed between two ships just off the sea bottom. Large electromagnets and barges with coils of wire were also used; even aircraft were employed. The first magnetic mine was detonated in the Bristol Channel, but although the sweepers were rapidly fitted with new devices and the officers given instruction in their use, none was wholly satisfactory and the sinkings continued at an alarming rate.

A doctor cannot prescribe a remedy until he has had the opportunity of diagnosing the disease, and the officers of the Mine Experimental Department of H.M.S. *Vernon* could not find the effective antidote to the magnetic mine until they had studied a specimen and discovered its mechanism. Every effort was made to recover a magnetic mine intact, but for some time without success.

Then it appeared that the enemy was dropping the mines from aircraft. This was all the more serious, because it rendered our own mine barrages, which were a protection against surface-layers and submarines, of no avail. Between 18th and 22nd November, fifteen merchant ships were mined, including the Japanese liner *Terukuni Maru* and the Dutch steamer *Simon Bolivar*. H.M.S. *Belfast* was damaged and the destroyer *Gipsy* sunk.

The danger to shipping had suddenly become intensified, and it seemed that merchant traffic would be paralysed unless the remedy could be found. The men in the sweepers did all they could, but they were powerless against this weapon new to their experience. They looked to the scientists to give them the means to combat the offensive, but that the scientists could not do until they had discovered exactly what they had to fight. . . .

Shortly after midnight on the morning of the 23rd, Lieutenant-Commander J. G. D. Ouvry, R.N., of H.M.S. *Vernon*, was called to the Admiralty from London. . . . He was told that at ten o'clock that night sentries at Shoeburyness, on the Thames Estuary, had seen a German aircraft drop an object into the sea near the beach. At first they believed the dark shape to be a parachutist. They waded out into the water to investigate, but the incoming tide forced them back. A report had been made to the naval authorities, who realized that the chance of recovering a magnetic mine intact had come at last. . . .

Led by one of the soldiers, the party set off in the darkness, splashing through the pools left by the ebbing tide. At length the light of the torches revealed a black object lying partially embedded in the sand. The two officers advanced to the attack, while the soldiers in the rear illuminated the mine with an Aldis signalling-lamp.

They found the mine to be cylindrical in shape, about 7 feet long, made of some aluminium alloy, with tubular spokes on the nose and a hollow tail containing a massive bronze spring for projecting the parachute. There were two sinister fittings near the fore end. One was evidently a hydrostatic valve. The other was impossible to identify. It was made of polished aluminium and secured by a screwed ring sealed with black wax. As this fitting seemed more likely to harbour a primer and detonator, Lieutenant-Commander Ouvry decided to tackle it first.

Lieutenant-Commander Lewis took an impression of the securing ring on a sheet from a signal pad in order that a brass (non-magnetic) spanner might be made to unscrew it. Flashlight photographs of the mine were taken from all angles, and measurements made for purposes of description. It was then decided to wait until noon, when the mine would be again uncovered, and the soldiers tenderly lashed it down with the ropes and stakes. On their way back to the car the party came upon the parachute spread out on the sand. It was made of white silk and took eight men to drag it above high-water mark.

At 6 A.M. the *Vernon* officers had just finished breakfast when they received a message that another mine had been sighted about 300 yards from the first. They immediately set off again and waded out in the deepening water to find it. The occupant of a moored hulk nearby told them that it had been submerged for some minutes, and they decided to wait for the falling tide.

A preliminary report was then framed and sent by car to the Admiralty, together with copies of the photographs which had been developed and printed. At one o'clock both mines were uncovered. By that time the special mine-recovery party had arrived from H.M.S. *Vernon*, with Chief Petty Officer C. E. Baldwin in charge, bringing a set of non-magnetic tools as an addition to those which had been made at Shoeburyness during the night. A tractor lorry with a crane fitting was kept in readiness in a sheltered position on the foreshore. While daylight photographs were being taken of the first mine, the officers examined the second; it was found to be on a different slew from the first, with its nose inclined downwards, and was more battered. . . .

Lieutenant-Commander Ouvry and Chief Petty Officer Baldwin tackled the first mine. They started on the aluminium fitting on the upper part of the mine. The keep-ring unscrewed easily and there was no difficulty in raising the fitting. This Lieutenant-Commander Ouvry did, however, with the greatest caution, since he believed he was handling either a detonator or some sort of magnetic needle. It proved to be a detonator.

Confident that this operation had removed the principal danger, he summoned Lieutenant-Commander Lewis and A. B. Vearncombe to help him turn the mine so that he could reach the fittings hidden by the sand. This they accomplished without mishap, and a second detonator was discovered, of a type similar to that of the German horned mine. The fangs had now been drawn.

"We felt on top of the world!" wrote Lieutenant-Commander Ouvry afterwards.

By 4 P.M. they were satisfied that they had made the mine innocuous. It was hoisted on to the lorry, for despatch with the parachute to the *Vernon* the following morning, and an hour later a report was made to the Admiralty that the mine had been recovered intact. Lieutenant-Commander Lewis returned to London that night, and at 11 P.M. attended a Board of Admiralty conference at which the First Lord, Mr. Winston Churchill, heard the full details.

The mine reached the *Vernon* next day. Its total weight was 1,128 lbs. and it carried an explosive charge of 660 lbs. in the fore end. The conical stern became detached when the aircraft dropped the mine, thereby releasing the parachute. When stripped down by the experts of the *Vernon*, its mechanism proved to be what one of them called "a scientist's paradise." Mr. Churchill had given orders that work was to proceed night and day until the answer had been produced. In twelve hours the solution was passed to the Admiralty: it was indeed a magnetic mine, and all its secrets had been laid bare. . . .

As soon as the secrets of the magnetic mine had been discovered it was possible to provide the counter-measures. A new sweep was evolved, the principle being to create a magnetic field which would activate the needle of the mine, and the sweepers soon began to achieve satisfactory results. Moreover, since the paravane could give no protection against ground mines, they were provided with a simple but effective device known as a "degaussing girdle," which could be fitted to vessels of any size: a band of wire fastened round the hull, level with the upper deck and energized by an electric current, which has the effect of neutralising the ship's magnetism and giving her almost complete immunity. At one time 1,200 miles of wire cable were being used weekly to fit the ships.

It was this degaussing gear which made it possible to send R.M.S. *Queen Elizabeth* on her maiden voyage to New York, and it has saved countless other vessels, great and small, from destruction. It seems ironical that the unit of magnetic flux, which is one of the means of countering the magnetic mine, should derive its name from a German scientist, Carl Frederick Gauss (1777–1855). One Senior Officer of a minesweeping flotilla found it a name to conjure with when, after an abortive search for a magnetic minefield, he had been sent on "a wild gauss chase."

Once these remedies had been found, the losses were far less disastrous.[11]

Only a few ships, however, could be equipped with degaussing mechanism; for the thousands of merchant and cargo ships bringing supplies to the British Isles the mines remained a menace. They were cheap to make, easy to lay, hard to detect or avoid. Upon the minesweepers of the Royal Navy rested the responsibility of clearing a path for the convoys, and throughout the war they went about their dangerous duty with efficiency and simple heroism. Most dangerous of all was minesweeping in the British Channel, for here the sailors were exposed not only to the mines but to attack from the air and bombardment from the coastal batteries.

The U-boat danger remained the most serious menace, for notwithstanding continuous raids on submarine pens and on the plants manufacturing parts, submarine production increased during the war, and their cruising and striking power became more formidable. By March 1940 Britain had lost over 200 ships and neutral countries 200 more. During the summer and fall of 1940, losses ran to about 240,000 tons a month. 1941 saw a sharp increase in sinkings: from April to June the tonnage sunk was three times the combined British and American construction. Destroyers afforded some protection to the convoys but sometimes the U-boats penetrated to the merchant ships. And sometimes they got the destroyers themselves. Thus on October 31—over a month before Pearl Harbor—a U-boat struck the U.S.S. *Reuben James* on convoy duty out of Iceland. Commander Griffith Coale has given us a firsthand account of this tragedy.

October 30, 1941—Just as near to England as we are to Iceland. Subs are ahead of us so we have detoured far to the south. Message just received—SALINAS TORPEDOED. We were on that exact position two days ago. Another message—CONVOY BEING ATTACKED THREE DAYS ASTERN OF US. On the bridge all day, lots of bearings coming in. All ship's company alert. Same tanker strayed astern. We went back two hours, found her repairing engines. Left her, and rejoined. Getting quite used now to the peremptory da-da-da-da-da, sounding General Quarters throughout the ship. Men are on the run to their battle stations before the sound is finished. Three-quarter moonlight bright on water, making ships good targets. With a strange feeling of impending disaster, I printed a letter to my little daughter, turned in mostly dressed, and fell instantly to sleep.

October 31, 1941. Attack—Half awake because of the unusually easy motion of the ship, in the unaccustomed quiet I am conscious of the monotony of her listening tubes. A sudden loud explosion brings me upright. Know instantly that it is a torpedo and not a depth charge. Spring from my bunk, jump for the bulkhead door, spin the wheel releasing the dogs, and land on the deck in a split second, with General Quarters still rasping. It is not us. A mile ahead a rising cloud of dark smoke hangs over the black loom of a ship. With a terrific roar, a column of orange flame towers high into the night as her magazines go up, subsides, leaving a great black pall of smoke licked by moving tongues of orange. All the ship forward of No. 4 stack has disappeared. We move rapidly down upon her, as her stern rises perpendicularly into the air and slides slowly into the sea. A moment, and two grunting jolts of her depth charges toss debris and men into the air. Suddenly my nostrils are filled with the sickly stench of fuel oil, and the sea is flat and silvery under its thick coating. Before we know it, we hear the cursing, praying, and hoarse shouts for help, and we are all among her men, like black shiny seals in the oily water. The Captain leaps to the engine telegraph and stops her, rushes to the bridge side, sees all at a glance, and gives a sharp order to put her slowly astern, for our way has carried us through them and over the spot where she just has been. In a minute we have backed our way carefully among them and stopped again. Orders calmly barked, and every man acting with cold precision. Cargo nets rigged over the side, lines made ready for heaving. "We are the *Reuben James'* men!" comes a chorus from one raft, and then we know. The spirit of these huddled greasy forms, packing the overloaded life rafts, is magnificent, and their team work in shouting in unison is a fine example of quick return to initiative and organization in a crisis. But the bobbing blobs of isolated men are more pitiful. Thrice blown up and choking with oil and water, they are like small animals caught in molasses. We are now in a black circle of water, surrounded by a vast silver ring of oil slick. The men to port are drifting toward us and the hove lines are slipping through their greasy, oily hands. Soon many eager hands are grasping our cargo net, but our ship's upward roll breaks their weak and slippery hold. Instantly officers and men are begging permission to go over the side, and in no time three of our officers are ten feet from the ship on a reeling raft, and several chief petty officers are clinging to the net, trying to make lines fast around the slimy bodies of the survivors so that dozens of strong arms above on the deck can heave them aboard. The first man is hauled over the amidship rail vomiting oil. Forward from the lofty bridge I see an isolated man below me and hear his choking curses. Half blind, he sees the bridge above him. His cursing ceases—"A *line*, please, Sir!" I cup my hands and shout. A line is hove and he is towed amidships to the nets. Crossing to the starboard side, I see the obscure mass of another loaded raft. One man ignites a cigarette lighter and waves it in the darkness. They shout in chorus, but our lines fall short. They are drifting away to leeward. We shout through megaphones: "Hang on! We'll get you!" One man alone is trying to swim toward us. "Come on, buddy!" I bellow, "you can make it!" But the line hove with great skill falls short—and we chart the course of their drift. It is a lengthy and desperately hard job to get these men aboard. Our men are working feverishly, but less than half have come over the rail and thirty-eight minutes have passed. The horizon is dull red with the coming of the dawn, and the increasing light makes the mass of our inert ship an easy target for the submarine which must be lurking near. One of our destroyers is continually circling us, as the Captain bellows from the bridge: "Get those men aboard!" After sixty-five minutes a few exhausted men still bob along our side. The Captain says to me: "We are in great danger. I cannot risk the ship and her company much longer." Now there are two or three left. . . . A contact directly astern with a submarine! The telephone buzzes in the wheelhouse—the other destroyer gets it too! There is nothing for it. We order the ensigns on the raft aboard with all haste, the engine telegraph is snapped full ahead, and we leap away, leaving two survivors to swirl astern. We roar away and the other destroyer lets go a pattern of depth charges, the white rising columns of water tinged with blood color in the dawning. We search, lose contact, and return, and the other ship picks up eleven men while we circle her. We hope she got the two we had to leave! A third destroyer comes back to relieve us with orders to search the spot until noon, and we with thirty-six survivors, and the other rescue ship, catch up with the fleeing convoy at twenty-five knots.

"Secure from General Quarters!" Ten-thirty and we can go to breakfast! Hot coffee—Lord, it's nectar! We have been on the bridge since five twenty-three! The ship is a mess—her decks, rails, and ladders are covered with oil and the smell of it. At lunch I am amazed to see two perfectly naked ensigns walk into the holy precincts of the wardroom, their eyes, hair, and ears still plastered with oil in spite of the scrubbing that they have given themselves! Ropes, life jackets, and the men's clothes are piled along the decks in black and soggy masses. Four men with hemorrhages are put into officers' bunks. We learn that all the officers died with the blowing up of the forward part of the ship, and we had many friends among them.[12]

In spite of everything the Nazis could do, the ships went through. New destroyers joined the British and American navies; fast PT boats—the thunderbolts of the sea—took on escort duty; planes operating from flat-tops joined the bombers flying from newly built—or newly acquired—bases in Labrador, Greenland, and Iceland to furnish air protection. Sinkings declined sharply and by June 1943 one U-boat a day was being destroyed. By September of that year Churchill was able to announce that no merchant vessel had been sunk by enemy action in the North Atlantic for four months. The U-boat was still a menace, but the situation was well in hand.

Lend-Lease

During the dark days of Dunkirk, the fall of France, and the blitz, many Americans all but despaired for Britain. The overwhelming majority hoped for a British victory and gradually, as British fortitude endured all that the Nazis could do, and as Britain gathered her resources to strike back, the conviction grew that the Nazis might be stopped, and ultimately defeated. More important was the growing realization that Britain's fight was, in the end, our fight; that Britain defeated would mean America isolated in a hostile world. From the beginning President Roosevelt was frankly anti-Nazi, and in this he faithfully reflected the attitude of the American people. Bolder than most of his followers, however, he was prepared to translate attitude into conduct. In his Charlottesville speech of June 10, 1940, he promised to "extend to the opponents of force the material resources of this nation, and at the same time . . . harness and speed up the use of those resources in order that we ourselves in the Americas may have equipment and training equal to the task of every emergency." In September came the first important contribution from the United States—the famous arrangement whereby the United States transferred to Britain fifty over-age destroyers in return for 99-year leases on a series of bases from Newfoundland to British Guiana. It was, said Roosevelt, "the most important action in the reinforcement of our national defense that has been taken since the Louisiana Purchase." But this was not enough. British funds were running low, and some way must be found to supply Britain with the ships, planes, munitions, and food so desperately needed.

That fall President Roosevelt ran for re-election on a program of all aid to Britain; his opponent, Wendell Willkie, attacking him on the domestic side, resolutely ranged himself alongside the President on this foreign policy. Roosevelt was elected, and when, that winter, Willkie went to Britain, he carried a personal message to the Prime Minister. Churchill said:

The other day, President Roosevelt gave his opponent in the late Presidential Election a letter of introduction to me, and in it he wrote out a verse, in his own handwriting, from Longfellow, which he said, "applies to you people as it does to us." Here is the verse:

Sail on, O Ship of State
Sail on, O Union, strong and great!
Humanity with all its fears,
With all the hopes of future years,
Is hanging breathless on thy fate!

What is the answer that I shall give, in your name, to this great man, the thrice-chosen head of a nation of a hundred and thirty millions? Here is the answer which I will give to President Roosevelt: Put your confidence in us. Give us your faith and your blessing, and, under Providence, all will be well.

We shall not fail or falter; we shall not weaken or tire. Neither the sudden shock of battle, nor the long-drawn trials of vigilance and exertion will wear us down. Give us the tools and we will finish the job.[13]

A plan, brilliant, bold, and far-reaching, to give Britain the tools, had already been formulated. Early in January, Roosevelt submitted to Congress his proposal for a lend-lease arrangement, and after two months' heated discussion the plan became law, and this beneficent scheme was started upon its epoch-making career. Roosevelt hailed its passage in one of the most notable of his addresses:

The British people . . . need ships. From America, they will get ships. They need planes. From America, they will get planes.

Yes, from America they need food and from America they will get food. They need tanks and guns and ammunition and supplies of all kinds. . . .

Our country is going to be what our people have proclaimed it must be—the arsenal of democracy.

Speedily the vast industrial potential of the United States was harnessed to war. A trickle, a stream, then a flood of supplies flowed towards Britain—and, after our entry into the war, toward other United Nations. This was the great weapon for victory which enabled Britain—and then Russia—to hold out until we could bring the full power of our military force to bear.

Edward Stettinius, for a time Lend-Lease Administrator, summarized the first two years' operation of the plan:

The United States has put into lend-lease about twelve cents out of every dollar that we have spent to fight this war.

What does $12,900,000,000 of lend-lease by June 30, 1943, actually mean in terms of fighting strength? First of all, it means about 13,000 airplanes sent to our allies—a few hundred big four-motor bombers, 4,000 medium bombers, 5,000 fighters, many trainers, and some military transport planes. It means also the spare parts to keep these planes in the air, and many motors for airframes built in the factories of our allies. Of these airplanes, more have gone to Russia than to any other battlefront.

The lend-lease planes being sent from the United States represent about 16 out of every 100 that our factories are turning out. The proportion of our tanks that we are sending to our allies has been much higher—about 38 of every 100 produced in the U.S. Tanks account for more than $1,000,000,000 of lend-lease aid. Three hundred thousand trucks, jeeps, scout cars, and other vehicles account for another $500,000,000. The planes, tanks, and trucks together with more than $1,500,000,000 worth of guns and ammunition, $1,000,000,000 worth of fighting ships, landing craft, and merchant vessels, and thousands of smaller items total up to a little over $6,000,000,000.

During this period the U.S. was able also to lend-lease over 5,000,000 tons of food. In addition about 700,000 tons of other agricultural products were sent. Together, these account for another $2,000,000,000 of the total of lend-lease aid. We have spent a little over $1,000,000,000 to provide shipping and the air transport and ferrying service that our allies need.

Since March 11, 1941, all the governments-in-exile have become eligible for lend-lease, except that of the Philippines, whose forces are merged with our own until the day of liberation.

The men of the undefeated nations brought with them to the Allied cause more than 10,000,000 tons of merchant shipping. These merchant fleets have played a decisive role in the battle of the sea lanes. From the Norwegian merchant marine of more than 5,000,000 tons, through the sizable fleets of the Netherlands and Greece, down to the six Philippine ships which escaped from the Japanese, all have counted. On June 6, 1941, the defense of Norway was declared vital to the defense of the United States under the Lend-Lease Act. Many Norwegian vessels were armed and repaired under lend-lease in American shipyards. As the other undefeated nations were declared eligible for lend-lease, these services were extended to the merchant ships of Greece, the Netherlands, Yugoslavia, Poland, and other countries.

This is the breakdown of the $12,900,000,000 total of lend-lease aid— $6,200,000,000 worth of planes, tanks, guns, ammunition, ships, trucks, and other fighting supplies; $2,800,000,000 of raw materials and industrial equipment; $1,900,000,000 of food and other agricultural products; $2,000,000,000 of shipping, ship repairs, factories, and other services. We provide these things under lend-lease because they fight for our cause just as our own soldiers do.

The total impact of lend-lease on the economy of the United States has been relatively small. The dividends it has paid have been enormous. We are, it is true, drawing heavily upon our national resources to fight this war, mostly to arm and equip our own fighting men, but also to aid our allies. If we had not had lend-lease, however, if Britain had gone under, Hitler had isolated Russia, Japan had completed the conquest of China, and finally we in the Western Hemisphere had stood alone against an Axis-dominated world, who can measure the expenditure of men and of our material wealth we would have had to make if our liberties were to survive?

The United States is receiving reverse lend-lease in many parts of the world through supplies and services provided for our forces stationed in allied countries. The British, who have developed this aid most extensively, spent $871,000,000 in reverse lend-lease from June 1, 1942 to June 30, 1943, not including provision made for U.S. forces outside the British Isles.[14]

The most urgent demand on America's productive capacity was for ships—for without ships the planes, the tanks, the food so badly needed by Britain and her Allies could not reach their destination. And in no field— not even in that of plane production—did America reveal her industrial might and genius more clearly than in ship-building. Applying the technique of mass production, American shipyards turned out 8 million tons of merchant ships in 1942, almost 20 million in 1943.

Through the combined efforts of the British and American navies, and their air arms, of merchant seamen, of shipbuilders, of statesmen who formulated lend-lease and workmen who provided the material and services to lend and lease, of scientists who fought secret weapons, and provided some of their own, of soldiers and airmen on lonely outposts in the Arctic, of thousands and thousands of heroic workers and fighters, the Atlantic life line was held and Britain transformed from a last outpost of defense to a forward base of attack.

4

WAR IN THE MEDITERRANEAN

Britannia Rules the Waves

EVER SINCE HIS rise to power Mussolini had dreamed and boasted of building a great Italian Empire in Africa and making the Mediterranean an Italian lake. In 1935 came the beginning of the realization of that dream. That year he launched an army of half a million men against helpless Ethiopia, while the League of Nations stood by paralyzed by indecision and Haile Selassie solemnly warned the assembled delegates that their countries, too, would be victims of the breakdown of collective security. The Spanish revolution of 1936 offered an opportunity to extend Italian influence—and the Italian type of government—to the Iberian peninsula, and in the course of that war Mussolini sent over 100,000 of his legionnaires to fight and die for Franco. In 1937 Italy left the League of Nations and joined the rival organization—the Anti-Comintern Axis. In the spring of 1939, envious probably of Hitler's giant strides, into Austria and Czechoslovakia, Mussolini picked an easy victim for his next act of aggression— little Albania. The outbreak of the war found him committed to Hitler, but wary of fulfilling his commitments until he could be sure that he was on the winning side. The speedy conquest of the Low Countries and the destruction of French and British armies in Northern France afforded him that assurance, and then, on June 10, 1940, with France on the verge of collapse and Britain reeling from Dunkirk, Mussolini boldly declared war. "On this day," said President Roosevelt at Charlottesville, Virginia, "the hand that held the dagger has struck it into the back of its neighbor."

The entry of Italy into the war, together with the collapse of France, enormously increased the difficulties that faced Britain. Not until he had conquered the Balkans and immobilized the threat from Russia could Hitler cut Britain's life line to the Far East or obtain Persian oil. But Mussolini was now in a position to achieve these objectives. Could Britain, fighting for her life, spare sufficient forces to resist Mussolini? At first glance the task seemed insuperable. Mussolini clearly dominated the Mediterranean. He had built up the Italian navy to a first-class battle fleet; he boasted over one hundred submarines. His planes, taking off from flying fields in southern Italy and Sicily could cut far-flung British communications to Egypt. In Africa, his flank was secured by the surrender of France; he had a friendly government in Spain and his western flank was secured by the surrender of France. His control of Libya threatened Egypt from the west; his control of Ethiopia, Eritrea from the south and east.

The most immediate threat was naval, for if Mussolini could really make the Mediterranean his sea, the jig was up. By itself the Italian fleet was no match for the British. But now the British fleet was engaged in defending the home island and the Atlantic life line, while there was grave danger that Italy and Germany might get control of the French fleet which had found refuge in Oran and Alexandria in the Mediterranean and turn its guns upon the British. French ships fought beside the British against air raiders over Alexandria, but at Oran the French commander refused even to see Captain Holland, the British officer sent to negotiate. The following ultimatum was therefore delivered.

Sail with us and continue to fight for victory against the Germans and Italians.

Sail with reduced crews under our control to a British port. The reduced crews will be repatriated at the earliest moment.

If either of these courses is adopted by you, we will restore your ships to France at the conclusion of the war or pay full compensation, if they are damaged meanwhile.

Alternatively, if you feel bound to stipulate that your ships should not be used against the Germans or Italians unless these break the Armistice, then sail them with us, with reduced crews, to some French port in the West Indies—Martinique, for instance—where they can be demilitarized to our satisfaction or be perhaps entrusted to the United States and remain safe until the end of the war, the crews being repatriated.

If you refuse these fair offers, I must, with profound regret, require you to sink your ships within six hours.

Finally, failing the above, I have the orders of His Majesty's Government to use whatever force may be necessary to prevent your ships from falling into German or Italian hands.[1]

This was reasonable enough, but French pride, or folly, forbade the acceptance of terms. Two hours after Captain Holland had presented his ultimatum, a battle squadron under Vice-Admiral Somerville arrived at Oran and at 5:53 of July 3 began to fire upon the French. In the engagement which followed, the battleship *Bretagne*, two destroyers, and a seaplane carrier were sunk and the battle cruiser *Dunkerque* damaged. The *Strasbourg* escaped, but was pursued by the aircraft carrier *Ark Royal*, whose planes struck her heavily. There were still powerful elements of the French fleet at Toulon, and some warships at Madagascar and Dakar—though here the new battleship *Richelieu* was damaged—but with this "melancholy action" at Oran the threat of Axis control of the French fleet passed, and Britain was left to deal with Italy alone in the Mediterranean.

Although outnumbered in almost every category of ship, and constantly subject to attacks by land-based planes, the Royal Navy promptly took— and kept—the offensive. On November 11 Churchill was able to announce that planes of the Naval Air Arm had caught important elements of the Italian fleet at Taranto. In one of the first torpedo-plane attacks of the war, British fliers sank half the Italian battle fleet at a cost of only two planes, one officer killed and three taken prisoners.

The Royal Navy itself had not yet engaged the enemy which, notwith-standing heavy losses at Taranto and from subsequent torpedo plane raids on Sicily and Naples, was still formidable. Late in March 1941 reconnais-sance planes reported a force of Italian warships in the Eastern Mediter-ranean. The Mediterranean fleet met this Italian force off Cape Matapan, southwest of Crete, on March 29 and inflicted on it a crushing defeat.

The Commander-in-Chief, in deciding to engage in a night action, had to accept certain risks. Apart from the powerful force screening his quarry, there was Force Z—two cruisers and five destroyers—somewhere in the darkness to the northward. On the other hand, the enemy were only 300 miles from home and by daylight would be under cover of their dive-bombers. Admiral Cunningham could not afford to subject his fleet to air attack on such a scale. He therefore accepted the hazards involved in a battleship night action, and at 8:40 P.M. sent his destroyers in to the attack.

The necessity for providing protection for the vital Aegean convoys had reduced the number of destroyers available for fleet work to an absurdly small force, and only eight destroyers, in two divisions, formed the attack-ing force. The odds were dead against them, and they knew it. . . .

At 10:25 P.M. two large cruisers and a smaller one were unexpectedly sighted by the *Warspite* steaming on an opposite course, about 2 miles away. Although they were clearly visible through night-glasses, it was apparent, though incredible, that they were serenely unconscious of the presence of the Battle Fleet. They had presumably turned back in search of the dam-aged *Pola*. The *Greyhound*, the screening destroyer nearest to them, switched her searchlight on to the second large cruiser in the line; the merciless glare revealed that her guns were trained fore and aft; every detail of her construction stood out vividly in the illumination of the *Grey-hound*'s questioning stare. Almost simultaneously the *Warspite* and the *Val-iant*'s 15-in. guns opened fire. The enemy ship was seen to be the *Fiume*. Both broadsides hit. She appeared to change into a sheet of flame that was only extinguished half an hour later when she sank.

The leading ship in the enemy line, as seen from the *Barham*, was silhouetted against the beam of the *Greyhound*'s searchlight. Captain G. Cooke opened fire and hit her with the first broadside. She turned away to starboard, a dull glow of internal fires partly obscured by smoke. Her identity and subsequent fate are unknown. She was not seen again.

Captain C. E. Morgan of the *Valiant* shifted his fire to the second ship in the line, now illuminated by searchlights and starshell. This was the

Zara. Fire from all three battleships was concentrated on her at 3,000 yards range. She was hit by at least twenty 15-in. shells. The *Jervis* found her a burning hulk still floating at about 2:30 A.M. and sank her with a torpedo.

Meanwhile, in the terrible illumination of starshell, blazing ships and gun flashes, a number of enemy destroyers appeared astern of the *Fiume* and fired torpedoes at the battleships before making off to the westward. The leading destroyers were hit by 6-in shell from the *Warspite*, as the Battle Fleet swung to starboard to avoid the torpedoes. The Commander-in-Chief, with the battleships and the *Formidable*, then withdrew to the north-eastward to avoid the possibility of being torpedoed, in the confusion of a destroyer *mêlée*, by his own forces. That a contretemps of this nature was already taking place in the ranks of Tuscany was indicated by starshell and heavy firing on a bearing that none of our ships had reached. The *Vittorio Veneto* is believed to have shelled one of her own cruisers in this action.

Before turning, the Commander-in-Chief launched his screening destroyers to the attack. The 10th Flotilla went off in pairs—the *Stuart* led the *Havock* towards the burning cruisers; the *Greyhound* and the *Griffin* went off after the fleeing destroyers.

Just before 11:00 P.M. the *Stuart* saw an enemy cruiser, probably the *Zara*, stationary and ablaze. Another, apparently undamaged, was circling her and solicitously making signals. The *Stuart*, judging her moment, fired her full outfit of torpedoes at the pair of them. She also opened fire on the burning ship, which provoked brief response, followed by silence.

The Captain of the *Stuart* proceeded to turn his attention to her consort, who was found to be lying stopped 1,500 yards away, with a heavy list. At this moment, in the glare of the burning cruiser another appeared, apparently chasing the *Stuart*, who was busy shelling the victim of the heavy list. As if this was not crowding the moment with incident enough, an Italian destroyer shot past the *Stuart*, illuminated by a convenient explosion in one of the damaged cruisers. The *Stuart*, who had to dodge to port to avoid collision, put three salvoes into her as she swept past with the *Havock* in pursuit.

The *Stuart*, still swinging to port, now narrowly escaped collision with the cruiser Captain Waller of the *Stuart* previous thought to be chasing him. Apparently taking the *Stuart* for a friend, she ignored her, and Captain Waller, who had fired all his torpedoes, did nothing to disillusion her; instead he went off soft-footed to look for his earlier victim. She was on fire when he found her. A few salvoes produced nothing but explosions, and in his own words, "I considered her good enough to leave till morning." He had then lost touch with the *Havock*, and, as he puts it, "was feeling somewhat alone." This gallant unit of the Australian Navy then retired to the north-east and the cover of the Battle Fleet. On the way she engaged yet another cruiser and left her on fire.

We last saw the *Havock* disappearing in pursuit of a destroyer that the *Stuart* had severely mauled. Lieutenant C. R. G. Watkins, in command of the *Havock*, managed to get a torpedo into her, which brought her to a standstill. The *Havock* then circled her, pouring in a heavy fire until she blew up and sank.

It was now about 11:30 P.M. The *Havock* had lost touch with the *Stuart*, which was retiring on the Battle Fleet. Passing through a number of rafts and survivors Lieutenant Watkins, who had by now released his remaining torpedoes, saw, by the light of a starshell, what he took to be yet another cruiser. This was the crippled *Pola*, bagged at dusk by the Fleet Air Arm. He fired a few rounds at her, which provoked no reply; she appeared undamaged, and in some bewilderment he ceased fire. . . .

At this juncture the *Greyhound* and the *Griffin* appeared on the scene. The *Pola*, her ensign still flying, her guns trained fore and aft, was apparently undamaged. But a large number of her crew had unaccountably taken to the water, and the remainder, a disorganized rabble on the upper decks, were bawling surrender. The problem was either to sink her, to carry her by boarding, or to go alongside and take the crew grateful prisoners. His consort, Lieutenant-Commander J. Lee Barber in the *Griffin*, was for boarding her with bayonet, cutlass, and revolver. The *Havock*'s captain had changed his mind about boarding and was preparing to blow the *Pola*'s stern off with depth charges, having no torpedoes left.

Commander Marshall A'Deane was rescued from his quandary by the arrival of Captain Mack and the 14th and 2nd flotillas. They had failed to establish contact with the enemy fleet due to its timely "jig" to the southward, and now returned to the scene of the action, sinking the burning *Zara* on the way. Ordering his ships to pick survivors out of the water, Captain Mack took the *Jervis* alongside the *Pola*. Her upper deck was a scene of incredible demoralisation. Many of those who had not jumped overboard were half-drunk. The deck was littered with bottles, clothing, packages; the guns were abandoned—indeed had not fired a shot.

By 3:30 A.M. this strange rescue work was completed. Casting off from the *Pola*, the *Jervis* put a torpedo into her. As she settled very slowly, the *Nubian* followed up with another. The *Pola* sank at 4:10 A.M. and the flotillas rejoined the Battle Fleet.[2]

Taranto and Matapan effectively disposed of the Italian surface fleet, but the menace of the submarine and the plane continued. The task of supplying the armies in Egypt was difficult enough even through Gibraltar and the Mediterranean; if all supplies had to be convoyed around Africa it would be all but insuperable. At all costs, then, the supply lines through Gibraltar and across the Mediterranean must be kept open. Astonishingly enough, Hitler failed to move through Spain and seize Gibraltar. Perhaps one reason for this failure—a failure which in retrospect seems as fatal as any which he made in the course of the war—was his belief that Italian planes and submarines, operating out of southern Italy and Sicily, could take care of any convoys that attempted to run the gauntlet. This assumption seemed sound enough, but its realization required the early reduction or neutralization of the island fortress of Malta.

But Malta did not fall, nor did she ever cease to serve as a base for offensive action against the Axis. Within easy flying distance of Sicilian airfields, Malta was the most vulnerable, and perhaps the least defensible, of all Britain's outposts. Altogether, to the end of 1942—when the Italians and Germans had other things to think about—Malta sustained and fought off more than 3,200 air raids. Completely isolated, she depended entirely on convoys for the necessities of life as well as for planes, guns, and ammunition. And through the dark months of 1941 and 1942 the convoys came through, and planes flying from the island airfields became an increasing menace to the German supply lines to North Africa.

Desert and Mountain Victories

Meantime the Italians had already begun the great offensive in North Africa that was designed to win them a vast empire and assure them a position as one of the great powers of the earth. The prospects were, indeed, splendid. Altogether the Italians had perhaps half a million soldiers in Africa: against them the British could muster barely one hundred thousand. The British, too, were badly outnumbered in tanks and planes, and while the Italian lines of communication were short, those of the British were almost 2,000 miles, all of them perilous. The Italian plan envisioned an invasion of Egypt from the south and easy by the army in Ethiopia under the Duke of Aosta and, simultaneously, an attack from the west by the large and well equipped army under Graziani. The first step in this plan was the occupation of French and British Somaliland, duly made in August, 1940. Then on September 13, Graziani began his advance through Libya and into Egypt. But the attack, so triumphantly begun, bogged down at Sidi Barrani. There, two months later, on December 9th, General Wavell struck the Italians 60 miles inside Egypt and sent them hurtling back across the frontier. In rapid order Bardia, Tobruk, Derna, and Benghazi fell to the victorious British army, which did not pause until it reached El Agheila in Cyrenaica. In this brilliant campaign of two months, Wavell had wholly destroyed Graziani's army, capturing over 130,000 prisoners and enormous quantities of material, at a cost of some 1,800 casualties.

Italy's plans for the conquest of Egypt from Ethiopia were going badly, too. Here the Duke of Aosta had at his disposal some 200,000 troops, many of them veterans of the earlier Ethiopian campaign. Against this vast army the British could muster only two divisions, though, in addition, they could count on aid from the native population. Early in 1941 the British launched their offensive, striking westward from the Sudan towards Eritrea, and north from Kenya into Italian Somaliland, and occupying French and British Somaliland from Aden, across the straits. All at once the hapless Italians found themselves attacked from all sides. Within less than three months all Italian resistance in Ethiopia was wiped out, and Haile Selassie was once more on his ancient throne. This all but forgotten campaign, fought against odds of 7 to 1, over all but impassable terrain, was one of the most brilliant in military annals. Here is the story of the last battle, the fall of Gondar:

It must be realised that Gondar was not an isolated stronghold but the centre of a large district in which the Italians held numbers of strong positions. It is easy to grasp the essential features of the country. Gondar stands about 7,000 feet up, amid mountains that rise to some 10,000 feet to the east, west and north. Southward the mountainous plateau falls away to the blue waters of Lake Tana. Our men, on the high ground to the east of the city, had magnificent panoramas of green rolling country in which maize and millet grew, for it was the harvest season and, throughout the battle, Ethiopians were busy attempting to tend their crops with that supreme unconcern for war that they have inherited for generations, to whom both the sword and the spade were all in the day's work.

Although to Gondar roads of a kind ran from all points of the country, an army powerful enough to overcome Nasi's 34,000 men could only approach along two routes, one of which ran north-west from Debra Tabor and one south-west from Asmara. The two main Italian outposts were established respectively at Kulkaber on the southern road and at Wolchefit on the northern. . . .

The new plan was to concentrate the 25th and 26th East African Brigades with various supporting arms at Amba Giyorgis approximately 30 kilometres north-east of Gondar, while a small force called "Southforce," of two battalions with a battery of medium guns backed up by dummy tanks and quantities of wireless sets belonging to non-existent units, should launch a sham offensive along the Dessie-Debra Tabor road. This offensive was not intended to be entirely sham, for it was hoped that the "Southforce" would succeed in driving in the enemy's outposts at Kulkaber. . . .

Heterogeneous, but highly efficient bodies helped in the reduction of Gondar. There were the 2nd Ethiopians who, under Lieut.-Colonel Benson, had marched from Debra Markos round the western shores of Lake Tana. On 11th November they fell on the post of Gianda, captured the position, and later contained a large body of Italians in Gorgora. There was the Sudan column which, advancing from the west, cut all communications between Chelga and Gondar. There were also in the field no fewer than five different Patriot groups, each of which, under European leadership, played a most effective part in the operation. One group was led by a Bimbashi shepherd, who in peaceful times was a Professor of Poetry in Cairo University. First he established headquarters at Amba Giyorgis; later he descended the escarpment into the "Badlands"—a strange Walt Disney country just north of the Gondar mountains. There he fought a curious three-day mediæval war against the Kamant chiefs, who finally said, "You win," and came over to his side. Then he turned on the Italian outposts north of Gondar and was besieging Ghindi Merea when Gondar fell. . . .

The main conception of the attack on Gondar is not difficult to grasp. North-east of the city our strongest force faced Italian concentrations in the Ambazzo area. South-east of the city our weaker units faced the strong Italian positions on the Kulkaber-Feroaber line, where the natural defences provided by steep slopes had been considerably improved by fortifications, land mines and booby traps. Against these on the 13th November a combined attack was launched by "Southforce" and Douglas' Patriots. This first attack failed after an initial success. But Kulkaber had to be taken otherwise one-half of the scheme would have to be abandoned and our medium guns would have to be left behind to waste their sweetness on the rarefied Ethiopian air miles from the scene of the main attack on Gondar.

The problem was solved by a combination of enterprise and engineering. An old track was found, in terrible condition, but possessing the supreme merit of offering a short cut between Amba Giyorgis and Kulkaber. Everybody got to work and by 19th November a road of a kind could definitely be stated to exist. It was so steep in places that tractors had to be used to haul lorries up the more severe gradients, but it was just out of artillery range and it was also screened from Italian observation, save along one single stretch. The first thing that General Nasi knew of the development of this road was a glimpse of the lorries of the 25th Brigade passing along it to the south, and he could give no assistance to the isolated garrison in the new battle which began almost immediately—on 21st November. . . .

The final attack on Gondar came mainly from the east and from the south-east in partial reversion to the original plan, which had to be abandoned on account of the poor condition of the Debra Tabor road. Since a route had now been opened up southward from Amba Giyorgis and so much material and so many men had already been moved along it, it was no longer desirable to attack along the Asmara-Gondar road, where the enemy had not only his finest positions, but also his greatest strength. A small containing force was therefore left at Amba Giyorgis and the remainder of the 26th Brigade moved southward to Aiva.

Most of the 26th Brigade had to cross difficult country in which no roads existed, and in which for reasons of secrecy no reconnaissances had been attempted. For this purpose the Brigade was put on a "pack" basis, and it travelled on improvised resources and locally requisitioned horses, mules and donkeys. Each man carried fighting equipment and rations for three days. The final approach had to be made down a slope in full view of the enemy and the route had to be camouflaged by cutting down shrubs at night and replanting them so as to cover the track—a device used by the Japanese in the 1904 war.

At dawn on 27th November began the last battle of the East African campaign. Artillery fire was concentrated on the enemy's registered positions; the South African Air Force was soon active. The 26th Brigade crossed the river Megech, and began their assault upon Defeccia ridge. Further south, the 25th Brigade were attacking up the main road towards Azozo, and between the Brigades Douglas' Patriots flung themselves upon the series of enemy positions known as the Fanta Posts.

The country before the 26th Brigade turned out to be much more cut up and difficult than it had seemed; at times it was so precipitous that they had to go upon their hands and knees, even midst vast anti-personnel mine fields. However, they reached their objectives at last and captured them after a certain amount of fighting, despite casualties from mines and heavy shell-fire.

Immediately south of the 26th Brigade, the Patriots were meeting with very great success. But most spectacular of all were the achievements of the 25th Brigade, still further to the south. In a manner which one staff officer has described as "beautiful in its regularity," they took in steady succession the positions south and south-east of Azozo, and at last Azozo itself. Our armoured cars and light tanks roared across the river after the bridge had been repaired and found that Italian resistance had so far collapsed that they could push on to Gondar, interfered with only by small arms and rifle fire. The Patriots, who need not wait for bridges, had, however, got there first.

Meanwhile General Nasi had realized that the campaign was at an end. He had been deceived as to the direction of the attack and, though his guns were numerous, he was short of reserves. His only course was to send in envoys to ask for an armistice, but they arrived too late, for already Patriots and regular troops were getting into Gondar. In the end the last and best of the Italian commanders surrendered unconditionally to an officer of the Kenya Armoured Cars.[3]

Terror in the Balkans

Meantime, Wavell's rapid advance along the Libyan coast came to an abrupt end as he was called upon to send half of his meager forces to the defense of Greece.

In October of the previous year, Mussolini, hoping to win new glory and secure new outposts for his attack on Egypt, had launched an utterly unprovoked attack upon Greece. He had anticipated an easy victory, but in the mountain passes of Albania and Greece, as on the deserts of Cyrenaica, his armies met defeat and humiliation. The first Italian advance had pushed into the Pindus mountains along the Albanian border, but by the end of winter, the Greeks had thrown the invaders back across the border and themselves overrun almost half of Albania. Then the situation changed radically. Hitler, who had already determined to attack Russia, prepared to launch an invasion of the Balkans designed at once to secure his southern flank, rescue his Axis partner, and tie up with the Vichy forces in Syria and the pro-Axis elements in Iraq and Iran. All through 1940 he waged a war of nerves against the Balkan countries, and one by one Rumania, Hungary, and Bulgaria caved in. Only Yugoslavia and Greece remained unintimidated.

Through February and March pressure on Yugoslavia increased until it became, in the end, intolerable. On March 25 the government of Yugoslavia, under the Regent Prince Paul, yielded. But the people, divided as they were by internal dissension, refused to yield. Rallying under the youthful King Peter, they overthrew the government that had betrayed them and prepared to fight.

Despite public speeches, despite what the controlled radio said and what the weak-livered Yugoslav press told us, we all knew that Prime Minister Cvetkovich had at best only twenty per cent of the population behind him when he joined Yugoslavia to the Axis. But it had been the same in Rumania. There the eighty per cent had remained dumb. And we all expected the same pattern to be followed here in Yugoslavia. There was no reason to believe the eighty per cent would dare speak out in denunciation. But none of us had considered the possibility of a "Diaper Revolution." Yet that is just what it was, a Diaper Revolution. It all started with boys and girls ten, eleven, and twelve years old letting off steam with typical Balkan gusto. Sit-down strikes. Riots. A young revolution in the

classrooms of the grammar schools. Hitler pictures torn to shreds. Cvetkovich denounced as a traitor. Slogans deriding the weakness of the government scrawled in childish writing on walls and doors. Thousands of
hungry youngsters barricading themselves in their schoolhouses and re-
fusing to obey orders from anyone.

Belgrade was never prouder of its young than that day in March when
its young said things the whole city wanted to say but didn't dare. . . .

"Interesting handbills the kids put out," I said casually but with a wink
(to a Yugoslav) as we bumped into each other coming out of the booths.
He looked a bit startled; then he took me off into a corner of the lobby.

"You're an American, aren't you? All right. We're on the same side
then. I tell you those kids out there may be making history today. Don't
you see what this means?"

"What?" I asked dumbly.

"If this were just a few hundred kids writing a lot of nonsense it wouldn't
mean anything, but these kids are only parrots. They're just repeating
stuff they hear at home. That's why my office"—he looked around
nervously—"that's why my office is watching this thing. This shows how
the country feels. This is important. You newspaper boys better keep your
pencils sharp. Things are going to happen in Yugoslavia yet! . . ."

Just then I saw a squad of soldiers bringing in a familiar figure. Milan!
Good old Milan, our favorite barman at the Srpski Kralj Hotel. Milan was
one of my best sources of information. If anyone knew the answers, he did.
We went off into the bushes and had a hooker or two out of a bottle of
slivovich Milan always carried in his hip pocket for emergencies, and then
he opened up.

Simovich, the commander of the air force, was behind it all. The retired
captain was right. We were watching the unfolding of a first-class, full-
dress *coup d'état*. On the stroke of two o'clock army units all over the
country had been ordered out. At two-thirty they struck, surrounding the
royal palace, the regent's palace, the home of every cabinet minister, all the
police stations, the gendarmeries, city halls, and other public buildings.
They had all their tanks, light artillery, and motorized equipment ready
for action in case of opposition. Simovich was pro-British. He was convinced the country would be with him in his attempt to throw out the
government that had sold Yugoslavia to Hitler and Mussolini. He was
playing a dangerous game and he knew it. Prince Paul, who was ruling as
regent for the boy king, Peter, was a "tough old bird," as Milan put it. . . .

Milan said the coup was really being directed by the officers of the air
force. Simovich trusted them down to the last man. Their plan called for
the coup to be completed, for the country to be entirely in their hands, by
dawn, which meant five o'clock.

The more Milan talked the more my blood pressure rose. This began to
look like the biggest story in all of Yugoslavia's history. I remembered what
the plain-clothes man had told me in the Srpski Kralj lobby. Out of the
mouths of babes had come a call for the overthrow of the treacherous
Cvetkovich government, and now Simovich and his air force boys were
answering that call with tanks and cannon and machine guns. The Diaper
Revolution![4]

It was magnificent, but it was not war. Though her army was—on paper—large, and her soldiers brave, Yugoslavia was hopelessly unprepared for modern war. Even before her armies could be mobilized, Hitler struck. Belgrade, which had been declared an open city, was the first victim. Robert St. John describes the attack:

Back in the square we saw one place where a bomb had made a hole in the street big enough to bury a couple of railroad cars. I mean big American railroad cars. We walked up as close as we could to it, but still we couldn't see down to the bottom. You never saw such a mess as Terrazia was. I don't think there was a piece of glass more than a few inches square within half a mile. The bombs had torn the fronts right off a lot of buildings. I know that's old stuff. Everyone's seen pictures of buildings like that in Spain and in France and Rotterdam and, of course, in London. But it was different seeing it right in front of your eyes. Especially when the bombers were still over your head and you didn't know if they were through with the job or not. Those naked buildings made us think of Eugene O'Neill's *Desire under the Elms*, where they had a house on the stage and took away parts of the front wall so you could see what went on inside. . . .

We counted two or three hundred bodies right in Terrazia. And Terrazia isn't half as big as Times Square. Terrazia proved to me that this was all intentional. These planes that were bombing Belgrade had everything their own way. They weren't releasing bombs from up in the clouds. Every one of them came down in a dive or a glide and planted his bombs just where the crew wanted to plant them. From what we saw in Belgrade that day we decided they could have dropped a bomb right down the flue of a chimney, their aiming was so accurate. There wasn't any mystery about why Terrazia was one of the "military objectives" they hit, as Berlin called them in the communiqués after it was all over. Hitler was getting his revenge for the humiliation of ten days ago. He was showing the Serbs that no one could tear up his picture in public and get away with it. This was a mass execution of the guilty, of those who had demonstrated in Terrazia. It was a mass execution carried out on orders from Berlin, with the executioners riding the clouds. . . .

The people we felt really sorry for were those who had everything they owned tied in bundles on the ends of sticks they carried over their shoulders. Instead of following the winding highway, those footloose people trudged across the fields, because that way was shorter, even though they did have to struggle down through little valleys and then up steep hills. That ribbon of people is still one of the most vivid pictures of the whole war.

About ten miles from Belgrade there was a spot where the highway circled around a hill. When we got up there we could get a good view of the whole scene. Behind us we could see Belgrade. Burning Belgrade. Belgrade already well on the way to becoming a city of silent people. Except that a lot of those men and women lying around the streets were probably still moaning for help and a drink and something to stop the pain. We could see the smoke from dozens of fires. And up through the smoke the red flames. It looked as if there was another air raid going on. We were too far away now to hear sounds distinctly, but what we did hear was a dull noise that probably was a brew of all the noises of war mixed together. The noises of planes and guns and sirens and falling buildings. But what made us think the raid was going on in earnest again were the little black dots in the sky and the puffs of white smoke, which we knew came from the shrapnel sent up by the ack-ack guns as they tried so hard and generally so futilely to pin one on the bombers.

Then from the hill we could see that human ribbon stretching across the countryside. We couldn't see individual people and we couldn't see any single movement, but the ribbon seemed to move just like a piece of string as you drag it across the floor when you're playing with a cat. Or like a snake slithering slowly through the grass. One end of that ribbon was back ten miles, in Belgade. The other end was lost in the distance the other way. We figured that some of those people way up ahead must have started out the minute the first bombs fell, to be that far by afternoon. Silent, resigned people who knew it wouldn't be any use staying in their own city. Once out in the country they'd be safe from bombs, probably, but where would they sleep tonight? I kept thinking, where will they sleep tonight? And I kept wondering what they would do for food when they had cooked up all the cornmeal they had and there was nothing left.[5]

From Bulgaria, Rumania, and Hungary mechanized armies poured across the frontiers, scattering the Yugoslav forces, and cutting the country to pieces. In eleven days it was all over. Formal resistance ceased, and the stricken country was divided up among her neighbors. Yet resistance, implacable and relentless, went on. Guerilla bands, under General Draja Mihailovitch and General Tito harried the invaders, immobilizing many divisions of Nazi troops and exacting an ever increasing toll of Italian and German lives.

Even before Hitler struck, the plight of the Greeks had commanded the sympathy and enlisted the support of the hard-pressed British. In January, Wavell conferred with the Greek General Metaxas about problems of defense, and when, the following month, the Greek government promised to resist German aggression, the British gave assurances of aid. During March, Wavell managed to shift approximately half of his forces from North Africa to Greece—a total of some 60,000 men, British Australians, and New Zealanders. These men were equipped with courage, but little else: they had practically no armor and were almost entirely without air support. They were, therefore, wholly unable to stem the Nazi advance. One prong of that advance thrust down from Bulgaria to the Aegean Sea; another raced down the Vardar valley to Salonika, isolating three Greek divisions to the east; still a third drove through the Monastir pass, splitting the British and Greek forces. The British tried to form a line from historic Thermopylae to the Gulf of Corinth, but after three days of ferocious fighting German armor cracked this line and sent the British reeling to the evacuation ports of Piraeus, Megara, and Nauplia. On April 27 as the

Nazis raised the swastika over the Acropolis, the British, hammered relentlessly by the *Luftwaffe*, were pulling out of Greece in what was another, and no less glorious, Dunkirk.

The news was received April 22, that the Greek Army of the Epirus (that which had been isolated from the British force by the original Monastir split)had capitulated, that the Greek King and Government had departed for Crete, and that the Greek Government had requested the British Government to withdraw all British forces from the Greek mainland. The order was given for the troops to abandon the Thermopylae-Lamia Line at once and the Navy was told to rush ships across from Crete and Egypt for another Dunkirk evacuation. The British commanders in Greece had no option but to obey the order; indeed, it relieved them of an immense anxiety that had been growing ever since the news of the successful German drive through Libya, ever since their promised reinforcements from Egypt had failed to arrive. The task of organizing the evacuation of the troops devolved largely upon General Blamey, the Australian.

And Blamey revealed qualities of organization in the next few days that placed him among the greatest of staff officers, the more so as evacuation arrangements had not been discussed with the Greek military authorities until a few days before. . . .

Yet for all Blamey's fantastic brain-work and ceaseless enterprise, the operation came more than once to the fringe of disaster. New Zealanders, possibly because they were the most amateur, therefore intrepid soldiers present, were again given the place of doubtful honour. They were sent down to that covering pass, Erythria, then the village of Kriekouk between Athens and Thebes, to hold the fort while the other troops left the Thermopylae positions and made for safety. Some Australians, particularly gunners, went with the New Zealanders. The British armoured brigade, its gallant remnant, acted as moving rearguard to the main body of the British forces.

Athens was avoided as much as possible in the Blamey plan. The troops were sent instead straight down the motor-road from Thermopylae to the port of Megara in the Gulf of Aegina opposite sweet Salamis. A certain number were detained there and embarked, while the rest continued over the Isthmus of Corinth and across the Morea to the port of Nauplia, for more transports. Simultaneously another column was switched to the east after Thermopylae and sent through Marathon (history repeating itself) to the Aegean port of Rapthis and many other small havens down that rugged coast.

Meanwhile gunners of both the Australians and New Zealanders had last-minute excitements. Some Australian batteries remained on the Thermopylae heights till the very last, when they were rewarded by the spectacle of a German column as it halted and started to make camp on the plain directly beneath them. Waiting till the camp in those green meadows was complete, the gunners opened fire. It was a chastening spectacle of desperate confusion, but pleasant to the Australians who had themselves been made to suffer so much.

Similarly the New Zealanders, after lying in the gullies and among the olive groves of Kriekouk for two days, constantly attacked by dive-bombers, were able on Friday, the 25th, to catch an unwary advance-guard of German embussed infantry and annihilate some fifty lorry-loads of the troops (Australians at the guns again). That enabled the brigade to start its own retreat to the sea. The main body had passed down in comparative safety, so there was nothing to wait for. Megara was the chosen port for this brave rearguard.

But the evacuation of so many others from Megara already, had progressively exposed that port to German air-attack, and the New Zealanders were told to continue across the Isthmus of Corinth and make for Nauplia. Unfortunately the Germans got in first.

They descended early on the Saturday morning under parachutes and calmly (though their leader abandoned himself to uproarious laughter when the job was accomplished) occupied the vital bridge across the Isthmus Canal. When this news was brought to the New Zealand brigadier, approaching with his tired forces a few miles up the Athens road, that laconic officer promised to redeem the situation and the pride of all Britons by advancing at once on the impudent parachutists and rounding them up. Unfortunately he was ordered to not make the attempt, but to re-direct his troops to beaches on the Attica coast, where they were transported soon after to Crete.

But one New Zealander was allowed to show his paces at the end. This was Sergeant John Daniel Hinton, and he was shivering with other New Zealanders and many tommies on the beach at Kalamai during the muddled night of April 28–29. A German armoured column entered the town, then, with several armoured cars and many large guns, came down to amuse the evacuees—who were immediately ordered to retreat still further.

But Sergeant Hinton, shouting, "To hell with this, who'll come with me?" ran to within a few yards of the nearest German gun, which fired and missed him. Hinton hurled two grenades at the gun crew and they were dead. He fixed his bayonet and continued to charge, followed now by several other New Zealanders. He forced the Germans to abandon all their guns and take refuge in two houses. Hinton rushed at one, smashed the window and the door, and led his New Zealanders in to transfix the Germans with their bayonets. He led a similar attack on the other house and silenced that also.

Thus Hinton was able, with his men, to hold the German guns and the position for some time, while other New Zealanders and British escaped, and until the Germans sent down a stronger party, who found the extraordinary sergeant himself with one of their first bullets, wounding him in the abdomen so that he could be taken prisoner. They told him in Germany many months later that he had been awarded the Victoria cross.[6]

Miraculously, the British managed to evacuate to the near-by island of Crete some 45,000 of their 60,000 troops, along with remnants of the Greek army and King George II of Greece. If the Germans were to realize their plan for the conquest of North Africa and the control of the Middle

East, possession of Crete was essential. Yet if all the power of Italy and Germany could not subdue Malta, how did the Nazis hope to conquer Crete? Its people were loyal; it was garrisoned, now, by substantial British and Greek forces; the waters around it were controlled by the Royal Navy based on Alexandria. It was, or seemed, impregnable.

Yet ten days sufficed for its conquest. On May 20 the Nazis launched against the island the first airborne invasion in history. First parachute shock troops seized the airfields, then fleets of glider and troop-carrier planes, shuttling back and forth from Greek airfields, brought in additional thousands of mechanized troops. Loss of the airfields was decisive, for the British were forced to withdraw their pitifully small air force to Egypt, thus leaving the defenders of the island without aerial support. The Royal Navy, to be sure, destroyed two convoys of Nazi ships advancing on the island, but in the end, punished cruelly by the *Luftwaffe*, it too was forced to limp back to its African bases. By the end of the month Nazi control of the island was complete, and the British, leaving over half their forces dead or prisoners, were engaged in yet another evacuation.

Defeat

Things were going badly in North Africa, too. Not only had Wavell's army been reduced, by the Greek gamble, to half its strength, but the Italian army of some seven divisions had now been reinforced by the powerful Afrika Korps, under the command of one of the ablest of German generals, Field Marshal Erwin Rommel. Late in March the Germans attacked, and rapidly pushed the British back into Egypt. The retreat, however, was not complete, for the British left one Australian division in Tobruk. These "rats of Tobruk," as they came to be known, were a constant threat to Rommel's flank, and upon the effort to dislodge them Rommel frittered away time and strength. Alexander Clifford describes them:

The story of the desert during the summer of 1941 is the story of Tobruk.

In the middle of April the Australian Ninth Division, retreating at top speed through Cyrenaica, had stopped inside the perimeter defences of Tobruk and turned and fought. From the Germans' point of view it was not a fully staged attack on a fortress, but an incidental attack on some defences. The Commander of the Twenty-first German *Panzerdivision* was convinced that he could get the place easily. He attacked strongly. But when he ran into difficulties he swerved aside from Tobruk and drove on to the frontier in pursuit of the rest of the British army.

For fifteen anxious days the Australians, under the command of General Morshead, redug the defences and drew up their plans. Then on May 1 Rommel made the biggest attack he ever did make on Tobruk. His forces were at that time not very great and this was his first desert campaign. He had left himself only a little time to spy out the ground and reconnoitre the enemy defences. And he picked a spot on the south-west boundary which was naturally strong and strongly held.

The German attack, when it came, was a powerful one. But the Aus-

tralians had improvised a supple, resilient form of defence and they deliberately followed the German tanks to make a penetration. Then they
rushed mobile anti-tank guns from all the near-by sectors and formed
them up in a corridor on either side of the enemy thrust. The Germans
found themselves suddenly caught in a blistering crossfire and they turned
back and relinquished the attack. But they retained a dent they had made
in the perimeter, and this "bulge" or "blister"—or if you prefer it
"salient"—stayed there until Tobruk was finally disengaged.

Now it may well be argued that the Australians, in repelling these two
attacks, justified the Italians' fortress-area theory. But there are these
points to be considered: Rommel was new to the desert and so were his
men. They were not numerous or experienced. Part of the German forces
had to be detached to keep at bay the British forces along the frontier. The
attack was quickly planned and quickly staged. And the Australians met it
with a supple, mobile form of defence inside the perimeter, not with the
rigid, outward-facing fortifications of the Italians. The Australians had
proved that, given certain circumstances and a bold, intelligent defence,
these fortress areas need not necessarily collapse even when a penetration
has been made. They had proved that in a modified way the fortress area
can be useful in the desert, for while Rommel had not been prevented
from thrusting ahead to Bardia and the frontier, he had been prevented
from marching on into Egypt afterwards. Tobruk, the first British exper-
iment in the theory, was already paying dividends as far as defence was
concerned. It still remained to be seen whether the place could have any
more than a purely negative value.

In May Rommel sat down to besiege Tobruk. He gave up land attacks
and tried the air. The Stuka dive bombers and high-level bombers came
over in layers. Night and day the harbour and the little white town rocked
under the impact of the explosions. The enemy planes only had fifteen
miles to fly. The defenders of the southern perimeter could actually hear
the bombers warming up their engines at El Adem before coming to bomb
Tobruk.

Geographically the Tobruk area was twice the size of the district of
Columbia and the shape of a wooden clog standing level and with the toe
pointing to the right. Tobruk itself—a plain white town of one-story stucco
buildings arranged in half a dozen crisscrossing streets—lay with its back to
the open sea, facing south across the inlet which forms its harbour. From
it one metalled road ran east to Bardia, one west to Derna, and one south
to El Adem Air-Port.

The defences ran in a semicircle from coast to coast, concentric rings of
barbed wire, tank traps, trenches, mine fields, concrete pillboxes. Dotted
all round were high lookout posts like ships' crow's-nests, from which
artillery observers could survey the countryside. The whole was divided
into two levels by the steep escarpment which ran right across it, parallel
with the sea, a mile or so inland. Nothing grew there except in a fertile
little oasis down by the shore called the Wadi Auda, where the Public
Relations Unit had its camp.

Tobruk had no fighter protection. Its own air fields inside the perimeter could not possibly be used, and the Egyptian air fields were too far
away. It only had its anti-aircraft batteries to fight off these cascades of

planes. Between April 9 and July 31, for instance, actual bombing raids totalled 437. Forty-eight of these were dive-bombing attacks, 277 were high-level daylight raids and 160 were at night. It was calculated that 458,000 pounds of high explosive had been dropped during the day raids, and 320,000 pounds during the night.

Yet in the face of this Tobruk was not only fed and maintained but it was turned into a dump. The navy ferried in shipload after shipload of food and petrol and ammunition which was stored against the day when an army advancing from Egypt should need it. More than eighty tanks were brought in. Thousands of tons of matériel were unloaded at night on the battered quayside by workers who retired into caves when the bombers came. A complete repair workshop was established. Tobruk settled down to a noisy, hectic routine.

Lord Haw-haw called the defenders "the self-supporting prisoners," and "the rats of Tobruk," but Rommel gave up trying to take the place. He built the "Achsenstrasse," a forty-mile bypass road round Tobruk, so that his convoys could get through to Bardia. He brought up siege guns—long-barrelled 155-millimetre French guns and even a 210-millimetre cannon. He pounded the harbour with shells and bombs and of course he sank a ship now and then but Tobruk never starved.

They lived a life there of simplicity so stark, so primitive, that its rhythm was even governed by the phases of the moon. For it was only on a few black moonless nights that Tobruk had contact with the outside world. In the dead of those black nights, men would stand on the quayside, straining their eyes into the darkness, seeing and hearing nothing until voices hailed them from just twenty yards ahead across the water, and they saw the faint phosphorescence of the inky sea as it swished round the bows of a destroyer. Then men would stream ashore and march away, and others would embark in a swift, steady exchange. Newcomers would be afraid to talk aloud, so near did the enemy seem. They jumped when they were told to and marched ahead into the opaque darkness when they got the order, obeying blindly like children because they were in a place with rules of its own which they did not understand.

Few of the men in Tobruk ever had a roof over their heads. They lived in a picnic not as a reaction or an escape from civilized life, but merely because there was no civilized life. They were almost unimaginably devoid of luxuries. Strip life of everything that makes it worth-while, and you will have the standard of living in Tobruk. The water was scanty and brackish and the tea tasted salty however strong it was made. The rations were just a means of keeping alive in the most economical way and Vitamin C came in little white pills. Beer appeared once in a blue moon—there is the story of the only Tobrukian who ever achieved a hangover. His unit decided to make one man thoroughly happy instead of getting a tantalizing mouthful each, so they drew lots for the entire ration. On one famous occasion two tins of beer were issued to every man in the garrison, and the sounds of rejoicing were so loud that the Italians uneasily doubled their sentries, then ordered "Action Stations" all night, and finally laid down a non-stop artillery barrage, just in case.

The nearest they ever got to women in Tobruk was when they cut pictures of film actresses out of old magazines, or painted the names of their girl friends on their trunks. No Tobruk sock was ever darned by a woman's hand, no button was ever properly sewn on. They never saw a tree or a flower or bought themselves a drink or sat around a table to eat a meal, or heard a note of music. They very rarely had much to read, for shipping space was worth its volume in gold. But they got their mails and parcels, and that was a bigger comfort to them than anything else. I still think one of the most pathetic stories of the war is the one about the private in Tobruk who unwrapped a parcel from England and out tumbled a tin of bully beef. For bully beef was one of the very few things they did have in Tobruk, perhaps the only thing in the world that was infinitely more precious in England than there.

The surprising thing is that they did not go crazy with boredom. There were front-line positions which could not be reached in daylight, and the outposts had to crawl there before dawn and just sit and wait all through the torrid day for evening to relieve them. It is a wonder that sandstorms and bombings and eternally salty water and boredom did not drive them to despair. But there was not a moment when Tobruk's morale was not higher than Cairo's.

These men grew tough and lean and seasoned. The summer suns burned them the colour of shoe leather. They bathed in warm sea and played football and organized sports. Gradually their bodies grew accustomed to this hard living and monotonous eating. The raids caused astonishingly few casualties. Men said that they got used to the bombs much more easily than to the flies. And there were even people who claimed that they liked the place.

Towards the end of July and the beginning of August, British, Indian and Australian patrols began to take the offensive. At first they went out just to obtain information. They checked up on the dispositions of the enemy fortifications and the changes in his position. Then they found that it was rather more effective to destroy enemy observation posts and strongpoints than merely to plot them on their maps. Next they discovered that Italian morale was beginning to crumble as the night raids continued. Finally the patrols realized that they themselves enjoyed the business.

As a rule each raid provoked a hysterical artillery barrage big enough to stop a division. Sometimes the Italians wore out their guns and used up their shells for two hours on end. Then the patrollers would silently rise from the dug-outs where they had been waiting and carry on with their job.

One Indian patrol attacked and took four enemy positions in a night. An Australian patrol spent a whole day outside the perimeter in a captured strong-point and then came home to read about its own exploits in the daily paper, *Tobruk Truth* (or *Dinkum Oil* to Australians). The best patrol story of all was that of the eighty Italians who stood one night watching Tobruk being shelled, rubbing their hands and exchanging congratulations. So intent were they on watching that they did not hear a faint shuffling in the sand behind them. In fact, they heard nothing at all until an electrifying war-cry made their blood run cold. They spun round to see the moonlight gleaming on Australian bayonets. Most of them were so horror-struck that they did not even try to flee.

Amateur "Bush Artillery"—cooks, orderlies and such like—doing stunts with guns captured by the Italians from the Austrians in the last war, was another of Tobruk's features. The first salvoes of these patched-up cannons seem to have caused consternation. Puzzled German gunners ranged feverishly, trying to contact this mystery battery which their Intelligence had failed to locate. But the "Bushmen" were able to keep up their hobby for weeks and were finally given a place in the line.

At the end of August the garrison was relieved. The Australians came out, all except one battalion, and they were replaced by the Polish brigade, the Thirty-second British Army Tank Brigade, the King's Dragoon Guards (with armoured cars) and men from the Black Watch and an assortment of British country regiments. General Morshead handed over to General Scobie.

The Poles livened up the pace at once. Their pleasure at the prospect of fighting Germans could hardly be restrained. Sometimes a deafening clamour would break out at night from the Polish sector and men would stir uneasily in their sleeping-bags and wonder whether the Germans were attacking. But they soon got to understand. The Poles were apt to interpret a patrol as an offensive. Or someone had thought they had seen a German. Or simply the Poles had felt like having a barrage.

A friend of mine once went to the Poles to explain to them where the enemy's guns lay. They listened politely but without enthusiasm while he pin-pointed the Italian batteries. Then he mentioned a German battery.

While he was still speaking three Poles left the tent at the double. Outside he heard urgent words of command. And before he had finished talking the Polish guns were in action, all aimed at the Germans.

When he could hear himself speak, the Englishman showed the Poles where an Italian division was being relieved. Again they listened politely. Then he pointed out three German sentries. Within a couple of minutes the three bewildered sentries had gone to ground with a hail of fire screaming about their ears. The Italians were left in peace.

As the summer wore on the defence system was worked out with elaborate detail. The place was divided up into interdependent sectors and all the defences were designed to swivel round to the flank or the rear and form a new front inside the perimeter at a moment's notice. All signal wires and communications were duplicated by alternative routes so that if one line were cut another could instantly be switched on. There was a complex technique of mutual assistance among the closely interlocked subdivisions of the front line, and forces for counterattacks were always held ready in the rear.

And Tobruk was also being groomed for offence as well as defence. All its defenders knew that the fortress was to play its vital part in the winter offensive—for it was morally certain that there would be a winter offensive. The tank force mounted up and the caves became stuffed with food and petrol. The nightly patrols were recognized as rehearsals for the day when the garrison should really break out in earnest. From being an isolated remnant of a retreating army, Tobruk increased in stature and confidence as the summer burned on. It became the forward outpost, the vanguard of a new army that was growing daily stronger away in Egypt. And when Russia came into the war, Tobruk was the extreme left wing of an Allied front that ran from its own sun-parched patch of desert to somewhere on the Arctic Ocean.

So the epic of Tobruk was built up, out of a multitude of human details all co-ordinated towards one end. A life that had been stripped nearly beyond its bare essentials grew somehow rich and dramatic on this barren soil. The Rats of Tobruk became almost proud of their prison and they cursed it with a certain affection. But their greatest hour was yet to come.[7]

In all this black chapter of defeat there was but one encouraging page. In the vast and strategically important Middle East which stretches from the eastern shores of the Mediterranean to India, the British had out-guessed, outmaneuvered, and outfought the Axis and its agents. The importance of this area can scarcely be exaggerated. If the Axis came to dominate Syria, Iraq, and Iran they could secure for themselves the precious oil that supplied the Mediterranean fleet, immobilize Turkey and perhaps force her into partnership, interpose an insurmountable barrier to lend-lease supply to Russia via the Persian Gulf, and threaten India from the west. The outlook for Axis success in this area was bright. Vichy forces in Syria were hand-in-glove with the Germans; Axis agents engineered a palace coup in Iraq, and hundreds of other agents were pouring into Iran with the same purpose.

The British moved with admirable promptness to frustrate these dangerous designs. Immediately after the palace revolution in Iraq the British reinforced their Habanniya airfields, and within a month Bagdad was occupied and the pro-British regent, Abdul Illah, restored to power. In June, General Sir Maitland Wilson invaded Syria from Palestine and Iraq and, after sharp fighting, defeated the Vichy forces and ousted them from power. By that time Russia was at war with Germany and, realizing the crucial importance of the Persian Gulf route through Teheran to the Caspian Sea, British and Russians moved simultaneously into Iran and established effective and lasting control of that country.

General Sir Claude Auchinleck had succeeded Wavell in command of the British forces in North Africa, now consolidated into the ever-famous Eighth Army. By November, reinforced with new armored divisions and equipped with American lend-lease supplies, he felt strong enough to take the offensive against Rommel in an effort to relieve the long-besieged garrison at Tobruk. The offensive got off to a bad start when British tanks were outfought at Sidi Rezegh and Rommel cut across Auchinleck's rear to invade Egypt. But Rommel, too, overplayed his hand, and soon he was forced, by British armored superiority, to pull back in a retreat that did not stop short of El Agheila. There he received rank reinforcements and the British, who were by this time overextended, were in turn forced to fall back towards Tobruk.

The ensuing months witnessed a race between the opposing armies to build up their armor—a race the first lap of which the Germans won by virtue of their short line of communications. On May 26 Rommel, heavily reinforced, mounted his most dangerous offensive. In this campaign the British were both outclassed and outfought. First outflanking British mine-fields along the Gazala line, Rommel won the tank battle of the Cauldron.

Then, on June 10, the French were forced, by incessant bombing, to evacuate their outpost at Bir Hacheim which had so long threatened Rommel's southern flank. Three days later, on "Black Saturday," June 13, the Desert Fox lured the British army into a trap at Knightsbridge and destroyed all but 70 of 300 tanks. It was one of the most stunning defeats of the war but worse was still to come. On June 21 Tobruk, which had held out for so long against Axis attacks, was surrendered, with 25,000 men, by its South African commander, General Klopper. Winston Churchill, then in Washington, admitted publicly that the fall of Tobruk was "a bit disconcerting"; privately he confessed that he was the most miserable Englishman in America since Burgoyne had surrendered at Saratoga. The Axis exulted that Africa was theirs, and even the most optimistic British wondered whether it would be possible for the Eighth Army to form a defense line anywhere short of Alexandria or the Suez Canal.

El Alamein and Beyond

Fortunately this defeat of the Eighth Army was not irretrievable. Indeed at this moment, which seemed so fraught with peril, the Allies were approaching one of those grand climacterics which mark the shift in the fortunes of war. With admirable energy and skill General Auchinleck set up a defense line in the narrow neck between El Alamein and the impassable Quattara Depression and here, barely sixty miles from Alexandria, the Eighth Army hung grimly on. Gradually, as Alexander Clifford points out, the desperate situation improved:

Mussolini arrived in Africa with uniforms, flags, bands and a white charger ready for entry into the cities of Egypt. He brought his flashiest regiments, the Novara Lancers and the Sardinian Grenadiers, with fragile parade tanks that broke down hopelessly in the desert but would probably have negotiated the streets of Cairo. The German and Italian radios began to announce high-sounding proclamations promising complete independence to the Egyptian people. Medals were struck and occupation money prepared. Experts worked on a scheme for civil administration. The German radio made dates for the Afrikakorps with the ladies of Cairo and Alexandria. At night in their messes, while they ate British food taken in Tobruk, weary German officers discussed the baths and clean sheets to come. The Italians wrote home and said they could already see the towers of Alexandria.

It looked a practical certainty for Rommel. But day by day, hour by hour, two sets of forces were at work with cumulative strength. It was hard to calculate mathematically the exact influence of these forces, but it was certain that both were working against Rommel. One set was acting as a brake on his army, holding it back, dulling its impetus, draining its strength. The other set was tending to endow the Eighth Army with fresh power and order and energy.

The influences working against Rommel were these: his men were growing more tired every hour. Already the Ninetieth Light, who had fought magnificently, were rocking on their feet with weariness. Every day a few German tanks were being lost, and no new ones were coming up. British bombers scored annihilating hits on a tank recovery workshop. Supply lines were stretching and stretching. Transport was wearing out. The wells of Egypt had been salted or oiled or blown up, and every drop of water must come by land. The *Luftwaffe* had lagged dangerously behind in the advance, and when it had made a supreme effort to get ahead, it had come too fast, without proper protection, and the R.A.F. had made mincemeat of its planes on the ground. The British had put every plane they could in the air, and were concentrating fiercely on the fragile, elongated Axis supply routes. British mobile columns were hitting hard at weak spots, and in particular a force which drove westwards south of the eastward-moving Germans was wreaking great havoc.

All those things were holding Rommel back. These things were renewing the British strength: the convoy of eighteen ships had reached Suez and was being frantically unloaded. Every gun and tank as it was unpacked was rushed straight across to the front. Since every man possible was needed for fighting, girl A.T.S.'s drove new trucks for fourteen hours a day from the ports to Cairo and handed them over to the army drivers. The New Zealanders, with the emblems on their trucks painted out and their distinctive hats packed away for the sake of secrecy, came racing down from Palestine and up to the desert. They first went into action near Mersa Matruh—fresh, vigorous troops without the memory of hundreds of miles of retreating immediately behind them—and when they got surrounded, Maoris went in with bayonets at night to chop a way out for them. The Australian Ninth Division, too, was on its way to the front. With every day's retreating, the base workshops and the reinforcement dumps were nearer and the army was falling back onto its own strength. The R.A.F. was retiring onto its own well-equipped air fields and it was working without ceasing. Kittyhawks went out bombing, fighting and escorting all in one operation. Tedder and Coningham made a major effort which many people believed was the decisive element in the situation.

So the balance was swinging back to level.[8]

President Roosevelt, no less alarmed than Churchill himself, had promptly ordered every spare Sherman tank sent to the imperiled Egyptian front. Churchill himself came out to see personally how bad the situation was and to encourage the troops with is presence. And in August, Auchinleck was removed from command and the command of the Middle East entrusted to General Sir Harold Alexander and that of the Eighth Army to his devoted friend, General Bernard Montgomery. John Gunther here gives a glimpse of Montgomery in Egypt and reports a curious circumstance:

He was heartily disliked when he first arrived in Cairo. He was cavalier about his predecessors, which was considered bad form in the extreme, and many officers thought him insolent. Monty paid no attention. He went up forward and wandered around for a day or two, inspecting every position, talking to every man he met, making intimate personal contact with the troops. What he had to pray for was time. "Give me a fortnight," he said, "and I can resist the German attack. Give me three weeks, and I can defeat the Boche. Give me a month, and I can chase him out of Africa." Meantime, he *took hold*. Within forty-eight hours the difference in spirit at the Alamein front was prodigious. The previous commander had scarcely ever visited or even talked to his own men. But within forty-eight hours of Monty's arrival, every man in Egypt knew that a fresh new wind was blowing, that their new commander was something quite different, something unique. He instilled into them, magically, his own magnificent superconfidence.

The plans for the Alamein battle, which opened on October 23, 1942, were made originally by General Wavell when the Italians were attacking in 1940; Wavell selected Alamein as a good position for a last stand, if a last stand should become necessary. Oddly enough, the original Wavell plans were unaccountably lost; when the Germans threatened Egypt two years later, they were unearthed just in time. The actual conception of the 1942 battle was Alexander's. Montgomery was simply the executant. But he executed the job supremely well.[9]

It was the Allies—and the United States could, by this time, be counted as an ally—who won the final lap of the battle for supply. During the summer months hundreds of Sherman tanks, thousands of jeeps and trucks, almost one hundred 105-mm self-propelled guns, and hundreds of planes arrived from the United States. The British, too, strained every nerve to rush in supplies—the major part of the Eighth Army equipment was British—and by October Montgomery had definite superiority in armor and in the air.

On October 3rd, Marshal Rommel said, "We hold the gateway of Egypt with full intention to act. We did not go there with any intention of being flung back sooner or later. You may rely on our holding fast to what we have got." Three weeks later, on the night of October 23, Montgomery hurled all his might at the enemy. The battle of El Alamein was not only, as Churchill said, "the end of the beginning"; it was one of the decisive battles of the war—and of history. Let Lieutenant-Colonel J. O. Ewert, one of Montgomery's intelligence officers, describe it:

The twenty-third of October, 1942, was a still and moonlight night in the desert. At 9:40 the roar of 800 guns broke the silence and marked the start of the battle of Alamein. Twenty minutes of flashing, deafening chaos, interrupted by a nervous silence while the barrage lifted from the enemy's forward positions to his gun line. For these twenty minutes the sky was lit by the winking flashes along the horizon, then a quiet broken by the sound of tank tracks and the rattle of small arms. The Eighth Army was unleashed. Since Rommel had left his hopes of taking Egypt with forty blackened tanks south of Alem Halfa ridge late in August, the army had been waiting and building. There had been endless activity round the back areas and in the workshops of the Delta. More tanks, new tanks—the Shermans—more guns, new guns—the Priests—more and more six-pounders, more men had been pouring up the switchback road. Tracks had been constructed leading up to the assembly area carefully camouflaged, and behind the lines there were as many dummy tanks as real ones to mislead the enemy as to the point of our attack.

The Germans, too, had been busy. Rommel had fenced himself in behind barriers of mines and wire, sandwiching Italian battalions between German battalions. It was the deepest defence that either side had constructed in Africa, and there was no possibility of outflanking it. In front of the main position, a strong line with great keeps, there was a forward line. It was not so strong, but was joined to the main ladder. The front parts of the line between the "rungs" were weaker, so that our attacks would be canalized into a series of hollows and would lose direction. Into these "Devil's Gardens," as Rommel named them, a murderous defensive fire was to be laid down. In some areas there were as many as nine successive minefields to overcome.

General Montgomery had decided to make a break-in in the north, using the 30th Corps which now included the 9th Australian Division (the Rats of Tobruk), the 1st South African Division, the 51st Highland Division (newly arrived in the Middle East) and the New Zealand Division. He chose the north because a break-through in the north threatened the coastal road, the enemy's life, and imperilled the security of all his forces on the southern part of the line. The 30th Corps was to make the gaps, mainly by grinding away at the German defences with infantry supported by some heavy tanks. Then the 10th Corps, consisting of the 1st and 10th Armoured Divisions, which had been reorganized and retained in the Wadi Natrun area half-way from Cairo to Alamein, was to go through the gaps into the open country beyond and there deal with the enemy's armour. On the southern part of the front the 13th Corps with the 7th Armoured Division was to attack to contain the enemy reserves opposite them.

By first light on the 24th the greater part of the objectives had been gained, and we had bitten deep into the enemy's main defences. Gaps had been made in the minefields and the armour of the 10th Corps had started to move up. We had broken in, but not through. On the enemy side there was confusion. Rommel's deputy, Stumme, had been killed by a stray shot in the first moments of the battle. The Axis command was taken over by von Thoma, who was comparatively new to the desert. His handling of the situation was indecisive. He could not make up his mind whether the main attack was in the north or in the south, or whether it was a seaborne landing west of Daba where light naval forces had been demonstrating. And so he failed to concentrate his reserves. He left the 21st Panzer and the Ariete Divisions in the south, and the 90th Light and Trieste along the coast near Daba, and tried to plug the gap in the line with only the 15th Panzer and the Littorio Divisions.

The first phase of the battle continued until the 26th. While our infantry ground down the enemy defences slowly and steadily and beat off the counter-attacks of the 15th Panzer Division, the sappers were making corridors for the armour behind. The second phase began on the 27th. A purposefulness appeared in the enemy's movements. We guessed that Rommel was back. Subsequent evidence proved we were right. He took an immediate grip on the situation, and concentrated all his reserves in the north. Meantime Montgomery was building up a hitting reserve behind the "bulge" as it was now called. There were some desperate moments during these days, especially when a battalion of the Rifle Brigade in an advanced position we called Kidney Ridge was counterattacked five times in a day by the 15th Panzer Division, but held out.

Montgomery was making his plan for the break-through. The threat from the 7th Armoured Division in the south had paid its way, and the division was now brought north into reserve. Everyone moved up one, with the result that there was a spare formation, the 4th Indian Division in the bulge. The plan had the simplicity of genius. It was to persuade the Germans that we were going one way, and then to go the other. It worked perfectly. On the 29th the 9th Australian Division after bitter fighting, advanced due north across the coast road almost cutting off an enemy force of about two regiments in a strong point known as Thomson's post. On the map it looked just like a thumb stretched up toward the sea. The Australians were exposed in this precarious salient, but they were told to stay there. Rommel was drawn. All day on the 30th and the 31st the enemy dashed himself against the Thumb. Gradually the whole of the enemy reserve, including the 21st Panzer and the 90th Light, was concentrated astride the road, right in the north. It was tired and battle worn. The Australians had not yielded an inch.

It was the moment Montgomery was waiting for. After a night attack by the Highlanders and the New Zealanders, gaps were made farther south, and on November 2nd the whole weight of the Eighth Army's armour poured west straight out of the bulge. The Germans were caught off balance. Their attention was toward the north, and the Thumb had become an obsession to Rommel. Before he could re-concentrate to meet the threat from a new direction, the 1st and 10th Armoured Divisions were among him. A fierce battle was fought at El Aqqaqir, and it was here in this flat out, hammer and tongs fighting on murderously open and featureless ground that the final pressure was applied. By nightfall the enemy had cracked, and was starting to disengage.

But Montgomery had another trump in hand. The 4th Indian Division broke south-west through the Trieste and Trento Divisions, now ripe for surrender, and through the gap poured the 7th Armoured Division. Meantime the armoured cars of the South Africans and the Royals were clean through. Like pirates back in their element after months of waiting they preyed on the enemy soft skinned transport and caused pandemonium in his rear.

Rommel's main stocks and dumps and workshops were at Daba, some twenty miles up the coast road. To cover their evacuation he tried to stand, but the old, old story had begun. There was no longer a line with two firm flanks. The southern desert flank was open and the 7th Armoured Division was round it before Rommel could call a halt. The Afrika Korps commander, von Thoma, was in the bag, and the retreat for the moment became a rout. Tanks, guns, vehicles, stores were abandoned, burnt out and scattered along the roadside, while Rommel tried to break right away. Past Daba, where the tank workshops were left almost intact, and a train was still steaming in the station, past Fuka, the Axis remnants streamed, pounded ruthlessly by the R.A.F. Tanks were abandoned in panic when they ran out of fuel, aircraft abandoned intact on the Daba landing grounds.

Nose to tail, two deep, the Eighth Army poured west, back past the old familiar places, tanks, guns without number, without an enemy aircraft disturbing them. In the other direction marched long columns of tattered, tired, dejected Germans and Italians, to join the four divisions Rommel had abandoned in the southern part of the line, and to continue their dreary march into captivity in Egypt, the land they had so nearly conquered. The Axis had suffered its first great defeat and the tide had turned.[10]

For the Axis it was a disaster, complete and irretrievable. Hastily Rommel pulled back his shattered forces, hoping to make a stand, as so often before, at Tobruk or Derna or Benghazi. But the pursuit was relentless—an epic of courage and endurance and supreme co-ordination of the various arms with their technical and supply services. By April—

Egypt was saved; the waters east of Malta were clear for sea traffic; and the Eighth Army was knocking at the gates of Tripoli. The long, brown shore was safe behind them now; the great airfield at Castel Benito with all its dainty buildings was full of wreckage; and the harbour mouth was blocked with sunken ships. A little after dawn on January 23 the wide streets beyond the ochre dunes saw them arrive. It was three months to a day since the guns opened at Alamein. . . . The Desert war was over; and, two thousand miles from end, to end, the Mediterranean danced in the winter sunshine of 1943.[11]

Invasion!

Meantime even more momentous events were taking place on the other end of the continent. Shortly after Pearl Harbor President Roosevelt and Prime Minister Churchill, both of them eager to assume the offensive at the earliest possible moment, had planned an attack on the Axis through Africa and the "soft underbelly" of Europe. The plan had much to recommend it. It involved fewer risks and quicker results than a direct attack on Fortress Europe. The expeditionary force could count on aid from the Free French and the local population and, if all went well, from Montgomery's Eighth Army. From vantage points in North Africa the Allies could invade Sicily and Italy, with every likelihood of knocking that weak Axis partner out of the war.

But before this dazzling plan could materialize it was necessary for the United States and Britain to prepare on a scale and with a precision never before equalled in military history. The grand strategy of the campaign was worked out by the Joint Chiefs of Staff and, particularly, by Lieutenant-General Dwight Eisenhower, commander-in-chief of the operation; its detailed planning engaged the energies of thousands of military and civilians. Hundreds of thousands of troops had to be trained for mountain and desert warfare; hundreds of ships had to be built, armed, and supplied with some 700,000 separate items of equipment; mountains of materiel and supplies had to be stockpiled; the most meticulous co-ordination of British and American plans arranged; the most delicate diplomatic and secret services negotiations conducted.

On October 24, as Montgomery broke through the Afrika Korps at Alamein, a vast troop convoy set sail from American ports to North Africa; the next day two great convoys sailed from Britain. At 3 A.M. of November 8th a great armada of 85 cargo and war ships converged, with machine-like precision, on their objectives: Oran and Algiers. Every effort had been made to win over the French authorities in North Africa, for it was realized that ultimate success depended in large part upon the speed with which the Allies could get from Morocco and Algeria to Tunisia—and beyond. The American counsellor, Robert Murphy, had secretly won strong support among the Free French and pro-Ally elements; the American General, Mark Clark, had landed by submarine to confer with French officers; as a trump card the famous General Henri Giraud, spirited out of a German prison, had been brought in to lead the Free French forces. Notwithstanding all these preparations, the Allies encountered stiff resistance, especially at Casablanca and Oran.

Resistance might have been prolonged to the point where it imperiled the success of the expedition, but on November 11 Admiral Darlan, one of the most notorious of Vichy collaborators, gave the word to cease resistance and went over to the Allies.

With Darlan's capitulation went not only undisputed control of Morocco and Algeria, but Dakar—so long a threat to Allied shipping—and the whole of French West Africa. The resistance movement in France, too, was vastly encouraged: when Hitler, occupying the whole of France, tried to take over what remained of the fleet at Toulon, French officers and men scuttled their ships.

Swiftly the Allies raced forward through Algiers towards the Tunisian border, hoping to capture the ports of Bizerte and Tunis before the Germans could smash them from the air—or rush over enough reinforcements to hold them. The Nazi reaction was characteristically swift. Strong forces seized the Tunisian ports, and carrier planes rushed over thousands of reinforcements from Sicily and Italy while other thousands were ferried over from southern France. When American forces, struggling through mud and rain, advanced at Mateur, five hundred miles from their nearest bases, they were held, and then forced back. That winter they stabilized a line running north from Medjez-el-Bab to the sea.

While the Allied and German forces were building up strength in Tunisia and the Eighth Army was racing westward from Libya, Churchill and Roosevelt, together with high ranking officers of the Allied armies, met at Casablanca to plan future military operations and formulate large political policies. The auspices were propitious: the Russians had turned the tide at Stalingrad, Montgomery had saved Egypt and destroyed the Afrika Korps, the Allied landings promised total victory in Africa and throughout the Mediterranean, the battle and the landings on Midway marked the beginning in the Pacific of that offensive which would end only with the conquest of Japan. The Allied chiefs were therefore in a position to announce that they would demand from the Axis powers "unconditional surrender."

The arrival of Rommel and the Afrika Korps to reinforce von Arnim more nearly equalized the opposing forces. Yet the Germans realized that time fought on the side of the Allies, and determined to strike before they could bring up reinforcements. The blow came on February 14, with a powerful armored thrust, westward from Faid Pass towards Sbeitla. Next morning the Americans launched two counter-attacks, which were severely mauled. On the 20th, supported by a heavy artillery barrage, the Nazis poured through the Kasserine Pass and turned northward towards Tebessa, threatening to cut the Allied armies in two. For four days the fighting raged back and forth. Two American infantry divisions raced eastward from Oran in one of the most spectacular forced marches of the war; Allied planes flew thousands of sorties; powerful new Churchill tanks joined the Grants and Shermans to hold off the enemy. By February 25 Rommel acknowledged defeat and fell back through Kasserine Pass to defensive positions. It had been a near thing, but during the battle of Kasserine Pass the new and untried American army found itself. Confident, determined veterans, skilled in the business of war, began the push on Bizerte and the destruction of the Afrika Korps.

Death of an Army

Now Montgomery from the south, Patton and Anderson from the north, closed in for the kill. The stiffest fighting was still ahead. To the south the Germans were protected by the all but impenetrable Mareth Line; to the west they could count on some of the toughest terrain in the world to nullify the advantage of superior armor and air power. Realizing how desperate was his position Rommel, always an offensive fighter, hurled himself at the Eighth Army in a series of unco-ordinated attacks at Medenine that were bloodily repulsed. Two weeks later, on March 21, Montgomery took the offensive. In a brilliant operation, reminiscent of Lee's at Second Manassas, he sent his Northumbrian Division on a frontal attack against the Mareth Line and his New Zealand division on a wide sweep around its southern flank to strike from the rear. These tactics were completely successful. Threatened by encirclement, Rommel abandoned the Mareth Line and retreated towards Cape Bon.

Then began the last great push which ended in the annihilation of the German army. The American II Corps and the British First Army fought their way, in a series of bitter engagements, from one mountain range to another, while from the south the Eighth Army and the French IXI Corps pushed towards Cape Bon. The hardest fighting came at Hill 609, dominating Mateur, which the Americans captured on May first. On May 7th the British First Army broke through to Tunis, cutting the Axis forces in two. That same day, at almost the same hour, the triumphant Americans entered the great port of Bizerte. The German Army was still strong and potentially dangerous, but it had no fight left in it. On May 11, abandoned by its commander, it surrendered. Here is Clifford's account of the death of an army:

The guns were still firing in the hills as we drove back through Mateur and then wound among the sunset valleys to Thibar. But there was no front left here, no organized resistance. It was nothing but a very big-scale job of mopping up. Bizerta would be made safe to-night as Tunis had been last night. For Tunis was now a town of mad delirium. When I went back there next day it was still in a permanent state of carnival. Every scrap of red, white and blue bunting the place possessed was hung out. The streets were so full of crowds and celebrations that traffic could barely move. It was the very antithesis of Tripoli. This was a vivid, genuine, alive town with smart shops and good buildings and clean streets and a fine broad central avenue where the people strolled in the evening beneath thick trees. There was nothing of Tripoli's pretentious façade with the tawdriness behind. This was no anticlimax at all. It was a climax that was being maintained for days. The London Irish played their bagpipes in the avenue in the afternoon. The Americans gave people rides in their jeeps. The compositor of the local paper piled up all the blocks the German printers had been using and swept them off his table into the corner with one superb gesture. A wildly pro-Allies paper was being sold on the streets almost at once and the Allies put a notice in it increasing the bread ration and announcing a distribution of coffee. Political refugees crept out of hiding. The first member of General Giraud's forces who reached the city was nearly suffocated with kisses—literally nearly suffocated. It was sunny and gay and lastingly exciting.

North-west of Tunis the Fifteenth *Panzerdivision*, hard-bitten veterans of the desert, surrendered en masse to the Seventh Armoured Division. They got themselves cornered in Porto Farina, between Tunis and Bizerta, and they made a half-hearted attempt to start evacuating by sea. But the air force quickly stopped that and this whole *Panzerdivision* made formal surrender. It sent out envoys with a white flag to negotiate, and it capitulated with its Generals and its vehicles and its men.

That was one of the significant things that happened on this day. The other was that the Germans retiring from Tunis where showing signs of resistance at Hammam Lif, a few miles farther east along the coast. Hamman Lif was a sort of Thermopylæ position—a little town on a narrow coastal shelf with cliffs towering above it. The mountains ran down from there to Zaghouan and round to Enfidaville and there was no easy way through. It might be a very strong line indeed.

These two facts together made the situation suddenly clear. The speed and strength of the great armoured drive down the Medjerda Valley had indeed split the Axis armies in half and dislocated their main defensive positions. The surrender in toto of the Fifteenth *Panzerdivision* proved that the dislocation was complete and irretrievable. But the enemy still had some good troops and the secondary defensive position might conceivably be held. Already at Hamman Lif they were making ready to hold it. Given time to pull themselves together and reorganize, the Germans might still be able to buy a few more weeks of time.

That was the essence of the thing—time. The General who had steered that swift sword thrust down the Medjerda Valley and rammed it home even though his flanks were not absolutely safe saw the full implications of it. Once already he had dislocated the enemy by speed. Perhaps it could be done again. He must strike hard and quickly at Hammam Lif, and get through it before the enemy were properly installed there.

He said to the Sixth Armoured Division, "You will get in your tanks and you will travel night and day eastwards." Someone objected, "You cannot travel with tanks by night." Said the General, "You will travel by night and you will reach Hammamet, on the other side of Cap Bon Peninsula, by five o'clock to-morrow morning."

So in the evening they moved up against this Thermopylæ position. Hammam Lif was a town of six parallel streets, and there seemed to be a sniper in every house. There was one five-story building, and there was a sniper in every window. There were at least twenty 88-millimetre guns ranged at the far ends of these six streets.

They waited till night fell. The moon was very young, but it was bright enough to show the way. And by its faint radiance men with fixed bayonets climbed onto the Sherman tanks and they charged together down the six streets. At each corner the infantrymen leaped down and scattered right and left, routing out the snipers house by house and room by room. The tanks charged down on the 88-millimetres duelling at point-blank range. Hand-to-hand fighting surged up and down the staircase of the five-story building and through the gardens of the villas beyond the town. But the battle was won and in the darkness the Sixth pressed on. The sea was milky-grey with dawn when they reached it at Hammamet. It was just light enough for them to see by their watches that the time was 5 A.M.

So it had been done again. A second time the British had beaten this Axis army by speed, had split it in two and thrown it into utter confusion. Now the remnants of the Afrikakorps in the Enfidaville Hills were cut off from their comrades in the Cap Bon Peninsula. And the whole structure of the enemy forces crumbled and collapsed.

The thing was so big that the process of collapse took three more days. Inevitably there were knots of brave men who fought on because they did not know of the collapse, or because they preferred to fight. It was not until eight minutes to eight on the evening of May 12 that G.H.Q. announced the end of organized resistance. And even then a large part of the Afrikakorps still had not surrendered. . . .

This was the ending no one had foreseen. There was no Dunkirk. There was no fight to the finish. There was not even an organized surrender. It was a complete, muddled collapse—a collapse as swift and as wholesale as had been Graziani's collapse against Wavell. . . .

Rommel's old army in the Enfidaville Hills was the last to surrender. Its commander was an Italian named Messe who just at this very last moment was made a Marshal, and as such the highest-ranking Axis officer in Africa. On the evening of May 12 he tuned in to the British wave length and radioed an offer of surrender. His Headquarters were unfortunately bombed just at that minute, but he made his offer again and said he had no hard feelings. He made just one stipulation: that he should be allowed to surrender to the Eighth Army, not to the First. And we realized that that strong desert solidarity which had welded the Eighth Army into an intimate confraternity had extended even to the enemy. The Eighth Army was very pleased with Marshal Messe for this gesture. . . .

Tunis, as I write this, is still *en fête*. And the exhilaration of this finale is the right note on which to end the story—an ending beautifully clean and complete and thorough, without any false notes or untidy aftermaths. It was a very great victory.[12]

It was the greatest German disaster since Stalingrad. At a cost of some 70,000 casualties the Allies had captured 266,000 and killed or wounded another 60,000 enemy soldiers. But this was only a small part of the victory. All Africa was now cleansed of the Axis stain and restored to Allied control. The danger of Spanish intervention was past. The Suez was safe. The Near East was secure. Italy was in mortal danger and from Africa, Sicily, and Italy the Allies would have a springboard to Berlin.

5

FROM THE VISTULA TO
THE VOLGA

The Attack on Russia

ON JUNE 22, 1941, Hitler took his greatest gamble.

"I decided today again," he said to his people, "to lay the fate and future of the German Reich and our people in the hands of our soldiers." As he spoke his armies were rolling across the plains of eastern Poland into Russia, his airmen bombing towns and cities whose names were soon to be famous throughout the world.

Why did he do it? Germany had a non-aggression pact with Russia and, presumably, her eastern frontiers were safe. Yet clearly neither Germany nor Russia put much confidence in that pact. Already Russia had moved in to create a defensive barrier in eastern Poland, Finland, the Baltic states, and Bessarabia. Already Germany had extended its influence to Hungary, Bulgaria, and Rumania and smashed its way into Yugoslavia and Greece. The non-aggression pact was a mere "marriage of convenience," to be broken when it suited the parties to break it. Hitler wanted temporary security in the east while Germany fought in the west.

Stalin wanted time in which to heal internal dissensions, build up Russian industries and transportation, and prepare for defense. He explained his position in a speech two weeks after Germany had attacked:

It may be asked, how could the Soviet Government have consented to conclude a non-aggression pact with such treacherous fiends as Hitler and Ribbentrop? Was it not an error on our part? Of course not. No peace-loving state could decline a peace treaty with a neighboring state even though the latter was headed by such fiends and cannibals as Hitler and Ribbentrop, provided that treaty did not infringe on the territorial integrity, independence, and honor of the peace-loving state. By concluding the pact we gained for our country peace for a year and a half and the opportunity of preparing our forces to repulse Fascist Germany should she risk an attack on our country despite the pact.

To Hitler, planning not for a peaceful world but for world dominion, there appeared to be sound reasons for war. As the historians Haines and Hoffman put it:

Hitler had apparently come to his decision to attack Russia after the most careful calculation of the existing military situation. By the spring of 1941 he was in position to choose one of several alternatives: to wage an all-out war against Great Britain and the British Empire; to seize the Mediterranean lands and march into the Middle East; or to start a new war against Russia. There were some strong arguments in favor of the first. Conditions for air warfare over the Channel had improved, the submarine campaign was progressing favorably for Germany, and the German army was much better prepared for invasion that it had been the preceding autumn. There were equally good reasons for a Mediterranean and Middle Eastern campaign. Germany had the power to make Gailani's adventure in Iraq a success, if she wished; she could have supplied Rommel with the men and matériel to march to Suez; and had she so chosen, Vichy France and Franco Spain and with them the whole of North Africa would have fallen into Hitler's grasp. But both of these courses of action were eliminated because Hitler had concluded that a preventive war against Russia was an urgent and compelling necessity. He wanted most of all to avoid a two-front war. The Soviet Union, which had annexed the Baltic states, Bessarabia, and the Bukowina and had then connived with the enemies of Germany in Jugoslavia and Bulgaria, was not to be counted upon to stay its hand if Germany moved into Britain or the Mediterranean in force. On the other hand, Great Britain was still not strong enough to create a second front if Germany attacked Russia; certainly she would not be strong enough until American industry was adequately organized to supply her needs. This latter possibility dictated speed: Russia was to be conquered before Britain, with the aid of the United States, could create a serious diversion. If this could be accomplished, then all other conquests could be assured. These were the principal considerations which motivated the attack upon Russia.[1]

There was another reason. Hitler doubtless hoped that by transforming his war of conquest into a crusade against Bolshevism he could confuse democratic opinion in Britain and America. As he himself entertained psychopathic fears of communism, he deluded himself that leaders in other capitalist countries would share those fears: this, apparently, was behind the fantastic flight of Rudolph Hess to Britain in the month preceding the assault on Russia. In this expectation he was grievously mistaken. The leaders of the democracies were not confused or deceived. Said Churchill to a hushed House of Commons:

Can you doubt what our policy will be? We have but one aim, and one single irrevocable purpose. We are resolved to destroy Hitler and every vestige of the Nazi regime; from this nothing will turn us—nothing. We will never parley. We will never negotiate with Hitler or any of his men. We shall fight him by land, we shall fight him by sea, we shall fight him in the air, until, with God's help, we have rid the earth of his shadow and liberated its peoples from his yoke.

Any man or state who fights against Nazidom will have our aid. Any man or state who marches with Hitler is our foe. This applies not only to organized states but to all representatives of that vile race of Quislings who make themselves the tools and agents of the Nazi regime against their fellow countrymen and against the lands of their birth. These Quislings, like the Nazi leaders themselves, if not disposed of by their fellow countrymen, which would save trouble, will be delivered by us on the morrow of victory to the justice of the allied tribunals.

That is our policy and that is our declaration. It follows, therefore, that we shall give whatever help we can to Russia and to the Russian people. We shall appeal to all our friends and allies in every part of the world to take the same course and pursue it as we shall, faithfully and steadfastly to the end.

And in the United States, Under-secretary of State Sumner Welles made America's position equally clear:

The immediate issue that presents itself to the people of the United States is whether the plan for universal conquest, for the cruel and brutal enslavement of all peoples and for the ultimate destruction of the remaining free democracies which Hitler is now desperately trying to carry out, is to be successfully halted and defeated.

That is the present issue which faces a realistic America. It is the issue at this moment which most directly involves our own national defense and the security of the New World in which we live.

In the opinion of this government, consequently, any defense against Hitlerism, any rallying of the forces opposing Hitlerism, from whatever source these forces may spring, will hasten the eventual downfall of the present German leaders, and will therefore redound to the benefit of our own defense and security.

Hitler's armies are today the chief dangers of the Americas.

At first glance the invasion of Russia had the appearance of recklessness. Russia, after all, was a nation of 190 million, with vast, almost limitless, resources of territory and wealth. Yet if ever there was to be a test of strength now was clearly the moment when that test might be made most advantageously by Germany. With his allied, vassal, and conquered states Hitler could muster formidable power. He had not only the resources of Germany, the most highly industrialized and highly militarized nation on the continent, but those of most of Europe from the Arctic to the Mediterranean, from the Atlantic to the Black Sea. With immunity in the west, he could hurl against the Soviet Union a larger initial force—and a far better equipped one—than it could mobilize.

The risks, to be sure, were great. The prize was dazzling. So Hitler took the road to Moscow that another world-conqueror had taken.

The Bloodiest Front in History

The Germans launched a three-way offensive with three great army groups totalling perhaps 180 divisions, thousands of planes, tanks, and armored vehicles. One offensive, under General von Leeb, drove through the Baltic states towards Leningrad and a juncture with the Finns—who had joined in the war—coming down from the north. The second and major offensive, under General von Bock, headed straight west towards Moscow. The third and, as it turned out, most successful, under the skillful von Rundstedt, smashed through southern Poland towards the Ukraine, the Crimea, and the Black Sea.

At first all three offensives met with spectacular success and it seemed, as many foreign observers predicted, that the *Wehrmacht* would indeed "go through Russia like a hot knife through butter." The northern army plunged into Lithuania and by August was striking at the outskirts of Leningrad. The central army swept past Bilaystok, penetrated the Stalin line, and attacked Smolensk. The southern forces overran Lwow and Kiev, while eager Rumanian divisions swept down on Odessa. Even the blitz in France had nothing to show like this.

The trouble was that the Russians didn't know when they were licked. Joseph Grigg tells of the early fighting:

The first of these huge battles developed within a week after the beginning of the invasion. Flinging in the entire weight of his tanks and dive bombers, Field Marshal von Bock broke through the Russian lines at two points simultaneously on the central front and encircled a huge body of Red troops in a gigantic caldron between Bialystok and Minsk. But then something occurred which had not been provided for in Hitler's battle blueprints. Instead of surrendering en masse after being surrounded the Russians continued fighting. This was not at all according to plan. In the Western Front campaign the mere fact of knowing they were encircled frequently had been enough to make whole bodies of French troops lay down their arms. But the Russians did not fight according to the book of rules. When surrounded they kept on fighting back and killing Germans until they themselves were destroyed. And another point where the Nazi calculations went sadly astray was on the number of troops and quantity of war materials at the Red Army's disposal. On June 3rd, the German High Command communiqué announced the end of the caldron battle of Bialystok-Minsk, in which it was claimed 324,000 prisoners had been taken. The communiqué went so far as to describe the victory as a "decision on a world-historic scale" and to add that "unimaginable chaos has overtaken the Soviet armies." It was evident from these tones of triumph that Hitler was convinced that the main strength of the Russian armies already had been smashed. He was soon to discover that the campaign had barely begun.

After the first two weeks or so of fighting Hitler found that his original blitz tactics simply would not work in Russia. Instead of stringing out his armies along the whole frontier to be pierced, encircled and captured by the Nazi panzer and motorized forces, Stalin had adopted the only form of strategy suitable to a country of the vast dimensions of Russia, namely the "feather pillow" or "defense in depth" system. Each time they slashed through the Russian defenses the Germans found themselves confronted by new Russian armies in the rear. Furthermore, the Russians themselves were trying out a new means of dealing with the armored spearheads. When encircled themselves, instead of surrendering immediately, they tried to encircle the encirclers with their own tank forces. The result time and again was a fearful mix-up of caldrons within caldrons, with Russian and German tank and motorized forces swinging wildly around, each trying to encircle and destroy the other in a chaotic free-for-all over a battle field sometimes covering several hundred square miles. As a result, Hitler and his marshals were compelled to make a radical change in their plan of campaign. Instead of trying for a quick knockout by driving straight through to Moscow, Leningrad and the Caucasus, the Nazis had now to attempt to win by destroying the Soviet armies one after the other in a series of bloody *Vernichtungsschlachten* or "annihilation battles." In place of speedy, comparatively bloodless victories which he had pictured to himself, Hitler had to drive the youth of Nazi Germany to the fearful slaughter of a conflict in which each side was out only to wipe out its opponent.[2]

The Germans gave great blows—and received heavy blows. In a war of attrition the Red Army could outlast the *Wehrmacht*. It was, as Frederick Oechsner pointed out, the bloodiest front in history:

When Hitler, culminating six months of secret preparation, hurled the German army across the Russian frontier, it attacked with an unparalleled mixture of hatred and fanatic zeal. This spirit had been implanted by twenty years of Nazi vituperation against Communism—except for a cynical two years of Nazi-Soviet "friendship" on paper—and the conviction that German *Kultur* must be brought to the benighted east. Also by a very great yearning for Russian food and raw materials. Millions of young fighters were impelled by this fanaticism, which had been lacking in the western campaigns.

The utterly ruthless character of the Nazi attack was best illustrated for me by an incident told me by a Nazi soldier. On the morning of the attack, that twenty-second of June, 1941, the Russian and German guards at a bridge straddling the frontier were due to be changed as usual. The German sentries approached their Russian colleagues for the customary meeting and salute in the middle of the bridge, but, instead of the usual civilities, whipped out their guns and shot the Russians dead.

That was the style of the onslaught along the whole huge front. It enabled the Germans to chalk up the victories of Bialystok, Minsk, Smolensk, Bryansk, Uman, Nikolaev, and finally Kiev and Odessa. But the Russians held eventually at Leningrad and Moscow, constantly inflicting huge losses on the attackers.

No, this campaign in the east was not like the march through Holland, Belgium and France, as I was able to see on a 2500-mile tour of the southern sector last autumn. I had been on the western front a number of times, too, and even for me, a non-participant, it had been different. In Belgium and in France there had been numerous towns and cities with beds to sleep in. The food had not been bad. In Russia I slept on straw and ate raw bacon; I didn't have my clothes off my body for ten days running. There were miles upon miles of empty country with only here and there a small, dirty village.

I could see why the German soldiers didn't like the Russian show. It was a tougher war, resistance was more bitter, losses were greater, there was incredible punishment of equipment on the Russian roads. In the east there were not things to buy in the conquered territory: no silks or wine or chocolate to take home when you went on leave. Nor were the girls the same. I could see distaste written in the grim, weathered faces of thousands after thousands of German youngsters moving forward to the battle lines; I had seen these same youths in France, and their faces were different there.[3]

By mid-July the Germans were at Smolensk and there occurred the first great battle of the war, a battle which ended with the Russians in headlong retreat and the Germans in possession of a ruined city. Meantime von Rundstedt's armies had taken the great bastion of Zhitomir and moved on to Kiev. Here Budenny put up a stubborn resistance but, after two months, was forced to fight his way out of a vast encirclement and retreat as best he could towards Kharkov.

The Germans announced fabulous captures—324,000 prisoners on July 10, another 310,000 at Smolensk in August, 103,000 at Uman that same month, 675,000 in the Ukraine in September. But somehow the Russians managed to extricate themselves and escape to fight another day. Colonel G. N. Filonov of the Red Army explains how he learned to escape from encirclement:

In July, 1941, while commanding an artillery brigade on the southwestern front I was forced to withdraw eastward after heavy fighting in the western Ukraine. The brigade was the last unit to withdraw, and with its complementary infantry formations fought its way over several hundred kilometers and finally succeeded in breaking through the enemy encirclement without suffering heavy casualties either in men or guns.

The favorite tactics of the Germans—pincers and spearheads—are intended to break their opponents' forces up into small groups and encircle each of them. The Nazis take advantage of everything that enables them to maneuver for encirclement. . . .

Withdrawal from an encirclement isn't to be compared with retirement from battle although both maneuvers have a similar objective—withdrawal from a place where the enemy is dealing a heavy blow. The methods employed, however, are different. . . . The operations of units fighting a withdrawal may be placed in the category of defensive operations. But avoiding or escaping encirclement is solved instead by decisive offensive action. The task is not to get away from the enemy but to attack him on a given sector of front, break through the hostile ring, and then retire. . . .

With what tasks is a commander faced when he has to organize withdrawal from encirclement? The first problem I came up against when my brigade was encircled was to decide where I could break through the hostile ring. My intelligence units brought me my answer to the problem. They were at work over a very extensive front. Naturally the longer the front over which reconnaissance is carried out, the easier it is to discover the best sector through which a breach can be made. Experience has taught us that every form of intelligence must be used from ordinary agents to reconnaissance. Intelligence must also discover the weak link in the enemy ring in the shortest possible time, and by any means at its disposal get this information to headquarters fast. Delay in getting the information in may give the enemy time to strengthen the weak sector of front before the blow can be delivered.

The second problem was distribution of forces for actual operation of making a breach. . . .

The last problem I had to solve was how to organize the thrust by our main forces, make the breach into and through the enemy ring, and withdraw quickly under the cover of my rear guard. . . .

Artillery regiments composing a brigade, with infantry to cover its action, formed my rear guard. They fought the rear guard action until they were again encircled by tanks and tommygunners. The artillerymen had to blow up their guns and were lost trying to break through the newly formed ring around them.

In consideration of the fact that the burden of battle lies on the flanks and rear of troops forcing the breach, all guns capable of combating tanks must be concentrated on the flanks and rear of main body. Experience has shown that these artillery units must be decentralized. The fire of heavy artillery must be directed to making the breach and supporting the attacking troops. Its place is in the center of the formation attacking the enemy line. If there are tanks at the disposal of the troops breaking out of encirclement, they can be used to attack the enemy line and fight the enemy tanks. It is apparently best to concentrate some tanks at the flanks of the leading troops forcing the breach, and others in rear for support of the rear guard. For at the beginning of an operation the enemy will attempt to frustrate the attempt to withdraw from encirclement by attacking from the air. All ground defenses against air attacks must be applied for the protection of attacking troops. Experience has taught us that small caliber antiaircraft gun and antiaircraft machine gun installations should be kept as close as possible to advanced troops. This is the most advantageous disposition of antiaircraft guns particularly for action against dive bombers.

After the first few volleys dive bombers usually begin to shorten their dives. This, of course, leads to greater inaccuracy in bombing. The enemy also usually withdraws a number of planes from battle.

While the troops are still encircled and preparations are being made for the breakthrough, every soldier must be confident of success. There must be the strictest discipline. Any panicmonger or provocators weakening the morale of troops must be shot without mercy. And if all ranks carry out their operations accurately and show the utmost initiative, a successful escape from encirclement will always be assured. The authority of the commander, his willpower and determination, must be felt everywhere—on the gun positions, in the tanks, and in the infantry trenches.[4]

The Battle of Moscow

As German armies to the north opened the siege of Leningrad and to the south the siege of Odessa, von Bock prepared for the knock-out blow against Moscow. By October the stage was set for one of the greatest battles of the war—and Hitler's first defeat. The government moved to Kuibyshev, on the Volga, and Moscow prepared to fight for its life. The Red Army fell slowly back, meeting blitz war with what one Russian officer called "blitz grinding." C. L. Sulzberger describes the nature of the fighting on the approaches to Moscow:

In the vastness of this struggle, there have been few pitched battles on static lines. But day after day, night after night, thousands of men are dying, while others crawl to the rear wounded. The terrain over a 2000-mile front varies only in foliage and climate. It is a monotonous flatland from the southern Ukraine to the wooded shores of Lake Ladoga, rarely broken by geological highlights. There is only this fundamental difference: from the Arctic to the central front the fields are enveloped by great forests . . . while to the south there is the open steppe.

As a result, Soviet communiqués never mention *sectors* but talk instead about fighting "in the direction of." There is no real front and hence there are no sectors. When the battle is joined, the opposing troops come out of their slit trenches and dugouts and fight it out until the tide swings backward or forward. The struggle on both sides is to envelop, outflank and crush enemy units, to capture or maintain strong points but not areas or lines.

My diary, describing a typical region northeast of Yelnya on the Moscow front, reads:

"Here and there batteries garlanded with birch branches nestle in wooded spots. Single antitank and anti-aircraft guns, among clusters of trees, are guarded by sentries carrying bayoneted rifles or Tommy guns. Behind the lines light tanks guard the highways and key positions.

"Most of this area has been reconquered, and the slightly sour smell of death hovers over it. Enormous bomb craters scar the roadsides, some of them 18 feet deep and more than 30 feet across. Fields have been chewed by tractor and tank treads, and pitted by shell bursts.

"Soldiers drive herds of cattle forward to fill the stewpots at soup kitchens. Privates labor in some of the fields. Crows and magpies peck at the blood-soaked earth.

"This is gray, gloomy, desolate territory. Villages have been smashed and leveled, and trees ripped apart. Fragments of wrecked machinery are seen everywhere. Here is a piece of a Messerschmitt hurled into the ocher-colored earth. There is a Skoda reconnaissance car or a Mercedes gun hauler; cases of mortar shells, tattered uniforms, rifle butts.

"The front half of an armored car is parked in the shadow of what was once a house. A bent, bullet-riddled fragment of a tank lies near a dirt-caked helmet.

"To the southwest a rutted road winds through a field of rye, decayed in the rain. Puffs of smoke are billowing from the trees. Goats munch peacefully as shells scream occasionally overhead. A flight of light bombers roars over a forest. On an open road the Germans put a shell a hundred yards from the car; it bursts with a sharp noise and a puff of dirt."

These words describe a quiet day in a quiet area. In general the Russians remain on the defensive, making the Germans pay heavily for every attack, chipping down the size of the *Wehrmacht* day by day. They realize that Hitler's greatest weakness, manpower, is their own chief strength—that no matter how much matériel the Führer can squeeze out of the slave factories of Europe he must have soldiers to use it. General Vassily Sokolovsky, Timoshenko's husky chief of western staff, described the Russian tactic to me as one of "blitz grinding." The object is to chew the enemy slowly to pieces.[5]

The major battle was launched, after thorough preparation, on October second: it involved a series of grand encirclements designed to end in the destruction of the Red Army on the central front, the capture of the capital, and the end of the war. H. S. Cassidy analyzes the grandiose plan and its faulty execution:

Before the battle the front ran straight from north to south, through the Yartsevo sector, roughly three hundred and fifty miles west of Moscow. It was stabilized there during the summer battle of Smolensk. The rains came in September, soaking the dense pine and birch forests, spreading bogs in the turgid earth, washing out the dirt roads, and making mass movements impossible. Then came the autumn, freezing a firm, fast track again for Blitzkrieg. That was the situation when the Germans started their first general offensive against Moscow October 2, 1941.

A powerful force of German armies had been aimed at Moscow from the very start of the war. This "central group of armies," commanded by Field Marshal von Bock, included the fourth and ninth regular armies of Generals Kluge and Strauss, and the second and third tank armies of Generals Guderian and Goot, later to be joined by the fourth tank army of General Hepner from the Leningrad front.

The striking force, seventeen infantry divisions, two motorized infantry divisions, about a thousand tanks and nine hundred aircraft, was concentrated against Viazma, in the center of the front. The general plan was to drive northeast from Smolensk toward Kalinin, outflanking Moscow from the north; southeast toward Orel and Tula, outflanking Moscow from the south; and east through Viazma, taking Moscow by frontal assault. The date fixed for the fall of the capital was October 16. . . .

The German armies, by weight of numbers and machines, smashed the Russian first line, broke into the open and raced more than two hundred miles northeast to Kalinin, east through Viazma and southeast toward Tula. The sharpest advance was made in the center, where they reached the Viazma sector within a week and occupied the city in ten days. They reached the Kalinin region October 14, the Tula region, October 29. They were rolling fast, recklessly, sending out individual tanks with small groups of motorcyclists or cavalrymen to scout, then flinging columns of tanks, with companies or battalions of motorized infantry, into spurting advances.

Suddenly the Red army's resistance stiffened on the flanks. Kalinin fell, but in the forests behind the upper Volga fresh Russian armies converged on the German spearhead, stopped it in the suburbs of Kalinin. Tula refused to fall. The German center, receiving no support from the flanks, dared not advance alone on Moscow. Thus, in mid-October, ended the first general offensive.

The Germans now held a great bulge around Kalinin, northwest of Moscow, and a lesser salient to the southwest, below Mojhaisk. They spent the last days of October and the first of November straightening their lines. They filled in their upper fold north of Rzhev and their lower bend from Volokolamsk west of Narofominsk. They drove twice at Tula, starting November 6 from the northwest and November 11 from the south. There they were repulsed. Their line formed an arc roughly one hundred miles north, west, and south of Moscow. That was the setting for their second general offensive.

They drew up, this time, thirteen tank, thirty-three infantry, and five motorized infantry divisions. Their plan was to take Moscow by encirclement, rather than by frontal assault. Snow was falling, the thermometer was dropping, the winter campaign, on which the Germans had not counted, was starting. There was need to hurry, for the Germans, but this time, there must be no mistake, for a mistake would mean disaster.

But Stalin, in his Kremlin, had another plan. The Red army command, either from direct information or from deduction, seemed to have known or to have figured out the second German offensive in advance. Stalin's plan to meet it provided for concentration in depth of reserves both before Moscow and outside the ring of encirclement, strong defense along fortified lines to drain enemy strength, and finally a powerful, perfectly timed counteroffensive to defeat the enemy.

Moscow, meanwhile, had been declared in a state of siege October 19, the capital had been emptied of industries, commissariats, and civilians not essential for its defense, and General Zhukov was announced to be in command of the western front—a post he had already been holding throughout the battle—while Marhsall Timoshenko went to bolster the sagging southwestern front.

The people of Moscow were called upon to play a major part in the drama of life or death of their city. . . . Thousands of women, mobilized by their house committees and still wearing their city clothes, went by train, bus, and truck into the mud, slush, and cold west of Moscow, there to dig tremendous trenches and anti-tank ditches, running like scars across the countryside. The fortifications extended back into the city itself, where steel, sandbag, and earthwork barricades were raised. The Palace of Soviets, a naked skeleton of steel girders, which was to have risen as the world's highest building, started to come down as raw material for defense. The Moscow Métro, most modern subway system in the world, was given over to movements of troops and supplies.

In all small shops which were not evacuated, work was turned entirely to war orders. One, which had been making pots and pans, started turning out hand-grenades. Another, which usually made cash registers and adding machines, began producing automatic rifles. Its first delivery of arms was ready November 7.

The Russians, being intensely human, did not undergo this strain without a tremor, any more than they had faced their first bombing without a qualm. When the mass evacuation began October 15, there were three days of stampede. People swarmed the railroad stations, seeking transportation, and when there was none, started on foot into the vast spaces of the east. Queues formed at food stores for the extra rations of bread, sausage, and cheese allotted to evacuées. There was a boom on the matrimonial market, as people married to go along with others whose offices or factories were being evacuated. In some organizations, the state circus, for example, there were cases of executives taking the cashbox and evacuating themselves without permission. Outside the city, on the roads east to Gorky and Vladimir, cars were stopped and looted. Inside the city, maids, relatives, or acquaintances helped themselves to the belongings and better apartments of those who had left.

The Germans started their second general offensive against Moscow November 16. The great armies collided, the plan and counter-plan started working.

The Germans struck their first blow on the Russian right flank. The third and fourth tank armies attacked in the Volokolamsk sector and farther north toward the Moscow Sea, the artificial body of water forming part of the Moscow-Volga canal system forty miles north of the capital. The panzer divisions drove the Russians behind the Volga, north of the Moscow Sea, and covered their own left flank under this great lake.

Then the offensive spread southward. Part of the German left wing descended on Moscow through Klin, Solnechnogorsk, and Istra, part carried out the encircling maneuver through Yakhroma and Dimitrov toward Zagorsk.

The Germans hit the Russian left flank November 18, when the second tank army attacked southeast of Tula toward Kashira and Riazan. Part of this force pushed up toward Moscow, cutting the Tula-Serpukhov highway, reaching Venev and approaching Kashira; part struck through Stalinogorsk and Mikhailov toward Riazan and Kolomna, to complete the encirclement.

In the center the Germans broke through in the Narofominsk sector, penetrating the Russian defense twelve to fifteen miles, carrying their advanced forces within twenty-five miles of the capital.

So far the German plan seemed to be succeeding. But the Russian plan also was in full operation. It called, in the first phase, for a stubborn defense. What this meant was exemplified on November 16, the first day of the German offensive, in the Volokolamsk sector, by one of the grandest acts of heroism of the war.

Major-General I. V. Panfilov, a dapper little fellow who had been military commissar of the middle-Asiatic Khirgiz Republic, defended the Volokolamsk-Moscow highway with the 316th Red army infantry division, later to become the 8th Guards infantry division. General Panfilov died in the field. Twenty-eight of his troops, isolated at one point, died in their trenches. But they exacted, as the price of their lives, eighteen enemy tanks. And they checked the Germans.

Those twenty-eight became Soviet immortals. A year later, their names were inscribed on a gray plaque, rimmed in black, at the Moscow Historical Museum.

The four Moscow Communist divisions went into action in the first lines. They had had little training, there were not enough automatic guns to go around, but they sacrificed their bodies to the defense. Their losses were horrible, but their resistance was strong. In sheer desperation, they delayed the Germans, while in the rear and on the flanks, other forces were gathering. Those were black days for the Communist volunteers who did not know the plan of the high command. Their slaughter became one of the great glories of the defense of Moscow.

Those were bright days for the Germans. They had estimated the maximum strength of the Red army at three hundred and thirty divisions. They had counted that number, they thought, in defeat. Now, before them appeared a few ragged new divisions of hastily mobilized workers, fighting with the spirit of demons but without the arms, training, or experience of regular troops. The Germans thought the end was in sight. Berlin editors were advised, December 2, to leave space on their front pages to announce the fall of Moscow.

During the first week of December, the Germans reached their farthest points of advance, cutting the Moscow-Volga canal to the north at Dimitrov, spreading south through Istra, Svenigorod, and Narofominsk and looping around Tula, north almost to Kashira and east to Mikhailov and Yerifan. The nearest they came to Moscow was the outskirts of the little Moscow-Volga canal port Khimki, five miles north of Moscow connected with the capital by a commuters' bus line.

In the meantime, regularly, as often as every quarter of an hour, trains were passing along railway lines to the front, carrying fresh young troops, dressed in warm winter uniforms and armed to the teeth.

Inside and outside the German armored claws, these reserves stiffened the Russian resistance. The Germans began to scratch vainly for ground. Their left arm was pinned down on the Moscow-Volga canal. Their center was blocked east of Narofominsk. Their right arm was stopped before Kashira. They dangled awkwardly, in danger. The Russians' hour to strike, with their full force, had come.

The Red army launched its counter-offensive on December 6. . . .

In the battle of Moscow, from November 16 to December 10, the Soviet high command estimated the Red army killed more than 85,000 Germans, captured or destroyed 1434 tanks, 5416 vehicles, 575 field guns, 339 mortars, and 870 machine guns.

These estimates covered two periods. During the first, from November 16 to December 6, when the Germans were on the offensive, they included 55,170 dead, 777 tanks, 534 vehicles, 178 guns, 119 mortars, and 224 machine guns destroyed. During the second, from December 6 to 10, when the Russians were on the offensive, they included 30,000 dead, 386 tanks, 4317 vehicles, 305 guns, 101 mortars, and 515 machine guns captured, and 271 tanks, 565 vehicles, 92 guns, 119 mortars, and 131 machine guns destroyed.[6]

The autumn rains came in the middle of October. By the end of November the Germans had exhausted themselves in vain assaults against the deep defenses of Moscow. On December 7, Zhukov went over to the offensive, and after wiping out Nazi salients to the north and south, pushed the whole front back for varying distances from 50 to 200 miles. Walter Kerr has pointed the significance of this counter-attack which saved Moscow, and proved that the *Wehrmacht* was not invincible:

It was a tired Red Army when the snows began to go, but von Bock's and von Kluge's army of fifty-one divisions had suffered the defeat of their lives. New divisions that the German High Command had intended for the summer offensive were thrown in to hold. The flower of the German armored forces had been cut down.

During the Battle for Moscow they had suffered defeats in the far north around Tikhvin east of Leningrad, at Kalinin on the Moscow-Leningrad highway, and at Rostov in the far south. They had not been able to take Leningrad. Never again would this German army be strong enough to attack in more than one large sector at a time. The following summer it was not all Russia they were attacking, but only southern Russia.[7]

Guerrillas and Scorched Earth

Not only were the Germans balked of the victory which Hitler had promised them. They were denied, too, the fruits of victories already won. They had advanced hundreds of miles, smashed one army after another. But their resounding victories brought them only barren space, and in the areas they had conquered guerrilla armies sprang up like tares in wheat fields. As Joseph Grigg puts it:

However far they advanced into the depths of Russia and however many Soviet armies they destroyed, the Nazis still saw the mirage of final victory retreating tantalizingly from them. The Bolshevist system did not crack up with its first defeats as they had pictured to themselves. The "scorched earth" policy of the Red Army destroyed before their eyes those very treasures of raw materials, agricultural and industrial machinery, which they had come to steal for themselves. Hardly a factory was left standing, hardly a machine left behind which the Nazis could use. German officers admitted to foreign correspondents at the front that it would be at least two years before they began to obtain grain in any quantity from the Ukraine. Behind the front and in the fastnesses of the Pripet marshes Russian "partisans" carried out a ceaseless guerrilla warfare against German supply columns and isolated garrisons. And in the huge caldrons the Russians continued to hit back and kill Germans until they were wiped out themselves. This was a form of warfare with which the Nazis had never reckoned when they built their beautiful dream castles in the Ukraine and Moscow. Moreover, it was one which they could not understand and which they passionately resented. The Nazi newspapers and radio railed ceaselessly at the "bestial" Russians who continued this "senseless" resistance and had not the human intelligence to know when they were beaten. Only "sub-humans" could fight like this and keep on killing Germans, they wailed. The "senseless" Russian resistance whipped Hitler into such a fury that in a speech in the Berlin Sportspalast on October 3rd, 1941, he denounced them as a "cruel, bestial and animal opponent . . . the Mongolian horde of a modern Genghis Khan." In this same speech Hitler made for the first time the revealing and damaging admission that he had never dreamed the Russians possessed such reserves of man power and materials.[8]

This "scorched earth" policy, on the scale and with the thoroughness here practiced, was something new in the history of warfare, and the Germans were unprepared for it. Hugo Speck describes how the Russians ruined Kiev and Odessa before they evacuated those cities:

In the Ukraine, Kiev, with its peacetime population of about a million, was an example of the thoroughness with which the Soviets destroyed what they could not defend. Outside the city entire sections of woods had been cut to make tank barriers; rails had been encased in cement to block roads. Wires were strung waist-high through the trees—with a mine attached every few feet.

South of Kiev in the open fields the Soviets had constructed an intricate system of trenches, barbed-wire entanglements, tank traps and artillery emplacements camouflaged in shacks. These had all been bombed and blasted into ruins. In the city itself were formidable street barricades made of logs, sandbags, cobblestones and dirt. The outskirts showed the desperate measures to which the defenders had resorted. All railway and road bridges had been blown up, factories dynamited or burned. Streetcars stood abandoned where they were left when the power plant was destroyed along with other public facilities. Except where the Germans had managed to make repairs, Kiev was without lights, gas, water or heat. Blocks of the business section still smoked as the result of fires started by hidden mines which exploded four days after the city was surrendered.

When they left, the Soviets took all the city's fire-fighting apparatus as well as the firemen and all expert workmen who might be able to repair the power plant and waterworks. The Germans say it will take four years to rebuild Kiev after the necessary workmen and materials can be assembled.

In the hotel where I stayed, the Russians had even taken the bedclothes. Formerly called The Red Kiev Hotel, the Germans had ironically renamed it "Hotel Liberty"—but that couldn't make the elevator run or put blankets on the hard mattresses. . . .

What happened in captured Russian cities long after the Red army left proved the Russians to be the world's best saboteurs. So cleverly were time and incendiary bombs and mines hidden that expert German mine re-movers couldn't find all of them. In Kiev alone more than 10,000 mines were discovered and removed, but this still did not prevent a large section of the city from being blasted to bits by hidden infernal machines. The commonest type had plungers like hand grenades. They were hidden in stoves, clothes closets, under chair cushions, in beds—any place where a string or wire could be attached to the plunger. When the stove or closet door was opened, the mine exploded. It was the same if you sat on a chair, attempted to sleep in a bed or even raise a window. Other bombs were hooked up with telephones, electric light lines or water pipes. In the first two types the bombs were set off simply by taking the phone off the hook or turning on the light. Sometimes turning on a light on the fourth floor would set off a mine under the basement floor. Those mines hooked up with water pipes were set off by some pressure principle when the tap was opened.

In Odessa, the entire building occupied by the Rumanian General Staff was blown sky-high as a result of someone turning on a water tap. Both in Kiev and Odessa hundreds of bombs went off automatically four days after the Soviets evacuated the town. Most of them were "two-timers," meaning they first blew out the walls and then set fire to the wreckage.

There were even teleignition bombs. The fuses of these were attached to radio-receiving sets set to a certain wave length. These bombs were exploded by the Russians miles away and days later by broadcasting a certain signal to which the set was tuned. A mine of this type with three and a half tons of dynamite inside was found and removed from the big new Lenin Museum in Kiev, but another one, undiscovered, blew the place to ruins. The greatest and most complete sabotage job I saw was in the huge Nikolaev shipyards, where 25,000 men used to be employed. Only the two-thirds-finished hull of a 35,000-ton battleship, a steel-plate-cutting plant and two small power plants remain. And in that great hulk of steel there might still be a joker. Everything else—machinery, railway yards, work and tool shops, locomotives, the hulls of an 8,000-ton cruiser and two submarines were ruined beyond repair.

Whatever the Soviet regime was able to construct in twenty years its people destroyed in just so many hours.[9]

The Germans had met resistance movements in Poland, Norway, and France, and they were to find a formidable one in Yugoslavia. But this was their first experience with large scale, highly organized military resistance, and they were unprepared for it.

There are many realistic accounts by the guerrillas themselves. Here is one from "Batya," commander of the Smolensk guerrillas:

When the Germans invaded the Smolensk region we headed for the forests and marshlands, took up arms and struck out at the scoundrels wherever we could. Every day saw new detachments coming into being. To-day we number thousands.

We are steadily extending the so-called "small front" which stretches behind the battle line of the main Red armies. We have fought 300 engagements and liberated more than 300 villages. Six thousand Germans have met death at our hands. We burned or destroyed 17 tanks which were sent against us, and derailed five trains carrying reserves, tanks and other military equipment for the front.

We show no mercy to traitors who sell out to the foe. Wherever we set foot, Soviet power is restored and the people once again take up their peaceful labours. To-day we possess not only sub-machine guns, trench mortars and machine-guns, but also artillery and tanks, all of which we have captured from the Germans.

With the coming of spring we intensified our struggle. From April to July we fought 150 battles in the course of which we wiped out 1,600 Nazis and took 19 prisoners.

We fight in the localities where we were born and bred. This enables us to attack the foe suddenly. Moving through forests and marshland, we converge imperceptibly on German units and swoop down on them. Every day our men mine the ways by which the enemy passes. . . .

To-day our main problem is so to develop our tactics that we can harass, wear down and destroy piecemeal even big enemy units. The Germans now throw divisions, tank battalions and planes into action against us. Only recently they sent the "yellow elephant" division, supported by artillery and tanks, to destroy our detachments. We routed and dispersed this division and burned 12 of its 45 tanks.[10]

No less upsetting to Nazi grand strategy was the transfer of factories and machinery and the development of industry to the region east of the Urals. With her industrial area overrun and without adequate supplies from Britain or the United States, Russian armament production should have been paralyzed. That is what the Germans counted on. Instead, production seemed to increase.

And Harrison Salisbury, who accompanied Eric Johnston to Russia, saw for himself the miracles that had been worked in the Urals:

Millions of Soviet civilians were moved from the west to towns in Siberia, the Urals and Central Asia, where they had a chance to resume war production. The high tide of this evacuation has long since ebbed, and the majority of the workers have returned to their homes. At Sverdlovsk, for instance, the prewar population of half a million was doubled by the evacuation; now it is back to three quarters of a million. But the sacrifices these civilians made while in the Urals were unbelievable. These workers were not in danger of death as were the men of the Red Army, but in every other respect, their existence was just as Spartan. We saw how they lived in hastily erected huge barracks and sod huts. Enormous new war plants had to be built. All but the most essential buildings were taken over. Everywhere there was an acute shortage of water, food, shelter and fuel—and this in some areas that have winter temperatures like Minnesota. In Novosibirsk, housing for 300,000 persons was built in 75 days; Tashkent built 10,000 square yards of housing space and 100,000 square yards of industrial space. At Omsk, residents were allowed only 28 liters (a liter is about a quart) of water a day for all purposes; but Omsk also built 9 brick plants with an annual production of 86,000,000 bricks.

Johnston saw where, in some places, schools were used for living quarters; one hospital became a parachute factory; airdrome hangars were turned into aircraft factories. Heavy steel mills became tank factories within forty-five days. Streets were unpaved, permanent sewers virtually unknown, transportation hopelessly overburdened. Teenage youngsters swarmed over the Russian version of the Douglas DC-3; women and girls worked in potato fields four or five hours on food production after a long, hot day over drop forges and giant presses.

I went with Johnston through the 24-square mile integrated steel enterprise at Magnitogorsk which is scheduled to produce sixty million tons of steel annually after the war—about two thirds of U.S. production. It is typical of this area which closely parallels the Alleghenies fifty years ago.

Started in 1930, Magnitogorsk is due to be completed four years hence, and will have a larger plant than Gary, Indiana. Scores of thousands of workers in three shifts man its six huge blast furnaces, and prepare its seventh. Near by, a huge mountain (which contains three hundred million tons of ore that assays sixty per cent iron, plus another eighty-five million tons of forty-five per cent ore) daily feeds the plant's six blast furnaces, twenty open hearth furnaces, two blooming mills, eight rolling mills, six coke batteries and a small wire mill. . . .

The cavernous steel mills are completely mechanized and seemed almost vacant, as a comparative handful of workers manipulated great traveling cranes, giant ingot rollers and automatic presses. The average age of workers is thirty-two, and forty-five per cent are women; the accident rate is eight per 10,000 workers per month.

Centers of Soviet arms production in the Urals are Sverdlovsk and Omsk. For reasons of military security, exact locations and production figures of these plants cannot now be given, but it can be stated that we saw a huge machine-building plant which put out 30,000 tons of heavy machinery per year before the war; artillery, self-propelled artillery, tank and shell factories, some built before the war, some moved from west Russia and some built especially for this war. The men directing these plants, which employ from 30,000 to 50,000 workers each, are young—in their thirties or early forties. In one plant, 35 per cent of the workers are women and only 20 per cent are skilled enough to have had ten years' experience. All work eleven hours a day, many in plants with broken roofs which there has been no time to repair, with poor ventilation and bad light.

Compared to Youngstown steel plants, the Chrysler tank arsenal in

Detroit or the Consolidated assembly plant in California, we saw working conditions that are bad—not because anyone wants them that way, but because the war has been so tough and production demands so severe that there hasn't been time to think of conveniences for workers. All have plans for elaborate improvements after the war.

Despite these conditions, workers are enthusiastic. Typical of their spirit is the Ural Tank Corps. The workers in the Urals arsenal decided to make, outside their regular production, sufficient tanks and armored weapons for an entire brigade. After turning out the equipment, many of them joined the corps and went to the front with it.[11]

Leningrad

While the mighty armies of von Bock and Timoshenko were locked in combat before Moscow, von Leeb's armies were sweeping north on Leningrad. The left wing pushed along the coast into Estonia and bottled the Russians up at Tallinn which they captured after a short but sharp fight. The right wing drove through Polotsk, Velikie Luki, and Kholm towards Lake Ilmen and by the end of August had approached Leningrad. During the next two months these armies, together with a Finnish army under Mannerheim, all but completed the encirclement of the city. The siege of Leningrad was on, one of the most heroic in all history.

William Mandel gives us a general picture of the siege:

Six thousand cannon, 4,500 trench mortars, 19,000 machine guns, 1,000 planes and 1,000 tanks, armoring forty divisions of troops, or approximately 600,000 men were hurled against Leningrad by the Germans in August, 1941. Salvos from the Germans' huge railways guns reached every corner of the city. With all that huge power they expected to smash into the city in a short time. . . .

The Red Army dug in against the assault. As many as 160,000 workmen dropped their tools and took up rifles, women and children replacing them at the factories.

Twelve railroads, a modern canal system, a huge deepwater port, and three excellent highways had been built to supply the three million people of Leningrad and its industries. By the middle of September, the Germans had cut all of these except the water route across Lake Ladoga. Supplies of food, fuel and raw materials rapidly dwindled. When the lake froze and the Germans took Tikhvin on the railroad running to its shore, it seemed that all was lost.

Tikhvin, however, was recaptured, and a truck highway was laid across the ice of Lake Ladoga. This single road kept the city alive during the winter. Even here, munitions and industrial raw materials got priority. Rations were cut again and again, until, for a short period, they reached a low, for the non-working population, of four ounces (five thin slices) of bread and a little watery soup per day. . . .

Though freezing and weak from hunger, the population worked eleven hours a day, took military training in its spare (!) time and walked to and

from work through the uncleared snow-drifts and the rubble left by the
bombs. Had there been food other than bread and fish, there would have
been no way to cook it, for there was no kitchen fuel. Neither could the
water supply be maintained in the face of continual German bombardment and lack of power for the pumps. Water had to be brought from
wells, the river and the numerous canals.

Despite these incredible hardships, there were no epidemics, thanks to
the rising standard of living before the war, the maintenance of public
health services and the remarkable steps taken to distribute available supplies. . . .

Munitions were produced, not only for Leningrad, but for other sections of the front, and were taken out of the city on the ice road, although
it was under bombardment from German-held Schlusselburg, northeast of
the city on Lake Ladoga. On their return trip, these trucks brought the city
100,000 tons of supplies during the winter, although they could only run
at night.

Not only industry but science, arts and education continued to function.
Leningrad's colleges graduated 2,500 students during the siege. Its enter-
tainers put on 20,000 performances for the men at the front lines outside
the city. Its publishing houses issued, among other books, a 100,000 copy
edition of Tolstoy's "War and Peace," which people somehow found time
to read. And its artists put together mosaics for the new subway line just
opened in Moscow.

With the coming of spring the food situation improved. Shipping was
resumed on Lake Ladoga. The health stations were replaced by special
dining rooms serving high-calory diets to those whose health had suffered
most. Three hundred thousand people were served by these restaurants.
Even the guerrillas helped feed the city, smuggling in a 200-cart train of
farm products from districts they controlled to the west of Leningrad. Far
off in Central Asia, the people of Uzbekistan, donated sixty carloads of rice
and fifty-four carloads of canned meat, dried fruits and juices, to defenders of this city they had never seen.

As provisioning improved, there was garbage and the city began to raise
hogs. Lake Ladoga and the Gulf no longer frozen began to contribute fish
to the dinner table. A year after the siege began, restaurants were able to
post menus reading "codfish, soup with macaroni, roast pork with vege-
tables, cocoa," of which only the cocoa and macaroni represented supplies
brought from outside. . . .

Truck gardens were planted on every available foot of ground. Altogether 22,500 acres were planted by 270,000 families, after working hours,
although it was often necessary to crawl to and from one's plot to avoid
shrapnel. Improved supplies also enabled the resumption of street-car
traffic and other public services.[12]

When the Germans cut the railroads to Moscow and the east and the
Finns and their German supporters the railroad to Murmansk, it seemed
that Leningrad was doomed. Day and night artillery pounded the great
city while the *Luftwaffe* bombed it with a thoroughness reminiscent of the
blitz on London. But Russian planes and anti-aircraft guns brought down

more planes than the enemy could afford to lose, and Russian artillery proved superior to German. All through the winter, and the next year, fighting raged around the outskirts of the city and guerrilla bands plagued the invader.

It was estimated that, during the siege, over a million Russians lost their lives, mostly by starvation. But life and work went on. Alexander Werth gives us a series of conversations and vignettes of life in Leningrad.

Most of these people pulled themselves together when they were given work. It was a great thing. But on the whole men collapsed more easily than women and at first the deathrate was highest among the men. However, those who survived the worst period of the famine finally survived. The women felt the after-effects more seriously than the men. Many died in the spring when already the worst was over. The famine had peculiar physical effects on people. Women were so run down that they stopped menstruating . . . so many people died that we had to bury most of them without coffins. People had their feelings blunted, and never seemed to weep at the burials. It was all done in complete silence without any display of emotion. When things began to improve the first signs were when women began to put rouge and lipstick on their pale skinny faces. Yes, we lived through hell right enough; but you should have been here the day the blockade was broken—people in the streets wept for joy and strangers fell round each other's necks. And now, as you see, life is almost normal. There is this shelling, of course, and people get killed, but life has become valuable again. The other day I saw an unpleasant street accident: a man was knocked down by a tramcar and had his leg cut off by the wheels. Why, our Leningrad crowd nearly lynched the driver! It seemed so wrong that anyone who had lived through the Leningrad siege should lose a leg through the fault of another Leningrader; whose fault it was exactly I do not know, but you see the point? . . .

At the end of January and in February, frost also joined the blockade and lent Hitler a hand. It was never less than thirty degrees of frost! Our classes continued on the "Round the Stove" principle. But there were no reserved seats, and if you wanted a seat near the stove or under the stove pipe, you had to come early. The place facing the stove door was reserved for the teacher. You sat down, and were suddenly seized by a wonderful feeling of well-being; the warmth penetrated through your skin, right into your bones; it made you all weak and languid and paralysed your thoughts; you just wanted to think of nothing, only to slumber and drink in the warmth. It was agony to stand up and go to the blackboard. One wanted to put off the evil moment. It was so cold and dark at the blackboard, and your hand, imprisoned in its heavy glove, goes all numb and rigid, and refuses to obey. The chalk keeps falling out of your hand, and the lines are all crooked and the figures deformed. . . . By the time we reached the third lesson there was no more fuel left. The stove went cold, and horrid icy draughts started blowing down the pipe. It became terribly cold. It was then that Vasya Pughin, with a puckish look on his face, could be seen slinking out and bringing in a few logs from Anna Ivanovna's emergency reserve; and a few minutes later one could again hear the magic crackling of wood inside the stove. . . . During the break nobody would jump up because no one had any desire to go into the icy corridors. . . .

One of the greatest examples of how Leningrad fought for its life was when in the spring 300,000 or 400,000 people came out into the street with shovels—people who were scarcely standing on their feet, so weak and hungry were they—and proceeded to clean up the town. All winter the drains and sewers had been out of action; there was a great danger of epidemics spreading with the coming of the warm weather. And in a few days these 300,000 or 400,000 weak, hungry people—many of them were very old people who had never handled a shovel in their lives—had shovelled away and dumped into the river and the canals all those mountains of snow and filth which, had they remained there, would have poisoned Leningrad. And it was a joy to see the city streets a few days later all clean and tidy. It had a great moral effect. . . .

It was our people and not the soldiers who built the fortifications of Leningrad. If you added up all the anti-tank trenches outside Leningrad, made by the hands of our civilians, they would add up to as much as the entire Moscow-Volga canal. During the three black months of 1941, 400,000 people were working in three shifts, morning, noon and night, digging and digging. I remember going down to Luga during the worst days, when the Germans were rapidly advancing on Luga. I remember there a young girl who was carrying away earth inside her apron. It made no sense. I asked her what she was doing that for. She burst into tears, and said she was trying to do at least that—it wasn't much, but her hands simply couldn't hold a shovel any longer. And, as I looked at her hands, I saw that they were a mass of black and bloody bruises. Somebody else had shovelled the earth on to her apron while she knelt down, holding the corners of the apron with the fingers of her bruised, bloodstained hands. For three months our civilians worked on these fortifications. They were allowed one day off in six weeks. They never took their days off. There was an eight-hour working day, but nobody took any notice of it. They were determined to stop the Germans. And they went on working under shellfire, under machine-gun fire and the bombs of the Stukas.[13]

Odessa and Sevastopol

The most successful of all the German offensives, in terms of distance travelled, territory taken, prisoners captured, and production destroyed, was von Rundstedt's drive to the south—a drive in which the Germans had the aid of powerful Hungarian and Rumanian divisions. After the destruction of Budenny's army east of Kiev, the whole rich Ukraine fell into German hands. The Russians withdrew from the industrial region of the south, abandoning the Dniepropetrovsk dam, largest in Europe, and fell back to the south on the Crimea, to the east on the Donets River. Kharkov, a city of almost a million, was defended heroically, but fell late in October, threatening the Donets Valley. Meantime Rumanian troops had laid siege to the great Black Sea port of Odessa which finally fell after two months of desperate fighting—but not until the Russians had evacuated everything that was movable and destroyed the rest.

With Odessa in their hands, and the main Russian forces retreating to Rostov, German forces under von Mannstein turned south to take the strategically important Crimea with its mighty naval base of Sevastopol. Late in October they stormed the defense lines strung across the Perekop peninsula, then seized Simferopol, capital of the Crimea, and in December laid siege to Sevastopol itself.

The first assault on Sevastopol, in December 1941, had cost an estimated 35,000 German and Rumanian casualties. The final attack, which raged all through June, took a far larger toll.

Life during the siege was as grim here as in Leningrad, though the successful evacuation of most of the civilian population made the final casualty figure much smaller. Nowhere, not even at Stalingrad, did the defenders fight with greater heroism or endure with greater fortitude than here. Boris Voyetekhov, who came to the doomed city by destroyer in time to witness the final attacks, recalls the last days of Sevastopol:

Night came on swiftly as our destroyer approached battered Sevastopol. The Chersonese Light began to flash—it was the only light that was not permanently blacked-out. As soon as it took up its sacrificing task of showing us the way, the sides of the lighthouse were illuminated by the flash of exploding shells.

Our sailors knew that familiar welcome beam did not beckon to rest and a cozy hearth. The quivering light said: "Soon you will cross the thresholds of your destroyed homes. Soon you will see what the Germans have done to your city."

We reduced speed and began to worm through the channel's complicated mine fields. At the beginning of the offensive the Germans had strewn the crowded harbor with mines, threatening many ships with destruction. But Russian sailors had jumped overboard and pushed the floating mines before them to shore. Many men were torn apart by exploding mines as they thus cleared a path for our ships to depart and return with munitions for the defenders of Sevastopol.

When we at last reached the inner harbor we saw Sevastopol enveloped in the flame and smoke of fires set by German incendiaries. The fascist knife was at the unhappy city's very throat. High in the sky hundreds of beams from searchlights, Russian and German, crossed like silver swords in an aerial duel. Tracer bullets wove their deadly pyrotechnical pattern. The still surface of the bay mirrored the inferno raging along the shores. To the left of the mole where we landed, barracks and warehouses were blazing. As I watched, the only remaining wall of a building slowly lurched into the sea.

"We are lucky. It is a quiet night," said our captain.

"What is it like when it is not quiet?" I asked.

"Tomorrow in the daytime you will find out," he replied.

The operation of putting our men and munitions ashore, and of reloading the destroyer with wounded and evacuees, was carried on with incredible dispatch. My business was with the Admiralty ashore, to which I was guided by a commissar.

The entrance to Naval Headquarters, the nerve center of Sevastopol's defense, was a tunnel which opened in the face of a steep cliff. Inside, narrow corridors led deep into rock. Dim electric lamps helped one to grope one's way in the gloom. Many doors opened off the corridors into small rooms where tense, energetic people worked and lived. You heard snatches of telephone conversations, the rattle of typewriters, the occasional screams of the wounded, the abrupt answers of officers on duty, the harsh snores of the sleeping.

Radio operators were dictating urgent messages. I overheard snatches: "O–24 searchlight crew: Light the entrance of the bay for incoming transport. Women and children evacuees from a sunk transport are being picked up by following warships. Germans are firing on the harbor. Instruct the 35th Battery to shell the Germans."

These underground chambers had a drinking system, a drainage system, a restaurant, a barbershop, and many other services deep in the rock. But air was lacking. When the ventilators broke down it became difficult to breathe. Many of the workers were women, and it was tragic to see their unsparing toil. Their pale sallow eyes inflamed, they gasped for breath at telephones or typewriters. Occasionally relieving one another at work, they took in their arms their children, who sweated in their sleep, and stood in the trenches outside, breathing deeply the sharp sea air. But such relief was rare and often interrupted by shrapnel or bombs.

Underground, all voices and sounds were drowned by the fearful noise of the explosions on the rock above. So heavy was the bombardment, which resumed regularly just before dawn each day, that in places the rock was cleft and it seemed that at any minute these corridors, rooms and dugouts would cave in to bury completely these tireless toiling people.

During the next four days I did not leave the underground headquarters and saw nothing of what was happening outside. But an officer who had been out on duty described the city's destruction.

"There is no town left. The houses are all roofless, the streets are nearly all blocked by avalanches of rubble."

There was no place in the town where instruments of death did not prevail. No place was safe from bombs, land mines, or shellfire. Everything that moved—cutters, cars and motorcycles—was pursued and attacked. Enemy air squadrons sought out women and children who were sheltering among the rocks, awaiting their turn to be evacuated. Powerful explosives buried them in the debris beside the sea.

Every day the divers reported to the Admiralty commissar about material recovered from the bottom of the harbor. These experts in underwater mysteries dived every night and, amid old wrecks and skeletons of the dead, they loaded their baskets with unexploded bombs and shells.

The commissar was insatiable. He carefully thumbed rescued bills of lading, asking persistently: "Where are those six airplane engines? Where are the bandages, the cotton, wool and drugs? What are you doing down there? Playing chess with the dead?"

"Just that," replied the chief diver, "and you had better take a hand down below; then you will be satisfied that it is impossible to get up those motors. They are covered with piles of dead horses and cavalrymen in the hold. Drugs—" he hesitated—"I can't go there."

"Why not?"

"I have been a diver for 30 years. I have seen things that drove people who were working next to me mad, but to go into that cabin where, if I open the door, dead bodies of children will rush toward me—no, I can't."

"Well," said the commissar, "that means you are letting living children die for lack of food and bandages."

The discussions always ended with the divers going back down below. And in the morning the airplane motors were taken to the airfield, and the bandages were drying in the sun, and the salvaged shells were on the way to the enemy through Sevastopol's sky.

Night after night our ships would steal into the harbor bringing reinforcements and supplies, evacuating women and children. The Germans illuminated the landing stages with parachute flares and searchlights, and shelled them unmercifully. The scene was indescribable: oil tanks blazed; cases of ammunitions exploded; truck drivers rushed overloaded machines through the flames and smoke while the fire-fighters strove to check the fires.

Always there was the effort to maintain the tremendous tempo of loading and unloading. Faster, faster, faster. At dawn every vessel must be far away from the quay. The stakes were high and the methods used had to be ruthless. Among the dock laborers were a number of convicts. One of them had organized a group of malcontents who delayed the work. A communications officer came up to the convict leader and said: "Open your mouth and say 'Ah'!" Whereupon he shot the man in the teeth, spattering those around with blood and brains. Then turning to the others, he said: "I want tempo."

When, finally, I plucked up courage to leave the Admiralty's underground shelter by daylight, I felt my nerves quailing before the frightful, gigantic panorama. Half-submerged ships showing stern or bow projecting from the water still held trapped cargos of unfortunate fugitives. A fully loaded schooner lay on its side with its masts sprawled on the surface stretching toward the coast like the arms of a helpless drowning man.

The inhabitants of the houses nearest to the sea used to take refuge among these hulks during air raids. They believed naively that bombs do not fall in the same place twice. They were wrong, for the Germans bombed the wrecks.

Within the city there was no time for funerals. The dead were covered with a thin layer of earth. On a hillock, where a damaged plane lay, I read these words written on a piece of a propeller: "Make room, you in the graves. Shift, you old soldiers. A newcomer has joined you to prove his love of battle. Take him into your graves. He is worthy."

In search of oil reservoirs, the Germans had completely desolated a cemetery. The remains of the Crimean War dead were scattered, and fresh blood drenched their ashes. Behind the cemetery lay a region which had been so badly bombed that it was impossible to determine where streets or houses had been. Here were craters that contained bloodstained water in which floated hands, limbs, torsos of children. . . .

Reconnaisance photographs proved conclusively to the German Command that Sevastopol had ceased to exist. German troops were told they would be bathing in the bay within two days' time, and after that they would be given a long leave.

Yet the town survived. Boiling with energy and hatred, it gnawed at the earth with bleeding gums. Deprived of its life above ground, Sevastopol continued its struggling existence in cellars, abandoned quarries, or dugouts.

Typical was a mine factory I visited. The noise was incredible. The vast cellar was subdivided by heavy metal screens where hundreds of lathes hummed and rattled. A roaring tractor motor, puffing and smoking like a bad old samovar, was generating electricity. When the motor stopped, the lights went out; immediately every worker lit a cigarette, and the cave glowed with hundreds of faint lights. It had been agreed among them that only when their work was held up by a failure of current should there be smoking.

The machines ran 24 hours daily. Everybody was working. Before me was an elderly woman at a stamping machine. She had no right hand. It had been torn away by a bomb blast. After leaving the hospital she refused to be evacuated. Beside her was a beautiful young woman with a nursing baby at her breast, keeping control of a boring machine at the same time. Sometimes she charmed all by singing a lullaby.

On bunks built in three tiers along the walls, the workers of other shift slept, wedged in among personal possessions and luggage for which there was no room elsewhere. On the lower bunks pale sallow children played war games. The girls would wrap grenades in pieces of bright-colored cloth to make dolls.

Messengers, department chiefs, journalists, newsreel operators hurried through the lines of bunks along the corridors. Kneeling at a small table, an engineer was shaving. The cashier was paying out wages. A resting telephone switchboard girl was playing a guitar. These and many others lived and worked here.

From the fighting front itself came strange and terrible stories. One day in the harbor a passenger ship was sinking. An explosion in the hold had blocked the door to the messroom, where there were wounded lying. From the engine room burning fuel was flowing, leaking though the messroom door. It could not be stopped. Engulfed in the burning liquid, wounded men struggled to get through portholes too narrow for their shoulders. These wounded men were not armed and could not kill themselves. A sailor struggled along the deck outside to the porthole through which the head of an agonized friend appeared. His comrade begged him to kill him. The sailor drew his revolver and shot. He then turned away. He had done what he could.

And from a Russian commander of marines, I heard this story of front-line barbarity: "Last December when the Germans captured Height 615, they took the most severely wounded of our marines and arranged them in the shape of swastikas. Then they poured gasoline on them and set them on fire. All night the blazing starfish lit up the valley. . . ."

It was clear that an assault was about to begin. Entering an observation post I hear the chief's voice: "Zero hour. Be ready for the fireworks," and at the same moment I see tanks creeping out from the left side of the valley. They are followed by running figures. Through my glasses I see that they are half naked and have the butts of their tommy guns pressed against their sweating bodies. They have cotton in their nostrils because of the stench of the corpses. Some, I see, carry movie cameras recording the battle.

Suddenly everything is enveloped in smoke. Nothing is visible. Into this dusty soil we shoot blindly. Hours pass. The battle rages. The weight of the explosions presses down on one's head, squeezing one's brains, eyes and eardrums.

The leading tanks have reached the trenches. Somehow they are checked there, suddenly they wheel sharply, scrunching the bodies of German and Rumanian soldiers who have just been killed in the assault. But several of our batteries are silenced.

At this point the Germans strike decisively from the air. Our planes are outnumbered ten to one. The attack of the dive bombers is not a battle but an execution, a complete suppression of the earth and the men on it, and when the planes have swept on, enemy tanks surge forward. Those who defended the second line saw everything that happened; they saw their fellows wiped out, several of our batteries silenced; but they stood firm. No one ran away, although they knew that two or three more assaults would carry the enemy through the defenses.

The end is history, though I was not there to see it, for I was ordered out on the last submarine to leave Sevastopol. When the Germans came to the fourth sector of defenses they met with practically no resistance. There was no surrender, but out of the division that had been defending that part of the line only 130 men were left alive.

The advancing Germans were suspicious and fearful of the corpses. Stabbing and slashing the bodies with their bayonets or emptying their revolvers into them, they sneaked forward under the cover of light tanks towards the Konstantinovsky Battery. Capture of this battery would give the enemy complete control of the harbor, and the channel to the sea.

The 130 survivors had long since received an order to abandon their positions. They ignored it. They chose their narrowest sector and defended it so resolutely that the Germans were forced to pause for reinforcements. These 130 men fought for the lives of their wounded comrades who were being ferried across the bay.

The wounded, many of them horribly misshapen, lay along the beaches. The supplies of drugs and water had been exhausted—there was nothing to ease their distress. And this everyone knew—the doctors and the wounded. There were no reproaches, no complaints. The wounded suffered and died quietly. Young Russian women who had served in the army from the beginning of the war carried the wounded to boats, and swam or sank with them when their boat was hit.

The men who were fighting to let this go on, those 130, knew what the women were doing. Even when reinforcements arrived the Germans were still unable to break through this last stubbornly contested line of defense. But the ranks of the marines thinned rapidly and it was a mere 40 who made the final stand at Konstantinovsky Battery.

For three days and three nights 40 men held that battery—days and nights when the German attack was incessant. For three days and nights these sailors held shut the gates to Sevastopol, and only when all their bullets and shells had been spent did resistance on the fourth sector of the Sevastopol defense come to an end. Not one battery fell into the enemy's hands. One by one, as they exhausted their ammunition or were disabled, they blew themselves up. Everything which might be of use to the enemy was destroyed.

For eight months this town, which was not a very large place and which had been built and fortified to withstand danger coming from the sea, had stemmed the advance of the whole German and Rumanian Crimean Army toward the Caucasus. But now, before the enemy's relentless steam-roller advance, Sevastopol itself—for Sevastopol had ceased to be a city and had become a tradition which had winged its way to all Russia—fell back with those tortured, sweating, bleeding, swearing sailors, who, step by step, with their breasts to the enemy, retreated toward the last lighthouse in Crimea—the Chersonese.

At a port on the eastern coast of the Black Sea I watched the arrival of one of the last ships to leave Sevastopol. She was mastless, her bridge had been shot away, and her sides were riddled like a sieve, but the Germans had not managed to sink her. The first words of the wounded sailors on reaching land were: "We shall return to Sevastopol. We have seen how the lamps of the Chersonese Lighthouse went out, but we shall light them again."[14]

Stalingrad

With Sevastopol and the whole of the Crimea secured, the Germans prepared for a giant movement that was intended to outflank Moscow from the south, cut communications with the Urals, secure the Volga River and its valley, and capture the rich oil fields of the Caucasus. No campaign on a more prodigious scale, involving larger armies, and bringing richer rewards, had been seen.

At first all went according to plan. German armies swept north past Kharkov towards Voronezh on the Don, other armies crossed the Donbas towards Stalingrad on the Volga, and to the south still other armies swept down from Rostov and across the Kerch Peninsula into the Kuban and the Caucasus. By August the Kuban was cleared of Russians, who were forced to evacuate the great Black Sea naval base of Novorossisk. The Maikop oil fields were in German hands, and the path to the Caspian seemed open. Then Russian resistance stiffened, the Germans were denied the great Grozny oil field, and pushed slowly back.

The crucial battle, however, was at Stalingrad—one of the decisive battles of history.

Something of the character of the Stalingrad battle is suggested by Major Velichko's account of the fighting by the 62nd Army:

A light Yu. 2 plane soared slowly over the wide Don steppe. Down below foreign hordes crept eastwards along all the roads over the plain. Like metal worms the Germans crawled over the Russian soil, making their way to Stalingrad and the Volga.

The Yu. 2's passenger was making notes on a map. He was Lieutenant-General Chuykov, commander of the Soviet 62nd Army. He knew that it was not particularly safe to go cruising over the battlefield on his old coffee-grinder, as the Germans call the Yu. 2. He could easily have taken a faster plane. But during this leisurely amble across the sky he could see everything in perfect detail.

The enemy was forging ahead, pressing towards the city. Stalingrad was already ablaze. The headquarters of the 62nd Army was installed on a height which gave a view over the whole city and the expanse of the Volga.

Chuykov returned. He tramped Stalingrad's streets, looked over houses and basements, broke open the stone to make a fortress, dug a grave for the enemy in the hard soil. Every window must shoot at the enemy, every paving stone must crush him, every city square must strangle him.

The 62nd Army set about making Stalingrad into a shield that would bar the way to the Germans.

The Germans, incomparably superior in numbers, bit bloodily into the defences. At one time it seemed that the 62nd Army must crumble, that human flesh and blood could never withstand this trial. The Military Council discussed the situation. Chuykov, worn out yet unwearying, pointed to a line on the map and said: "The Guards must take up positions here."

At dawn the Germans struck. Their horseshoe had forced its way ahead some distance when the Guards launched a thunderbolt of a flank attack. The enemy had not even considered the possibility of such a blow. The German horseshoe was mutilated, its thrust diverted from its course. Only a narrow German tongue reached the Volga crossing and was at once forced to pass to the defensive. And that was as far as the Germans ever managed to get.

The scale of the Stalingrad battle grew day by day. Thirteen thousand machine-guns were at work on both sides sixteen hours a day. The *Luftwaffe* made 2,000 flights a day over the city. But the 62nd Army fought back.

It created a university of street fighting. Its Red Army men students sat in trenches. Blockhouses were their lecture halls. Hatred of the enemy was their text-book.

The Red Army and the enemy tested each other's mettle. It was in those days that Vasili Zaitsev, one of Stalingrad's most famous snipers, coined the phrase: "There is no land for us on the other bank."

It was a war of grenades. They were stored everywhere: at headquarters, in passageways, in messes and kitchens, near sentry posts, in special dumps. Every niche in every trench was packed with grenades.

The turrets and treads of German tanks could be seen buried under piles of brick and rubble. And under this layer was another and another of buried Germans and their armour. The counterattacks of the 62nd Army grew more and more daring. The Germans went mad. On October 14 the battle grew to monstrous proportions and all scale for comparison was lost.

Command posts and dugouts caved in. The bombardment was so terrific that men staggered in passage-ways as though on a ship in heavy seas. In the air bombers howled maliciously. Tens of thousands of bombs came down on the 62nd Army. It seemed that the Volga and her banks had moved from their places.

The terrible vibration shattered empty glasses. All the wireless stations went out of commission. Then the oil-covered Volga caught fire.

The Army and the city grew into one. Every soldier became a stone of the city, and a city cannot retreat.

Chuykov decided on a subterranean offensive. The first underground attack was launched by two sections under Vladimir Dubovoy and Ivan Makarov. Their blow was directed against a big centre of resistance from which the Germans kept the Volga under fire. They went down a well 16 ft. deep and from the base of the well began to make a tunnel 32 in. wide and a yard high. They probed for 45 yards. For 14 days oil wicks shimmered in the tunnel. The sappers forgot what daylight was, what it felt like to stand on one's feet. The air was foul. Their eyes grew sunken and their faces green.

At last they heard German voices overhead. Three tons of explosives were placed in a chamber under the Germans. An explosion of terrific force shook the Volga bank.

Strong winds blew at night. They brought the ruins of many-storied buildings crashing to earth. A Red Army man from Kirghizia looked at the debris of a house and said: "The city is tired, the house is tired, the stones are tired. We are not tired."

Meanwhile the balance of the battle of Stalingrad was growing ever more stable. Then came the hour when the shattering Soviet offensive overwhelmed the Germans near Stalingrad.

And the 62nd Army, too, went over to the offensive. A ring of death closed around the Germans. On December 20, for the first time since the beginning of the battle, the commander of the 62nd Army, Lieut.-General Chuykov, went to the other bank of the Volga.

He walked over the ice and stared for a long time at the city.[15]

Edgar Snow asked General Chuikov what important tactical errors the Germans had made, but he said he had observed none.

"The only great error they made was strategic."

"What was that?"

"They gave Hitler supreme command."

But it was more than that which decided the outcome, he said. "On any battlefield the contending forces are never absolutely equal. If there is numerical equality there is variation in countless other factors. But once you are given approximate equilibrium, the side with better training, better equipment and greater stability will win. We had greater *stability* and we won."

At one time the Germans possessed immense tank superiority. On October 9th, when the Germans attacked with two tank divisions, the whole 62nd Army had only nine heavy tanks and thirty-one light tanks. But the Russians had superior artillery and made good use of it. Everywhere it was the might of Russian guns that stopped, wore out, and finally pushed back the enemy, and this was particularly true in the winter, of course, when the Germans' mechanized equipment lost much of its greater mobility.

"The Germans underestimated our artillery," Chuikov said, "and they underestimated the effectiveness of our infantry against their tanks. This battle showed that tanks forced to operate in narrow quarters are of limited value; they're just guns without mobility. In such conditions nothing can take the place of small groups of infantry, properly armed, and fighting with utmost determination. I don't mean barricade street fighting—there was little of that—but groups converting every building into a fortress and fighting for it floor by floor and even room by room. Such defenders cannot be driven out either by tanks or planes. The Germans dropped over a million bombs on us but they did not dislodge our infantry from its decisive positions. On the other hand, tanks can be destroyed from buildings used as fortresses."

The Germans learned that costly lesson at Stalingrad and later they were to apply it most effectively against the Allied troops in Italy. The tactics Chuikov used were employed a year later, with little variation, by the Germans who held up our advance for weeks at Cassino despite our complete mastery of the air. There is an answer to this kind of ground-hog defense, but our generals had not learned it, and Chuikov told us that, too.

"Our counter-attacks," he said, "were not led by tanks but by small storm groups of 'armor-piercers' who knocked out enemy firepoints, assisted by tanks. These small groups, of from five to eight men, were equipped with tommyguns, rifles, anti-tank rifles, hand-grenades, knives, flame-throwers and shovels. They usually attacked at night and they recovered each house as a fortress."[16]

By November the Red Army was ready to go over to the offensive. Albert Parry tells the story of the frustration of the German attacks and the beginning of the Russian counter-offensive:

The Russian resistance alarmed Hitler's generals no less than it heartened Stalin's allies. The Nazi high command wanted more of Germany's strength to reinforce the battering ram at the Volga gates. The *Wehrmacht* chiefs told their Fuehrer that the German Sixth Army at Stalingrad had to be protected in the rear. But he gave them only one-fourth of the troops they requested for such protection.

The generals then demanded that before real winter set in the German line must be shortened. Both the Caucasian and the Stalingrad groups must be withdrawn a few hundred miles, possibly to Rostov, but if necessary even farther west, they insisted. Hitler refused, in a customary rage.

The debacle began.

When the Russians outside Stalingrad finally struck, it was mid-November, the beginning of the dreaded winter of the steppe. They hit not only from the north and northeast, as feared by the Nazi generals, but also from the southeast—from the bare Kalmuck plains where the Germans did not at all suspect the presence of any Russian bases of troops and supplies. The courageous Sixty-second Army inside the besieged city took fresh heart.

The timing was perfect. Winter weather was grounding whatever Nazi planes had not been taken from this front to the new menacing lines then being established by the Americans and British in North Africa and at

Italy's doorstep. And air power was practically the sole weapon in which the Nazis had superiority in the Russian steppes. The Red offensive was opening under most propitious circumstances, with the Nazis overextended and overexpended in more than one sense.

In mid-November 1942 the German-Russian front stretched some 2,000 miles all the way from the Baltic Sea to the Black Sea. The figure would have been closer to 3,000 if every twist of the line were counted. A much longer front than a year earlier, it placed the Reichswehr chiefs at a disadvantage, for, with their depleted forces, they had to guard a far greater line. The difference in distance was nearly 650 miles!

Also there was this added drawback for the Nazis: in November 1941 they had a fairly straight line. Where it curved or twisted, it did so to the Germans' benefit, since the curves and twists formed a number of pincers or near-pincers threatening the Russian lines. But in November 1942 the Nazi line was overdrawn in the southeastern direction, in the shape of a bag or a pocket surrounded on three sides by the Red Army units and vulnerable to a puncture on the fourth.

And now the Nazi generals began to worry about the Stalingrad winter in earnest. True, the winter is short in this area, as for nine months out of every year the temperature remains mostly above the freezing point. (But this is valid not so much for Stalingrad itself as for the area immediately to the south of it.) On the other hand, both the Russian and German chiefs knew that this winter, although brief, can be extremely violent. Unlike the winter at Moscow and central Russian generally, at Stalingrad—and especially southward—it is not a period of evenly distributed snows and steady frosts. The Stalingrad winter varies frequently and abruptly from slush to storms, from rains to a brief but deep snowfall which, on melting, contributes to the mire left by the preceding rains to freeze temporarily beneath the snow. The mire, the slush, the sudden rains and violent snowstorms play havoc with communications unless you are a native and know how to prepare for every eventuality.

The main reason for the contrasts in the weather is that the Stalingrad region is at a crossroads of two different climates. To the north and east there are the vast and icy steppes and forests of Siberia. The intervening Urals are not high enough to stop the Siberian winds from descending onto the Lower Volga plains. There they meet the warm currents that come up from down south—from the Caspian, from the direction of Iran and other balmier parts. In the conflict between the warm currents and cold winds the Stalingrad winter is born with all its convulsive changes, and all its damage to supply communications for those who have not made ready for whatever it brings between late October and early May.

But besides the winter there were two other factors the Nazis feared in Russian: night fighting, and bayonet charges. At least the first two fears were overdone by the Nazis in a curious sense, namely: a precise military mind should neither overrate nor underrate fighting in any season of the year. The Germans should have been afraid of the Russian ability to fight at any time—in the summer as well, as the Soviet counter-offensives in the Orel-Kharkov-Bryansk areas proved later, in July and August 1943. And with regard to night fighting, some Red Army men confess that they do not like it either—to grope for the enemy's forts and flesh in the dark is no easy thing, but it must be done. Thus the cold steel of the bayonet remains the only unexaggerated advantage of the Soviet infantryman.

The Germans might have been able to cope with the Russian winter and the Russians' night fighting had they faced them more calmly, with less desire to find alibis for their defeats, and so create unduly frightful myths out of these two obstacles. The Nazis defeated themselves psychologically when they babbled excitedly and self-pityingly about the hardships of winter and night battles in the steppes. It was only in the matter of bayonet charges that they truly lacked the stamina and training of the Russian foot soldier.

At Stalingrad, the Red Army infantryman used all three bugaboos of the Nazis to Russia's best gain. His success was most notable because at that juncture—by 1942–43—he was to a considerable degree a different fighter from what he had been in 1941. At the outset of the Nazi-Soviet war, the Russian infantryman was bound too much to the orders of his superiors, and so, on occasion, he failed to extricate himself from difficult situations. By the time of Stalingrad, fortunately, the error of excessive supervision was realized by the Red Army's chiefs. The rank-and-file soldier was very soon given more leeway to exercise his individual ingenuity, depending on the emergencies of the battle, all of course within the larger strategic and tactical designs of the Soviet command.

By November 1942 the average "Infantry Ivan" had experienced this change in his relationship with his commanders—in his personal responsibility at the height of a heated battle—as clearly as he had discerned the three main weaknesses (and quite a few minor ones) in his Nazi opponent. Of equipment this Soviet Ivan had had enough or nearly enough from the very beginning. But now he really knew how to use it to best advantage, and he was free to employ these weapons in his own ways.

As the Russians attacked in November, they proceeded to do precisely what the Nazi generals had nervously expected they would do. The Red Army began to drive from two directions at once in a gigantic pincer movement designed to cut off the German Sixth Army at Stalingrad from the Nazi bases in the Don Cossack land. The drive succeeded.

A partial encirclement of the Sixth Army was accomplished on November nineteen. Four days later the ring was closed. A German prisoner related sadly to his Russian captors that neither he nor any of his mates had at first comprehended the gravity of the situation. "We treated the news of the Russian break-through very calmly and attached no particular significance to it," he recalled. "We regarded it only as a temporary Red Army success, never suspecting it was so serious."

From the chief, Colonel General Friedrich von Paulus, down to the lowest subaltern, the Nazi officers told their soldiers not to worry. A Nazi sergeant, when taken prisoner, testified at the interrogation: " 'We have to hold firm, soldiers,' they said, 'large forces of reserves are coming to our aid. They will cut through the Russian encirclement and relieve us.' " In December, a panzer division, sent by Field Marshal Fritz Erich von Mannstein, indeed tried to break the ring southwest of Stalingrad, at the town and railroad station of Kotelnikovo, but was knocked out by the troops of General Rodion Malinovsky and retreated ignominiously.

The Nazi high command then put its hope in the air transport as a means of supply. Perhaps, reinforced by air with food and weapons, the Sixth Army and other trapped units would be able to counter-attack and smash through to freedom on its own. But the hope went for naught. . . .

Food shortly became a thorny problem. The diet of horse-flesh was not improved by a terrible-smelling soup, made of pressed cabbage. A Nazi machine gunner, surrendering to the Red Army outposts, revealed that, from one liter per man daily, the ration of the horrid soup was cut to one-quarter liter. Other captives related that dogs and cats were being eaten by the beleaguered Germans.

Munitions, too, gave out. The same captured machine gunner also complained: "Instead of the normal issue of nine thousand rounds of ammunition per day to each machine gun crew, already toward the end of November only six hundred to one thousand rounds were being doled out. Later it was reduced to three hundred or two hundred rounds, and the command further demanded they should not be fired except in extreme emergency. . . .

On January 8 von Paulus was presented with the Soviet ultimatum to lay down his arms by the tenth. The Nazi general refused, blindly obeying his insane Fuehrer. At that time the Russians did not quite perceive what a rich prize they had within their ring of steel and fire. For they thought that the trapped armies had originally contained from 200,000 to 220,000 men. Actually the number was close to 330,000, as it later turned out. . . .

On January 25 the southern group of the Nazis gave up. The next day the Russians cut their way through the remainder, cleaving it into two smaller pockets. Hitler still urged von Paulus to keep on fighting. Promotions to non-commissioned ranks were radioed to all the S.S. and other soldiers in the northern group. At the end of January, von Paulus himself was made a field marshal. But this was also the end of von Paulus. He and his staff had sought refuge in a department store basement. He had only a few thousand soldiers left, and most of them were lying in cellars near by—hungry, in rags, suffering from frostbite.

On the last day of January, von Paulus directed one of his generals to tell the Russians to come and take him and whoever else of the Nazis was yet alive and in the vicinity. A young Russian lieutenant—aged only twenty-one!—marched in with a group of his infantrymen and accepted the surrender. "The road of German shame!" exclaimed one of the Nazi generals, as the small but significant band of prisoners proceeded through the ruins of Stalingrad, past the thousands of German dead and piles of discarded equipment.

One field marshal and fifteen generals were gathered that day, including two Rumanians. Twelve thousand Russian civilian prisoners were freed from the basements where they had been kept ever since November, awaiting shipment as slaves to Germany should the ring be broken. In twenty days alone, from January 10 to 30, an incomplete count established that the Red Army had annihilated more than 100,000 German officers and men in and near Stalingrad. The booty seized in approximately the same period consisted of 750 airplanes, 1,550 tanks, 6,700 field guns, 1,462 trench mortars, 8,130 machine guns, 90,000 rifles, 61,102 trucks,

7,365 motorcycles, 470 tractors and troop carriers, 5,700 parachutes, 320 radio transmitters, three armored trains, 56 locomotives, 1,125 railroad cars, and 235 ammunition and arms dumps.

On February 2 the last small segment, separated from von Paulus on January 26, capitulated. Two days later, in the strange silence of the main plaza of the city, heroes of the Sixty-second Army held a meeting with the troops who had come up from the south and north, also with the surviving civilians of Stalingrad. Both Chuikov and Rodimtsev delivered brief speeches as the infantrymen and natives marked the victory and honored their dead. General Rodimtsev, the symbol of his infantry's stand at Stalingrad, was especially moved as he slowly spoke his few words.

Thus perished the infamous Sixth Army of the Nazis which in the summer of 1940 had rolled treacherously into Holland and Belgium, crushing those peaceful countries quickly and completely. Retribution had to wait more than two years, but it came. Hitler's Germany had good reason to mourn, indeed![17]

6

THE RISING SUN

Pearl Harbor

ON NOVEMBER 17 the Japanese Ambassador, Admiral Kichisaburo Nomuro, brought his colleague, Mr. Saburo Kurusu, to the office of Secretary of State Cordell Hull. Mr. Kurusu had just arrived. Alarmed by the unfavorable American reaction to her southward expansion into Thailand and Indo-China, the Japanese government had rushed this special "peace envoy" over to Washington to explain away all misunderstandings and restore harmony to Japanese-American relations. If this was to be achieved there was need for haste, but the conversations dragged along without appreciable results. The Japanese demands were extreme, the American attitude inflexible, and late in November Mr. Hull informed the cabinet that the situation had passed beyond diplomatic control and would have to be handled by the army or navy. Yet President Roosevelt did not give up. On December 6 he addressed a personal note to the Japanese Emperor pointing out the "tragic possibilities" of the situation. At 2:15 the next day, Sunday afternoon, December 7th, the two Japanese emissaries appeared once more at Mr. Hull's office with their final reply, a reply which charged the United States with scheming for the extension of the war. Hull glanced at this fantastic document. "In all my fifty years of public service I have never seen a document that was more crowded with infamous falsehoods and distortions on a scale so huge that I never imagined until today that any government on this planet was capable of uttering them."

Even as this interview was going on, bombs were raining down on Pearl Harbor.

The Japanese plans were well laid and skillfully fulfilled.

Sometime late in November, when attention was fastened anxiously upon Japanese troop movements into Thailand and Indo-China, there put out from the harbors of Japan every ship that was available. A segment of this fleet, a task force composed of carriers and guarded by cruisers and destroyers, struck off north and east behind a cold weather front. At sunrise, December 7, one hundred and fifty miles north of Oahu in the Hawaiian Island group, the air was alive with the roar of enemy planes. At 7:02 a private, listening on a radio plane detector, reported the large flight of planes to the north, but it was assumed that these were American, and no action was taken.

In fine homes on the heights above Honolulu, in beach shacks near Waikiki, in the congested districts around the Punchbowl, assorted Japanese, Chinese, Portuguese, Filipinos, Hawaiians and *kamaainas* (long-settled whites) were taking their ease. In the shallow waters lapping Fort de Russe, where sentries walked post along a retaining wall, a few Japanese and Hawaiians waded about, looking for fish to spear. In Army posts all over Oahu soldiers were dawdling into a typical idle Sunday. Aboard the ships of the Fleet at Pearl Harbor, life was going along at a saunter. Downtown nothing stirred save an occasional bus. The clock on the Aloha Tower read 7:55.

The Japs came in from the southeast over Diamond Head, the Rising Sun insignia clearly visible in the early morning sunlight. Civilians' estimates of their numbers ranged from 50 to 150. They whined over Waikiki, over the candy-pink bulk of the Royal Hawaiian Hotel. All that they met as they came in was a tiny private plane in which Lawyer Ray Buduick was out for a Sunday morning ride. They riddled the lawyer's plane with machine-gun bullets but he succeeded in making a safe landing. By the time he did, bombs were thudding all around the city. The first reported casualty was Robert Tyce, operator of a civilian airport near Honolulu, who was machine-gunned as he started to spin the propeller of a plane.

Single-engine Jap bombers picked out ships and naval centers in Pearl Harbor, blanketed the area with explosives. Under subsequent attack were the Army's Hickam Field, Wheeler Field, Schofield Barracks, Bellows Field, Kaneohe Naval Air Station and that portion of the Fleet offshore.

Shortly after the attack began, radio warnings were broadcast. But people who heard them were skeptical until explosions wrenched the guts of Honolulu. All the way from Pacific Heights down to the center of town planes soared, leaving a wake of destruction. With anti-aircraft guns popping and U. S. pursuits headed aloft, pajama-clad citizens piled out of bed to dash downtown or head for the hills where they could get a good view. Few of them were panicky, many were nonchalant. Shouted one man as he dashed past a CBS observer: "The mainland papers will exaggerate this!"

After the first attack Governor Poindexter declared an emergency, cleared the streets, ordered out the police and fire departments. Farrington High School, the city's biggest, was converted into a hospital. But the Japanese attackers returned. Obvious to onlookers was the fact that Pearl Harbor was being hit hard. From the Navy's plane base on Ford Island (also known as Luke Field), in the middle of the harbor, clouds of smoke ascended. One citizen who was driving past the naval base saw the first bomb fall on Ford Island. He said: "It must have been a big one. I saw two planes dive over the mountains and down to the water and let loose torpedoes at a naval ship. This warship was attacked again and again. I also saw what looked like dive bombers coming over in single file."

Incoming passengers on an American liner, watching the planes swoop down, commended the U. S. Navy's thoughtfulness in staging a big-scale war game on Sunday morning. An American automobile salesman, en route to Tientsin, gawked admiringly as a bomb whooshed into the harbor a scant 100 yards away: "Boy! What if that had been a real one?" The perspiring ship's officer who finally broke the bad news flubbed his lines: "It seems there's a state of undeclared war between Honolulu and the United States."

After the first stunning shock, Pearl Harbor's defenders swung into action. Spotters in the Navy Yard signal tower picked up the attackers, flashed air-raid warnings via visual signals. Working coolly under enemy bombs and machine-gun fire and shrapnel from defending anti-aircraft batteries, the signalmen routed scores of orders to ships standing out to sea or fighting from berths.

A recruit seaman is credited with the first blow against the enemy. "General Quarters" had not yet sounded when he fought off an attacking plane single-handed with a machine gun. A battleship captain had his stomach laid open by a shrapnel burst as he went from conning tower to bridge to direct his ship's fight. He fell to the deck, disdained attempts to lift him to safety, continued to command until the bridge went up in flames. Two officers attempting to save him were themselves saved only after a third officer climbed above the fire, passed a line to an adjoining battleship, another to the trapped men, thus led them to safety.

Ten members of a 5-inch gun's crew fell before a strafing attack. The lone remaining bluejacket took over: three times he grabbed a shell from the fuse pot, placed it in the tray, dashed to the other side of the gun, rammed it home, jumped into the pointer's seat and fired. A terrific bomb blast finally carried him over the side. He was rescued.

When the brig door blew open, a seaman confined earlier for misconduct dashed to his post at an anti-aircraft gun. A hospitalized officer brushed aside his nurses when the first alarm was sounded, ran across the Yard to his ship. So effectively did he fight, despite his illness, that his captain recommended promotion. One tough sailor, unable to find a mount for a heavy machine gun, fired the weapon from his arms despite terrific concussion.

A moored aircraft tender, blazing under repeated attacks, downed a Japanese plane on her own decks. Simultaneously her captain spotted a midget submarine's shadow within yards of his vessel. Hits were immediately scored and, as the sub's conning tower emerged, a destroyer administered a *coup de grâce* with depth charges. The tender then shot down a second plane. Motor launches from a vessel laid up for overhaul braved a steady hail of bullets and shrapnel, rescued scores of victims from the oil-fired harbor. Almost without exception officers and men exhibited quick thinking, coolness, coordination.[1]

Washington, which had for so long lived in an atmosphere of crisis, reacted to the news with courage and energy.

The blow that was about to fall cast no shadow into the unseasonably

warm sunshine of December 7, 1941. At midday Washington was the
capital of a people technically at peace, psychologically at war: a "white"
war against overseas aggressors and, at home, among themselves on the
question of how far to pursue the war abroad. The first note of menace
reached the capital almost inadvertently at 1:45 P.M. It came by way of an
alert, intercepted at Mare Island and relayed to the Navy Department,
which read:

> From CINCPAC (Commander in chief Pacific fleet) to all ships present Ha-
> waiian area: Air raid on Pearl Harbor. This is no drill.

In the final sentence. Admiral Husband E. Kimmel was correcting the
incredulous reaction of Hawaii, which had accepted the first Japanese
bombs as evidence of a particularly realistic maneuver.

At the Navy Department, Secretary Frank Knox, about to depart on a
routine visit to the Washington Navy Yard, received the message from one
of his companions, Admiral Harold S. Stark, Chief of Naval Operations,
who had it from a panting Communications officer. By a rueful irony, the
Secretary's annual report, attesting the Navy's fitness, had appeared in that
morning's Sunday newspapers, which now lay strewn through millions of
American living rooms. Handing the message to Knox, Stark failed to
comment.

"What," demanded the Secretary, "does this mean?"

"It's the beginning," replied Stark, somewhat vaguely, whereupon Rear
Admiral R. K. Turner, of War Plans, standing alongside the Secretary,
broke in with the definitive: "By God, sir, they've attacked us!"

Back into his private office hurried the Secretary. In private life a
Chicago newspaper publisher, he nevertheless keeps his office as nautical
as a man-of-war's wardroom. Behind his desk stands a bank of telephones,
one a direct wire to the White House. He lifted that receiver and jiggled
the hook. . . .

At the moment when Knox lifted the White House phone, half of
Washington was lingering over Sunday midday dinners. Such was the case
with the President, who was eating from a tray on his desk in the oval
study, a large, littered, intensely personal chamber on the second floor of
the White House. With him were his friend, Harry L. Hopkins, lounging
on a couch in a V-necked sweater and slacks, and the President's Scottie,
Falla, expertly pouching morsels from the tray. After an exhausting week
with the Far Eastern crisis, aggravated by clogged sinuses, Mr. Roosevelt
had dedicated this day to rest. Saturday he had worked late, clearing his
desk while the White House staff took a half day for Christmas shopping.
Today, tieless and in shirt sleeves, he hoped to catch up with his neglected
stamp collection. After a late breakfast, Hopkins, whose health is poor, had
strolled in from his bedroom down the book-lined corridor for some re-
laxed talk. The President might have been any one of a million Americans
putting in a loafing Sunday afternoon with a crony and a hobby.

The White House, therefore, was, like the country, at peace. Elsewhere
in the great Regency-Georgian mansion, Mrs. Roosevelt was giving a lunch-
eon for an American radio commentator recently home from London, but
the President's calendar was bare and the executive staff scattered. A "do

not disturb" order had been confidently placed with the switchboard. Mr. Roosevelt was topping his dinner with an apple when his desk telephone jangled disobediently.

The President lifted his receiver oh an apologetic operator agitatedly saying that Secretary Knox had insisted on being put through . . . the call was most urgent. The President cut the operator short: "Put him on," and then, "Hello, Frank."

In a tone and at a pace the President still regards as a model of casualness on the brink of crisis, Knox began: "Mr. President, it looks like the Japanese have attacked Pearl Harbor. . . ."

"NO!" the President interrupted.

"It's true," said the Secretary. "I'll read you the message," which he did.

The hands of the brass ship's clock on the President's desk stood at 1:47. The message, which was, as we have seen, a service alert to the fleet and not an official report to Washington, did lack explicitness, and its terse language gave no insight into how the attack was being met, no hint as to the extent, weight, or gravity of the air raid. Yet its meaning was plain to the President: the flag had been fired upon, Hawaii, not Siam, had been subjected to the overt act, and the war, so long dreaded, so exhaustively debated, had come to America. Directing that Knox see at once to safeguarding the Panama Canal and the Alaskan bases, and to doubling the guards at all Naval establishments against sabotage, the President rang off, bidding the operator to get him Secretary Hull. Thrice that afternoon he lodged anxious inquiries about the Canal with the Navy Department.

Just before Hull lifted his receiver at the State Department, Hopkins said: "This is it." For a long while the President's *fidus Achates* had predicted that World War II would overtake America in the Pacific rather than in the Atlantic. . . .

To Mr. Hull the President said: "Frank Knox has just telephoned a report of an air raid over Pearl Harbor. We haven't confirmed it yet." The Secretary, a man of fire and storm under a gently benign manner, uttered a profane comment. In is graphic phraseology, the Japanese war party had, for some time, been succinctly characterized as "Dillinger."

Of all the ranking officials in Washington, Mr. Hull should have been the least surprised. Five weeks earlier, before the arrival of Kurusu, he had warned the Army and Navy that the Far Eastern crisis, having passed outside the bounds of diplomacy, was now in their lap. A fortnight before he had been more precise. Reminding his War Cabinet colleagues of Japan's proclivity for beginning wars by stealth, he had suggested that all hands in the Pacific be on watchful guard lest a shock attack on a wide front "stampede the hell out of our scattered forces."

But with Mr. Hull foresight never lapses into imprudence. He is not, by nature, a jumper at conclusions. The President had said the report was unconfirmed. So little did the Secretary relax his customary caution that he withheld from his associates the news that the country constructively was at war and the next day, at a press conference, recalled only that an "unconfirmed report" had reached him from "an official source" before the arrival of the Japanese envoys. Because the report lacked corroboration, he had elected to see them.

In turn the President telephoned Henry L. Stimson, Secretary of War;

General George C. Marshall, Chief of Staff; Viscount Halifax, the British Ambassador; and Sumner Welles, the Under Secretary of State. Ten years earlier, Stimson, as Hoover's Secretary of State and Hull's immediate predecessor, had labored to arouse the Western World against the explosive implications of Japan's "Manchuria incident." Today he observed the cycle of aggression begun at Mukden conclude its march around the globe.[2]

Five battleships, three destroyers, a minelayer, and a target vessel were sunk; three battleships and three destroyers as well as numerous smaller vessels damaged; most of the 273 army planes and 150 of the 202 navy planes were destroyed. Casualties totalled 2,117 killed, 1,272 wounded, and 960 missing. It was a disaster of the first magnitude but not, as the Japs had hoped and planned, an irretrievable one. A substantial part of the Pacific fleet was not at Pearl Harbor. Of all the ships sunk and damaged every one but the ancient *Arizona* was back in active service within a year. "The essential fact," said Secretary of the Navy Knox, "is that the Japanese purpose was to knock out the United States before the war began. In this purpose the Japanese failed."

The nation as a whole heard the news first with utter incredulity, then with indignation and an implacable determination to avenge the infamy. Republicans and Democrats, interventionists and isolationists, labor and capital closed ranks in a solid phalanx, and the nation moved from peace to war with a unity which it had never known before in time of crisis. Undismayed by the initial setback, it faced the prospect of a long and arduous war with complete confidence in ultimate victory. That confidence was eloquently voiced by President Roosevelt as he appeared before a joint session of the Congress, at noon of December 8, to ask for a declaration of war against Japan.

Congress responded with but a single dissenting vote. The next day Great Britain and the Netherlands—the beginning of a long array of United Nations—ranged themselves alongside the United States in war against Japan. On the evening of December 9 President Roosevelt addressed the nation. Reviewing the American efforts for peace and the events that led up to Pearl Harbor, he reminded the American people that this was a war not only for the survival of the nation but for the survival of all those spiritual values which Americans had so long cherished and defended.

The true goal we seek is far above and beyond the ugly field of battle. When we resort to force, as now we must, we are determined that this force shall be directed toward ultimate good as well as against immediate evil. We Americans are not destroyers—we are builders.

We are now in the midst of a war, not for conquest, not for vengeance, but for a world in which this nation, and all that this nation represents, will be safe for our children. We expect to eliminate the danger from Japan, but it would serve us ill if we accomplished that and found that the rest of the world was dominated by Hitler and Mussolini.

We are going to win the war and we are going to win the peace that follows.

And in the difficult hours of this day—and through dark days that may be yet to come—we will know that the vast majority of the members of the human race are on our side. Many of them are fighting with us. All of them are praying for us. For, in representing our case, we represent theirs as well—our hope and their hope for liberty under God.

In the South China Sea

The disaster at Pearl Harbor assured the powerful Japanese navy temporary supremacy in the Pacific—and especially in those western waters where warships could be supported by land-based planes. The task of defending Allied outposts from Hawaii to the Philippines, Malaya, and Burma, from the Aleutians to New Zealand and Australia, was a herculean one. From Kiska to Midway, fogs and foul weather made it hard for patrol planes to operate effectively. From Honolulu south to New Caledonia, our island outposts were vulnerable to attack from Japanese mandated islands. Midway, Wake, and Guam, controlling our lines from Hawaii to the Philippines, were but feebly garrisoned and everywhere our air power was inadequate to the task now placed upon it.

Some help might be expected from the British navy, based on the great fortress city of Singapore, Gibraltar of the Pacific. Some months before the outbreak of the war, the British Admiralty, anticipating difficulties, had reinforced their navy there with the battle cruiser *Repulse* and the great new battleship *Prince of Wales*. When, on December 7, Japanese bombers struck at Hong Kong, Penang, and Singapore and Japanese soldiers swarmed down by land and along the coastal waters from Thailand to Malaya, Admiral Phillips, commander of the British Far Eastern fleet, put to sea in an effort to smash the invaders before they could build up forces strong enough to attack Singapore by land. As the two great ships and their destroyers steamed northward, Japanese reconnaissance planes spotted them. What happened is told by O. D. Gallagher who was on board the *Repulse*.

It was a thin, Oriental dawn that I saw when bugles awoke me with "Action stations!" at 5:5 A.M. A cool breeze swept through the fuggy ship that had been battened down all night. The sky was luminous as a pearl. . . .

At 6:30 A.M. the loud-speakers said: "A signal has just been received to say the enemy is making a landing one hundred and forty miles north of Singapore. We are going in. . . ." At that moment I almost lost an eye. The shock of an explosion made me jump so that I nearly pushed it out with the eyepiece of the telescope. It was 11:15 A.M. The explosion came from the *Prince of Wales*. She had opened fire with her portside secondary armament at a single airplane.

We opened fire too. There were now about six aircraft. A three-quarter-inch screw fell on my tin hat from the bridge deck above me at the shock of the guns.

"The old tub is falling to bits," remarked the yeoman. That was the beginning of a superb air attack by the Japanese—by an air force that had been until then an unknown quantity, never before having met an equal power. . . .

There was a heavy explosion, and the *Repulse* rocked. Great patches of paint fell from the funnel to the flag deck. We all saw then the planes which had sneaked up on us while our attention was focused on the low-flying aircraft which we supposed were going to attack.

They were high-level bombers—17,000 feet up. The first bomb, the one that rocked us, was a direct hit on the catapult deck. It went through the port hangar. Parts of the ship scattered into the air. I stood behind a multiple Vickers gun, of the type that fires 2,000 half-inch bullets a minute. At the after end of the flag deck I saw a cloud of smoke. It came from the hangar hit by the first bomb. Another came down—again from 17,000 feet. It exploded in the sea close to the port side and churned up a creamy blue-and-green patch about ten feet across. The *Repulse* rocked again. . . .

Two planes seemed to be coming directly at us. A spotter saw another at a different angle, but much closer. He leaned forward his face tight with excitement. He urgently pounded the back of the man who swiveled the gun.

He hit that back with his right fist and pointed with his left, his fore-finger stabbing at the new plane. Still blazing, the whole gun platform turned quickly in that direction and rained its hail of death on the Japanese. It was about 1,000 yards away.

I saw the tracers rip into its fuselage, dead center. The fabric opened up like a rapidly spreading sore with red edges and yellow center. The fire swept to the tail. In a moment the stabilizer and rudder became a framework skeleton. The nose dipped down, and the plane crashed into the sea. . . .

There was a short lull, and the boys dug inside their overalls for cigarettes.

The loud-speaker again: "Enemy aircraft ahead!"

Lighted ends were nipped off, and the ship's company went back into action. There were twelve planes. The boys on the flag deck whistled.

"One—two—three—four—five—six—seven—eight—nine—ten—eleven—twelve. Any advance on twelve, gentlemen? No? Well, here they come!" It was the wag of the flag deck, and he leveled his signaling lamp at the *Prince of Wales*.

It was 12:10 by my watch. All concentrated on the *Prince of Wales*. They were after big ships all right. A mass of water and smoke rose from the *Prince of Wales*'s stern. They had hit her with a torpedo.

A ragged mass of flame belched without a break from her Chicago pianos, as well as heavier, instant flashes from her high-angle, secondary armament. She listed to port. It was a bad list. We were about six cables from her. . . .

The *Prince of Wales* signaled us and asked if we had been hit. Captain Tennant replied: "No, not yet. We have dodged nineteen." Six stokers arrived on the flag deck. They were black with smoke and oil. The skin hung from their hands like dirty muslin. They had been caught down below when the bomb exploded. They were being taken to the armored citadel, at the base of the mast, for treatment. The list on the *Prince of Wales* had increased. There was a great rattle of two-pounder cordite cases as the boys of the Chicago pianos gathered the empties.

A new wave of planes appeared at 12:20 P.M. The end was near, though we did not know it. The *Prince of Wales* lay about ten cables astern of our port side. She was helpless. Not only was her steering gear destroyed by that first torpedo, but her screws also. Unlike the German *Bismarck*, caught by the navy in the Atlantic, which lost only her steering gear and was able to keep moving in a circle, the *Prince of Wales* was a hulk.

All the aircraft made for her. I do not know how many there were in this last attack, but it was afterward estimated that there were between fifty and eighty Japanese torpedo bombers in operation during the action. The *Prince of Wales* fought desperately to beat off the determined killers, who attacked her like a pack of dogs would a wounded buck. The *Repulse* and the destroyers formed a rough circle around her, to add our fire power. All ships fired with the intention of protecting the *Prince of Wales*, and, in doing so, each neglected her own defenses.

It was difficult to make out her outline through the smoke and flame from all her guns except the fourteen-inchers. I saw one plane drop a torpedo. It fell nose-heavy into the sea and churned up a thin wake as it dove straight at the immobile *Prince of Wales*.

It exploded against her bows. A couple of seconds later another hit her—and another.

I gazed at her turning slowly over on her port side, her stern going under, and dots of men jumping into the sea, and was thrown against the bulkhead by a tremendous shock as the *Repulse* was hit by a torpedo on her port side. . . .

With all others on the flag deck, I was wondering where the torpedo came from, when we were staggered by another explosion, also on the port side. . . .

My notebook, which I have before me, says: "Seven Japs down so far. *Repulse* got third torp. Listing badly."

The loud-speakers spoke for the last time: "Everybody on the main deck. Abandon ship!"

I noted the time. It was 12:25 P.M.[3]

The sinking of these two vessels was a catastrophe only less stunning than Pearl Harbor. It changed the whole situation in the Far East and spelled the eventual doom of Singapore with all the fateful consequences that were bound to flow from the loss of that outpost. These consequences Winston Churchill explained to a hushed House of Commons:

In my whole experience I do not remember any naval blow so heavy or so painful as the sinking of the *Prince of Wales* and the *Repulse* on Monday last. These two vast, powerful ships constituted an essential feature in our plans for meeting the new Japanese danger as it loomed against us in the last few months. These ships had reached the right point at the right moment, and were in every respect suited to the task assigned to them. In moving to attack the Japanese transports and landing craft which were disembarking the invaders of Siam and Malaya at the Kra Isthmus or thereabouts, Admiral Phillips was undertaking a thoroughly sound, well-considered offensive operation, not indeed free from risk, but not different in principle from many similar operations we have repeatedly carried out in the North Sea and in the Mediterranean. Both ships were sunk in repeated air attacks by bombers and by torpedo-aircraft. These attacks were delivered with skill and determination. There were two high-level attacks, both of which scored hits, and three waves of torpedo-aircraft of nine in each wave which struck each of our ships with several torpedoes. There is no reason to suppose that any new weapons or explosives were employed, or any bombs or torpedoes of exceptional size. The continued waves of attack achieved their purpose, and both ships capsized and sank, having destroyed seven of the attacking aircraft. . . .

Naturally, I should not be prepared to discuss the resulting situation in the Far East and in the Pacific or the measures which must be taken to restore it. It may well be that we shall have to suffer considerable punishment, but we shall defend ourselves everywhere with the utmost vigour in close co-operation with the United States and the Netherlands. The naval power of Great Britain and the United States was very greatly superior—and is still largely superior—to the combined forces of the three Axis Powers. But no one must underrate the gravity of the loss which has been inflicted in Malaya and Hawaii, or the power of the new antagonist who has fallen upon us, or the length of time it will take to create, marshal and mount the great force in the Far East which will be necessary to achieve absolute victory.[4]

Bataan

Even as the *Repulse* and the *Prince of Wales* went down, Japanese forces were moving confidently upon the Philippines.

Without complete control of the air and the surrounding waters, these islands were indefensible. And it was the Japanese who controlled both sea and air. Airfields and naval bases in Formosa to the north, Indo-China to the west, the Caroline and Mariana islands to the east, all but surrounded the Philippines. From their home islands the Japanese could land a large-scale invasion force across the troubled seas with complete impunity. To challenge invasion by sea, Admiral Hart had in his Asiatic fleet only a feeble force of cruisers, destroyers, and patrol boats. To oppose it on land, General Douglas C. MacArthur had, in Luzon, some 60,000 native troops, 11,000 highly trained Filipino scouts, and about 19,000 Americans made up of men from the National Guard, army air forces, marines, and navy; his air force consisted of 35 Flying Fortresses, 107 P-40 fighters, and almost 100 other planes.

The attack on the Philippines was not unanticipated. During the previous year Hart and MacArthur had planned the strategy of defense, increased patrol activities, and put the defenders of the island on the alert. Work on new airfields was going forward and troop and plane reinforcements were on the way from the United States. But the Japs struck before these arrived, and with a weight and ferocity that made effective defense all but impossible.

Nine hours after the attack on Pearl Harbor came a series of aerial attacks on Clark and Nichols fields that destroyed most of the American planes before they could get into the air.

Early in the afternoon of the third day—a black day memorable for the sinking of the *Repulse* and the *Prince of Wales*—and the first landings on Luzon—came the bombing of the great naval base of Cavite.

With Cavite destroyed, Admiral Hart ordered his remaining naval vessels southward where they later gave a good account of themselves in the Java seas. His destroyers convoyed 200,000 tons of merchant shipping to safety. Only a few submarines remained to harry Japanese invasion boats and bring in meager supplies: the nucleus of a great underwater force that was eventually to sink over 1,000 Japanese ships.

With our air force destroyed and our navy out of the way, the Japanese were ready for invasion. On December 10 an advance guard, almost unopposed, landed at Aparri and Vigan on the northern coast of Luzon. A few days later a large force tried to come ashore at Lingayen Gulf, north of Manila, but most of the 154 landing barges were sunk by Major General King's artillerymen. Then the Japs came on in full force, under the protection of heavy naval and air bombardment. As Frazier Hunt tells it:

At dawn on December 22nd, eighty Japanese transports steamed into Lingayen Gulf, north of Manila on the China Sea—and the great invasion was on. With superb skill every landing was beaten off, save the one made at Agoo. Here the exhausted defenders were suddenly struck on their right flank by a body of the enemy that had worked its way southward from the initial landing at Vigan. The defenders were forced back, and at San Carlos they made their stand. But many thousands of Japanese troops had now landed and were hurried into position. There had been little air opposition, and the defending forces were meager.

Simultaneous with the heavy landings on Lingayen, the Japs sent forty transports into Lamon Bay, to the south of Manila, at the narrowest point of the peninsula. Quickly they poured thousands of troops into the beachhead they already held at Atimonan. But already those good old Manila busses were roaring up from the south, bringing out the soldiers that would be trapped below, once the heavy Japanese force cut the narrow peninsula.

The battle was joined both on the north and the south. The great Jap prongs now moved toward the restricted Manila area, each attempting to drive the converging defending forces together and prevent their retirement to Bataan.

Rapidly pushing straight eastward across central Luzon from Lingayen Bay, a heavy Japanese force soon contacted a second Japanese army that had come down the Cagayan Valley from Aparri, in the far north. These combined Japanese forces in the north had no less than five complete infantry divisions, with a brigade of tanks, and other supporting troops. For months they had been specially trained in Formosa and in China. They were the cream of the Japanese Army.

Against them MacArthur had his hastily organized and incomplete First Philippine Division, with its American and Philippine Scout units; and his partially trained, half-equipped infantry regiments of three Philippine divisions, supported by certain artillery units. Already in the Cagayan Valley, the brilliant 26th Calvary regiment of the Philippine Scouts had played a heroic role of defense; they were to be helped by a rag, tag and bobtail bunch of American and Philippine mining engineers and demolition experts, whose story reads almost like a fantastic Alice in Wonderland epic of war.[5]

The exploits of this group of demolition experts, known as "Casey's Dynamiters," have become legendary.

The day after Christmas General MacArthur declared Manila an open city—a futile gesture as it proved—and executed a long-planned withdrawal to the wilderness peninsula of Bataan and its rock fortress of Corregidor island. Casey's Dynamiters expertly destroyed the great Calumit bridge, and on New Year's day, 1942, MacArthur's forces took up their desperate positions on Bataan.

Given proper weapons and supplies, Bataan is almost ideal for defensive purpose. Its mountainous terrain and thick vegetation afford good cover for defenders and present formidable obstacles to the effective use of armor or air power. But MacArthur's fifty thousand men, only 3,200 of them Regular Army, had neither weapons nor supplies. They lacked effective artillery, their ammunition was low, their air force consisted of a "bamboo fleet" of six P-40s. Even more serious, food and medical supplies were from the beginning dangerously low. Before the end came the men were eating horses, mules, and monkeys; 20,000 were down with malaria; and dysentery, scurvy, and beri beri had taken a heavy toll. It is fair to say that in the end the defenders of Bataan succumbed as much to hunger and disease as to the Japanese army.

General Homma had expected to make quick work of Bataan. But for ten weeks—weeks of painful suspense and of anguish to the American public, the American and Filipino troops held him off, again and again seizing the offensive, and exacting a bloody price for every mile gained. John Hersey describes the opening phase of the battle for Bataan:

It was the dry season. There was a moderately warm sun by day and the nights were cool enough to make woolen blankets comfortable. The only discomfort was the dust, kicked up by man-made vehicles on the man-made roads.

By the end of the first week in January the Japanese were recovered from their surprise at having Manila given them and had regrouped their forces above Bataan. They were ready to strike.

In a month of successes they had grown very confident. Here at the gate of Bataan they thought they had the possum up a tree. On the 10th Japanese planes dropped leaflets over MacArthur's lines bearing this polite, almost affectionate message to the General:

"You are well aware that you are doomed. The end is near. The question is how long you will be able to resist. You have already cut rations by half. I appreciate the fighting spirit of yourself and your troops who have been fighting with courage. Your prestige and honor have been upheld.

"However, in order to avoid needless bloodshed and to save your 1st, 31st Divisions, and the remnants of other divisions, together with your auxiliary troops, you are advised to surrender. . . ."

General MacArthur declined the invitation. He was ready—far readier than the Japanese imagined—to take the blow.

The battle began that same day with the first of a series of attacks, each of which was intended to end MacArthur's resistance. After each one failed in the face of General MacArthur's anticipatory tactics, the Japanese tried a new type of assault.

First they tried frontal attack. For obvious reasons, this is the most expensive kind of attack, but having done a lot of pushing, the Japanese thought they could push MacArthur and his men right off Bataan into the sea. Their first frontal attack, in which they used artillery ranging up to 105-mm. mortars, plenty of machine guns, automatic rifles, tommy guns, grenades, and, along the roads, tanks, struck hard at General MacArthur's right flank. His communiqué called it "tremendous." But after a quick concentration of his own artillery, General MacArthur reported the enemy thrown back "with heavy casualties and at relatively slight cost to the defenders." The attack subsided into an artillery duel in which the defenders' artillerymen, groping out with explosive fingers for enemy guns, silenced eleven batteries.

Next the Japanese tried infiltration, the tactic which won the Malayan campaign. Specially trained men slipped through the American-Filipino lines under cover of night and vegetation, met at previously appointed rendezvous, and tried to cut off sections of the defending units. Some of the infiltrated men acted as solo snipers, gunning especially for American officers. Infiltration failed on Bataan for two reasons. First, General Mac-Arthur did not let his men consider the Japanese who slipped through a threat to their rear; second, the defenders were indefatigable and incredibly courageous in beating the bush and wiping out the infiltrated posts.

Next, in the words of General MacArthur's communiqué, the Japanese "adopted a policy of continuous assaults, without regard to casualties, hoping by great superiority in numbers to crush the defending forces." From January 14 General Homma kept on the attack for ten days in succession, with just one short lull. He threw weight now on MacArthur's right, then on the left, then in the especially tangled center.

Under the prolonged pressure General MacArthur withdrew to his second line. Tokyo broadcasts said that Japanese airplanes had spotted American and Filipino artillerymen abandoning their battery positions, and large columns joining in the general retreat. The Japanese assumed that the defenders were scurrying for Mariveles, to try to evacuate to Corregidor; but they were not yet acquainted with MacArthur.

They got to know him on January 25. That was the day of his brilliant counterstroke when, desperately pressed on his left, he lashed out at the enemy not where they were attacking, but, daringly and incredibly, on his right.

This was the way of the man. . . .

Homma fell back, exhausted and frustrated, for three days. Then he made his supreme try. His plan was to strike MacArthur from all sides with all of his tricks—with frontal attack, with infiltration, with landings from the sea. Again MacArthur scored a victory, probably the most important of the whole campaign. The defeat of the Tatori, specialists in infiltration who attacked from the sea and almost succeeded in turning the American-Filipino flank, broke Homma's spirit.

Homma now resorted to almost incessant artillery fire and dive-bombing, apparently hoping by a kind of siege fire to exhaust his enemy since he could not outwit him. The Japanese entrenched some of their positions. This phase continued for over two weeks. MacArthur's men were undoubtedly badly tired by the endless bombardment, but they showed no inclination to quit.

And so the Japanese tried still a new tactic. Gunfire had failed: they decided to try plain fire. Their bombers came over with incendiaries to try to start jungle fires and smoke the defenders out, like foxes from their holes. It was the dry season; perhaps it would work. This time the tactic failed through no merit of Douglas MacArthur, but mainly because the Japanese used inferior incendiaries. Their burning agent was not the one used by the Western nations, magnesium, but white phosphorus, which burns weakly and fast—too fast to light up Bataan's green jungle. . . .

Homma's passivity was too much for Douglas MacArthur, who thinks that it is more fun to give than to receive. He decided it was time to attack.

He spent one day in aggressive patrol action, feeling the enemy out. Then he struck, all across his line. And all across his line he went ahead—a few yards here, five miles there, everywhere a little ahead. The attack did not, could not, amount to much, but it was an attack and a thrill.

The Japanese did not even counterattack. They were busy with adventures on other islands in the archipelago, apparently fearing that America might wake up to Douglas MacArthur and try to send him some help, which they might be able to land on the many islands south of Luzon which had not yet been attacked. The Japanese put a force down on Mindanao, the biggest island on the southern end of the group. They had had Davao, Mindanao's principal city, from the first days of the attack, and had used it as a hopping-off place for drives to Dutch and Australian islands; but American-Filipino forces were still intact on the northern part of the island. The invaders also landed on Mindoro, just under the chin of Luzon and the closest spot at which American help might prize a hold; and they shelled certain other islands, notably Cebu.[6]

Washington knew that it was impossible to get help through to the men on Bataan, and as early as February 22 General MacArthur had been ordered to make his way to Australia. Not until March 11 did he make his escape to Mindanao, whence a Fortress flew him to Australia. On his arrival there he made an historic statement:

The President of the United States ordered me to break through the Japanese lines and proceed from Corregidor to Australia for the purpose, as I understand it, of organizing the American offensive against Japan. A primary purpose of this is the relief of the Philippines. I came through and I shall return.

Gradually hunger and disease wore down the intrepid defenders to the point where further resistance was suicidal.

On April 8th the Japanese launched a mass attack on the American lines. Major General Jonathan Wainwright, who had succeeded Mac-Arthur, promptly ordered a counter-attack. It was the last flicker of the flame of defiance. The end came next day, when Wainwright and some 36,000 Americans and Filipinos surrendered.

A handful of the men of Bataan managed to make their way to Corregidor, to join the 11,000 defenders of that tunneled island rock. For almost a month the Japanese blasted it from planes, ships, and land-based artillery. At last, on May 6, they swarmed across the narrow channel and fought their way into the tunnel. From Australia General MacArthur paid tribute to the gallant defenders:

Corregidor needs no comment from me. It has sounded its own story at the mouth of its guns. It has scrolled its own epitaph on enemy tablets. But through the bloody haze of its last reverberating shot I shall always seem to see a vision of grim, gaunt, ghostly men, still unafraid.

Wake Island

Between Hawaii and the Philippines, at intervals of thirteen, twelve, and fifteen hundred miles, lay the three strategically important islands of Midway, Wake, and Guam. If Japan were to control the Pacific west of Hawaii, capture of these island outposts was essential. The prospect was inviting. Congressional tenderness for Japanese sensibilities had left Guam unfortified: Marines had landed on Wake only a few weeks before the opening of the war; the defenses of Midway were weak. Arrangements to strengthen the defences and reinforce the defenders of all these islands were under way but, as the Japanese well knew, had not yet been effected. Simultaneously with the attack on Pearl Harbor—as on Hong Kong and Singapore and Manila—came the first attacks upon these islands.

At 8:45 on December 8 (the calendar is one day later west of the international date line) eighteen light and medium bombers, wings spotted with the red sun of Japan, smashed most of the few military installments on tiny Guam. The tiny garrison of some 400 Navy personnel and 155 Marines had neither anti-aircraft batteries nor coast defense guns. Their few planes were quickly put out of action. The first landing came before dawn on the 10th, and within a few hours all resistance had been overcome.

The story of Wake, the Alamo of the Pacific, is one of the heroic and already almost legendary chapters of our history. Gilbert Cant's account gains intensity by its very sobriety.

The attack on Wake began a few hours after that on Pearl Harbor, but since the atoll lies on the far side of the international date line, the time was 11:58 A.M., December 8. A scant four hours earlier, the Philippine Clipper had left Wake for Guam in the performance of its last peaceful mission in a peaceful Pacific. Upon receipt of news that Pearl Harbor had been attacked, Major James P. S. Devereux, commandant of the Marine Corps garrison and of the island, had called the Clipper back. Except for the twelve Grumman F4F3 fighter planes which had been flown in from the *Enterprise* a week earlier, the Clipper was the only aircraft at Wake. There were no scouts, no bombers. There were no warships. There were six 5-inch naval guns and twelve 3-inch anti-aircraft guns, but with only two directors to control the fire of eight of the latter. There were eighteen .50-caliber and thirty .30-caliber machine-guns, plus rifles and side-arms. Military personnel comprised 378 Marines in addition to 62 in the fighter squadron, and 74 officers and men of the Navy under Commander Winfield Scott Cunningham. The majority of Wake's inhabitants, however, were noncombatants—1,200 civilian construction workers whose task of building up the defenses of this small and remote but vital outpost had barely begun.

Four Grummans were sent up to reconnoiter. The lumbering Clipper, never intended for military duty, was to have been dispatched later on a similar mission, but the enemy intervened. Twenty-four medium bombers flew from the south, out of the sun, eluding the Grummans, and since Wake had no aircraft warning equipment they were not detected until they began to level off at 3,000 feet to make their bombing runs. There was nothing amateurish or myopic about their performance. They knew exactly what they would find, where to find it and how to hit it. Their record against the grounded Grummans was 99.44 per cent: seven planes destroyed and the eighth rendered useless, at least temporarily. There were many casualties among the ground crews: twenty-five dead and seven wounded. Pan American Airways' hotel and radio transmitter, machine shop and other installations were destroyed, along with much oil and gasoline. The Clipper miraculously escaped with no structural damage, although scores of bullets fired in one of the Japs' characteristic strafing sprees hit her. To make matters worse, one of the four Grummans which had been aloft damaged its propeller in landing on the bomb-pocked runway. The Clipper was re-loaded and sent back east to Midway. Major Devereux's men were on their own.

None of the Japanese bombers in the first attack appears to have been hit, but the enemy had been buffeted by the anti-aircraft fire, and when twenty-seven bombers returned to the attack the next day they flew at a more respectful height. The four hardy Grummans tore into them and shot down one, but they could not divert the enemy from his objective. More buildings were destroyed and the hospital was hit. The commandant reported by radio to his superiors at Pearl Harbor: "Terrific bombing. Living quarters afire."

The Japanese evidently were based on Taongi Island, 352 miles to the south, for each day they came from precisely the same direction and each day they timed their arrival so as to approach Wake from out of the sun, the glare of which would blind the defenders. On December 10 they sent twenty-seven bombers but lost two of them to the Grummans and caused little damage. Major Devereux radioed to Hawaii: "Can civilian employes be removed? Seventy-five casualties already." On December 11 the Japanese arrived in force, determined to flatten out this pinpoint of resistance. It was about time for them to make good, since their Shanghai propaganda department had claimed its capture on December 8. The force dispatched should have been more than adequate: two transports, escorted by cruisers, destroyers and gunboats. The cruisers began to shell the island. Their 6.1-inch guns enabled them to stay for a while beyond the defenders' range. So the Marines waited for them to close in to 4,700 yards before opening fire. As the Americans' first shells crashed down on the smaller warships which were in the van, the fighter squadron roared in with 100-pound bombs fitted in emergency racks. The enemy pressed forward until he came within range of the 3-inch artillery which the Marines now began to use for the first time against a surface target. One destroyer and a gunboat were sunk by shellfire. A second destroyer was sunk by the Grummans' bombs and then the fighters concentrated on a light cruiser. They hit her with eight bombs and fired 20,000 rounds of ammunition as they strafed her decks. Fires broke out in half-a-dozen places and evidently reached her fuel or magazines, because she soon broke up and sank. The Tokyo radio already was announcing the capture of Wake for the second time, as the battered invasion force turned tail. During this operation the Marines had enjoyed the luxury of having five fighter planes in the air, since the one severely damaged on December 8 had been made serviceable by the extraordinary skill and perseverance—not to mention ingenuity—of the ground crew, working under the most adverse conditions. But this unexpected reinforcement was to be short-lived. The enemy bombers were back on schedule at noon, and although two were shot down, they so damaged one of the Grummans that it crashed in landing on the beach. And then there were four again.

For the sake of the morale at home, the Navy Department announced an exchange of messages in which the commandant at Wake was asked whether he needed anything, to which he replied: "Send us more Japs. . . ." They were back later this day, the 12th, with a flying boat which was shot down, twenty-seven bombers which inflicted further damage, and a submarine which was sunk by Second Lieutenant David D. Kliewer, dropping 100-pound bombs from his Grumman. December 13 was quiet, but to maintain their average the Japs sent three seaplanes and forty-one medium bombers on the 14th. They lost two—4½ per cent. The Marines lost one Grumman—25 per cent. On the 15th, the Japanese again tried a dawn patrol with flying boats and followed it with the regulation noon attack by twenty-seven bombers. Again they lost two—6.9 per cent—and again the Marines lost one—33⅓ per cent. As the defending forces diminished, the enemy stepped up the fury of his attack. Toward evening of the 16th forty-one bombers and several four-engined seaplanes criss-crossed the island, systematically bombing everything which bore the faintest resemblance to a military objective. They got a dynamite store, gutted the storehouse with spare parts for aircraft, and blasted the machine shop and blacksmith shop. They lost a seaplane, but came back next day to see what they had missed. Thirty-two bombers scored hits on one of the encampments and destroyed the diesel oil supply, the mess hall and the pumps for extracting fresh water. Their cost was one bomber.

On December 18 the Japanese sent only a reconnaissance plane, and on the 19th a U. S. Navy patrol plane arrived. It brought but little in the way of supplies, no reinforcements, and no good news—rather, a sentence of death. It had come to evacuate Major Walter L. J. Bayler, who had been responsible for the airfield and communication installations on Wake, and whose services were required elsewhere. Its departure under cover of bad weather on the 20th gave Commander Cunningham an opportunity to send headquarters a report on the activities of the Marine fighters and gunners:

> Our escape from more serious damage may be attributed to the effectiveness of anti-aircraft fire and the heroic action of fighter patrols, which have never failed to push home attacks against heavy fire. The performance of these pilots is deserving of all praise. They have attacked air and surface targets with equal abandon. The planes are full of bullet holes. The anti-aircraft battery is fighting with about 50 percent of the necessary fire control equipment. Four guns are useless against aircraft. One four-gun unit is actually being controlled by data received from another unit several miles distant. Only one and a quarter units of AA [3-inch ammunition] remain. . . .

On December 21 Wake underwent another heavy bombing which reduced its anti-aircraft defenses to a single battery of four 3-inch guns.

Reports of the last twenty-four hours are but fragmentary. They disclose, however, that the Japanese followed the technique which had since given the United Nations many golden opportunities, not all of which have been utilized. Having taken a drubbing on the 11th, they came back with a force which was literally overwhelming. Since they had not been able to knock out the Marines' 5-inch guns by level bombing, they brought up carriers whose dive-bombers could operate, virtually unhampered by fighters or anti-aircraft fire, against the coastal gun emplacements. Apparently they sought to soften up the already pulverized island with an intensive aerial assault during the night of December 21–22, for a report to headquarters said: "Attacked middle of night by land planes with carrier bombers and fighters. Our two remaining fighters aloft. Several enemy accounted for."

Escort vessels in the approaching Japanese fleet must have attacked an imaginary American submarine, for Major Devereux radioed to Pearl Harbor during the evening of the 22nd: "Apparent naval action in progress off shore." But there was no action, for, as the acting Commander-in-Chief of the Pacific Fleet was obliged to reply: "There are no friendly ships in waters near Wake." The scene during the dark hours of the morning of the 23rd can only be reconstructed from our knowledge of the many and determined Japanese landing operations in other theaters. The garrison was exhausted beyond all ordinary endurance. It was outnumbered. It had virtually no serviceable artillery and little or no ammunition. It had few machine-guns at best—not more than one for every quarter-mile of beach—and probably even these were by now reduced in number. Before

Major Devereux and Commander Cunningham surrendered, preferring to share life in a Japanese prison camp with their men rather than condemn them to useless slaughter, their radio sent its last, its most gallant and its most forlorn message, a masterpiece of understatement: "Urgent! Enemy on island. The issue is in doubt."[7]

Midway, too, was attacked on that fateful day, but there the shore batteries were so effective that the task force assigned to the job turned and ran. They lived to fight another day.

Singapore

Simultaneously with the attack on the American islands in the Pacific had come a carefully planned and co-ordinated assault on British outposts in the Orient.

Hong Kong was the first to fall. This great naval base formed, with Singapore and Manila, a triangle of Anglo-American power in the Orient. As early as 1940, however, Japanese occupation of nearby Canton had made it all but indefensible. The Japanese attack came off, as scheduled, on December 8, and for two weeks the great city was subjected to continuous bombardment from land and from air. The British garrison might have stood up to this, but far more serious was the cutting of the water supply. Confronted with responsibility for misery or death of hundreds of thousands of civilian inhabitants, the British commander, Sir Mark Young, surrendered.

Next came Penang, then Singapore.

Already poised in Thailand and Indo-China, a Japanese army of 200,000 specially trained jungle fighters swarmed down into the Malay peninsula towards the Gibraltar of the Pacific. British and Malay troops raced to meet them, but were outwitted and demoralized by the infiltration tactics of the enemy and by their skillfully conducted amphibious operations on both sides of the peninsula. Within two months the Japanese had covered 580 miles of rice fields, swamps, and rubber forests, and were at the gates of Singapore. That great island fortress was all but impregnable by sea, but dependent as it was on the mainland for water, highly vulnerable by land. The British rushed in reinforcements—Australians, Indians, regiments newly arrived from England—just in time to share the debacle.

For a month Singapore was raided every day. Then, from nearby Johore, the Japs pushed across to Singapore and captured the reservoirs. There was nothing left but surrender.

It was, said Winston Churchill, the "greatest disaster to British arms which history records." But he spoke not with despair, but with defiance:

Tonight I speak to you at home; I speak to you in Australia and New Zealand, for whose safety we will strain every nerve; to our loyal friends in India and Burma; to our gallant Allies, the Dutch and Chinese; and to our kith and kin in the United States. I speak to you all under the shadow of a heavy and far-reaching military defeat. It is a British and Imperial defeat. Singapore has fallen. All the Malay Peninsula has been overrun. Other dangers gather about us out there, and none of the dangers which we have hitherto successfully withstood at home and in the East are in any way diminished. This, therefore, is one of those moments when the British race and nation can show their quality and their genius. This is one of those moments when it can draw from the heart of misfortune the vital impulses of victory. Here is the moment to display that calm and poise combined with grim determination which not so long ago brought us out of the very jaws of death. Here is another occasion to show—as so often in our long story—that we can meet reverses with dignity and with renewed accessions of strength. We must remember that we are no longer alone. We are in the midst of a great company. Three-quarters of the human race are now moving with us. The whole future of mankind may depend upon our action and upon our conduct. So far we have not failed. We shall not fail now. Let us move forward steadfastly together into the storm and through the storm.[8]

Java Seas

So far Japan had been checked only at Hawaii, and that check she regarded as temporary. Her ambitions embraced far more than merely the Philippines and the eastern Asiatic mainland. They looked westward to the conquest of China, Burma, and eventually, India; eastward to the conquest or control of the vast archipelago which stretched four thousand miles from Malaya to the Solomons and included Sumatra, Java, Borneo, the Celebes, New Guinea, New Britain, and thousands of smaller islands. From these island outposts she would dominate Australia, whose seven million inhabitants could not resist for long the mounting Japanese might. Within her grasp lay an empire stretching from the Arctic to the Antarctic, from Hawaii to India—an empire with a population of a billion slave workers, infinite raw materials, and fabulous wealth. Never before in history had so splendid a prospect unfolded before the eyes of conquerors.

With a speed that bore eloquent testimony to the thoroughness of their planning, the Japanese swept down into this great archipelago from Malaya, from Mindanao in the Philippines, from the Marianas, Marshalls, and Carolines. The delays at Bataan and Singapore were but eddies in the southward stream.

As early as December the Japanese were swarming into the archipelago, one force landing at Sarawak on the northern coast of Borneo, another coming down from Mindanao to the great naval base of Amboina in the Banda Sea, only 650 miles from Port Darwin, Australia; still another swinging far eastward to New Guinea. Another month and they had landed in Sumatra and the Celebes, New Ireland, New Britain, and Bougainville in the Solomons. Timor, Lae, and Salamaua had been abandoned after heavy air raids.

To this combined land and sea blitz, speedier and on a larger scale than anything Hitler had imagined, the Allies could put up but feeble resistance. Their best and best-equipped ground forces had been lost at Bataan,

Hong Kong, and Singapore; their air forces were feeble, and a major tragedy occurred when bombers sank the U. S. tender *Langley* carrying fighter planes for Java. But the Allied navies, though they had lost all their best ships, exacted a heavy toll from the invader. The first engagement came in the narrow waters of the Strait of Macassar. Here, January 23–25, four American destroyers caught a Japanese convoy and dashed in and out among the bewildered ships, sinking them right and left with torpedoes and gunfire.

Macassar Strait was a brilliant victory, but it could not stem the Japanese tide, beating now against Java. Early in February Admiral Doorman took a small task force through the narrow Strait between Java and Madoera, but it was intercepted by Japanese bombers and badly mauled. Far more disastrous was the battle of the Java Seas, the last effort of the Allies to save Java. Admiral Helfrich of the Dutch navy was in command of the Allied force of five cruisers and nine destroyers when, on February 27, it ran into two enemy flotillas, far superior both in numbers and fire power to the Allied fleet. Fletcher Pratt tells the story of the holocaust that followed:

The Dutch Admiral turned northwest and worked up to twenty-five knots, forming his line of battle. The British destroyers *Jupiter* and *Electra* led it, followed at a mile's distance by the flagship *De Ruyter*; then came *Exeter, Houston, Perth,* and *Java.* . . . Off to the port of the battle line ran the Dutch destroyers *Witte de With,* and *Kortenaer,* with the British *Encounter;* astern of it came the American destroyers *Edwards, Ford, Alden,* and *Paul Jones,* with Binford of Bali in command of the division.

At four o'clock Jap spotting planes began to appear in the sky and *De Ruyter* announced by short-wave to the fleet: "Many ships two points on starboard bow." The Japs became visible as eight cruisers in a long line of battle, headed by two big ones, which the men in our fleet took for battleships till their shells began to come and were found to be only 8-inch.

They opened the ball at 4:30 from 25,000 yards, running parallel at a range where only 8-inch guns would bear. Of these the Japs had ten apiece, but our ships only six. Still things were not too bad at this stage; both *Houston* and *Exeter* were on with their early salvos, and gouts of flame leaped up from the Japanese heavies. They were firing on Doorman's ship without an answer; he ordered a ninety-degree turn-in, closing the range to under 20,000, and as our ships straightened on the new course the action took up all along the line. On *Kortenaer* they were counting splashes, up to fifteen in a salvo, which meant that some enemy light cruisers belonged to the *Mogami* class with that many guns. Our ships were outweighted two to one, and being hit too.

But we had the better armor and gunners at least as good. The enemy heavies were burning furiously, beginning to stagger out of line; one of them fired a salvo with only four shells in it, and a big black puff of smoke went up from one of their light cruisers where *De Ruyter* hit her as the crews of the destroyers cheered. It was an even fight or better than even till five o'clock, when the Jap Admiral, whose line had pulled a little ahead while Doorman was turning, suddenly shot eight big destroyers from the tail of his formation in a torpedo attack on the Allied ships. At the same time, down from somewhere ahead of their formation, came another mass of Japanese ships, destroyers in the lead.

Jupiter and *Electra*, at the head of our line, were the only ships available to repel it. They rushed into the smoke screens of the charge, and in the dramatic phrase of the British communiqué *Electra* "was not seen again." Later that night an American submarine unexpectedly surfaced and picked up thirty-five survivors.

Now things went from bad to worse; *Perth* and *Java* had to shift targets to take care of the destroyer rush, and at 5:15 one of the Jap heavies, firing her last gun as she staggered from the line, had the luck to hit *Exeter* squarely in the fire room, bursting the main steam line. The British cruiser swung sharply out to port away from the enemy torpedo attack. Amid the smoke and splashes *Perth* behind turned with her, ninety degrees, to lay smoke. And Doorman and *De Ruyter* could not but conform, breaking up the battle line. *Witte de With*, *Kortenaer*, and *Encounter* rushed in to screen the damaged *Exeter*. Binford in the American destroyer division saw a torpedo take *Kortenaer* squarely amidships and the ship break in half under a column of smoke.

Her survivors floated all night on Carley rafts, up to their chests in water and vomiting: "Fuel oil simply is not fit for consumption in any form, not even diluted with sea water," said one of them afterward. The Japanese destroyers came charging past, made a turn, and fired salvos all together; the survivors saw one of them, then another, take torpedo hits amidships and break up as their own ship had done.

. . . The men in the water were there all night and saved toward morning when a flare dropped by *Houston* enabled *Encounter* to pick them up. Two days later Binford thought he was seeing a ghost when a man in shorts and sneakers walked into his room in Surabaya and he recognized the Captain of the *Kortenaer*. . . .

The four American destroyers covered the retreat. The Allied ships were now much scattered, and *Exeter* under the escort of *Witte de With* making for Surabaya, and Japanese seaplanes appearing from time to time to be fired at. Doorman came sweeping around to an easterly course to assemble his fleet; did assemble it, and about 5:30 had another contact with a small enemy formation at long range. There was a Jap light cruiser in it, afire from the previous engagement. *Exeter* punched her again, she turned away, and a strong stream of enemy destroyers came charging in to cover.

It would be about this time that our destroyers let go their torpedoes at extreme long range, turning south behind Doorman later. They never saw what happened, but one of *Kortenaer*'s survivors did, floating on a life-raft. One, then another of the Jap destroyers blew up. "There was just a big cloud of dense, black smoke, and then nothing more." But our people did not know about this; damaged *Exeter* was on the way to Surabaya, and Binford's division had to go there, too, so nearly out of fuel they could not possibly make the rendezvous point at Tanjong Priok.

Doorman carried on, first easterly, then northeast, finally south, seeking for the enemy transports, hoping to find them uncovered. In the falling light there were a number of partial contacts, a number of shadows and flashes on the horizon, but always those of numerous ships, heavy ships, too many to engage, and not the transports he wanted. At 9:00 he turned northwest under a full tropical moon to have another try at catching Jap transports near Bawean Island, and at 11:15, clear under the moon, he sighted another line of Jap cruisers. "Target to port, four points," he signaled, and an engagement began, in which *Houston* at once began to hit.

But he was without destroyer cover now, all gone in for fuel and *Jupiter* sunk on the way in by a submarine's torpedo. As the Allied line executed a turn *Java* at its stern suddenly blew up; then *De Ruyter* at its head, with Doorman aboard, probably torpedoed by submarines, possibly mined, we do not know. The other two cruisers, all that was left of the fleet, turned away and were in Tanjong Priok by morning. . . .

Useless. Before dawn ABDAFLOAT took its decision—to get everything out of the sea that could be got out and to organize a new striking force with Tjilitjap as a base. Orders went out that night. *Houston*, *Perth*, and *Evertsen* were to run through Sunda Strait. The shortest route for the others from Surabaya would be by way of Bali Strait, and the U. S. destroyer division went that way; but the channel east from Surabaya past Madura is narrow, shallow, and excessively rocky—it would not do for damaged *Exeter*. Since she had to go north in any case, she was ordered through Sunda Strait with *Pope* and *Encounter* as escort.

Exeter and her group left at dawn, after emergency repairs to the cruiser. Before noon *Pope* reported herself shadowed by planes, then Bandoeng took in a radio message from *Encounter*, much garbled, reporting contact with the enemy, and since then there has been silence unbroken from around those three ships.

At dusk on the same day, February 28th, *Houston* and her group tried running the Strait from Priok, while Helfrich with silver-tongued Glassford and British Palliser on their mountain top at Bandoeng spread maps on the table and spent the night trying to see some way out, something that could still be done. Around midnight a report came in from a U. S. Army bomber: a hundred and fifty miles out in the Indian Ocean southwest of Tjilitjap she had sighted strong enemy forces, probably battleships with at least one carrier and transports, headed toward Java. How many planes had Patwing 10 left? Less than half a squadron, said the staff member in charge of that information.

. . . And no carriers and no fighters. The Japs were closing in on Java from every side at once; Tjilitjap would hardly do as anything but a temporary stopping place for the units from the Java Sea. They were not yet sure about *Exeter*, but as they discussed the new orientation this threw on affairs another message came in, a night message from *Perth*, saying she was engaging the enemy, and then one from *Evertsen* with news of a furious naval battle in Sunda Strait. There was another, briefer brush out in Bali Strait, where clever, lucky Binford's division got through after a ten-minute running fight; and another, not lucky, for the little old gunboat *Asheville* the next morning, in which she was sunk.

But these were not known either; there was only the melancholy conference, which lasted all night and broke up with day and the news that *Evertsen* had been beached in Sunda Strait in sinking condition. Of *Houston* and *Perth* there was no sign then or ever after. Perhaps some of their crews got away to the hills in Sumatra or Java and perhaps they are there yet; but for practical purposes ABDAFLOAT's fleet was dissolved, as ABDAFLOAT itself dissolved on that gloomy March morning. Admiral Glassford and his chief of staff, Rear Admiral William R. Purnell, went down to Tjilitjap, and the last, repaired, rickety plane of Patwing 10 took them off to Australia for the beginning of another campaign.[9]

After that there was nothing to stop the Japanese conquest of Java. From Sumatra and Borneo the Japanese poured one hundred thousand troops into the all but defenseless island. The end came on March 9, with the surrender of all the Netherlands East Indies and 98,000 prisoners.

Australia was next.

Defending Australia

As early as February 19 the Japanese had bombed the daylights out of Port Darwin, Australia's only major military and naval base on the north. All through March and April the isolation of Australia went on, as the Japanese occupied New Guinea, New Ireland, New Britain, the Solomons, the Admiralties, the Bismarcks, and the Gilberts far to the east. By herself, Australia would be in no position to repulse a determined Japanese assault. Fortunately prompt steps had been taken to strengthen the supply lines from the United States and heavy naval and military reinforcements were already on the way.

MacArthur arrived in Australia on March 17 and took up at once the defense of Australia. Where should the stand be made? It would be possible, even feasible, to retire to the south and east and trust to the desert, or to long lines of communication, to frustrate invasion. But MacArthur's was not the defense psychology. He preferred to take the offensive, and possession of Port Moresby on New Guinea gave the opportunity.

His forces were a corporal's guard compared to the Japanese arrayed against him. But by late July heroic engineers had built air fields and bomber strips at sweltering Moresby. Then they moved 150 miles down the coast to Milne Bay at the extreme southwestern tip of New Guinea. In this "green hell" a base was built, intended as a jumping-off place for a drive on the Japanese concentrations at Buna, Sanananda, and Gona on the island's northeast coast. General MacArthur did not believe it feasible to attack over the towering, jungle-clothed Owen Stanley mountains which divide New Guinea as the breastbone divides a chicken; only one muddy, narrow trail leading through the village of Kokoda crossed this forbidding range.

The Japanese, however, thought otherwise. On July 29 they advanced up the Kokoda trail and, on reaching the reverse slope, began to drive MacArthur's Australian outposts before them. The fighting was prolonged and bitter. On August 25 Australians and Americans—including anti-aircraft and engineer units—repulsed an attempted Japanese landing at Milne Bay. But it was not until September 16 that starvation, bombing and stiff resistance on the ground halted the advance against Port Moresby and

the Australians took the long trail back to Kokoda and the other slope of
the Owen Stanleys.

Vice-Admiral Halsey—the "Bull" Halsey who was later to be the scourge
of the Japanese—had already seized the offensive. On January 31 he sent
his carriers and cruisers on a raid into the Gilbert and Marshall Islands,
sinking 17 ships and destroying forty or fifty planes. Three weeks later the
carrier *Enterprise* led a force that bombarded Wake and Marcus Islands,
and in March came heavy raids on enemy bases at Salamaua and Lae in
New Guinea. On May 4 planes from the carrier *Yorktown* smashed thirteen
vessels in Tulagi harbor.

As our naval strength grew, we were prepared to call a halt to Japanese
expansion eastward or southward. Things were shaping up for a major
battle. It came May 7–8 in the Coral Sea, which washes the shores of New
Guinea, the Solomons, and New Caledonia. On that day carrier planes
from an American task force under Vice-Admiral Frank J. Fletcher sighted
a large Japanese force steaming towards the Louisiades. Planes from the
Lexington and *Yorktown* at once sped to the attack. The ensuing Battle of the
Coral Seas was, in the words of Admiral King, "the first major engagement
in naval history in which surface ships did not exchange a single shot." In
the ensuing action American planes sank the carrier *Ryukyu*, four cruisers,
and two destroyers; and heavily damaged another carrier, three cruisers,
and three destroyers. Our own losses, too, were severe. Most serious was
the loss of the giant carrier *Lexington*.

The Battle of the Coral Seas was not a clear-cut victory. But with it Jap
expansion was checked. Within a month the United States navy was to win
a victory which would mark ebb tide for Japanese power everywhere in the
Pacific.

Midway

Early on June 3rd a PBY patrol plane sighted a large flotilla of enemy ships
some 700 miles west of Midway. It was part of a vast armada of fifty-three
warships and over twenty transport and supply ships heading for Hawaii
and ready to deal a knock-out blow to the American navy. But this time
neither naval nor ground forces were caught napping. Our intelligence
had broken the Japanese code and as reports of a concentration of enemy
forces came in to headquarters prompt counter-measures had been taken.
Rear Admiral Spruance concentrated all available warships in the waters
around Hawaii, the *Yorktown* was hurriedly summoned from the Coral
Seas, every available Flying Fortress was rushed over from as far east as
Ireland, and the defenses of Midway reinforced. Even the Japanese attack
on Dutch Harbor on June 3 was not allowed to distract the navy from its
main job.

The Japanese force had divided into three squadrons: a striking force
with 4 carriers, 4 cruisers and 12 destroyers; a support force with 2 battle
cruisers, 4 light cruisers and 10 destroyers, and a landing force of transports and troopships supported by at least 4 cruisers and 12 destroyers.
This great armada definitely outnumbered anything Admiral Spruance
could send against it. But the Americans had the advantage of air bases in

Midway and Hawaii, and, as in the Coral Seas, this great battle was to be fought entirely by planes and submarines.

Our first attack came on the afternoon of June 3 when Flying Fortresses from Midway attacked the squadron of landing ships. The enemy reacted sharply with a heavy bombing of Midway the following day—an attack which did severe damage to shore installations but failed to knock out the island air fields. Then Marine Corps dive bombers hit back at the Japanese force; it was in this attack that Major Lofton R. Henderson guided his blazing plane into the superstructure of the carrier *Soryu*.

By this time our fleet had come within striking range of the Japanese squadrons, and swarms of planes, including the famous Torpedo 8 from the *Hornet*, set out after their prey. The opening phase of this attack is described by Gilbert Cant:

Forty-one torpedo planes were among the many groups sent out from the American carriers: fifteen from Torpedo Squadron Eight, attached to the *Hornet*; fourteen from Torpedo Squadron Six (*Enterprise*) and twelve from Torpedo Squadron Five (*Yorktown*). From the *Enterprise* there were, in addition to the fourteen torpedo planes, thirty-six dive-bombers (eighteen each from Bombing Six and Scouting Six, the latter armed with a 500-pound bomb and two 100-pounders), ten fighters, and an extra scout plane for the group commander, Lieutenant-Commander Clarence McCluskey. Presumably similar groups were flown from the other carriers.

Torpedo Eight, flying obsolete Douglas Devastators—not the new Grumman Avengers used by its reserve—was led by Lieutenant-Commander John C. Waldron. It became separated from the other formations in the long search for the Japanese ships. A group of bombers and fighters which failed to find the enemy at the assigned position and followed an extension of his reported course toward Midway failed completely to make contact, and finally had to be ordered to land on the island as they were running out of gasoline. Still, some were forced down at sea, and not all of these were picked up. But Waldron reasoned that if the Jap ships were not where they were supposed to be, it was probably because they had found the welcome too warm for their comfort and had decided to retire some distance, if not entirely. He therefore backtracked along their previously known course. McCluskey arrived at the same conclusion, but not until after he had overshot the enemy's reported position by seventy-five miles or more. Then he too set out to intercept them to the northwest. The effect of these identical decisions made at different times was to bring Waldron's squadron within sight of the enemy while the torpedo planes lacked fighter protection, and there were no dive-bombers to disperse the Japanese anti-aircraft fire.

Waldron found the main enemy force with few fighter planes in the air, but his squadron had been out a long time and was running short of gas. It had accomplished part of its mission merely by locating the retiring Japanese and reporting their position. Waldron radioed his information and added: "Request permission to withdraw from action to refuel." The admiral to whom the request was passed had an awful decision to make. To permit these planes to withdraw might make all the difference between sinking or crippling three carriers (Waldron had not sighted the fourth) and giving them a chance once more to slip out of sight under a squall. Three carriers could determine the balance of power in this 1942 sea war, in which the carrier was a capital ship at least equal in importance to the battleship, and actually of greater importance judged by performance in these first six months. Hypothetical scores of ships and hypothetical thousands of lives were on one side of the scale; on the other side were fifteen planes and the lives of their three-man crews. The admiral ordered: "Attack at once."[10]

It was in this attack that Ensign George Gay was shot down and from his rubber raft saw the subsequent attack:

Gay had not long to wait for the next act. Indeed, it may have begun before he scrambled out of his sinking plane, for Lieutenant Dickinson, who was in Lieutenant-Commander McCluskey's group, saw what appears to have been the end of the action against Torpedo Eight. Dickinson had a personal interest in what preceded the attack by his squadron, for the annihilation of Torpedo Eight released Japanese fighter planes (all but those which had been shot down by Waldron's men) for operations against Bombing Six and Scouting Six. But these squadrons had the advantage of fighter plane cover, and their story was far different from that of the torpedo planes.

They approached from the same direction, so that the *Kaga* and *Akagi* were in the foreground. McCluskey led the eighteen planes of Scouting Six to attack the *Kaga*, and ordered Lieutenant Richard H. Best to take Bombing Six against the *Akagi*. At this time the only other carrier visible was the one identified as the *Soryu* (despite the unsullied sweep of her flight deck), and by good fortune Bombing Squadron Three reached the scene in time to bring her under simultaneous attack. Just before Scouting Six began its attack, Dickinson saw a fourth carrier sliding out from the cover of a squall off to the southwest—the *Hiryu*.

The *Kaga* was making 30 knots, indicating that she had not been hit by Torpedo Eight, and was going straight upwind. She made no attempt to change course, for she was still trying to fly off fighters to increase her aerial protection. McCluskey led a section of three planes whose bombs bracketed the carrier but made no direct hits. Lieutenant-Commander Earl Gallaher was the next man to drop, and scored the first hit, on the flight deck aft, among planes still waiting to be flown off. Their gasoline was ignited and kept a fire burning long after the original explosion. Ensign Reid W. Stone soon marked up another hit, along the center line of the flight deck. His bomb, fitted with a delayed-action fuse, crashed through to the hangar deck before exploding, and tore up a section of the flight deck. Dickinson dropped his 500-pounder in the middle of the flight deck alongside the island, and his two smaller bombs among airplanes parked forward. There were other hits on the *Kaga* which have not been reported in detail, and one member of the squadron used his small bombs to harry a destroyer in the screen which was exhibiting too great proficiency in anti-aircraft fire. The destroyer lost way and appeared to be on fire in her engine rooms.

Best's Bombing Six set fire to the *Akagi* and Bombing Three achieved the same result with the *Soryu*; two battleships were hit, and one was seen to be blazing fiercely. The *Kaga* is described as having been on fire from end to end, and as the attack ended the flames evidently reached a magazine or a gasoline store, for there was an explosion amidships which sent a column of fire and smoke more than 1,000 feet into the air.

During most of this triple attack, torpedo planes from Squadrons Five and Six were in the vicinity, and at one stage they may have been launching their projectiles simultaneously with the dive-bombers. The Navy communique says that our "torpedo planes engaged the attention of the enemy fighters and anti-aircraft batteries to such a degree that our dive-bombers were able to drop bomb after bomb on the enemy ships without serious interference."[11]

The Japanese were battered, but still capable of fight. Planes from the carrier *Hiryu* struck back. Fletcher Pratt tells what happened:

There was life in those Japanese yet; there was one punch left in the *Hiryu*. Our carriers had turned and were steaming southwestward, keeping their distance from those fast Japanese battleships, since they had nothing stronger than fighters left aboard and nothing better than cruisers to cover them. (The *Scharnhorst* had sunk the *Glorious* in a few minutes off Norway under such conditions.) The three carrier groups were spread very wide, hull down from one another which kept the Japs from hitting all of them at once as theirs had been hit, but also increased the enemy's chances of finding and hitting at least one—a variation in method that will doubtless long exercise tacticians. Put it that this was a special case; there was no longer any chance of concealment in that clear, still day with our planes battering the Japanese ships, and Spruance's spread formation allowed the fighter planes from all to go to the aid of the first carrier attacked.

It was the *Yorktown*, the northernmost ship, that was struck just after 1 o'clock by 36 dive bombers from the *Hiryu*, which may have followed some of our planes home from their foray. . . . "Stand by to repel air attack," said her loudspeakers, and the fighter patrols of the other carrier joined the *Yorktown*'s. "It was damned spectacular," said an officer of one carrier. "On the horizon there would be a flash of flame and a mass of thick black smoke plunging downward to the sea. There would be another flash and another downward pencil; finally it looked like the sky over there was covered by a curtain of smoke streamers."

Only seven Jap planes came through that hornet's nest of American fighters, but they came in a mood of Oriental desperation, and despite losing three more at the ship, they planted bombs. One hit the *Yorktown* just abaft the island, smashed up the guns there, and started a fire; another hit in the forward elevator well and started more fire from the tanks of the planes on the hangar deck; and still another bomb went through the side of the funnel, blowing out the fires in the ship's engine room. The *Yorktown* stopped; watching her from the *Hornet*'s deck they could see a tall column of smoke shoot straight up. But on the damaged carrier the fires were got in hand and Engineer Officer John F. Delaney said he could work her up to fifteen knots after repairs. . . .

All the planes in the fleet still fit for work were refueled and remunitioned, while the pilots grabbed sandwiches and coffee, and then took off again to get that last Jap carrier, the *Hiryu*, and break up her flight deck. She and her escort, which now seems to have included most of the support force (since it had two battleships and a heavy cruiser besides destroyers), had steamed right away from the rest of the dolorous Japanese armada, northeastward. A good trick if it worked, but we had practical command of the air now, and our scouts found her. Whoever it was that first saw her, a *Yorktown* man, Lieutenant Sam Adams, scuttling along the edge of the clouds with his radio key open, described the course, speed, and composition of the *Hiryu* and her escorting group of ships so accurately that the tactical officers back on our carriers could assign precise targets to every man. Thus it happened that this was the most carefully worked-out attack of them all.

It must have been 2:30 in the afternoon, or later, before our attacking group of planes got away; and since the two fleets were now farther apart and steaming away from each other, it must have been after 4:00 before they reached the *Hiryu* group. Now the day-long losing battle that the Japanese airmen had fought began to have its effect. Their fighter opposition was weak. Their antiaircraft fired furiously enough, but the men who fired must have reached the point of black despair over the endless procession of star-marked planes that came out of the clouds to pound their dying ships. Hardly a blow from all that group of American planes missed its target; the *Hiryu* was hit and hit again with bombs timed to pierce her deck till she burned from end to end. Both battleships were hit, the cruiser and the destroyer were hit, while our loss was next to nothing.[12]

The *Hornet* and the *Enterprise* raced westward after the battered Japanese forces which split up to make detection more difficult. But neither this strategy nor the dirty weather which set in saved them from further punishment. The last phases of the great battle and the final score are given in the formal but no less stirring words of the official navy communique:

WASHINGTON, July 14.—A local bad weather condition to the northwest of Midway hampered the search operations of our carrier planes, which were seeking the enemy in that area. Throughout the night of June 5–6 our aircraft carriers steamed to the westward in pursuit of the enemy.

Early in the morning of June 6 a search by carrier aircraft discovered two groups of enemy ships, each containing cruisers and destroyers. Between 9:30 and 10 A.M. our carrier planes attacked one group which contained the heavy cruisers *Mikuma* and *Mogami* and three destroyers. At least two bomb hits were scored on each cruiser. One of the destroyers was sunk. The attacks were carried on until 5:30 p.m. The *Mikuma* was sunk shortly after noon. The *Mogami* was gutted and subsequently sunk. Another enemy cruiser and a destroyer also were hit during these series of attacks.

It was during this afternoon (June 6) that the United States destroyer *Hammann* was torpedoed and sunk by an enemy submarine. Most of her crew were rescued. . . .

The following is a recapitulation of the damage inflicted upon the enemy during the battle of Midway:

Four Japanese aircraft carriers, the *Kaga*, *Akagi*, *Soryu* and *Hiryu*, were sunk.

Three battleships were damaged by bomb and torpedo hits, one severely.

Two heavy cruisers, the *Mogami* and the *Mikuma*, were sunk. Three others were damaged, one or two severely.

One light cruiser was damaged.

Three destroyers were sunk and several others were damaged by bombs.

At least three transports or auxiliary ships were damaged, and one or more sunk.

An estimated 275 Japanese aircraft were destroyed or lost at sea through a lack of flight decks on which to land.

Approximately 4,800 Japanese were killed or drowned.

Our total personnel losses were 92 officers and 215 enlisted men. . . .

The battle of Midway was a complex and widespread action involving a number of engagements lasting more than three days and nights. Even our active participants in the numerous attacks and counter-attacks are unable to give confidently an accurate account of the damage inflicted by any one group in the many individual and unified attacks of our Army, Navy and Marine Corps personnel.

Retreat in Burma

If the outlook in the south Pacific was brighter, it was black elsewhere in the East. Even while the Japanese were besieging Singapore other powerful armies struck for Burma.

The prospect for the speedy conquest of Burma was favorable. Main British forces had been concentrated at Singapore. The British navy, already stretched to the breaking point by duties in the Atlantic and the Mediterranean, had its hands full guarding the supply route to India. Many of the native Burmese were loyal to Britain, but discontent with British rule was widespread and fifth column activities gave effective aid to the yellow invaders.

From Lashio in northeastern Burma runs the Burma Road, connecting at one end with Mandalay and Rangoon, at the other with Chungking. After the Japanese occupied all the main Chinese ports, in 1937–38, this road was China's life line to the outside world. Burma, too, was the key to India, seething with discontent. Nor was it without value in itself: its oil fields alone produced 8 to 10 million barrels annually, and its tin was badly needed for military purposes.

The invaders, too, were prepared. By December, 1941, Japan had massed some 200,000 troops, especially trained in jungle warfare, in Thailand, and Indo-China and had powerful air forces operating from airfields conceded them by the Vichy government in 1940 and hastily constructed in Thailand.

The first invasion came in December and Rangoon was heavily bombed on the 23rd of that month. The major attack, however, was launched late in January by Siamese puppet troops from Thailand. The British evacuated Moulmein and fell back on Rangoon, Burma's largest port. Ceaselessly attacked by air, they called upon the Flying Tigers to defend them. And the Flying Tigers came.

They came with a brilliant record already behind them. They had been hired by Generalissimo Chiang Kai-shek in the summer of 1941 to defend the Burma Road. Their record, from the time they went into action in December 1941 until they were absorbed into the American army air force in July 1942 is summarized by Robert Hotz:

The Flying Tigers . . . had officially destroyed 297 Japanese aircraft of all types and actually accounted for twice that number. They had killed more than 1,500 Japanese airmen and soldiers and destroyed thousands of dollars' worth of Japanese supplies.

Of the 300-odd men and 2 women who had left the United States a year ago, 22 were dead and 4 were prisoners. Four had been killed in aerial combat; 5 on strafing raids, and 3 by enemy bombers. Ten pilots had been killed in crashes.

It cost the Chinese Government approximately $3,000,000 to recruit and operate the American Volunteer Group for one year plus the $8,000,000 paid for the planes. With this money it purchased a series of strategic and timely victories. The Flying Tigers swept Japanese bombers from the northern end of the Burma Road and then almost alone kept the Japanese out of Rangoon for two and a half months while thousands of tons of vital war supplies were rushed up the road to China. They smashed the Japanese offensive into southern China in the Salween gorge. They cleared Japanese planes from the skies of bomb-battered Hunan and Kwangsi provinces and gave Chungking its first bomb-free summer in 4 years.

Their feats were acclaimed by the representatives of 3 governments. British, Chinese, and American medals were awarded their outstanding pilots. Almost all of the Flying Tigers were decorated with the Cloud Banner medal of China. American and British Distinguished Flying Crosses were won by Bob Neale, Bob Sandell, Jack Newkirk, Bob Little, Ed Rector, Frank Schiel, Charlie Bond, and Tex Hill.

From the British, Chennault received the rank of Commander of the Order of the British Empire. From the United States came the Distinguished Service Medal. This was the outfit that the experts predicted "wouldn't last three weeks in combat."[13]

Although in the battle for Rangoon Chennault's men shot down 46 Japanese planes at a cost of 5 planes and 2 pilots, there was no stopping the enemy onslaught. Late in February, in heavy hand to hand fighting, they crossed the Salween River and drove British Indian troops back to the Sittang. Rangoon was fired and evacuated in March, severing all supply routes for Allied troops in the interior. Chinese forces under Lieutenant-General Joseph Stilwell came down from the north to help hold the Sittang line, but the Japanese brought another army in from Thailand, cut the Burma Road north of Lashio, and forced Stilwell to retreat. That epic retreat is described by Jack Belden:

Our group consisted of about 115 persons, twenty-one of them women. For purposes of easy handling on the march, the group had been divided into four sectors. They were:

1. American—18 officers, 5 enlisted men, and 3 civilians (Lilly, Case, and myself).
2. British—11 officers and men and 2 civilians.
3. Seagrave Unit—2 doctors, 7 British Quaker members of the Friends Ambulance Unit, 19 Kachin, Karen, and Burmese nurses, 2 women refugees, and servants, totaling about 40 persons.
4. Chinese—Brigadier General Tseng and about 15 soldiers.

Furthermore, there were Indian cooks and mechanics, the latter being formed into a pioneer unit with the American group. In addition, there were twenty mules and one dog.

The area we were to traverse was part of a great triangle of jungle, bounded on the east by the Irrawaddy River, on the northwest by the Bramaputra River and the Himalaya Mountains, and on the south by a dry belt tapering off into Shwebo. This area differed in many places. In some sectors there was nothing but an impenetrable forest, a wet jungle, dissected by torrential mountain streams; in other places were plains and a dry dead jungle. In parts of the area were to be found heavy timber such as teak, kanyin, ingyin, and thayet; in other places were palms, giant ferns, banana, mango, and bamboo trees. The level land abounded in elephants. In the whole area were innumerable tribes of monkeys, tailed on one side of the jungle, tailless on the other side. Russel's vipers, hamadryads, and king cobras—all of them poisonous snakes—were also known to be present in fairly large numbers. Villages were scarce and the population sparse.

Our plan was to head west across part of this area to Homalin on the Chindwin River, and to cross the river before the Japanese coming up from the south in gunboats could cut across our path. We originally estimated that it would take us four days to reach the Chindwin, but we were inclined to increase this estimate because we had no certain information concerning the exact distance. Using guides, with Case as an interpreter, we planned to cut across country through the jungle and come out a day's boat ride from Homalin, when we would look over the lay of the land and see if any Japanese were around.

Our chief problem before we started seemed to be food. When our party had originally set out from Shwebo, we had been equipped with thirty days' dry rations for sixty-five people. But during the journey, stray groups fastening on us here and there had increased our numbers to almost double their original total. In addition, in examining the stores that afternoon, Captain Eldridge had discovered that they contained an abnormally large amount of butter and jams, which were useless in the hot jungle. Thus, facing a trip the duration of which was unknown, we appeared to be short on adequate food stocks. . . .

I looked at the general.

"I'm also radioing the British to get police, guides, food, and water on this road. If they don't, there's going to be a catastrophe. Everyone trying to get out and everyone out of hand. Thousands will die."

Stilwell was right. Thousands did die.

The retreat from Burma was one of the bitterest retreats in modern times, ranking only below the Long March of the Chinese Communists in point of physical hardship and duration of march. Even as late as October 1942, as I wrote these lines, it was still going on. Remnants of the Allied armies, six months after the finish of the Burma campaign, were still lost in the jungles, wandering at the base of the Tibet fastnesses, fed by airplane drops, but slowly dying of malaria, exhaustion, and starvation, still unable to escape. . . .

At half past three on the morning of the 7th of May, while sleep still gripped our tired camp like a disease, I rose from a blanket on the ground, turned my jeep headlights across the yard where weary men lay, and shouted: "Rise and shine!"

Men blinked, shoved their heads under the blankets, and growled when I shook them, saying: "You'd make a good sergeant, you've got a nasty voice."

Slowly everyone rose. Indian cooks started breakfast bonfires, revealing cans of discarded butter in the yard. Over the fires Pinky Dorn, the general's aide, burned codes—our radio had been destroyed during the night. The girls marched into the camp from the village, singing, already wide awake before the drowsiness had left the eyes of the men. Carriers came into camp by ones and twos, their shirts hanging loose over their skirts. Dahs were suspended from their rope belts. Rags were wrapped around their heads. They sat quietly smoking white cheroots.

We lined up for breakfast. Not having a mess kit, I borrowed a flat tin cover from someone and shoved down all the rice I could get. Plates were washed in a gasoline tin of water; canteens were filled with boiled water. Those who didn't get any used cold well-water, placing a few iodine drops in it to decontaminate it. The lights from the bonfires died. The lanterns of the muleteers shone on the horse-hair covering of their mule packs. To these they strapped baggage, the larger of the bedding rolls, and the heavier boxes of food. The carriers put bamboo ropes around boxes and lifted them up on poles. There were not enough carriers, and some baggage was left over, so that Frank Merrill had to shoulder his own large pack. Many of the others were carrying two water bottles, two pistols, rucksacks. I had made my pack purposely light, thrown away a heavy blanket, put the rest of my stuff on a mule pack, and carried only a canteen, which I slung around my neck by a cord, as I had no regulation army belt to which it could be fastened.

General Stilwell shoved a carrier guide out in front of him on the path and called to General Sibert: "Okay, Si! Let her go."

Sibert held a police whistle to his lips and blew a sharp blast. "Fall in," he shouted.

Dorn and I fell in behind Stilwell with the rest of the American group behind us; then the British, then the Seagraves, and at the end the Chinese and the carriers.

Stilwell slung a tommy gun over his shoulder, called: "Forward march," and started down the path at a slow pace.

We were off to India. . . .

The jungle along the banks grew thinner, the sun beat down harder, and the water became deeper. It washed sand and gravel into our shoes, crept up around our knees, and pressed like a wall against our legs, which grew heavier. We splashed, stumbled, and went slower. Men began to waver, complain, and curse. And suddenly Colonel Holcombe faltered, grew pale, and fell out of column. Half-supporting him on his shoulder, Dr. Williams took him over to the bushes beside the stream, poured a slug of whiskey down his throat, and waved an ammonia-soaked rag under his nose. From his body we took a heavy ground sheet, two water canteens, and a pistol, and, thus lightened, he came slowly on again. But once more he faltered, and Williams ran to the general and said: "Holcombe can't go any further, general."

Without stopping, the general turned his head and said out of the side of his mouth: "He's got to come on. This column can't stop. Take him out of line and bring him along. . . ."

The sun beating down with a naked flame on that open beach drove us to seek refuge among the trees, brambles, and bushes on an embankment hanging over the other side of the stream. Here, on top of a coarse prickly undergrowth, beneath trees from which great lianas hung down like raided ropes, Stilwell, Dorn, and I lay on a blanket together, shifting our position every fifteen minutes as the sun found a hole in the overhead shade and mercilessly burned us, and a regiment of ants and bugs crawled into our clothing and prevented us from getting any sleep.

Looking at . . . the tired bodies around him, the general audibly wondered "if this gang can march three hours tonight." Half to himself, he said: "If we don't go on, that mob in back will come down on us and that's going to be bad in this narrow stream."

A meal of rice, bully beef, and tea was served on the sands about four o'clock. Men and women lined up before black iron pans, looked at the white grain mixture spotted with red bits of meat, and then gobbled it down greedily. Then we started marching once again.

Although the hot fire had gone out of the air, the accumulative effects of the morning's march plus the abrasive action on our feet of the sand and gravel in our shoes made the evening hike for most of us a grueling affair; and in the end we went even slower than we had in the morning. The general sloshed with the same steady pace through the water, the tommy gun still on his back, but the main group could not keep up with him. Stragglers began to fall behind so that we had to form a stragglers' detachment to pick them up. At one of the halts the general put his gun down for a moment, leaning it against a rock, and at a nodded signal from Pinky Dorn I picked it up and wandered toward the rear; for both of us knew that if the general saw me, he would not let me carry his gun. . . .

At the start of the trip it had been generally feared that our rate of march would be dictated by the comparative slowness of the girls, but here on the first day, at any rate, they not only were marching as fast as anyone else, but were doing so in high spirits, bouncing, splashing and playing in the water, kicking up their legs, holding their skirts high, and singing like chorus girls. Yet they were not at all like Follies beauties—save in age, as all of them fell between seventeen and twenty-three—for the faces of most of them, while attractive and full of expression, were on the whole quite plain and were hidden by sun helmets which came down over their ears and under which many of them had placed towels to absorb the sweat from their foreheads. Yet in that atmosphere and environment they were the perfect companions. And their high-pitched, girlish voices, raised in song and echoing through the cliffs enclosing the stream, provided in moments of drooping morale and excessive fatigue marching rhythms, varying in mood and effect from the soothing to the stirring, that no military band could have equaled. Their own native Karen songs, war songs they had learned from Chinese soldiers, Christian hymns, and ancient American jazz were, save for General Stilwell's dogged, cool perseverance, the one invigorating influence we had on the march. With a feeling of nostalgia I can still hear them sloshing through the river, stumbling through the jungle, and streaming down steep mountain sides, singing in their childish, abandoned way. . . .[14]

By the end of May the Japanese conquest of Burma was complete, and so, too, the isolation of China. With the Burma Road gone, and the Stilwell Road still in the future, the only supply route to China was by air "over the hump"—one of the most hazardous air routes in the world.

7

OCCUPIED EUROPE
FIGHTS BACK

Signed with Their Honor

HITLER'S GRAND POLITICAL and military strategy had, from the beginning, a certain mad logic. Alone, Germany was no match for the whole of the rest of Europe. But Germany was to roll along like a snowball going downhill, gathering strength as she went. She would devour her enemies and her victims, one by one, add to herself the wealth and resources of each, and grow constantly more powerful while the combination which could be organized against her grew less powerful. To each of her conquered or vassal states she would extend the dubious benefits of the New Order. From each she would take what she needed—grain and coal from Poland, oil from Rumania, bacon and butter from Denmark, factories and skilled workers from Belgium and France, and so forth.

If this grandiose scheme were to work, it required at least the passive co-operation of the peoples of the occupied states. Dissident elements were to be rooted out: Jews exterminated; Poles, Russians, and other "inferior" peoples reduced to slave laborers; recalcitrant men and women put in concentration camps. Those who were left would become, so it was assumed, collaborators.

It was all logical enough. It merely left out of account such irrational things as love of country and hated of tyranny in whatever disguise it might appear. There were collaborationists in every country—more in some than in others. But the New Order never got under way. It was sabotaged by the patriots who, at the risk of torture and death, waged ceaseless war against the dark invader. Many of them are and will forever be unknown, their acts of heroism and sacrifice unrecorded by history. Stephen Spender's noble lines could be their epitaph:

Those who in their lives fought for life
Who wore at their hearts the fire's centre.

Born of the sun they travelled a short while towards the sun,
And left the vivid air signed with their honour.[1]

It is as yet too early to give more than a few episodes from this dramatic story. A more formal record waits upon the recollections of the thousands of men and women who made up the underground: the guerrillas of Poland and Russia, the Maquis of France, the Partisans and Chetniks of Yugoslavia, the Andartes of Greece, the others, unorganized and organized, who fought for freedom. Stevens Rayleigh explains something of the origin of the "little war makers":

While the guerrilla has always taken some part in the wars of mankind—and was probably the original soldier—never before has this hit-and-run warrior been multiplied into whole armies, or even into units operating with such deadly precision and effect. . . .

Why is all this happening? In a war where the very apex of organized armed might has been reached by armies prepared and trained for years, why do we observe the phenomenon of a world-wide return to what the American would call "Indian warfare"?

Military scholars explain. First, they say, war has no more a fixed character throughout history than any other phenomenon involving human beings. It changes and adapts itself to the needs of each epoch. It may even be said to have fashions and modes.

Second, they say, war is a matter of cause and effect—as with everything in Nature.

And, third, that it is a matter of David and Goliath, or Braddock and the Indians, or Lawrence of Arabia and the Turks in the first World War. . . .

German military might . . . produced its own antidote. . . . The antidote was the guerrilla who slipped in and cut and ran; the guerrilla who crept by night and blew up bridges; the guerrilla who sniped from dark hillsides and fled; the guerrilla who fired incendiary bullets into gasoline tank cars and then wasn't there; the guerrilla who fell silently on sentinels and small patrols and cut their throats; the guerrilla who cut telephone lines, tore rails from rail lines, burned commissaries, dynamited headquarters, and did ten thousand other things. But the guerrilla that the most efficient army could no more pin down than you can trap a drop of quicksilver with your thumb. . . .

Cause and effect. When a people without sufficient armament, armies and training could not stand up to the Germans and Japanese, because their armies were too well equipped and efficient after years of evil designing, the effect was to produce a whole nation, a rabble, in arms—the effect, in turn, of an aroused fervor of patriotism.

Thus the guerrilla. He is an interesting fellow. Throughout history he has been called brigand, *Freischütz*, partisan, *franc-tireur*, freebooter, bushwhacker, irregular, *komitaji*, *condottiere*, moss-trooper, and many other names. Yet the guerrilla has a recognized and lawful position in warfare.

The word itself is Spanish in origin, being the diminutive of the Spanish word for war, *guerra*. Freely translated, it means "little war maker."[2]

Here are glimpses of the people who fought the secret war against the Nazis, and stories of their deeds. Not every country is represented, nor every type of underground activity. But the illustrations are typical.

Poland

Of all conquered countries Poland was treated most savagely. Literally millions of its people were killed. Its territory was carved up; its towns destroyed; its wealth confiscated; its industries moved. Yet the spirit of resistance was never crushed—and Poland never had a real fifth column movement or a Quisling. Tens of thousands of its soldiers and airmen escaped to fight in Africa, Norway, the Low Countries, Italy, and France. Hundreds of thousands fought back from their native soil. Xavier Pruszynski tells of their operations:

Poland is frequently referred to as the country in which the Germans have shown what Europe would look like after a Nazi victory. Nowhere has the Nazi terror reached such monstrous proportions. In Poland the Germans see no reason for controlling their savagery in the slightest degree and they make no effort to restrain instincts on which they are still putting some brake in France and some other occupied countries. The world Press is full of reports about horrible massacres, executions and deportations which follow each other relentlessly. The world hears less about the stubborn resistance which is largely responsible for many of the brutal reprisals. Poland is thought of as a country which suffers, but it is also a country which still fights. Just as the German terror is reaching in Poland a height of ferocity unknown in other countries, so the underground resistance and struggle of the Polish nation has an intensity unique in Europe. It's a work which by its very nature must remain secret and unknown, but sometimes a fact like the escape of the three British officers from East Prussia reveals the existence of an organization that outgrows the frontiers of Poland and maintains contact with the Poles in all countries, including Great Britain.

The origin of this organization, the work of which has to remain concealed until the end of the war, can probably be traced to the transfer, immediately after the Polish campaign of 1939, of scores of thousands of Poles from the occupied provinces to Central Poland. The traditions of patriotic conspiracy, which thrived in Poland throughout the XIXth century, were revived on a scale made possible by modern civilization. The spies of the Gestapo met with an espionage even more subtle than their own. The German terror can never reach to the roots of the danger which threatens its rule. The concealed work goes on, and very few people know much about its nature and its scope.

There is every reason for not divulging even the little we do know about this clandestine activity. But the German Press noticed in 1940 that a considerable number of railway accidents happened on lines passing through Polish territory. It seemed strange that far more accidents happened on lines from the East to the West than on those from the North to the South. It was found that the Soviet-German traffic, so vital for German industry, was particularly affected. Soviet Russia had been not merely providing Germany with raw materials of her own, but had also served as helpful intermediary for the supply of certain goods from America. It was the last stage of a long journey, that passing through Polish territory which proved to be the most dangerous for the goods despatched to Germany from the other hemisphere. The Germans resorted to savage reprisals and executions, but the accidents continued to happen. The lines had to be closely guarded with German soldiers on every mile of track—the accidents were fewer but they still occurred with a disconcerting regularity. Finally the Germans were compelled to replace the whole personnel of the railways with staff imported from Germany. It was an expensive matter for a country which is beginning to feel a shortage of labor, but it didn't work either. There were still many accidents on the East to West lines, and the few roads between the empires of Stalin and Hitler are continuously undermined by the mysterious work of Polish moles, burrowing deep underground.

During the first year of the occupation German officers and officials used to meet their death in the dark, shot or stabbed by unknown killers. The German Press was indignant against Polish "bandits," and the Gestapo executed hundreds of people. Now the method has changed. There are fewer assassinations, but their victims are more carefully selected. No German is killed merely for the sake of revenge, but those who have managed to worm their way too deeply into Polish life and are beginning to understand the working of the national organization never live long. That was what happened to Igo Sym, the film actor of German origin, who entered Himmler's service offering to the Gestapo his knowledge of the country. Swift justice overtakes all those who could be dangerous informers for the German authorities. The tentacles of the Gestapo which try to probe too deeply into the living tissue of the nation are promptly cut off. Thus the wall between Germans and Poles become higher and more impenetrable every day. Every German knows that he is surrounded by hate more virulent than in any other of the occupied countries. He finds it hard to discover the nuclei of this dark hate, but he knows that a day may come when it will submerge him like a flood let loose by broken dykes.[3]

Norway

Norway had its Quisling, and the name, synonymous with treason, suggests that the fifth column was more active there than elsewhere. Such was not the case. There were traitors in Norway, but the overwhelming majority of the people did not forget their traditional love of freedom nor repudiate their democracy. The Norwegian government moved to London; thousands of Norwegians trained in the armies and air forces of Britain and Canada; tens of thousands of Norwegian seamen manned

warships and cargo ships that fought for the Allies. And at home passive
resistance and sabotage were an endless vexation to the conqueror. Walter
Taub celebrates some of the heroes of the Norwegian resistance movement:

It was Hauge who organized a daylight attack on a well-guarded lorry
carrying 90,000 ration cards along one of Oslo's main streets. Suddenly
five patriots jumped onto the lorry, one behind each guard, with a revolver
ready to silence him should he make trouble. After that it was an easy job
to force the lorry into a side street, remove the ration cards to a waiting car,
and speed the five guards over the Swedish border, where police would see
that they didn't blab. Then the patriots drove the car into a forest where
hundreds of hunted young men, threatened by enforced mobilization and
having no new ration cards, were facing starvation.

This Christian Hauge, who held all the threads of the military resistance in his hands, had been under the Gestapo's nose all the time. He was
a police commissioner! One of his best assistants was a young man who is
still known only under the name of "Grenade" Larsen. He was the Home
Front's arms producer.

In May, 1943, Grenade Larsen attended an underground course in the
use of arms and came to the conclusion that he could start manufacturing
automatics himself. He took one gun to pieces and thought out for what
other purposes the various small parts could possibly be used. When he
succeeded in finding a camouflage for each part, he ordered them from 21
different workshops. The most difficult was to find a plausible explanation
for the barrel of the gun, but finally he hit on an idea: It could be a spindle
such as that used in a spinning mill—so he ordered spindles through a
middleman. When all the parts were delivered, he put them in a rucksack,
cycled out to a forest and set up a secret assembly workshop. During
twenty months he produced 1,000 automatic Sten guns costing $17 each.

In December, 1944, he noticed that he was being shadowed by the
Gestapo, and the Home Front immediately ordered him to be sent to
Sweden. To gain time, it was decided that a young man resembling Larsen
would play the latter's role for a while. This double slept at Larsen's home
evenings and by day attracted the Gestapo's attention by cycling at high
speed with mysterious, heavy bags on the carrier. Four Gestapo men were
continually after him.

At five o'clock one morning, they came to arrest him—but he had
already learned that Larsen was safely over the border. The next day, the
Gestapo received a letter from Sweden: "I thank you for your recent
attentions and apologize for taking a short holiday without permission. To
convince yourselves that I really am myself, look at some samples of writing in my flat. Yours, Grenade Larsen." Larsen took a short holiday and
returned in time for the capitulation. . . .

One of the most perfect organizations within the resistance movement
was that which carried out transportation over the border. Every day during the entire occupation, an average of twenty persons was transported to
Sweden with almost complete safety. The organization was well informed
as to the Germans' plans against Norwegians, and the Gestapo never dis-

covered how it was possible that a man about to be arrested, disappeared a few hours before the blow fell. The secret isn't revealed yet; I got on the track by pure chance. . . .

The Gestapo caught up with one of the leaders, and he was terribly maltreated and tortured. For several months he lay in prison unable to move. Later, when his captors realized he was crippled for life, he was moved to a hospital. Two years after, he was still immovably chained to his bed. Then he received a strange visit from the Gestapo man who had tortured him.

The latter motioned the nurse from the room and said in a soft, pleading voice, "I've come to beg your forgiveness and I won't go until you grant it. I heard that you will always bear marks from that unfortunate episode. I beg you to believe me when I say that this is because, at that time, the instruments hadn't been finally perfected. Believe me, this doesn't happen now. We are perfectly acquainted with our instruments and I can assure you there are no aftereffects; you must believe me. Otherwise, you will regard me as inhuman, and you mustn't do that."

Of all the true stories of the Gestapo's sadism, I think this is psychologically the most terrible. . . .

Henrik Groth, the publisher, who had been a member of the opposition from the beginning, calculated that approximately 15 to 20 percent of all Norwegian prisoners were victims of systematic torture. According to this calculation, 50,000 Norwegians have gone through the Gestapo's prisons. The majority were men; if you subtract women and minors from Norway's population of 3,000,000 you find that every thirtieth Norwegian has at least once been deprived of his freedom.[4]

Belgium

When Belgium's army surrendered and Belgium's King went into captivity, the outlook for further resistance seemed black. But the Belgians were old hands at underground activities: they had maintained them throughout the first World War. Some of the leaders of that earlier movement once more shouldered the burden of resistance. John Kobler explains how the Belgian underground press plagued the Nazis.

Early in the morning of August 15, 1940, less than three months after Von Falkenhausen took over, a man ambled casually past the *Kommandantur's* letter box. In passing, he deposited an envelope addressed to his excellency and ambled on, unnoticed by the sentries. A few minutes later the baron was peering through his monocle at a complimentary copy of the world's oldest underground newspaper, La Libre Belgique—Free Belgium. To underscore the fact of its rebirth after twenty-five years, it carried the volume number "One, New War Series." In the same vein which harried Belgium's first governor general into a nervous collapse, every column spat scorn, defiance and cocky Gallic humor. "Do not swallow their lies!" warned the lead editorial. "Let not the edge of your wrath be dulled! Never forget that they are criminals, barbarians, murderers. Whatever they do, keep up your resistance against their Order."

With traditional impishness, the editorial address was given in the mast-head as "Kommandantur, 1, Place du Trône"; the editor was listed as Peter Pan, symbol of Belgian spirit. Price? "The Boches having wrecked Belgium, this copy is free." A note from the business department added, "Business being nil, due to the low value of the mark, we have suspended our advertising page and we advise our clients to save their money for better times." Peter Pan promised to deliver uncensored news twice a month and urged readers to pass on their copies. . . .

As this is written, La Libre Belgique hasn't missed a dead line in more than two years. The first few copies off the press are scrupulously ear-marked for the top Nazi administrators, reaching them on the day of publication, sometimes by post, sometimes by hand. At enormous risk, additional copies are smuggled across three frontiers to the Belgian ministry in London, as proof that Peter Pan still lives. He now publishes two editions, one in French and one in Flemish, with an average printing of 50,000 each. The actual readership, however, embraces most of the population.

For the sole purpose of silencing Peter Pan, the Gestapo maintains some 500 special agents. Occasionally the agents make a haul. In Liège, in July of 1941, sixteen readers, five of them young girls, were thrown into solitary, after being tortured in a futile effort to make them reveal who delivered their copies. In Flanders two distributors were shot without trial. But this yielded results no more permanent than lopping off the heads of a hydra. For La Libre Belgique is organized as intricately as one of Himmler's own spy networks. At its center operates a handful of editors who identities are known to less than 100 proved patriots in Belgium and abroad. Many of them double as allied intelligence agents. Concealing their copy material in umbrellas, hollow canes, false-bottom satchels, a team of them farm it out among different job printers. In this way no one raid can prevent publication.[5]

France

France had its Pétain and Laval. France had, too, its de Gaulle, and it was this skillful and gallant soldier who typified the real France. In midsummer 1940 the French people were stunned by the suddenness and thoroughness of the catastrophe which overwhelmed them. Many resigned themselves to their fate and, misled by Pétain, or by their own misguided selfishness, actively collaborated with the conqueror. The great majority, however, rejected collaboration and the New Order. It was in the anguish and humiliation of defeat that France found her soul. On June 18 de Gaulle called upon all his countrymen to join him in resistance. Within a short time the Free French movement grew to vast proportions. Over a hundred thousand French soldiers had escaped to Britain where they trained for their return. French Equatorial Africa rallied to de Gaulle, as did New Caledonia in the Pacific. French soldiers fought with the British in Libya and Syria, and when Eisenhower landed in North Africa a new French army was organized, under General Giraud. In France itself the resistance movement gained headway steadily.

André Girard, who helped organize it, describes its activities and J. Kessel gives us some day-by-day impressions of its impact on the lives of ordinary French men and women.

The Underground is a real army, made up of the toughest and smartest of the old French *poilus* and their officers, as well as civilians organized into commando, sabotage, signal corps, intelligence and engineering units. They cover the country; they include men of all classes and political beliefs.

Organization began while thousands of civilians and former soldiers stumbled south along the roads ahead of the invading Germans. Families often became separated. The newspapers ran columns of ads imploring information of lost ones: "Urgent. If you have seen my brother, Charles Pettigny, last heard from on the road to Chartres, please write Box—"

The Underground organizers answered the ads, saying in effect: "You are grief-stricken and homeless. But the war goes on. Lift your hand for France! Copy this and send it to three friends. Be a link in the chain that will break our chains!"

The idea grew and spread. The organizers rounded up their friends, telling them of the plan, warning them of the danger. And to each they put the question: Have you a friend you can trust? Then tell him, instruct him.

Aid came from high military men. Theoretically, all French war matériel was turned over to the German Army; actually tons of munitions were secretly trucked away into hiding. A hoard of several million francs was seized and concealed. Also seized was a record of exultant telephone conversations between German officers and their French Quislings. This has been filed away for use in the days of reckoning that will follow victory.

In the mountains of France the Underground has constructed fastnesses which are called *Places d'Armes*. The passes and defiles are guarded by pillboxes, machine guns and artillery, and the terrain is such that one man can hold off a formidable enemy. Here is the France that has never been conquered. . . .

In the early days the Underground's organizers made the Paris subway their headquarters. They did their work in the cars as the trains went around and around. Then the Germans discovered the ruse and they had to abandon it. The conspirators moved frequently. Records were kept on tiny strips of paper. Each record gave the name of a recruit, his job, his connections, whether he owned a bicycle, how many persons he could lodge and feed, and what he enlisted for: sabotage, transport or commando duty. The cataloguing was done by bank accountants working at night.

Files were made for every community in France. A record was compiled listing every railroad tunnel, every place where trains were obliged to slow down, every factory, garage and shipyard. The secret newspapers, appearing first in mimeograph form, later in printed four-page tabloids, turned out on small presses concealed in attics and cellars, helped to crystallize opinion and inform the people. Today there are some 40 of these papers, with a combined circulation of about 500,000.

The Underground sent agents through the country to listen to what people said, to refute German propaganda, to enlist new workers. The thousands who registered with the Underground had to be trained. Instructors were sent to visit them. These men—former lawyers, schoolteachers, soldiers—traveled at night and across country, to avoid German road patrols.

The instructors held classes for only two persons at a time. They taught their pupils how to plant incendiary bombs; how to place a charge on a railroad track in order to derail a train; how to sabotage production in factories turning out goods for the Germans. They also taught the use of the garrotte (a way to strangle a man before he can make a sound); how to attach silencers to pistols; how to assemble and use automatic rifles.

To test the courage of a recruit, the instructors often have him deliver a machine gun—wrapped in an innocent-appearing package—to a town some miles away. This means going to a railroad station, checking the parcel into the baggage car, then checking it out and delivering it, all under the eyes of the police. Recruits are also asked to cut a telephone line or lay a charge of explosives on a railroad track. The instructors judge a man fit for service only after he has passed these primary tests for courage. . . .

Often three months are spent in planning an operation such as the destruction of Radio Paris, France's most powerful broadcasting station. London was asked to determine exactly what amount of explosive would be needed. To find out, the British built a full-sized model of the station and blew it up. Four men of the Corps Francs were chosen to do the job. They rehearsed their parts a hundred times under the eye of an Underground instructor. On the day set, the four men slipped over the wall, set the charges and escaped. Twenty minutes later—boom! The men were never caught.

Another instance of careful planning and successful execution took place after the American invasion of Africa. It was thought at the time that southern France itself was going to be invaded, so it became important to shut off the Axis troops in Italy from access to France by blocking the railroads that connected the two countries. One Underground group set charges in a curving tunnel, causing a train to crash and buckle, effectively jamming the passage for days. Another group dynamited a mountain cliff, creating an avalanche which demolished an important railroad bridge. A third group killed the guards at another bridge, then blew it up. . . .

The Underground laboratory . . . developed an abrasive for use in factories. The Germans, for purposes of safety, had spread out production. One factory made the chassis of a truck, another the engine, and so on. In all but one of these factories, production would be right up to the mark. But in that one, a member of the invisible army would smear some vital part, say the bearings, with the abrasive. The truck would roll off the assembly line—in fact, it might roll along smoothly for 100 kilometers; then it would break down mysteriously. For a period of ten months, 90 percent of the trucks put out by one big assembly plant developed these strange ailments. The same grim gremlins pursued airplane production, shipbuilding, and every other kind of machine manufacturer in France. One shipyard has yet to produce a sound vessel. . . .

One member of the Underground deliberately joined a shipment of slave labor rounded up in France by the Nazis, in order to discover the location of a secret submarine plant. Once in Germany, he escaped from his captors and wandered over the countryside for a month, half-starved, until he found the place. This plant built its submarines entirely underground. The agent fixed its location in his mind, then rode back into France "on the rods." Later, well-directed bombs crippled the plant for a long time.[6]

The number of those who refused to work in Germany were a few thousand when I went to England. Today you can count them by the ten thousand. Many are swallowed up by the countryside. But many more have fled to the natural strongholds or have taken to the *maquis*—the *maquis* of Savoy, of the Cévennes, of the Pyrenees, of the *Massif Central*. Each holds an army of young people. They have to be fed, organized, and armed so far as is possible. It is a new and terrible problem for the Resistance. Some groups have sorted themselves into communities. Sometimes they edit a paper. Like tiny republics, they have their own laws. Others salute the colors every day, the flag with the Cross of Lorraine. The next mail for England will include photographs of these ceremonies.

But most of these lads, young workmen, students, clerks, need strong and intelligent leadership, money, and outside connections. . . .

The French weren't ready, weren't disposed, to kill. Their temperament, their climate, their country, the state of civilization which they had reached kept them a long way from bloodshed. I remember how difficult it was for us in the first days of the Resistance to contemplate murder in cold blood, ambushes, planned assassination. And how hard it was to get recruits for that. There is no question of these scruples now. Primitive man has reappeared in France. He kills to protect his home, his daily bread, his loves, his honor. He kills every day. He kills the German, the accomplices of the German, the traitor, the informer. He kills rationally and unconsciously. I would not say that the French people have grown hard, but their edge has been sharpened. . . .

Off again. Room taken under a fifth alibi. My papers: colonial officer on leave. Inoculations against malaria. Mathilde, as a nurse, comes to give them.

Visited Lemasque's sector.

I am not emotional, but I do not think I shall ever forget what I have seen. Hundreds and hundreds of young people returning to savagery. They can't wash. They can't shave. Their long hair hangs over cheeks burnt by the sun and rain. They sleep in holes, in caves, in the mud. Their food is a terrible daily problem. The peasants do what they can, but that can't last indefinitely. I've seen boys wearing old bits of tire for shoes, or even bits of bark tied around their feet with laces. I've seen others whose only costume was an old potato sack split in two and tied round the loins. One can't tell any longer where these boys come from. Are they peasants, workmen, employees, students? They all wear the same hunger, the same misery, the same anger, and the same bitterness on their faces. The ones

I visited were well disciplined under Lemasque and his helpers. We get them as much food and as much money as we can. But there are thousands of fugitives in the various *maquis*. No secret organization can look after even their most primitive needs. Either they must die of hunger then, or take to looting, or give themselves up. And winter hasn't come yet. Cursed be those who put such a choice before our young men. . . .

I have thought about the cells of Fresne, the cellars of Vichy, about room 87 in the Hotel T——, where every day, every night, they burn women's breasts and break their toes, and stick pins under their nails, and send electric currents through the sexual organs. I have thought of the prisons and the concentration camps were people die of hunger, of consumption, of cold, of vermin. I have thought of the team of our underground newspaper, completely renewed three times over, of the sectors where not a man, not a woman, remains of those who saw the work begin.

And I asked myself as a practical thinker, as an engineer who designs a blueprint, do the results we obtain justify these massacres? Is our newspaper worth the death of its editors, its printers, its distributors? Are our little sabotages, our individual assassinations, our modest little secret army which will perhaps never go into action—are they worth our terrible losses? Are leaders like us, who inflame and train and sacrifice so many stout fellows and brave men, so many simpletons, for a war in secret, of famine and torture—are such leaders, in short, really necessary for victory?

As a practical thinker, as an honest mathematician, I have to admit that I have no idea; and even that I don't believe we are. In numbers, for all useful purposes, we work at a loss. Then, I have thought, we should in all honesty give it up. But the moment the thought of giving up has come to me I have known it was impossible. Impossible to leave to others the whole weight and care of protecting us, of rescuing us; impossible to leave the Germans with the memory of a country without a comeback, without dignity, without hatred. I have felt that an enemy killed by us who have neither uniform nor flag nor land, that such an enemy was heavier and more efficacious in the scales which weight a country's destiny than a whole holocaust on the field of battle. I know that we have waged the French people's most glorious war. A war of little material use, since victory is already assured us, even without our help. A war which no one compels us to wage, a war with no glory, a war of executions and assassinations, in fact a free war. But this war is an act of love and an act of hate. In short an act of living.[7]

Yugoslavia

When, in March 1941, the weak Yugoslav government gave in to Hitler's demand for subserviency, a revolution swept it out of power. Faced with certain defeat, the Yugoslavs chose to fight rather than succumb. Belgrade was bombed, the country cut to pieces, and Yugoslavia, by all Nazi calculations, disposed of. Instead, Germany faced implacable guerrilla warfare. From the mountain fastnesses of their country armies of Chetniks under General Draja Mihailovitch ceaselessly harassed the invaders. After a time the Chetnik movement—chiefly Serbian—got itself involved in internal disputes with other resistance—chiefly Croat—elements. By 1943 these, under the leadership of General Tito, were doing the major part of the fighting against Germans and Italians—and doing it so successfully that they held down, in Yugoslavia, over twenty Nazi divisions. Cyrus L. Sulzberger, one of the most penetrating of correspondents, traces the rise of Tito and his Partisans.

DECEMBER, 1943—There are now more than 250,000 men and women organized into approximately twenty-six divisions fighting a savage war against some of Adolf Hitler's best veteran units along Yugoslavia's frontiers. That front stretches approximately 350 miles across forests, ravines and snow-covered mountains ranging between the Julian Alps of Slovenia and the forbidding crags separating bleak Montenegro from Albania and the south.

Bound together by aspirations for freedom, these soldiers, no matter what ideologists may think of them or their leaders, are as admitted by Prime Minister Churchill opposing more enemy divisions than face the Fifth and Eighth armies in Italy. As a result of their stubborn fight they are receiving American material and military aid, and accompanying them are American and British missions that soon will be joined by one from Russia.

They are openly and boastfully influenced by communism. Their chief is a Communist, and the Communist party, as he declared in a public speech, initiated and coordinated the peasants in their instinctive yearning for liberty. They have proclaimed themselves for a federation of the southern Slav peoples without favoring one over the other as do some of their opponents.

This force, which calls itself Yugoslav People's Army of Liberation, has been in process of formation for two and a half years. It began with the gradual amalgamation of nationalist and patriotic guerrilla bands and their welding together by an underground political movement, fomented by a mixture of Communist and democratic party leaders headed by a Croatian metal worker named Josip Broz, who has a Russian Soviet background.

For months M. Broz lived a furtive life in Belgrade under the eyes of the Gestapo. He sat quietly in a corner of cafes smoking endless cigarettes with a revolver in pocket, spreading his organization slowly while Nazi police and Serbian collaborationist gendarmerie hunted the capital's streets for him in scout cars mounting machine guns. . . .

Today M. Broz as Marshal Tito commands the immense popular upheaval resulting and serves as the political president of its temporary Government, which demands full recognition from the United Nations. He sends and receives important military missions to and from abroad.

Allied aircraft based in Italy are placed at the disposal of his specific commands. Sizable shipments, which now number thousands of tons of Allied war material, are being sent to his troops; guns, munitions, trucks, uniforms, medicines and special apparatus.

His army includes a regular officer's corps with special insignia, from the rank of noncom to marshal. His artillery, made up almost exclusively of captured weapons, has cannon as large as giant gun howitzers and coastal rifles. Officers' training schools, medical corps, ordnance and adjutant generals' departments have been created within his Supreme Command. . . .

In June when the Nazis attacked Russia, the Parisans began their active fight. . . .

Revolutionary moves, big and little, spread. Marshal Tito drew up special operational plans for five partisan detachments in Serbia. In raids for firearms gendarmerie stations were ransacked. Armed with two cartridge-less rifles, a group from Kragujevac held up ten gendarmes and stole their rifles and revolvers. Today that same detachment has swollen to a brigade equipped with captured Axis tanks.

On July 13 a large uprising erupted in Montenegro and swiftly all the titanic little province except three main towns was freed of Italians. Montenegrins have always said "Together we and the Russians are 200,000,000," and now they arose to prove their fighting spirit. . . .

Croatian workers, encouraged by Communist organizers, commenced a sabotage campaign, resulting in the slaughter of hundreds by Gestapo and Anté Pavelitch's Ustachi. They began to join thousands of Serbs dwelling in that province who had fled to the forest to escape massacres fostered by the Nazis. . . .

By the end of 1942, after a series of swift assaults and forced marches, Marshal Tito had liberated large chunks of Slovenia, Croatia, Kordun, Lika, Gorski, Cattaro, west Bosnia and much of Dalmatia. . . .

Early in 1943 the Germans mounted a big new offensive with four crack divisions plus Italians and Ustachi, and some Chetnik units simultaneously but independently attacked. Terrific aerial bombardments and strafings were loosed against the People's Army, which had neither fighter protection nor anti-aircraft artillery.

Around the Bihac area and in Croatia and Lika Marshal Tito left the First Bosnian Corps of four divisions and the First Croatian Corps of four divisions, and with five of his best divisions—The First, Second, Third, Seventh and Ninth—began to fight a terrible retreat southward more than 200 miles into Montenegro. With him he took 4,500 wounded rather than risk their capture.

The full tale of this retreat remains to be told. Snow whipped up by a terrible "bora" wind bit into the ragged army. Hunger was with them day and night. Their diet was raw meat and leaves. Mass hallucinations drove the troops desperate. At one stage an entire battalion fancied it saw in the distance a vast castle, with warm smoke pouring out of chimneys.

Again a whole brigade, imagining it smelled cooking food, rushed up to a barren field kitchen with battered mess tins.

At Prozor and Imotski in southwest Bosnia the People's Army, forcing a passage southward, attacked and wiped out an Italian purge division, capturing quantities of arms and clothing.

March was a savage month, cold and cheerless. The Germans commenced a new offensive from the north and Col. Gen. Alexander von Loehr flew down from Belgrade to assume command. Three Nazi divisions took part, including the Thirty-sixth Grenadiers sent from Greece.

In a desperate strategic position, Marshal Tito assembled all available munitions and started a counter-attack. Despite continual *Luftwaffe* bombardment, in one day the People's Army fired 3,000 captured Italian howitzer shells and drove back the Nazis.

During the month of April Marshal Tito organized a new corps in Slavonia and another in Bosanska Krajina, while the Germans prepared a fifth offensive to destroy him. Seven Nazi divisions and five of Italians as well as Ustachi troops were employed. The enemy devised a new strategy, no longer marching in large columns with vulnerable transport, but specializing in small units with heavy automatic weapon firepower which could only be supplied from the uncontested air. After careful concentration a sudden attack was launched from all sides May 15—as the Axis was expelled from Tunisia.

This action took place on the high Piva plateau in Montenegro, surrounded by declivities and steep canyons. A British military mission—the first to Marshal Tito—was scheduled to arrive and before breaking out Marshal Tito lost three days waiting for them. Gales were so stiff that the first time planes bearing paratroops neared the position the weather was too abominable for them to land.

Finally, May 27 they arrived: Six of them jumping into a terrific, slanting wind amid the steady humming and flashing of artillery rumbling through the Black Mountains which give the province its name. Marshal Tito began his forced retreat prior to a counter-offensive.

As the march commenced bullets from Chetnik ambush whizzed by Marshal Tito and he said to a near-by British officer, "This is the way Mikhailovitch fights the invader."

During forty days of steady fighting Marshal Tito swung his troops northwestward, breaking through sixty kilometers of prepared German positions. Each height approached held enemy machine guns, mortars and field artillery, and the country is a mass of heights. Marshal Tito always was in the front line.

All Bosnia was liberated again just at the time the Germans were announcing that the Partisan movement had been wiped out. That was in July when there were two Nazi divisions in Sicily and seven against Marshal Tito. Winding from end to end of Yugoslavia was a long road of unmarked graves. But the movement that had grown by dogged persistence began to receive hundreds of new cohorts from ravaged areas. Homeless women and children flocked to it. When the People's Army entered the historically famous town of Jajce beneath the ancient castle of King Tvrtka of Bosnia beside a placid lake, some thousands of black-garbed peasant women clustered pitifully behind.

They were looking for salt they had done without for more than a year and for which their systems craved. In Jajce is a small chemical factory. Beside it were vast piles of salt. The miserable horde of womenfolk scrambled to it like animals and on all fours began licking it.

They came from an unbelievable, tortured hinterland of burned-down houses. The peasants had lived in make-shift shelters with jerry-built roofs. Whenever they heard the Germans were coming they destroyed roofs themselves and hid in the fields to avoid pillaging of what looked like might be their homes.

Across this landscape marched and counter-marched polyglot armies:

Germans, Italians, Bulgarians, Croat Domobranci, Ustachi, Serbian fascist troops of the government and Chetniks and Partisans.

Along the Belgrade-Zagreb Railway, once Europe's main thoroughfare to the East, moved slow chugging Nazi grain convoys, warily looking out for saboteurs. Traveling only by day and at reduced speed, they were preceded by armored trains pushing ahead of the locomotive carloads of sand. Planes flew overhead and on either side were tree trunks.

Special Partisan demolition squads laid their mines carefully against these. During the early months they had only a few mines, usually rebuilt from enemy bombs that failed to explode and in which holes were drilled for the fuse. Now they had large of mines of their own manufacture and special Allied-sent chargers. Hundreds of yards of mines were buried by night and, playing complex chargers like a piano, Partisan engineers blew up mine after mine engulfing German convoys. Tracks were littered with rotting goods. Neither side could remove the twisted locomotives. All stations were burned down.

During this period after June the counter-offensive of Marshal Tito's movement swelled enormously from Macedonia to Slovenia. Liaison with guerrillas in Albania, Greece, Bulgaria, Rumania and Italy was established.

By the time the capitulation of Italy arrived the Partisans were strong enough for swift action and several Fascist divisions—six in Slovenia alone—were disarmed and most of the troops sent back to Trieste. Some units joined Marshal Tito's forces. . . .

After gaining vast new material resources Marshal Tito swiftly liberated the entire Dalmatian coast except Zara and Sebenico where the Germans dropped paratroops and the First Partisan tank brigade to be organized drove up to the outskirts of Trieste. The people of Slovenia arose in mass with spades and pickaxes, destroying bunkers and barbed wire.

The Germans rushed Panzer units, including Tigers, into Slovenia, but aside from destructive raids they generally were ineffective.

Following enormous new strength taken from the defeated Italians, Marshal Tito felt strong enough for decisive steps in the military and political sphere and summoned delegates to an "Avnoj" congress which met in picturesque Jajce. The word Jajce in Serbian implies masculinity and with this meeting the Partisans boasted they had emasculated the enemy.[8]

8

REAPING THE WHIRLWIND

The Unrelenting Struggle

IT WAS NO ACCIDENT that for so many years Hermann Goering was second in command to Hitler. It was upon the *Luftwaffe* that Hitler relied to assure him dominion over Europe. The *Luftwaffe* had blazed a path for his armies in Poland, the Low Countries, and France, and it was the instrument that was to bring Britain to her knees. It failed because big as it was, it was not big enough; good as it was, it was not good enough. It was the first failure— but not the last. "Daedalus" has analyzed the role of the *Luftwaffe* and the causes of its decline as they appeared in 1943.

Every ground soldier who faces the Germans in battle has a vital interest in the German *Luftwaffe*. He would like to know how strong it is, . . . and above all he would like to know something about the quality of its planes and pilots. Having been overwhelmed by an avalanche of books and articles covering the Polish, Norwegian, French, and Pacific campaigns— when the United Nations were on the receiving end—and having heard the cry: "For God's sake send us planes!" arising from the lips of fighting men on widely-separated battle fronts, the average American soldier may have had a tendency in the past to overrate the Germans and Japs in the air and to underestimate our own air program and doctrines. . . .

The *Luftwaffe* was at first the prime Nazi terror weapon. Its threat was a principal element in Hitler's "bloodless" triumphs during the appeasement period, and its actual striking power helped bring Poland, Norway, Holland, Belgium, France, Greece, and Jugoslavia to quick defeat.

. . . [There is a] very great probability that the *Luftwaffe* was originally designed and built for a short offensive war. . . . The developments of the war, the types of German planes, the very operations of the *Luftwaffe*—all point clearly to its design for use as the spearhead of a *Blitzkrieg* and a final weapon to terrorize defenseless people. Of the main plane types with which Germany began the war: the Heinkel, Dornier, Junkers, Focke-Wulf, and Messerschmitt, only two were fighters. The rest were medium, short-range bombers with limited bomb load and defensive armament. She was entirely lacking in effective long-range heavy bomber types.

By freezing her basic designs at an early stage, Germany enjoyed the advantages of mass production in these types long before British and American aircraft industries reached their peak. These plane types sufficed in the early periods of the war when no appreciable air opposition existed and when campaigns were reckoned in terms of weeks. The *blitzkrieg* phase of the European war ended in 1941 when Germany attacked Russia. As a result of the Eastern stalemate, the *Luftwaffe* was called upon from 1941–43 to fight a kind of war for which it was not designed. But having frozen her plane types in order to achieve early mass output, the only new plane types Germany has put into use since the beginning of the war have been the Focke-Wulf 190 fighter and the Heinkel-177 bomber. It is significant that the ancient Ju-52 transport and the obsolescent Ju-87 (Stuka) dive bomber were employed in large numbers in Tunisia. . . .

Even while retaining a healthy respect for the FW-190, the He-177, and the Ju-88, it seems safe to say that the all-around qualitative worth of the *Luftwaffe* as a modern air force is less in 1943 than it was in 1941. The fact that Germany is using her FW-190s for bombing operations and her Ju-88s as night fighters may indicate that the lack of tested designs is forcing her to adapt uneconomical types to this work. . . . The proportion of Nazi fanatics in the *Luftwaffe* is somewhat higher than in the other services, but mere fanaticism could not offset the fundamental handicaps of the *Luftwaffe's* situation.

The second important reason for the probable present decline and future embarrassment of the *Luftwaffe* is to be found in its doctrines. The *Luftwaffe* was designed, it is most apparent, for close support of the ground army, as an essentially tactical air force, and its organization into air fleets (like army corps) made to facilitate this employment. As long as it functioned in close concert with a victorious tank-infantry blitz team in campaigns that required only a short operational range, the *Luftwaffe* looked unbeatable, but it was not organized for strategic tasks, as the Battle of Britain demonstrated. The Germans were willing to accept losses in order to push home the attack, and the *Luftwaffe* maintained the assault on Britain until the losses could no longer be borne. By bringing an end to it, the German High Command admitted the failure of their attempt to carry out a strategic air mission with a tactical air force. . . .

In terms of the land war in Europe this means that the German ground forces, in many past operations protected by the "umbrella" of the *Luftwaffe* are likely in most future operations to be without this cover.[1]

In the crucial Battle for Britain the RAF outfought the GAF. That was the achievement of the Spitfires and Hurricanes and Beaufighters—which were short-range, defensive planes. As yet the RAF was able to take offensive action only sporadically—the great Lancasters, Halifaxes, and Stirlings were still in the future. But even in 1940 and 1941 the RAF did bomb ports and industrial targets in Germany, and by 1942 the aerial offensive was in full swing. It should be remembered that for three years the RAF bore the entire burden of air warfare, defensive and offensive. Not until the spring of 1942 was the U.S. 8th Air Force created; not until August 17, 1942, did it fly a mission in its own aircraft.

British aircraft production increased mightily all through these early war years, but without American-made planes the RAF could scarcely have taken the offensive as it did, or held its own in the Mediterranean. The great problem in getting American-made planes to Britain was that of transport; while U-boats prowled the Atlantic lanes the losses in planes shipped by sea were dangerously high. The problem was solved by the construction of a series of air bases in Canada, Newfoundland, Greenland, and Iceland by way of which pilots could fly themselves and their planes directly to Britain.

Before Allied bombs could paralyze German economy and air power, it was necessary to build a vast organization, formulate an elaborate plan. An air force cannot be improvised, and bombing is no opportunistic matter. W. B. Courtney tells what is involved in the creation of air power:

Air power is a complex and diversified structure, of which an air force is only a part. Air power tramples forward upon the enemy with what General Eaker calls "its two big feet of Strategic Air Force and Tactical Air Force, which you must plant down one after the other in proper cadence." But air power is also reconnaissance—no part of enemy territory on this earth remains unseen by our observers, unmapped by our cameras or harboring activities which our photo experts cannot read. Air power is a massive airline: The Air Transport Command has drawn a net around the globe larger in volume and facilities than all the world's commercial airlines of all the rest of the great nations, military, air supply and service traffic combined. Air power is airborne land fighters: the Troop Carrier Command on the first day alone of the air invasion of Holland, last September, used five times more planes than there ever have been on all the domestic commercial airlines of the United States together, and it dropped more soldiers than George Washington ever had under his command, in a single engagement.

Air power is service—huge bases and repair depots at home and abroad and millions of acres of airfields. Air power is training—the possession by a nation of a fund of young manpower, healthy and intelligent and well educated enough for technical and specialized work under conditions and temperatures abnormal to man's natural physical equipment. Air power is the control, husbanding and exploitation of critical materials and resources. Air power is industry—the ability of a nation not only to build more airplanes than its enemy, but to devise, invent and keep ahead in research of every conceivable means of unloading disaster from the air upon that enemy. Air power is science and engineering and investment.[2]

Strategic bombing—which includes both the saturation variety which the British practiced and the precision which the Americans preferred—requires, too, meticulously thorough and comprehensive planning. It was—before the atomic bomb—obviously impossible to bomb everything,

so a scientific scale of priorities was established both for different categories of objectives and for specific objectives within those categories. Again
W. B. Courtney explains the system, and what he says of American strategic bombing applies equally to British:

The Americans never bombed by targets. They bombed by a deliberate,
scientifically and mathematically contrived, evaluated and executed *program*. . . .

The program itself was predicated, first, on destruction of the German
Air Force in order to win uninterrupted Allied air supremacy; second, on
the destruction or disruption of those German industries which contributed to the German ability to continue the war.

No responsible airman ever fancied or claimed that we could wipe out
the *whole bracket* of German industry. You could bomb the Ruhr into a
lifeless desert—it is almost that now—and German industry elsewhere
could have fed this war indefinitely. . . .

All the cities, all the factories of the Reich are not in ruins. Doughboys
marching in to occupy have been surprised to find, for example, certain
steel factories intact. The explanation is the steel produced therein was not
of a grade or type used in essential war materials. In one city, Yanks saw
the wreck of a building still holding the sign of a German rubber company.
"Oh, yes!" said the townsfolk. "Your bombers smashed this but we wondered why. This was only the company's office. The manufacturing plant,
a hundred miles from here, was not touched." What they did not know was
that this "office" was also a research center, and it was more important to
destroy that research than the actual production. Also, the usual ugly
stories are now circulating in Europe of German factories spared because
of British ownership. They are nonsensical. Any German factory spared
was spared for war, not economic, reasons.

At any rate, number one on the American air-power program was the
German Air Force. That was a "must." We had to win air superiority, not
only over occupied territories but over Germany itself, to insure both our
strategical bombing success and the ground invasion. To do that, we had
to knock down German planes as well as the factories that produced
them. . . .

Meanwhile, our bombers got on with their concurrent job of wiping out
German plane manufacturing. Their success was attested by the G.I.'s
favorite D-Day question: "Where is the *Luftwaffe*?" The effective neutralization of the latter is also detectable in the fact that German flak, not
German fighters, was responsible for more than 90 percent of the 55,000
incidents of battle damage inflicted upon our strategical aircraft in 1944.

Next on the air-power program came these essentially direct war sections of German industry, although not necessarily in this order, for order
changed with circumstances.

Oil, synthetic and natural—the blood of modern war. Transportation
and communications—its arteries. Ball and roller bearings. Rubber, tanks,
submarines, chemicals, ordnance, miscellaneous small arms, marine engines and naval equipment, signals, depots and testing, and research laboratories. . . .

It is in the results of the high-priority bombing of German oil and its by-product of gasoline, that nonprofessional observers can best judge our air power. . . .

This war as fought, on land and in the air, was the most petrol-dependent of all wars. The Germans appreciated this and, in their preparations, had set up huge fuel reserves, assured themselves of the Rumanian sources, drove early for the Caucasus and Middle East and, having abundant coal, established the earth's greatest synthetic oil plants for its extraction. Moreover, when they assessed the intentions of the American air program, they placed their heaviest flak and smoke-screen concentrations around the oil plants. Of about 12,000 heavy and 30,000 light flak guns defending the inner Reich, half of the heavy and a quarter of the light spat for the oil works. Luena, near Halle, had 450 heavies and 300 lights and was, perhaps, the most heavily defended single target in Germany. Yet we hit Luena 18 times and there is nothing left of it today but five blackened chimneys. . . .

Destruction of German oil not only grounded their air planes, it seriously interfered with their subs, tanks, motorized transport and the home life of their people. In five months, from May to September of 1944, we cut their gas production to 20 per cent of normal. Up to April of this year, we made more than 500 attacks on 120 different oil targets.[3]

By 1942 the RAF was ready to begin a program of saturation raids. The first great 1,000 bomber raid was on Cologne March 30. That year, too, Lubeck and Rostock were razed, Mainz and Karlsruhe devastated, large areas of Düsseldorf, Münster, Emden, and Frankfurt destroyed. Improvements in bombers and in technique made possible ever heavier bomb loads and ever better results. The bomb capacity of the giant Lancasters and Halifaxes was increased to ten tons; a special "pathfinder" force to go ahead of the bombers, find and illuminate the targets, was developed, and eventually methods were found for bombing with some accuracy through overcast—a discovery of more value to the USAAF than to the RAF. By 1943 these improvements were beginning to show results. A laboratory test case was made of Essen, home of the great Krupp armament works. Hector Hawton describes the results:

The target chosen for the first trial of the Pathfinder was Essen. It was a challenge testifying by its boldness to the confidence the authorities felt in a strategic arm that seemed at last to be almost perfected. If the results had been ambiguous, however, it would have appeared that there were limitations to night bombing that must be accepted, however reluctantly. . . .

The skies above Essen are besmirched by the smoke from innumerable chimneys but on the night 5–6 March 1943 they were unusually clear. Bomber Command had timed the attack for a night when weather conditions were highly favourable. The Pathfinders led the way, dropped their flares amid a maelstrom of flak, and as photographs subsequently showed they were dead on the target. No sooner were the factories and engineering shops illuminated than the great force of bombers streamed in and bombs of the heaviest calibre were rained on Essen at the rate of 25 tons a minute. . . .

The third raid on Essen was the signal for a series of blows in such rapid succession that it is usual to speak of this phase as the Battle of the Ruhr. In the strict sense it was not a "battle"; what is meant is that a whole area—250 square miles, with a population of 3 million—was selected for systematic demolition.

It could not be destroyed literally, building by building. Bombing is so extravagant that no matter how heavy the attacks may be, many buildings will be left standing. Fortunately, however, it is not necessary to reduce a town to ashes in order to paralyse its industries. To win the Battle of the Ruhr, it was sufficient to succeed in carrying out repeated attacks on the scale of the Essen raids and so deny to the enemy the usefulness of his greatest arsenal for some time to come, compel a large-scale evacuation, and so divert the labour-power that might otherwise have been employed on making armaments to repairing damage.[4]

Even more effective was the bombing of Hamburg during the last week of July, 1943—bombing which even the Germans admitted cost almost 30,000 lives. Hector Hawton resumes his story:

The Battle of Hamburg began on the night 24–25 July. The main damage then was in the western sections of the city. The ferocity of this first raid—with its obvious implication that Hamburg was threatened with the same fate as the Ruhr—sent a shudder of dismay through Germany. No attempt was made to belittle it. Indeed, on the morning after, a broadcast on the German Home Service took listeners on a conducted tour among the still smouldering ruins.

"It is now 8 A.M.," said the commentator, "five hours after the All Clear, but it is still impossible to comprehend the scale of the damage. Everywhere there are fires burning, the fronts of houses crumble with a great roar and fall across the streets. The smoke lies over the town like an enormous thundercloud, through which one sees the sun like a red disc. Now, at 8 o'clock in the morning, it is nearly dark, as in the middle of the night."

There could be only one reply, according to another propaganda talk: "Terror! Terror! Terror! Pure, naked, bloody terror! Go through the streets of the town which are covered with glass and debris. Set your teeth and do not forget who it was who brought you such misery! Let hatred glow in your hearts! Walk through the streets of Hamburg and from the smouldering ruins of houses see for yourselves at whom bombs and phosphorus were aimed. Forgiveness and conciliation are no longer possible here. The suffering of our heavily tried population has become a sacred vow of hatred."

There was no respite. On that same day the U.S.A.A.F. delivered a daylight attack, followed by another on the 26th, and bombing was so accurate that heavy damage was done to shipyards and docks. On the

27–28, again in excellent bombing weather, destruction was spread to the east, and on the 29–30 those areas in the north which had so far escaped were found by our bombers.

Over 8,000 tons of bombs were dropped on Hamburg, and the devastation was finally judged to amount to 1,250 acres in fully built-up areas, and 1,160 acres in areas partly built up. From this it could be computed that about 400,000 Hamburgers were rendered homeless. . . .

All these attacks occupied less than an hour. The concentration reached such intensity that on the night 27–28 July, 51 tons a minute fell on Hamburg; and during one attack the bombs released exceeded 2,000 tons. The method of concentration and illumination had been mastered; the enemy's defences had been pierced, so that it was possible to repeat the attacks although they were expected, and the cost was very far from prohibitive.[5]

The strategically most important raids were not necessarily the largest. Of all RAF raids perhaps the most important single attacks were those on the Eder and Moehne dams, May 16, 1943, and on the laboratories of the little town of Peenemuende on the Baltic coast, just three months later. From the British Information Service we take the story of the Ruhr dam raid:

Sir Archibald Sinclair, British secretary of state for Air, said in a speech on May 17, 1943:

> I've got news—great news—for you today. The RAF Bomber Command—the javelin in our armory—struck last night a heavy blow of a new kind at the sources of German war power. The two greatest dams in Germany, one containing 134,000,000 tons of water and the other 202,000,000 tons, were breached by our bombers. The walls of the Eder and Moehne dams were broken, and the water descended the valleys of the Ruhr and the Eder in huge waves.
>
> The operation was one of extraordinary difficulty and hazard. . . . It is a trenchant blow for the victory of the Allies.

The RAF had developed a new technique in aerial warfare . . . with complete success. On the night of May 16 nineteen Lancaster bombers flew deep into Germany and dropped mines from altitudes of one hundred feet and less against two of the most important dams of the Ruhr industrial area. These two dams—the Eder and the Moehne, two of the biggest in Germany—were breached by the mines, and floods were let loose in the Ruhr, Weser and Fulda valleys which spread ruin and devastation throughout vital districts.

The operation had been planned by Air Marshal Sir Arthur T. Harris, chief of the RAF Bomber Command, who had had special crews training for months. The tricky feat of blasting the dams was accomplished by dropping the mines into the reservoir close to the dam. The mines were set to explode at a depth of thirty feet, and, when carried to the dam by the current, exploded under water with terrific force to breach the massive concrete dam structure. Cool and skillful flying, accurate bombing, and the proper weather conditions combined to make the operation wholly successful. The loss of eight of the nineteen bombers, with their air crews of some 56 men, is not a high figure for the magnitude of the task accomplished—a task which, it has been estimated, would have been considered well worth the loss of a division or two in earlier wars. . . .

Reconnaissance reports by the RAF soon after the bombings showed that more than 100 feet of the Moehne dam had been breached and the power station below it swept away, while the river below the Eder was in full flood. . . . In effect, the whole result of this daring operation is cumulative and, unlike ordinary bombings, the destruction is likely to become worse as time goes on, even without further action by the RAF. But of course the RAF is taking further action.[6]

Wings over Germany

During 1942 and early 1943 most American aircraft went to North Africa rather than to Britain. They supported the invasions of Africa, Sicily, and Italy, and from bases in North Africa—and eventually in Italy—blasted at Axis Europe. One of the most spectacular of the raids from North Africa was the carefully planned and daringly executed attack on the Ploesti oil fields, August 1st, 1943. This was a highlight in the sequence of raids which seriously crippled Germany's petroleum production—life blood of the *Luftwaffe*.

The chief burden of the air war was to fall, however, to the Eighth Airforce, based in Britain, and joined in February 1944 by the Ninth Tactical Airforce. The Eighth had started modestly enough late in 1942; by January 1943 it was ready for its first attack on Germany proper. During its first year of operation it dropped 17,000 tons on enemy targets, destroyed 2,050 Nazi fighter planes, and lost 472 bombers. By summer its strength had mounted impressively, and by the end of 1943 it could boast a year's total of 50,000 tons dropped and 4,100 Nazi planes destroyed. The first great raids came on August 17, first anniversary of the Eighth's bombing, when one fleet of Fortresses made a shuttle bombing attack on Regensburg and another struck at the ball-bearing city of Schweinfurt. Bomber losses in these early raids were very heavy, in spite of the thicket of bullets with which the bombers surrounded themselves. What was needed was a fighter escort that could knock the German Air Force out of the skies while the bombers destroyed aircraft factories.

The development of long-range fighters was a triumph on the home front. What the labors of the engineers and factory workers meant in the skies of Europe is graphically told by one of America's greatest aces to Ira R. Wolfert:

Captain Don Salvatore Gentile, a Piqua, Ohio, boy, twenty-three, the only son of parents who emigrated to the United States from Italy, has been called by General Dwight D. Eisenhower, "a one-man air force. . . ." This boy has destroyed thirty German airplanes—the equivalent nearly of two whole *Luftwaffe* squadrons. . . .

He talked about his life to me, and I have tried to set it down within the limits of space as truly as I could, for it seemed to me an important life for the rest of us to understand. . . .

I started flying in Spitfires. June 22, 1942 was the day I put myself up against the Huns for the first time. The Spitfire of that day was a defensive weapon, which could not carry the war far into enemy territory. It could just about go into his front-line trenches. . . .

Our side was still on the defensive. We had to do more running away than running after. It was not until August 19, 1942, that I got my first German planes, a Junkers 88 and a Focke-Wulf 190. That was over Dieppe, if you remember, when our side was turned loose on the offensive, if only for a day.

Through all the long months that followed, while the Eighth Air Force was building itself up from the ground, we prepared to take the offensive away from the Germans, and then with the Thunderbolts really started to go out and get it.

The big bombers were the heavy guns in this phase of the war. Their job was to beat the German air force out of Western Europe, and our job was to help keep the German air force from stopping them.

In those days we flew close support for the bombers. When the German fighters came in on the bombers—not before—we turned into fighters and shot at them. As soon as an individual plane or a single formation broke off the attack, we hustled back to the bombers. The thing was, it was a limited offensive. We couldn't go all out. We had to peck and peck at them until they were weak enough to be trampled down. . . .

The score of the whole group was low in those days and it stayed low. It was April 2, 1943, when the group quit Spitfires for Thunderbolts, and about June or July of that year when we started noticing a kind of faltering in the *Luftwaffe*. The pecking of the bombers and ourselves was beginning to take effect. It looked as if the time would soon come when we'd be turned loose to trample them down.

But the German is a crafty foe and he began then one of those "planned retreats" of his. He took many of his planes out of France, Holland and Belgium, and there we were sitting in our Thunderbolts, unable to follow after them.

The Fortresses and Liberators barreled right into Germany after the *Luftwaffe*. We could go along with them only so far and no further. The bombers had to go the rest of the way without us. The *Luftwaffe* just waited for the bombers to go past our sphere of action. Then they hit and didn't stop hitting until our bombers were back with us. Then the *Luftwaffe* strutted back home like dogs which chase a marauder out of the front yard and are content to let it go at that.

Meanwhile, the home front was busy on the Mustang. With the Mustang there was no place for the *Luftwaffe* to retreat. That plane put the Huns' back right up against the wall, but we did not have enough fighter cover in the latter part of 1943, and the early part of 1944, to give anything but close support to our bombers. Fighter planes had to fly close formation to protect one another and had to devote themselves to breaking off enemy attacks, but could not follow through on the Hun making his getaway. . . .

The time finally came for us in late February, 1944. There was no more need to put all our planes in the close support of the bombers. There was no more need to keep the formation at any cost. We were sent out there to go and get and clobber the Nazis. If they wouldn't come up into the air we would go down against their ground guns and shoot them up on the ground. Get them, that was the idea; kill them, trample them down.

It was this time I, personally, was ready for. . . . I have a feeling now, looking back over the last few weeks, that all my life everything I have done in it has gone to fit me to take advantage of the weeks between February 20 and April 8. . . .

When the bell rang for the big fight against Hitler's *Luftwaffe* . . . our twenty-six-year-old Colonel Donald Blakeslee, another Ohio boy, led into action as fine a team as I think any nation has ever been able to gather together.

The boys had a lot of natural ability; most of them had been so eager to fly that they had joined the R.A.F. or the R.C.A.F. before we had got into the war. Now their ability was tempered with experience. Their enthusiasm for the fight was sweeping and contagious. Each man was confident he would survive. . . .

We started the offensive battles with 106 German aircraft destroyed to our credit, and by March 17 the group score had mounted to 200. By the second week in April we had 434 to our credit and were top scorers for the whole European Theatre of Operations. In the month from March 17 to April 16, we got more than twice as many German airplanes as we had in the two years of 1942 and 1943. Yes, there's no doubt that attack is the way to kill Germans. In my own case I shot down fifteen Germans from March 3 to April 1.[7]

"Now," said Winston Churchill, "those who sowed the wind are reaping the whirlwind." As tonnage was increased, accuracy improved, the overcast penetrated, and Nazi fighters knocked out of the skies, the raids became heavier and more damaging.

On January 7, 1944, the Eighth Airforce dropped 1000 tons on Ludwigshafen; on January 29, almost 2000 tons on Frankfurt; on February 20, 2218 tons on various German industrial centers. During February the Eighth and the Fifteenth Airforce—based in Italy—raided a score of industrial centers and shot 900 enemy fighters out of the skies. During March came a series of incendiary raids on Berlin—the attack of March 8, by over 2000 American planes, dropped 350,000 incendiary and 10,000 demolition bombs.

Altogether by the end of the war the United States Air Forces in the European Theatre had flown the astonishing total of 1,692,469 sorties over Germany and enemy occupied territory. In the course of these sorties they had dropped 1,550,022 tons of bombs and destroyed, in the air and on the ground, 29,916 planes. It was, indeed, as Winston Churchill observed, a splendid and prodigious achievement.

Surveying the effects of aerial warfare after the surrender, Allan A. Michie concluded that Germany was bombed to defeat.

The combined damaged areas of London, Bristol, Coventry and all the blitzed cities of Britain could be dumped in the ruins of just one medium-sized German city and hardly be noticed. The raid on Coventry in 1940 marked the peak of *Luftwaffe* destructiveness; and there the Germans dropped 200 tons of bombs. By that standard Berlin suffered 363 Coventrys, Cologne 269, Hamburg 200 and Bremen 137. . . .

The Eighth Air Force was assigned the job of destroying Germany's synthetic oil plants, and by November 1944 every such plant in the Ruhr was out of production. In the files at Hitler's headquarters there is a letter dated September 16, 1944, from Albert Speer, Reichsminister of War Production, to Reichsleiter Bormann, Hitler's deputy:

> The idea is spreading that reconstruction of synthetic oil plants and refineries is purposeless, since the enemy always finds a suitable moment, soon after resumption of work, to destroy these installations again by air attack. . . .

According to official German figures, 2,000,000 foreign slave laborers, in addition to the regular German railway workers, were employed in repairing railway damage. Fritz Knickenberg, chief inspector of the great Hamm marshaling yards . . . said, "Your bombers were far more punctual than our trains, and after January 1945 our repair gangs were unable to cope with the damage. . . ."

It was a newspaperman who supplied the apt definition, "tactical bombing is knocking over the milk pail every day, while strategic bombing is an effort to kill the cow." The day-to-day job of knocking over the milk pail was generally left to the United States and British tactical air force which operated from just behind the front lines. . . .

"Every ton of bombs dropped on Germany's industries will save the lives of ten United Nations soldiers when the invasion comes," said Chief Air Marshal Harris in 1943. The casualty count from D-Day to V-E Day is the proof of his prediction. . . .

But the aerial battle of Germany was not won without great costs. When the totals are drawn, it will be found that the combined losses of British and American airmen from September 3, 1939, to V-E Day, far exceeded the toll of dead in the combined British and American land forces from the invasion of Normandy to the end of the war in Europe.[8]

9

ONE UP AND TWO TO GO

Sicily to Surrender

WITH ALL AFRICA cleared and control of the waters of the Mediterranean assured, the Allies prepared the first blow against Europe. It was not, however, "Fortress Europe" but the "soft underbelly" that was the objective. As it turned out, it was not so soft as Churchill had suggested.

Yet the advantages of a conquest of Italy were clear, however high the cost. As Edgar McInnis put it:

Italy's military weakness had already been glaringly revealed. Her political structure was tottering under the impact of successive defeats. A direct blow might well bring the Fascist edifice crashing in ruins and complete the elimination of the junior Axis partner as a factor in the war.

Thus Italy presented a case where military and political factors were almost indistinguishable. Fresh military victories would serve political ends which in turn would have far-reaching military results. The Italian peninsula was still only an outwork of the European fortress. But its conquest would place the Allies before the walls of the German citadel. A breach at this point would open a way to the Danube valley and threaten a body blow at Germany proper. Meanwhile from Italy as a base the Allies could fan out against the Balkans or southern France, and their air forces could cover the whole of Axis Europe from the Baltic to the Black Sea. Even if the position was not exploited on a major scale, it could be used as a pivot for a series of diversions which would force Germany to disperse her strength; and if this should lead to a weakening of her reserves it would not only accrue to the advantage of Russia, but perhaps even ensure the prospect of decisive success to the coming invasion across the Channel. Whether all these possibilities would be fully realized only the outcome would reveal, but they were extensive enough to make it evident that a successful attack on Italy might lead to nothing less than a transformation of the whole balance of the war.[1]

First the tiny islands of Pantelleria and Lampedusa were reduced by air. Then General Eisenhower turned his attention to Sicily, defended by ten Italian and three German divisions. The conquest of this island was assigned to the XV Army Group—which included Patton's Seventh Army and Montgomery's Eighth—all under the command of General Alexander.

From North Africa, across the Mediterranean streamed an armada of 3,266 vessels carrying 160,000 men with 1,008 guns and 600 tanks. Heavy weather caused much seasickness among the troops, but they landed as scheduled at Licata and Gela on July 10, 1943, under cover of naval artillery. The following day landings were made at Scoglitti. British troops landed along the Sicilian shore from Cape Passero to Syracuse, quickly swept inland to take Syracuse on the 12th, and continued their advance to the north.

American troops swung west and north, to mop up the western half of the island, then turned east to meet the British coming up around the other side. The strategy called for trapping the enemy in the northeastern corner of the island to prevent escape across the narrow Strait of Messina.

After a sharp tank battle at Gela, in which naval guns helped break up the enemy attack, Patton's men met little resistance. On July 14th the Biscari airfield was captured, and air superiority assured. Advances by the Americans were rapid, partly because the Italians who faced them had no stomach for a fight, partly because of the effective work of paratroopers who had been dropped at strategic points behind the lines.

Agrigento fell to the swiftly advancing Americans on July 22. Infantry and tanks swept around the western corner of the island to capture Palermo a week later, then fanned along the northern coastal road. Troina was taken on August 5, after some of the heaviest fighting of the campaign.

Already the Axis forces were preparing to withdraw across the Strait of Messina. A race for the Strait began, the British pushing up from the south, the Americans driving in from the north. Allied air and naval forces bombed and shelled German communication lines and concentrations of troops and supplies at Messina. But in spite of the most energetic efforts—including even a series of amphibious landings behind the German lines, 88,000 troops, including most of the famous Hermann Goering Panzer Division, got away.

By August 16 Messina was in Allied hands and Sicily cleared of the enemy. It had taken just 38 days to capture the great island, and 100,000 prisoners.

Already the Fascist regime was tottering. The loss of Sicily and the imminence of invasion into Italy proper gave it the death blow.

On July 25 Benito Mussolini was ousted from the dictatorship he had held for twenty-one hard years. Confessing the futility of further resistance south of the Po Valley, he had presented to the Fascist Grand Council a plan to defend only the rich industrial north. The plan was voted down, Mussolini dismissed. King Victor Emmanuel appointed Marshal Pietro Badoglio to head the government.

With the conquest of Sicily the stage was set for the next move. Allied planes ranged the whole length of the Italian peninsula bombing communications, ports, factories, and airfields. The Italian people, now thoroughly sick of a war they had never really wanted, staged huge peace demonstrations. On September 3 Badoglio signed a secret armistice calling for unconditional surrender. Formal announcement was postponed until the 8th in the delusive hope that the Germans might be caught napping. In a report on the war, September 21, Churchill told the story of the secret negotiations that had led to the surrender:

With the approval of the War Cabinet, it was decided that General Eisenhower should send an American and a British staff officer to meet the Italian envoy in Lisbon. We at once informed Premier Stalin of what was in progress. On 19th August the meeting in Lisbon took place. The envoy was informed that we could accept only unconditional surrender. The military terms embodying this act of surrender—not so much conditions as directions following on the act of surrender—which had been prepared some weeks earlier, after prolonged discussions between London and Washington and General Eisenhower's headquarters, were now placed before the envoy. He did not oppose these terms, drastic though they were, but he replied that the purpose of his visit was to discuss how Italy could join the United Nations in the war against Germany. He also asked how the terms could be executed in the face of German opposition. The British and American officers replied that they were empowered to discuss only unconditional surrender. They were, however, authorised—and this was a decision which we took at Quebec—to add that if at any time, anywhere, in any circumstances, any Italian forces or people were found by our troops to be fighting the Germans, we would immediately give them all possible aid. On 23rd August, the Italian general departed with the military terms expressing the act of unconditional surrender, and with full warning that the civil and administrative terms would be presented later. He then made his way back to Rome, with great secrecy and danger. He promised to lay the terms before his Government and bring back their answer to General Eisenhower's headquarters by 31st August. . . .

On 31st August the Italian envoy returned. He had met General Eisenhower's representatives at Syracuse. The Italian Government were willing to accept the terms unconditionally, but they did not see how they could carry them out in the teeth of the heavy German forces gathered near Rome and at many other points throughout the country, who were uttering ferocious threats and were prepared to resort to immediate violence. We did not doubt the sincerity of the envoy nor of his Government, but we were not able to reveal our military plans for the invasion of Italy, or, as it had now become, the liberation of Italy. The real difficulty was that the Italians were powerless until we landed in strength, and we could not give them the date. We therefore timed the announcement for the moment which we deemed would give us the best military chance, and them the best chance of extricating themselves from the German grip.[2]

The immediate military consequences of the surrender of Italy were disappointing, for the Germans simply took over that unhappy country and continued the war on the Italian soil. The most substantial gain was the surrender of the Italian fleet, including many merchant ships and many submarines—an event which, said Churchill, "has decisively altered the naval balances of the world."

In that same speech of September 21, Churchill, speaking of the losses that Italy had sustained by her folly, predicted that: "Now their own beautiful homeland must become a battlefield for German rearguards. Even more suffering lies ahead. They are to be pillaged and terrorized in Hitler's fury and revenge." It was a true prophecy.

Salerno to Naples

On September 3rd two divisions of General Montgomery's veteran Eighth Army crossed from Messina to Reggio di Calabria and advanced up the Italian toe against slight resistance. On the 9th a British air-borne division captured the Taranto naval base and struck north to Bari, thus sealing off the Adriatic.

The main attack on Italy was to be at Salerno, somewhat south of Naples. Lieutenant-General Mark W. Clark's new Fifth Army was to make the assault. Montgomery hoped to sweep up, trapping all enemy forces between the toe and Salerno, while the main body of Clark's troops were to move north on Naples. Convoys bearing the Fifth Army put out from ports in Africa and Sicily on September 8, 1943. John Steinbeck pictures the struggle on the beaches:

There are little bushes on the sand dunes at Red Beach south of the Sele River, and in a hole in the sand buttressed by sand bags a soldier sat with a leather covered steel telephone beside him. His shirt was off and his back was dark with sunburn. His helmet lay in the bottom of the hole and his rifle was on a little pile of brush to keep the sand out of it. He had staked a shelter half on a pole to shade him from the sun, and he had spread bushes on top of that to camouflage it. Beside him was a water can and an empty "C" ration can to drink out of.

The soldier said, "Sure you can have a drink. Here, I'll pour it for you." He tilted the water can over the tin cup. "I hate to tell you what it tastes like," he said. I took a drink. "Well, doesn't it?" he said. "It sure does," I said. Up in the hills the 88's were popping and the little bursts threw sand about where they hit, and off to the seaward our cruisers were popping away at the 88's in the hills.

The soldier slapped at a sand fly on his shoulder and then scratched the place where it had bitten him. His face was dirty and streaked where the sweat had run down through the dirt, and his hair and his eyebrows were sunburned almost white. But there was a kind of gaiety about him. His telephone buzzed and he answered it, and said, "Hasn't come through yet, sir, no sir. I'll tell him." He clicked off the phone.

"When'd you come ashore?" he asked. And then without waiting for an answer he went on. "I came in just before dawn yesterday. I wasn't with the very first, but right in the second." He seemed to be very glad about it. "It was hell," he said, "it was bloody hell." He seemed to be gratified at the hell it was, and that was right. The great question had been solved for him. He had been under fire. He knew now what he would do under fire. He would never have to go through that uncertainty again. "I got pretty near up to there," he said, and pointed to two beautiful Greek temples about a mile away. "And then I got sent back here for beach communications. When did you say you got ashore?" and again he didn't wait for an answer.

"It was dark as hell," he said, "and we were just waiting out there." He pointed to the sea where the mass of the invasion fleet rested. "If we thought we were going to sneak ashore we were nuts," he said. "They were waiting for us all fixed up. Why, I heard they had been here two weeks waiting for us. They knew just where we were going to land. They had machine guns in the sand dunes and 88's on the hills.

"We were out there all packed in an L. C. I. and then the hell broke loose. The sky was full of it and the star shells lighted it up and the tracers crisscrossed and the noise—we saw the assault go in, and then one of them hit a surf mine and went up, and in the light you could see them go flying about. I could see the boats land and the guys go wiggling and running, and then maybe there'd be a lot of white lines and some of them would waddle about and collapse and some would hit the beach.

"It didn't seem like men getting killed, more like a picture, like a moving picture. We were pretty crowded up in there though, and then all of a sudden it came on me that this wasn't a moving picture. Those were guys getting the hell shot out of them, and then I got kind of scared, but what I wanted to do mostly was move around. I didn't like being cooped up there where you couldn't get away or get down close to the ground.

"Well the firing would stop and then it would get pitch black even then, and it was just beginning to get light too but the 88's sort of winked on the hills like messages, and the shells were bursting all around us. They had lots of 88's and they shot at everything. I was just getting real scared when we got the order to move in, and I swear that is the longest trip I ever took, that mile to the beach. I thought we'd never get there. I figured that if I was only on the beach I could dig down and get out of the way. There was too damn many of us there in that L. C. I. I wanted to spread out. That one that hit the mine was still burning when we went on by it. Then we bumped the beach and the ramps went down and I hit the water up to my waist.

"The minute I was on the beach I felt better. It didn't seem like everybody was shooting at me, and I got up to that line of brush and flopped down and some other guys flopped down beside me and then we got feeling a little foolish. We stood up and moved on. Didn't say anything to each other, we just moved on. It was coming daylight then and the flashes of the guns weren't so bright. I felt a little like I was drunk. The ground heaved around under my feet and I was dull. I guess that was because of the firing. My ears aren't so good yet. I guess we moved up too far because I got sent back here." He laughed openly. "I might have gone on right into Rome if some one hadn't sent me back. I guess I might have walked right up that hill there."[3]

The attack at Salerno was not unexpected. The Germans had stripped the Italian garrison of its arms and were waiting. In the sector where the Fifth Army landed there had been no preliminary naval bombardment to soften up the defenses. The British especially, to the north of the American beachhead, ran into tough opposition.

The German counter-offensive of September 12–13 threatened for a time to break through to the sea. But the Northwest African Air Force, flying 1,888 sorties over the beachhead in one day, checked the advance. Road junctions were blasted, the Foggia airfields bombed, and giant naval guns picked out German supply convoys and shattered them. By September 15th the counter-attack had lost its force. By the 18th the Germans began to withdraw to the north closely followed by both the Fifth and Eighth Armies. Salerno had been captured and our lines stretched across Italy to Bari.

Quickly the Fifth Army pressed back the German right wing, taking Oliveto on September 23rd, 1943. The Germans fell back and the Fifth Army, with the aid of a civilian uprising, entered Naples on October 7th. The Germans had withdrawn from the great port, but behind them they left smouldering ruins of the harbor facilities. They destroyed the water supply, mined buildings and streets, had seized everything on wheels. One of the worst of their crimes is described by Herbert L. Matthews:

On Sunday the Germans broke into the university after having carefully organized their procedure—squads of men, trucks with dozens and dozens of five-gallon gasoline tins and supplies of hand-grenades. Their objective was deliberate and their work was as methodical and thorough as German work always is. The university was founded in 1224 by Emperor Frederick II.

The soldiers went from room to room, thoroughly soaking floors, walls and furniture, including archives that went back for centuries. The part of the university chosen was that where the rector, the dean and wholly administrative personnel worked. That it happened to contain archives and valuable documents on law and letters was beside the point.

When everything was ready, the second stage began. The soldiers went from room to room, throwing in hand-grenades. At the same time, in an adjoining building a few hundred yards up the street, an even greater act of vandalism was being perpetrated. There was something apt about it, something symbolic of the whole German attitude. It did not matter to the Germans that they were destroying the accumulated wealth of centuries of scientific and philosophical thinking.

The rooms of the Royal Society contained some 200,000 books and manuscripts, from not only Italy but every country in the world. These books were stacked neatly and soberly on shelves along the walls; in the middle of the rooms were plain wooden tables with chairs. In several rooms there were paintings—some of them by Francesco Solimene of Nocera, the great baroque architect of the seventeenth century. These had been lent by the National Museum, but they will never be returned.

Like everything else they are now heaps of ashes that I plowed through today like so much sand on a beach. Here too the Germans used the same efficient technique—gallons and gallons of gasoline and then hand-grenades. . . .

Every one knows how difficult it is to burn one solid unopened book thoroughly until nothing remains but a heap of fine ashes. The Germans burned some 200,000 books in that way. Of course, the fire had to rage a long time and—also of course—the German thoroughness was going to see to it that nothing interfered with the fire.

They set it at 6 P.M. Sunday. At 9 P.M. Italian firefighting squads came up to extinguish the flames. German guards prevented them from entering the Via Mezzocannone. For three days those fires continued burning and for three days German guards kept Italians away.[4]

Slogging Forward

Withdrawing from Naples, the Germans retired to strong defenses on the steep northern bank of the Volturno River. Foggia had been captured by the Eighth Army on September 27th, and advances to Termoli on the Adriatic threatened the Germans on the Volturno. Commandos, landing north of Termoli, in the German rear, held out until the Eighth Army could rescue them ten days later.

With astonishing speed engineers repaired the wrecked port of Naples and supplies for the approaching battle of the Volturno streamed in. Artillery bombardment began on October 12, 1943. Ordinarily the Volturno is a mild stream, but that October it was swollen with rains. Muddy ground hampered ground operations. A number of bridgeheads were won from the coast to the Calore River and Capua, in the center, changed hands several times in heavy fighting. On October 16th the German flanks had been pushed back, and as they retired, they left behind them broken bridges, mines, and small knots of snipers to hold up the Allied advance.

This was the muddy season. Mud, quite as much as enemy action, prevented a rapid exploitation of successes in battle. Herbert L. Matthews draws a picture of fighting as it was now done by General Clark's men:

A battle is a long, slow process. . . . The picture you want to get into the mind is that of a plugging, filthy, hungry, utterly weary young man straggling half dazed and punch drunk, and still somehow getting up and over and beating the Germans, and hanging on against the enemy counterattacks.

That is what wins battles and wars, and only that. No doubt there is glory in it, but you had better not talk of glory to the G.I.'s who fought on La Difensa or La Maggiore. Glory is something that comes afterward. During the fight itself there are only fear, pain, discomfort and fatigue.

While the British were going through exactly similar experiences on the southern side of Monte Camino massif, Americans on the night of Dec. 2 and 3 began their assault on Difensa and Maggiore.

You must not think that even then the doughboy was fresh, rested and clean. That is one of the things which is inevitable—he goes into the fight already tired. In preparation for attack it has been necessary to build supply dumps as high up on the slopes as possible. That is terribly fatiguing work and it is heart-breaking when the enemy shoots shells into some of them and blows them sky high, as he is bound to do from time to time. . . .

Everybody must have read about the mud of Flanders in the last World War, and everybody is going to read about the mud of Italy in this war. No mud could be deeper or stickier or more persistent. On flat ground you plow disgustedly through it, often getting well over your ankles. But on a climb you do worse. You slide, slip, fall all over yourself and get covered with it from head to foot. The more tired you get the more you slither and fall, the dirtier you get and the harder it is to stand up again and plug on. . . .

New G.I. shoes get torn to pieces in a few days, and men walk with raw feet until they drop or somehow get another pair of shoes. In every evacuation or base hospital you will find cases which are due simply to fatigue, although they would take the form of insomnia, shell shock, broken arms and legs. So it is a great problem, and one that all armies fight as they do any illness. Wherever possible the troops are withdrawn to rest areas and replaced as soon as they get too fatigued.

Under normal conditions, for instances, the same soldiers would not be kept more than three days on the actual summits of front-line mountains. However, the conditions during a campaign like this are rarely normal. The Forty-fifth Division, for instance, fought from day to day on the Salerno beachhead for forty consecutive days without rest. The Third Division, which came in later, did fifty-seven consecutive days.[5]

The Eighth Army crossed the Sangro River on November 8th, the Moro River on December 9th. In November Clark's troops, fighting through extremely rough country, made their first attack on the Winter Line—a series of positions in depth located among the highest mountains of the Apennines. Ernie Pyle describes the mountain fighting:

The war in Italy was tough. The land and the weather were both against us. It rained and it rained. Vehicles bogged down and temporary bridges washed out. The country was shockingly beautiful, and just as shockingly hard to capture from the enemy. The hills rose to high ridges of almost solid rock. We couldn't go around them through the flat peaceful valleys, because the Germans were up there looking down upon us, and they would have let us have it. So we had to go up and over. A mere platoon of Germans, well dug in on a high, rock-spined hill, could hold out for a long time against tremendous onslaughts.

I know the folks back home were disappointed and puzzled by the slow progress in Italy. They wondered why we moved northward so imperceptibly. They were impatient for us to get to Rome. Well, I can say this—our troops were just as impatient for Rome. But on all sides I heard: "It never was this bad in Tunisia." "We ran into a new brand of Krauts over here." "If it would only stop raining." "Every day we don't advance is one day longer before we get home."

Our troops were living in almost inconceivable misery. The fertile black valleys were knee-deep in mud. Thousands of the men had not been dry for weeks. Other thousands lay at night in the high mountains with the temperature below freezing and the thin snow sifting over them. They dug into the stones and slept in little chasms and behind rocks and in half-caves. They lived like men of prehistoric times, and a club would have become them more than a machine gun. How they survived the dreadful winter at all was beyond us who had the opportunity of drier beds in the warmer valleys.

That the northward path was a tedious one was not the fault of our troops, nor of their direction either. It was the weather and the terrain and the weather again. If there had been no German fighting troops in Italy, if there had been merely German engineers to blow the bridges in the passes, if never a shot had been fired at all, our northward march would still have been slow. The country was so difficult that we formed a great deal of cavalry for use in the mountains. Each division had hundreds of horses and mules to carry supplies beyond the point where vehicles could go no farther. On beyond the mules' ability, mere men—American men—took it on their backs.

On my way to Italy, I flew across the Mediterranean in a cargo plane weighted down with more than a thousand pounds beyond the normal load. The cabin was filled with big pasteboard boxes which had been given priority above all other freight. In the boxes were packboards, hundreds of them, with which husky men would pack 100, even 150, pounds of food and ammunition, on their backs, to comrades high in those miserable mountains.

But we could take consolation from many things. The air was almost wholly ours. All day long Spitfires patrolled above our fighting troops like a half dozen policemen running up and down the street watching for bandits.

What's more, our artillery prevailed—and how! We were prodigal with ammunition against those rocky crags, and well we might be, for a $50 shell could often save ten lives in country like that. Little by little, the fiendish rain of explosives upon the hillsides softened the Germans. They always were impressed by and afraid of our artillery, and we had concentrations of it there that were demoralizing.

And lastly, no matter how cold the mountains, or how wet the snow, or how sticky the mud, it was just as miserable for the German soldier as for the American.

Our men were going to get to Rome, all right. There was no question about that. But the way was cruel. No one who had not seen that mud, those dark skies, those forbidding ridges and ghostlike clouds that unveiled and then quickly hid the enemy, had the right to be impatient with the progress along the road to Rome.

The mountain fighting went on week after dreary week. For a while I hung around with one of the mule-pack outfits. There was an average of one mule-packing outfit for every infantry battalion in the mountains. Some were run by Americans, some by Italian soldiers.

The pack outfit I was with supplied a battalion that was fighting on a bald, rocky ridge nearly four thousand feet high. That battalion fought constantly for ten days and nights, and when the men finally came down less than a third of them were left.

All through those terrible days every ounce of their supplies had to go up to them on the backs of mules and men. Mules took it the first third of the way. Men took it the last bitter two-thirds, because the trail was too steep even for mules.

The mule skinners of my outfit were Italian soldiers. The human packers were mostly American soldiers. The Italian mule skinners were from Sardinia. They belonged to a mountain artillery regiment, and thus were experienced in climbing and in handling mules. They were bivouacked in an olive grove alongside a highway at the foot of the mountain. They made no trips in the daytime, except in emergencies, because most of the trail was exposed to artillery fire. Supplies were brought into the olive grove by truck during the day, and stacked under trees. Just before dusk they would start loading the stuff onto mules. The Americans who actually managed the supply chain liked to get the mules loaded by dark, because if there was any shelling the Italians instantly disappeared and could never be found.

There were 155 skinners in this outfit and usually about eighty mules were used each night. Every mule had a man to lead it. About ten extra men went along to help get mules up if they fell, to repack any loads that came loose, and to unpack at the top. They could be up and back in less than three hours. Usually a skinner made just one trip a night, but sometimes in an emergency he made two.

On an average night the supplies would run something like this—85 cans of water, 100 cases of K ration, 10 cases of D ration, 10 miles of telephone wire, 25 cases of grenades and rifle and machine-gun ammunition, about 100 rounds of heavy mortar shells, 1 radio, 2 telephones, and 4 cases of first-aid packets and sulfa drugs. In addition, the packers would cram their pockets with cigarettes for the boys on top; also cans of Sterno, so they could heat some coffee once in a while.

Also, during that period, they took up more than five hundred of the heavy combat suits we were issuing to the troops to help keep them warm. They carried up cellophane gas capes for some of the men to use as sleeping bags, and they took extra socks for them too.

Mail was their most tragic cargo. Every night they would take up sacks of mail, and every night they'd bring a large portion of it back down—the recipients would have been killed or wounded the day their letters came.

On the long man-killing climb above the end of the mule trail they used anywhere from twenty to three hundred men a night. They rang in cooks, truck drivers, clerks, and anybody else they could lay their hands on. A lot of stuff was packed up by the fighting soldiers themselves. On a big night, when they were building up supplies for an attack, another battalion which was in reserve sent three hundred first-line combat troops to do the packing. The mule packs would leave the olive grove in bunches of twenty, starting just after dark. American soldiers were posted within shouting distance of each other all along the trail, to keep the Italians from getting lost in the dark.

Those guides—everybody who thought he was having a tough time in this war should know about them. They were men who had fought all through a long and bitter battle at the top of the mountain. For more than a week they had been far up there, perched behind rocks in the rain and cold, eating cold K rations, sleeping without blankets, scourged constantly with artillery and mortar shells, fighting and ducking and growing more and more weary, seeing their comrades wounded one by one and taken down the mountain.

Finally sickness and exhaustion overtook many of those who were left, so they were sent back down the mountain under their own power to report to the medics there and then go to a rest camp. It took most of them the better part of a day to get two-thirds of the way down, so sore were their feet and so weary their muscles.

And then—when actually in sight of their haven of rest and peace—they were stopped and pressed into guide service, because there just wasn't anybody else to do it. So there they stayed on the mountainside, for at least three additional days and nights that I know of, just lying miserably alongside the trail, shouting in the darkness to guide the mules.

They had no blankets to keep them warm, no beds but the rocks. And they did it without complaining. The human spirit is an astounding thing.[6]

Progress was slow all along the front. On December 6th newly formed units of liberated Italy came up to fight in the front lines against their former Axis partner. Clark's men cleared out the Camino hills early in December, then consolidated their positions for a drive on the Winter Line in mid-January. They broke this, only to run into a new German defense system south of Rome—the Gustav Line. There they were halted for the remainder of the winter. If progress seemed slow, there was some satisfaction in holding down over twenty Axis divisions, including some of Germany's best troops, that might otherwise have been thrown into the crumbling Russian front.

Cassino and Anzio

Twice during the first three months of 1944 the Fifth Army tried to break the Gustav Line and capture Rome. These two attacks were connected. A landing on the west coast of Nettuno and Anzio, thirty-six miles south of Rome, was intended to cut German communications and turn the flank of the Gustav Line. Attacks through the middle of the Line at Cassino were to carry through to join the Anzio beach-head and sweep on to Rome.

Three divisions landed at Nettuno and Anzio on January 22, 1944. The Germans, preoccupied at Cassino, were taken by surprise and quick Allied advances carried through Aprilia before gathering German resistance stopped the advance. At this stage three Axis divisions, including Italian Fascists, still held the heights commanding the beach-head. Ernie Pyle wrote of life on the Anzio beach-head:

On the beachhead every inch of our territory was under German artillery fire. There was no rear area that was immune, as in most battle zones. They could reach us with their 88s, and they used everything from that on up.

I don't mean to suggest that they kept every foot of our territory drenched with shells all the time, for they certainly didn't. They were short of ammunition, for one thing. But they could reach us, and we never knew

where they would shoot next. A man was just as liable to get hit standing
in the doorway of the villa where he slept at night as he was in a command
post five miles out in the field.

Some days they shelled us hard, and some days hours would go by
without a single shell coming over. Yet nobody was wholly safe, and anybody who said he had been around Anzio two days without having a shell
hit within a hundred yards of him was just bragging.

People who knew the sounds of warfare intimately were puzzled and
irritated by the sounds on Anzio. For some reason, we couldn't tell anything about anything. The Germans shot shells of half a dozen sizes, each
of which made a different sound on exploding. We couldn't gauge distance at all. One shell might land within our block and sound not much
louder than a shotgun. Another landing a quarter-mile away made the
earth tremble, and started our hearts pounding.

We couldn't gauge direction, either. The 88 that hit within twenty yards
of us didn't make much noise. I would have sworn it was two hundred
yards away and in the opposite direction.

Sometimes we heard them coming, and sometimes we didn't. Sometimes we heard the shell whine after we heard it explode. Sometimes we
heard it whine and it never exploded. Sometimes the house trembled and
shook and we heard no explosion at all.

But one thing I found there was just the same as anywhere else—that
same old weakness in the joints when they got to landing close. I had been
weak all over Tunisia and Sicily, and in parts of Italy, and I got weaker
than ever in Anzio.

When the German raiders came over at night, and the sky lighted up
with flares bright as day, and ack-ack guns set up a turmoil and pretty soon
a man heard and felt the terrible power of exploding bombs—well, his
elbows got flabby and he breathed in little short jerks, and his chest felt
empty, and he was too excited to do anything but hope. . . .

The land of the Anzio beachhead is flat, and our soldiers felt strange
and naked with no rocks to take cover behind, no mountains to provide
slopes for protection. It was a new kind of warfare for us. Distances were
short, and space was confined. The whole beachhead was the front line, so
small that we could stand on high ground in the middle of it and see clear
around the thing. That's the truth, and it was no picnic feeling either.

Back in the days of desert fighting around Tebessa, the forward eche-
lons of the corps staff and most of the hospitals were usually more than
eighty miles back of the fighting. At Anzio everybody was right in it together. From the rear to the front was less than half an hour's drive, and
often the front was quieter than the rear.

Hospitals were not immune from shellfire and bombing. The unro-
mantic finance officer counting out his money in a requisitioned building
was hardly more safe than the company commander ten miles ahead of
him. And the table waiter in the rear echelon mess got blown off his feet
in a manner quite contrary to the Hoyle rules of warfare.

Though the beachhead land was flat, it did have some rise and fall to it;
it was flat in a western Indiana way—not the billiard-table flatness of the
country around Amarillo, Texas, for example. A person would have to go
halfway across the beachhead area from the sea before the other half of it

came into view. Rises of a few score feet, and little mounds and gullies, and groves of trees cut up the land. There were a lot of little places where a few individuals could take cover from fire. The point is that the general flatness forbade whole armies taking cover. . . .

Space was at a premium. Never had I seen a war zone so crowded. Of course, men weren't standing shoulder to shoulder, but I suppose the most indiscriminate shell dropped at any point on the beachhead would have landed not more than two hundred yards from somebody. And the average shell found thousands within hearing distance of its explosion. If a plane went down in No Man's Land, more than half the troops on the beachhead could see it fall.[7]

As this constant shelling went on, powerful German counter-attacks to the north took Aprilia. British tanks, American flank attacks, naval fire, and a tremendous air bombardment were hurriedly concentrated and, in desperate fighting, the German offensive was checked. But the Allies could not break through, and a perimeter defense—a triangle with a shore base of some 19 miles and reaching inland about 15 miles—was set up. There, in March 1944, the Allied force was stalled.

Meanwhile, some of the fiercest fighting of the war was going on for the old monastery town of Cassino fifty miles to the south. Late in January the U.S. 34th Division had managed to breach the north end of the Gustav Line and the French Corps simultaneously captured key hills east of Mount Cairo, the lofty mountain dominating the Cassino area.

The first attack on Cassino was launched from the north on February 1st. The approaches to the town were well defended. Marshal Kesselring, commander of the German forces, had an estimated 100,000 men at his disposal, and elaborate fortifications, including innumerable mines of various types, had been constructed to supplement the natural defenses of the place.

In twelve days hills to the north and northwest of the famous Hill 516—on which stood the ancient Benedictine Monastery—were taken. Although the Monastery itself was partially destroyed in a bombing raid of February 15th, 1944, the German defenders drove off all attempts to capture it.

Early in February the New Zealand Corps, cream of the Eighth Army, together with the 4th Indian Division moved up to relieve the tired II Corps of the Fifth Army. Their job was to capture the town of Cassino itself. All through February these expert troops jabbed and drove at Cassino. W. F. Shadel describes the close fighting in the town from the viewpoint of a rifleman:

With Company I in one of the few captured houses was Private Fred Ratliffe, a soldier qualified with both the M1 and the carbine. Ratliffe found the carbine especially useful in snap shooting from windows. "We spent the first night barricading and building up shelters on the first floor out of rubble," he said. "We could hear Jerry moving in the houses just across the street. There were just five of us and we were pretty scared."

On the second day Ratliffe spotted a Heinie sneaking along a wall. He could just see the German's helmet above the wall but waited until he reached an opening where he made a bigger target. "I got off one quick shot and know I hit him, 'cause a couple other Jerries reached out to pull him back, and I got one of them, too. . . ."

Ratliffe, his company commander said, would stand at the side of the window until he saw a target and then snap his rifle to his shoulder, fire and duck back into the shadows. The lieutenant also told how, when bazookas were brought up to the house, Ratliffe, although he had never fired a bazooka before, got off some shots at a house that contained machine guns.

Another private, Wayne C. Bryan was a member of a 60 mm. mortar crew until more help was needed in Cassino. . . . Joining Company I in town, Bryan used an M1 from the windows. "When we started cleaning out the square and the Jerries started running back, I could lean right out the window and fire. I got quite a few shots and know I hit two. One of them almost reached the far side of the square but I dropped him. That was at about 200 yards. Three of us in that house gave as much covering fire as we could. The M1 is lots better than the carbine for that kind of work."

Out of the rubble from the broken-down walls Sergeant S. Bannon of Company K made a bunker for protection against more shelling. Then he stuck the muzzle of his BAR through an opening in the wall made by one of the German bazookas. Once he put a burst into a doorway across the street and saw a shadow go down. Again, a German in a house not more than fifty feet away started firing rifle grenades from a window. The German exposed himself enough to give Bannon a shot, and that was the end of the rifle grenadier.

One costly assault job was against an old schoolhouse. Three even costlier ones were against the jail. Not only was the jail heavily fortified but all avenues leading to it were covered by machine guns. In these assaults we often learned the cost of leadership—the loss of noncoms and officers out in front leading their groups on such attacks. In the first strike at the jail, one officer, new to his company, led a small group of seventeen men and succeeded in getting into one room with three of his men before the rest were cut off by machine-gun fire. But the next time he led, he was killed.

In the second attempt at the jail, Lieutenant X led twelve men to the left while another Lieutenant took fifteen to the right. Those on the left got four men across the road before the others were cut off by machine-gun fire. Those on the right worked along a wall but could go no farther because of enfilading fire. Two days later in a night attack five men gained one room of the jail. Still later, a part of one battalion took over the jail and a few adjoining houses.

Sergeant E. Drewis, a machine-gunner with Company L, was one of the best fighters at Cassino. Quiet, shy, none too willing to go into the details of his experiences, he gave us a modest account. But we learned later from his lieutenant that Drewis and another sergeant, J. Gaizzetti, tackled a machine-gun nest in some bunkers set up in an open space across a drainage ditch which covered the approach to the jail. Sneaking along the ditch, then rushing to within hand-grenade distance, they threw grenades and followed up with rifle fire. After cleaning up that job, these two sergeants got into a broken-down house, found two half-tracks parked in the court, threw grenades into them, set them afire, and then rejoined their company.

Sergeant Drewis was in a hot spot while giving supporting fire to those of his company who were making the assaults on the jail. In the ten days his machine gun faced the jail across the street, the house he was in had twenty-five direct hits. He made a pillbox for himself, however, out of timber and rubble, and the crumbling walls only piled up for his protection.

One morning a sergeant led six men in an attack on a house. They sneaked along a wall, dashed across the street and threw grenades into the house. Four of them got inside. The sergeant was the first man in and turned his tommy gun on one Jerry who showed fight. Another was taken prisoner, but then the Americans found themselves cut off. Unwilling to give up their positions they stayed where they were two days without supplies. When they were finally pulled out with their prisoner, they were then put into the attack of Company L on the jail.

These six with some nine other men, started to attack from the left. The group ran into a withering fire, hit the irrigation ditch alongside, then ducked back to the house they had started from. Soon after, a direct hit on a central beam overhead collapsed the entire second floor and buried ten of the group.

This is a sample of the first days in Cassino. From interviews with officers and men, one gets an idea of the fighting, of the endless days of waiting and watching, of the frequent desperate rushes to take more houses. Everyone talks about the clever defense of the Boche. All of them spoke of the devilish booby trap installations. One engineer officer who makes a specialty of the things told us he had found more than fifty different varieties.[8]

The New Zealand Corps managed to take roughly one third of Cassino, but could gain no more. The drive to take the rest of the city was postponed to March. In March a terrific aerial bombardment by some 500 planes practically levelled Cassino, yet when the New Zealanders tried to inch forward they found roads so cratered and choked with debris that tanks could not be used. Fanatical members of the German 1st Parachute Division, who had learned the lesson of Stalingrad, under direct orders from Hitler to hold at all costs, stopped the drive. The Indian troops still were not able to take the Monastery perched atop Hill 516. Again, on March 23rd, General Alexander called the battle off. The Gustav Line had held through the winter.

Rome and Florence

During the lull in fighting at Cassino Lieutenant-General Ira C. Eaker's Mediterranean Air Force was active. In the month of April, 1944, it flew 21,000 sorties, systematically wrecking enemy rail yards as far north as Florence. This was the same air force that in the course of a year's bombing from Africa and Italy had destroyed three-quarters of the output of Rumania's huge oil fields at Ploesti. While the army rested and the air arm plagued communications far up the peninsula, enormous preparations were made for smashing the Gustav Line in the spring.

On May 11th, the Fifth and Eighth Armies plunged forward. Opposing them were 25 divisions. Quickly, within a week, Clark's men drove through 12 miles to the Hitler Line. Cassino was encircled by May 17th and was captured. The Anzio garrison had meanwhile burst from their confines on May 23 and in wild fighting at Cisterna had repelled seven German counter-attacks and taken the town. They were joined in this operation by the Fifth Army which came up the west coast. The German 14th Army, retreating from Cisterna, joined the famed Hermann Goering Division to protect the Alban Hills guarding the roads to Rome. How Velletri, in the heart of the Hills, was captured is told by Eric Sevareid:

The City of Velletri lay white and lovely, like a brooch of old gold, strung upon the highway which held the town nestled in the breast of the Alban Hills. Velletri faces to the south; it is an ancient town, and Nero once sent his favorite mistress into exile there, but the tired and dirty men of the American Thirty-sixth Division didn't know about that and they wouldn't have cared. They had been dug in the vineyards before the town for several days, harassed by snipers and machine guns around them and eighty-eights from the German batteries above Velletri. They had to take the town somehow, they had to break the highway-railway defense belt here because these slopes formed the last German breastworks defending Rome.

They were getting nowhere very fast; nor was the Thirty-fourth, faced with the same problem just on their left. Further to the left, the First Armored was being badly shot up trying to get around the hills, and over to the right the Third and the Special Service "Commando" force were moving very slowly upon Valmontone in their attempt to skirt the hills on that side. Somehow, we *had* to take the heights dominating this semicircle of futility.

Early on May 31st we learned back at Anzio that a totally unexpected thing had occurred, that two regiments of the Thirty-sixth had silently pulled back from their frontal assault, had circled around to the right by side roads and had climbed the two-thousand-foot height behind Velletri before the Germans were aware of it. It was a gamble: If the Germans could close their lines again, these men might be lost. If not, we had surely turned the key in the lock of the great door barring us from the Roman plains and the capital. . . .

Another quarter-mile and we could go no further on the highway. Velletri lay only another thousand yards or so to the west. Machine guns were sounding again and it was sure death to proceed. Here now was the cut-off, a narrow "jeepable" trail, mounting sharply between high banks. . . . We began the upward hike, rounded a bend and found *tanks* chugging up, their massive breadth plugging the whole cut, scrapping down dirt and stones from the banks.

Here you had it; this was much of the explanation why the great natural barriers of Italy could never stop the Americans. I think few but Americans would dream of attempting this and none but American army engineers could ever make it possible. For, scrambling around the tanks, we found the ubiquitous bulldozer, simply carving the trail into a road, roaring and rearing its ponderous way at a forty-degree angle upwards.

The men themselves, bearded, silent with exhaustion, swung their shovels through the loose dirt and pitched it over the banks. . . .

We pulled away from the engineers and found ourselves now with a rifle company of a regiment which I had last visited in the fields before Velletri. They were completing the marvelous feat, their comrades ahead having already reached the crest. They had been pulled out from their old position at nightfall, gone a short way by truck, then had made a ten-mile hike around Velletri and gone straight up the mountain, carrying their heavy mortar shells in their bare hands, clutching them to their stomachs.

The weighty metal boxes of rifle ammunition they strapped to their backs and they had climbed all night, silently, like Indians, forbidden by their general to have a cartridge in the chamber of their guns. He would permit no firing, to avoid alerting the Germans. Only a grenade could be used, if absolutely necessary, for the Germans would easily mistake that for a mortar shell and remain ignorant of its origin. Later, we learned the Germans believed two companies had made the infiltration, not two regiments. . . .

In the night, the counter-attack came and failed. Our boys clung to the heights and fired down upon the desperate Germans inside Velletri. In the morning General Walker, his tanks and men rushed the town, entering upon the highway. Lieutenant Colonel Reese insisted upon walking ahead of the tanks and it was a shell that killed him. . . .

With Velletri gone, the Alban Hill defense line was irreparably penetrated and our Divisions smashed into the disorganized Germans around to the left, down Highway Six to the right—Rome lay shimmering and undefendable straight ahead.[9]

Two days later, on June 4, the Allies entered Rome, and all Christendom rejoiced that the Holy City had been spared the kind of fighting that other capitals—Warsaw, Moscow, Belgrade—had known. Said President Roosevelt: "The first of the Axis capitals is now in our hands. One up and two to go. It is perhaps significant that the first of these capitals to fall should have the longest history of all." And Churchill called it "a memorable and glorious event." As indeed it was.

Defeat on the outskirts of Rome placed the Germans in a strategically vulnerable position. They fell back, quickly and in good order, to defenses 150 miles north, along the Arno River. All through June and July Allied forces followed them, delayed by mines, mud, lengthening supply lines, their air forces destroying hundreds of planes and exacting a heavy toll of supplies.

The Germans made no real attempt to check the advance. Siena was occupied on July 3rd. Leghorn fell after a stiff battle on July 19th and on the same day Polish troops captured Ancona on the Adriatic. British troops, advancing up central Italy over difficult terrain, took Perugia in June. On July 16th they passed around both sides of Lake Trasimeno, taking Arezzo, and opening up the way to Florence. 75,000 German troops failed to halt the British advance, and patrols reached Florence on August 4th. The main body of the Eighth Army came up to outflank pockets of resistance in the northern half of Florence. In the city itself every bridge spanning the Arno was destroyed except for Ponte Vecchio. In the old Tuscan art center heavy street fighting wrought enormous damage to monuments of art. American AMG units did wonderful work in preventing further damage to art in practically every captured Italian city, but the permanent loss of the artistic world is heavy.

The Gothic Line

City by city the Allied armies moved forward. Gains were not dramatic, and were won with difficulty. In September, 1944, Pisa, Lucca, Prato, and Rimini were taken. Landings on islands off the Dalmation coast blocked a possible German escape route from the Balkans. In the mountains north of Florence the Fifth Army outflanked the Futa Pass and drove within fifteen miles of Bologna.

The Eighth Army, using Britons, Canadians, Poles, and Indians, in September punched through the powerful Gothic Line stretching across Italy north of Florence and Pisa. Martha Gellhorn describes the final push before winter weather made the front comparatively inactive:

The great Gothic Line, which the Germans have used as a threat ever since the Hitler Line was broken, would, under normal circumstances, be a lovely range of the Apennines. In this clear and dreaming weather that is the end of summer, the hills curve up into a water-blue sky: in the hot windless night you see the very hills only as a soft, rounded darkness under the moon. Along the Via Emilia, the road that borders the base of these hills, the Germans dynamited every village into shapeless brick rubble so that they could have a clear line of fire. In front of the flattened villages they dug their long canal to trap tanks. In front of the tank trap they cut all the trees. Among the felled trees and in the gravel bed and the low water of the Foglia River, they laid down barbed wire and they sowed their never-ending mines, the crude little wooden boxes, the small rusty tin cans, the flat metal pancakes which are the simplest and deadliest weapons in Italy.

On the range of hills that is the actual Gothic Line, the Germans built concrete machine-gun pillboxes which encircle the hills and dominate all approaches. They sank the turrets of tanks, with their long, thin snout-ended 88-mm. guns, in camouflaged pits so that nothing on wheels or tracks could pass their way. They mined some more. They turned the beautiful hills into a mountain trap four miles deep where every foot of our advance could be met with concentrated fire. . . .

It was the Canadians who broke into this line on the Adriatic side by finding a soft place and going through. It makes me ashamed to write that sentence because there is no soft place where there are mines and no soft place where there are Spandaus and no soft place where there are 88-mm. guns, and if you have seen one tank burn on a hillside you will never believe that anything is soft again. But, relatively speaking, this spot was soft, or at any rate the Canadians made it soft and they got across the mined river and past the dynamited villages and over the asphalt road and up into the hills and from then on they poured men and tanks into the gap and they gouged the German positions with artillery fire and they called in the Desert Air Force to bomb it and in two days they had come out on the other side of the Gothic Line at the coast of the Adriatic. But before that, many things had happened.

First of all, the main body of the Eighth Army moved from the center of Italy to the Adriatic coast in three days' time, and the Germans did not know it. That sounds very easy, too, written like that. What it meant was that for three days and three nights the weaving lateral roads across the Apennines and the great highways that make a deep V south from Florence and back up to Ancona were crowded with such traffic as most of us have never seen before.

Trucks and armored cars and tanks and weapon carriers and guns and jeeps and motorcycles and ambulances packed the roads, and it was not at all unusual to spend four hours going twenty miles. The roads were ground to powder by this traffic, and the dust lay in drifts a foot thick and whenever you could get up a little speed the dust boiled like water under the wheels. . . .

So this enormous army ground its way across Italy and took up positions on a front thirteen miles long. The Eighth Army, which was now ready to attack the last German fortified line outside the Siegfried Line, had fought its way to these mountains from the Egyptian border. In two years since El Alamein, the Eighth Army had advanced across Africa through Sicily and up the peninsula of Italy. And all these men of how many races and nationalities felt that this was the last push and after this they would go home.

We watched the battle for the Gothic Line from a hill opposite, sitting in a batch of thistles and staring through binoculars. Our tanks looked like brown beetles; they scurried up a hill, streamed across the horizon and dipped out of sight. Suddenly a tank flamed four times in great flames, and other tanks rolled down from the sky line seeking cover in the folds of the hill. The Desert Air Force planes, which cavort around the sky like a school of minnows, were signaled to bomb a loaf-shaped hill called Monte Lura. Monte Lura went up in towering waves of brownish smoke and dirt. Our artillery dug into the Gothic Line so that everywhere cotton bolls of smoke flowered on the slopes. Our own air bursts now rained steel fragments over the German positions on Monte Lura. . . .

All that day and the next the noise of our own guns was physically painful. . . .

Later—but I don't remember when, because time got very confused—we crossed the Foglia River and drove up the road our tanks had taken. . . . An American Sherman, once manned by an English crew, lay near a farmhouse: across the road a German Tiger tank was burned and its entire rear end had been blown off. The Sherman had received an 88 shell through its turret. Inside the turret were plastered pieces of flesh and much blood. Outside the Tiger, the body of a German lay with straw covering everything except the two black clawlike hands, the swollen blood-caked head and the twisted feet.... You cannot note everything that happens during a battle; you cannot even see what happens and often you cannot understand it.... A battle is a jigsaw puzzle of fighting men, bewildered, terrified civilians, noise, smells, jokes, pain, fear, unfinished conversations and high explosive....

Historians will think about this campaign far better than we can who have seen it. The historians will note that in the first year of the Italian campaign, in 365 days of steady fighting, the Allied armies advanced 315 miles. They will note this with admiration because it is the first time in history that any armies have invaded Italy from the south and fought up the endless mountain ranges toward the Alps. Historians will be able to explain with authority what it meant to break three fortified lines attacking up mountains, and the historians will also describe how Italy became a giant mine field and that no weapon is uglier, for it waits in silence, and it can kill any day, not only on the day of battle.

But all we know who are here is that the Gothic Line is cracked and that it is the last line. Soon our armored divisions will break into the Lombardy plain and then at last the end of this long Italian campaign will become a fact, not a dream. The weather is lovely and no one wants to think of what men must still die and what men must still be wounded in the fighting before peace comes.[10]

October came, bringing with it bad weather, before the Allied armies had progressed much beyond the Gothic Line. The *New York Times* pictured conditions in Italy as winter took over:

American and British troops in northern Italy moved slowly . . . in their drive for Bologna and the rich industrial Po Valley. There were several factors to explain the slow Allied progress. Factor No. 1 was the weather. Alternating rainy and clear days prevented the Allies from using their superior air power effectively, and heavy rain had turned the marshy, canal-webbed countryside on the eastern end of the line into a morass, had bogged down the troops inching their way through narrow mountain passes in the center of the line.

A second factor was the fury with which the Germans were resisting. Apparently the Germans were fighting for time—time to strip the industrial north of Italy of every piece of equipment that could be moved back to the Reich. An Italian Resistance Front communiqué confirmed that the Nazis were looting Italian factories in the north to insure that they would be of no use to the Partisans or the Allies. German resistance was spurred, also, by the real danger that if the Allies succeeded in getting through to the great plain of northern Italy the situation for the whole German Army there would become desperate since their escape routes would be endangered.

In any case, progress was slow and the pelting cold Italian rain combined with the snarling German machine-gun fire to make life none too cheerful for the Allied troops in the line. Thirteen months after storming ashore on the beaches of Salerno, they still had a big job before them.[11]

10

FROM THE VOLGA TO
THE ODER

Russia's Mounting Strength

AFTER STALINGRAD IT was all ebb-tide for the Germans. In part this was because Russia has inflicted upon the German army irreparable losses of manpower, tanks, planes, and military equipment. In part it was because Germany was now fighting a two-front—and preparing for a three-front—war, and because incessant bombing was seriously cutting into her production. But in part, too, it was because Russia, notwithstanding the cruel losses which she had suffered during the first eighteen months of the war, was growing steadily stronger. New armies were being raised, new generals were forging to the front, new arms and equipment were coming off her production lines, and pouring in from Britain and the United States.

Wendell Willkie, who visited Russia on his famous round-the-world tour, looked over one of the new Russian aviation plants and was impressed with its size and efficiency:

I spent one entire day looking at a Soviet aviation plant. I saw other factories in Russia, candy factories, munition factories, foundries, canneries, and power plants. But this aviation plant, now located outside of Moscow, remains most vivid in my memory.

It was a big place. My guess would be that some 30,000 workers were running three shifts and that they were making a very presentable number of airplanes every day. . . .

American aviation experts were with me on this inspection, and they confirmed my impression that the planes we saw wheeled from the end of the assembly line and tested on an airfield next to the factory were good planes. And, peculiarly enough, they pronounced the armored protection for the pilots the best of any they knew on any plane anywhere in the world. I am no aviation expert, but I have inspected a good many factories in my life. I kept my eyes open, and I think my report is fair.

Parts of the manufacturing process were crudely organized. The wings of the Stormovik are made of plywood, compressed under steam pressure, and then covered with canvas. The woodworking shops seemed to me to rely too much on hand labor, and their product showed it. Also, some of the electrical and plating shops were on the primitive side.

With these exceptions, the plant would compare favorably in output and efficiency with any I have ever seen. I walked through shop after shop of lathes and punching presses. I saw machine tools assembled from all over the world, their trade-names showing they came from Chemnitz, from Skoda, from Sheffield, from Cincinnati, from Sverdlovsk, from Antwerp. They were being efficiently used.

More than thirty-five per cent of the labor in the plant was done by women. Among the workers we saw boys not more than ten years old, all dressed in blue blouses and looking like apprentice students, even though the officials of the factory pulled no punches in admitting that the children work, in many of the shops, the full sixty-six-hour week worked by the adults. Many of the boys were doing skilled jobs on lathes, and seemed to be doing them extremely well.

On the whole, the plant seemed to us Americans to be overstaffed. There were more workers than would be found in a comparable American factory. But hanging over every third or fourth machine was a special sign, indicating that its worker was a "Stakhanovite," pledged to overfulfill his or her norm of production. . . . The walls of the factory carried fresh and obviously honored lists of those workers and those shops which were leading in what was apparently a ceaseless competition for more and better output. A fair conclusion would be that this extra incentive, which was apparent in the conversation of any worker we stopped to talk to at random, made up for a large part, but not all, of the handicap of relative lack of skill.

The productivity of each individual worker was lower than in the United States. Russian officials admitted this to me freely. Until they can change this by education and training, they explained, they must offset it by putting great emphasis on patriotic drives for output and by recruiting all the labor power, even that of children and old women, that they can find. Meanwhile, and there was nothing done with mirrors here, we could see the planes leaving the cavernous doors of the final assembly unit, testing their machine guns and cannon on a target range, and then taking to the air over our heads.[1]

The new Russian planes were good, especially the Stormoviks—heavily armored "ground strafers" equipped with rocket bombs effective against tanks. The new Russian tanks were powerful and mounted heavy guns.

Indeed the Red Army was steadily growing in power and it was, in the last analysis, the Red Army—and the Russian people—who were responsible for victory, not just a particular army, a particular weapon, the weather, Allied aid, or other subordinate factors. Lieutenant-Colonel Paul

W. Thompson, one of the most penetrating of all military historians, gives us a portrait of the Red soldier:

The most important piece of war material in the world today is the Russian private soldier—he of whom, praise the Lord, there are so many. What kind of fellow is this individual whose uncompromising resistance, like that of the Spaniard of Napoleon's day, has put the first chink in the armor of the would-be world-conqueror?

Der Russe, as the enemy calls him, is perhaps best described by that very enemy. After all, who could know him better? And the Germans have described him in countless tirades of unconscious praise and in an occasional grudging paean of reluctant acknowledgement. . . .

A German estimate of the Soviet fighting man is succinctly expressed in the following passage from an official training manual on the subject of combat in the woods:

"The Russian takes fullest advantage of his extraordinary sense of orientation, his mastery of camouflage, his willingness to engage in close combat. He never surrenders, even when the woods are surrounded and he is under heavy fire. He often leaves behind observers cleverly installed in trees, to direct artillery fire by radio, even when they themselves are endangered by that fire."

The Germans pride themselves on being "soldiers of iron"; but every once in a while one of the iron men finds himself looking in annoyed wonder on the iron in the make-up of the Russian. For instance, the German sergeant who presents, in *Deutsche Algemeine Zeitung,* a vignette from life in a bunker on the frozen winter front:

"In the burned-out derelict tanks scattered over no-man's-land there sit Russian snipers with telescopic sights, rifles against shoulders, waiting for one of us to show himself. Day and night and again day. There they sit and wait with the nervelessness and stubbornness that only the Russian has. Their pockets are full of grain, there is an occasional bottle of vodka, and by each is a sack of ammunition. So they sit and wait, Godforsaken—but deadly dangerous—behind two inches of steel in no-man's-land."

Things like this make the Nazi "iron men" wish for the good old days of the *Blitzkrieg.*

Another soldier-writer expounding in the staid columns of the military weekly, *Militärwochenblatt,* concludes that *der Russe* is not a normal being, worse luck, but is "something from without this world," possessed of "a strong, highly developed animal instinct," which in some unexplained way makes him "insensitive to freezing weather, imperturbable to pain and immune to suffering." Why else would the Russian "always attack, no matter what the odds are against him?" Any good old-line German knows that you only attack when you can bring overwhelming forces to bear.

These very tough guys are extremely handy with the strategy of war, too. When in 1941 invaders reached the area east of Leningrad, they found there fortifications *facing east.* Someone had anticipated the course of events, and had taken care to insure that there would be no parade into Leningrad from the rear. The German officer who reports this does so in tones of infinite disgust. This, he says in effect, is clearly a case of dirty pool, for the Russians must have begun work on the fortifications even before the start of the invasion. Such foresight, employed against the Germans, is unpardonable. . . .

Another thorn in the side of the German is the resolute industry of the Soviet soldier. He goes out of his way to keep busy, and is likely to "tear in and build a road in a location where there is no prospect of immediate action," while the Nazi soldiers "as the campaign drags on and on, are inclined to laziness." *Gott im Himmel!*

One German soldier, writing from the battlefront, compares the Russian to an unnamed "animal in South America which can burrow out of sight in the hard earth on the turn of a hand. At this operation, digging in, the Russian is our superior." The same exceptional ingenuity at improvisation led him to devise the Molotov cocktail from an empty vodka bottle, gasoline siphoned from a crippled tank, and cotton batting from his own quilted uniform. The outcome was an effective missile used to ignite enemy tanks and trucks. The Nazi commentator urges his *Kameraden* "to keep awake and on their toes—or to prepare for sudden death. *Der Russe* is likely to appear anywhere, materializing almost out of the thin air."

Another Russian characteristic—infinite patience even in the face of freezing weather—has been demonstrated on a thousand fields, but nowhere to better advantage than in the capture of a village during the 1941 winter counter-offensive from Moscow. The Soviet infantry actually managed to approach to within hand-grenade distance of this point across treeless, snow-covered plains, *undetected by the numerous German outposts*. How? Clad in white and with weapons wrapped in white, the Russians had confined their movements to succeeding nights. Before each dawn, they would carefully smooth over their tracks and burrow into the snow. There, under the very eyes of the German look-outs, they would lie in their burrows, *motionless all day long*. Come the night, they would pursue again the slow, silent approach to the town. Finally, at the zero dawn, the assault was launched from close quarters. The surprise was complete and the Germans once more took the count. . . .

There we have a picture of *der Russe* sketched by those who ought to know—his enemies. He is strong and tough, "insensitive to weather and terrain." He is aggressive, "forever attacking." He is resourceful and alert, and it is disastrous to make a mistake in his presence. He is industrious, "working continuously on his positions." He is brave and steadfast, "always choosing to fight it out." He is well armed, well led, and he is fighting under the best of strategy.[2]

From Murmansk to Persia

From Britain and the United States, meantime, came a steadily mounting stream of supplies. As soon as Germany attacked Russia, Britain sent over some token aid, and thereafter she gave generously of her own limited production. Lend-lease had been extended to Russia early in the war, and eventually its contribution was tremendous. Altogether, to January 1944, the United States sent Russia under lend-lease 7,800 planes, 4,700 tanks and tank destroyers, 170,000 trucks, millions of boots and shoes, over a million tons of steel and two and a quarter million tons of food.

It was one thing to allot supplies to hard-pressed Russia; it was another to get them there. There were three main supply routes: the Arctic Sea route to Murmansk, constantly harassed by German bombers and warships; the long route to the Persian Gulf and up through Persia to the Caspian Sea; and the Pacific route from the western coast to Siberia. Most dangerous of all was the Murmansk route. Robert Carse tells what happened to him when he went with a British convoy to Murmansk:

We stood north out to sea. Once more the tightening of nerves took place as we realized that along this coast the U-boats harried almost every ship and convoy. But danger had become for us monotonous. Every moment, every second outside port we might get it, so a man could only do his best and wait it out, try to work the ship through.

We came one day into another port. This was no place like our anchorage in the Clyde and was used only for the purposes of war. More ammunition was brought out to us for our machine guns, and we cleared and inspected our P.A.C. rockets, the ingenious and skillful device by which, through rocket fire, 500 feet of piano wire is suspended above the ship between two small parachutes to slice the wing right off a diving Nazi plane or wind and wind, snarling around his propeller blades. On our 'midships and after decks also were huge smoke-screen cans which would protect us from the enemy we were very soon to meet. . . .

From that port, again in convoy, we ran North. There was talk of the *Tirpitz* again, and of the *Admiral Scheer*, but we held to our course and came in good order up to that island which is one huge, smoky mountain thrusting from the fog swirl and surf rush of the sea. One more time we went to anchor, back in the tremendous depths of the harbor.

Our own bombers and patrol planes were overhead there. Our own battle wagons, cruisers, and destroyers and submarines came and went out again in ceaseless operation. We watched them, learning, studying, for we were with the Navy now, would fight with it. On the bleak shore, where the shaggy little Iceland ponies ran among the sod-walled houses and the humped khaki shapes of the fabricated huts, our Army jeeps jumped the ruts of the roads, and we could hear the racketing of machine-gun fire on the ranges; at night, sometimes see the enormous white lances of the Marine Corps anti-aircraft searchlights in the sky, hear a salvo burst in practice fire. . . .

Fog closed some hours after that, bringing obscurity and a kind of fulginous darkness. Allen and I were in our bunks in our room at two-thirty when blond Olë and "Sensation," the wild-eyed ordinary, came running to the door. "Get up on deck," they said, the same note of shock and horror in their voices. "The *So-and-So* has just got it. She's sinking."

We grabbed our shoes and coats and ran for deck. The *So-and-So* was over on our starboard hand, two columns away from us to the inboard. Fog was close about her, dimming her, but her hull still showed black against the gray shoulders of the sea.

That hull was in two pieces. She had broken in half 'midships, was sinking. The explosion we had dully heard as we ran up the companion ladder was her cargo of T.N.T., and she carried a lot of the stuff. Vapor in a low and white and then broad and high cloud rose from her as her cylinder tops and boilers gave.

She sank, and those two black halves went into the sea like swiftly withdrawn fingers. We stood there, the wind hard against us, the fog clammy on our faces and coat collars, the deck slightly areel under us, but firm, shaken only by the strong turning of our screw. We didn't speak. The horror and the sorrow were too great. They were dead, and we were alive, and our brains could take no more. . . .

During the fog, after the *So-and-So* had got it, the cruisers had pulled out of the convoy. Warning had been received by them that German surface raiders were out, and it was their task to find them. So that day and in all the rest of the battle we fought without the great aid of the cruisers' gunfire.

Raid after raid was made on us. The Messerschmitts were back, the jobs that had been on us yesterday and the same type that had done so much damage to London and the other cities in the Battle of Britain. But today, too, we had the Heinkel 111 K's, the twin-motored medium bombers that here were being used as aerial torpedo carriers.

They slanted down from the low ceiling at us through the snow and the sleet, and we hardly had our guns on them before they'd released their torpedoes and were up and away again. Those torpedoes they carried had a 21-inch warhead and weighed half a ton. In the air, they held the speed of the plane, 274 knots an hour. In the water, they made a speed of 35 knots, were fired from an approximate distance of 500 yards.

Our Commodore had warned us against them. We crouched tense watching for them, knowing just one would finish everything. The Heinkels came in a roaring dive, straight in the first part of it in the fashion of the dive-bombers. But then, as they released the torpedoes, they made a peculiar upward, flipping motion, and from under their broad wings the torpedoes took the sea.

There was a white splatter of spume as the torpedoes rushed into the sea. Then they went beneath the surface to leap and broach at intervals, porpoise-wise, as they raced towards the ships. We swung with hard right helm, hard left helm back and away from them. Our gunners, waiting, waiting, let go at the Heinkels just in that moment when they executed that upward-flipping swing.

Visibility was bad, though, and it was hard for us to see our enemy; the same for them. There were a lot of near misses that day from torpedoes, from bombs, and from the floating mines the Nazi planes dropped, but all of our ships came through safe. Tuesday was another good day for us. We had done all right. Yet the Nazis had discovered one major fact that a lot of us overlooked as we sat in our messroom after the "All Clear" was given; the cruisers were no longer with us. Our fire power was greatly reduced, particularly at high altitudes.

The snow and the sleet squalls passed. Wednesday gave a clear cerulean sky, a blue and gleaming sea, very little horizon or zenith cloud. This was their day, the Nazi's, we knew. We dragged our ammunition cases closer to the guns; got ready as well as we could.

They came early: the Heinkels, the Messerschmitts, the Stukas, the Junkers 89's, and all told there were 105 of them over us during that day's fight that was to last twenty hours. They used everything: 1,100-pounders, 550's, 250's, aerial torpedoes, mines, their cannons, and their machine guns; while outside, always trying to get in, their submarines rushed our escort.

That was hell. There is no other word I know for it. Everywhere you looked aloft you saw them, crossing and recrossing us, hammering down and back, the bombs brown, sleek in the air, screaming to burst furiously white in the sea. All around us, as so slowly we kept on going, the pure blue of the sea was mottled blackish with the greasy patches of their bomb discharges. Our ship was missed closely time and again. We drew our breaths in a kind of gasping choke.

At about half-past ten that morning, the long-shanked Fourth Mate and I were on the after guns on the poop. Two Messerschmitts came after us, off the bank of broken cirrus cloud on the Northern horizon. Since Monday, the Messerschmitt squadrons had given our ship a lot of attention, no doubt remembering their pal that we had nailed.

This pair came down in one-two formation, the after-most perhaps three hundred feet behind his partner. At the start of their direct dive on us they had about two thousand foot altitude.

It was my first time to fire at them, and, eager and excited, I shot too soon. My tracers curved off; I was out of range, so I cut the guns. But they kept on coming, bigger and bigger in the ring sights, their wings growing from thin lines to thick fierceness from which lanced gun flame. We could see the bombs in the racks; we could see the bombardiers. Together, the Fourth Mate and I cut in at them.

We were leaning far back, knees bent, hands hard on the rubber grips, fingers down on the triggers, eyes to the ring sights. We were no longer conscious of the empties clacketing out underfoot, of the cold, the trembling motion of the ship as the other bombs burst. Here was death, and we were throwing death back to meet it.

The aftermost plane peeled off, banking towards the ship astern. The other kept on, right into our fire, smack for us. Then he dropped it, a 550-pounder. He was gone, away from our fire, and, hanging to the guns, all we could do was look up at that bomb.

It fell, slanting with the pull of the plane's speed. It whirled, screaming and howling in the air directly overhead. We could very clearly see the cylindrical khaki shape, the fins, even the white blur that was the serial markings on the side. This was for us, we thought. This was death. Even should it miss, the concussion will take the T.N.T.

There was nothing to do but hang on tighter to the gun grips. We said good-by to each other, but the bomb held our ears, the sound of it seemed to possess all sound.

Then in some sudden and not-yet-strong gust of wind it veered a bit. It struck the sea no more than twenty-five feet astern of us. There was the impact of passage into the sea, an immense, rushing smack, then the det-

onation. My wife's image was before my eyes. I stood there waiting for the
T.N.T.

Water went tumbling over me in a dousing, blinding column. The ship
rose and fell, groaning, terribly shaking. Empty cartridges jumped under
the shock, pitched off into the sea. Beneath my feet, as the ship still jarred
from that awful violence, the deck seams opened, and the oakum lay loose.

Water dripped from my helmet brim into my eyes. I was soaked from
the collar of my sheepskin coat to my felt-lined boots. Beside me, still at his
station between me and the Fourth Mate's guns, was old Ben. He was the
oldest A.B. in the ship; Ben, a Baltimore man, who in the last war had seen
service at the front in France. He might have run as that bomb fell, taken
out forward for the life boats on the boat deck, anywhere away from the
bomb. But he stayed there; he just bent his knees and set himself and
waited, empty-handed and where he belonged.

For that moment of steadfastness, I loved Ben, and I always shall. We
looked staring, shaking, just about conscious, into each other's eyes, and as
the frightful tightness gave from our stomachs and lungs, spoke to each
other. I forgot what we said, and I guess it doesn't matter. We talked as
shipmates, that was all.

Allen, my partner, was the next man up there. He had been coming up
the companion ladder from the fo'c'sle below, and the shock had all but
hurled him back down the steps. He helped me dry and reload my guns,
and we tried them and they were all right. The ship was still going on,
although now there was a great, grinding thump from the propeller under
us. We were in a bad way, we knew. We had been damaged plenty below.

The Chief, quiet and bespectacled, came aft to look at her and told us
that nine of the ten main bearings on the shaft had been shattered. There
was a bad twist in the tail-shaft itself, and plates had been stove in the shaft
alleyway. She was taking water there, but, for the time being, the pumps
could handle that. We kept on going up to Russia.[3]

Eventually more important, especially after the Mediterranean was
cleared, was the Persian Gulf route into Russia. We have already seen how,
in 1941, Britain and Russia had cleared Axis agents and pro-Axis governments out of Iraq and Iran, and secured this all important bridge from the
Persian Gulf to the Caspian Sea. Before this route could be used, however,
much remained to be done: the construction of port facilities at Basra, the
improvement of the single-track railroad to Teheran, the liaison between
American, British, and Russian soldiers and technicians. Something of
what was involved in all this is described by Joel Sayre:

In 1942, the most feasible and almost the only way, geographically, of
getting the stuff to the Russians was across Iran. Iran, which we all used to
know as Persia, is big; its area, 628,000 square miles, is greater than Germany, France, and England combined, or a couple of Texases. The way
was clear politically, because in August, 1941, the British and Russians had
invaded Iran and forced the abdication of the late Shah, Reza Pahlevi, on
charges of harboring Axis agents and playing too much ball with them. He

was exiled to the British island of Mauritius, off Madagascar, and his son, Mohammed Reza, who had shortly before come of age, was put on the throne in his place.

Reduced to its simplest terms, this was the Persian Gulf Command's supply procedure: Ships were unloaded at the ports of Khorramshahr, Bandar Shahpur, and Cheybassi. This last is in Iraq, part of Basra, Sindbad the Sailor's old home town. The cargoes were hauled hundreds of miles up the western side of Iran by rail or truck to terminals where they were turned over to the Red Army. The P. G. C.'s rail terminal was Teheran, a city with a population estimated, catch-as-catch-can, at seven hundred thousand; its truck terminal was Kazvin, a town of perhaps fifty thousand and a favorite residence of the Caliph Harun-al-Rashid, who many of the boys in the P. G. C. were surprised to learn was a real person and not just a kind of Foxy Grandpa in the "Arabian Nights." Kazvin, today notorious for its vodka distillery, is ninety miles northwest of Teheran by a spine-grinding road.

But that is reducing the procedure to too simple a simplicity. If you had gone to Iran in the Command's early days and talked to one of its high-ranking officers about what it was up against, you might have heard something like this: "The distance between New Orleans and St. Louis is about the same as between the Persian Gulf ports and Teheran. On the New Orleans end of our theatre we have to keep our three ports going full blast on stevedoring and lighterage operations. In the port battalions that do the dock-walloping, the white personnel is largely professional, lots of them from the Pacific Coast, but among the Negroes there are many country boys who never even saw a ship before they were drafted, let alone helped unload one. However, they're shaping up well, since good long-shoring is largely a matter of horse sense. As for docking facilities, two of our three ports aren't much more than fishing villages yet. The Liberty ships have been piling up outside them something awful, some of them waiting to be unloaded for as long as two months. Russians are dying for lack of the stuff that is in them, so that bottleneck's got to be busted at once. We'll have to build plenty of berths and jetties as fast as we can. Don't ever forget for a second that every phase of our job here is a speed proposition.

"Between the Gulf and Teheran there's a single-track railroad the old Shah built, and whenever you dream of the tonnage that's got to be hauled over it, you wake up shaking. Normal peacetime traffic on this line is one light passenger train every other day and one freight a week, and the freight train is of the usual modest Middle East proportions. A lot of the passengers are pilgrims bound for the holy city of Qum, where Fatima's mosque is, with a gold dome on it that will strike you blind. Of course we've had to draw up a new timetable for the railroad, but that Qum prayer train mustn't ever be monkeyed with. Religion is something these people over here don't kid about. Back in the nineteen-twenties, they stoned an American vice-consul to death in Teheran just for taking a snapshot of a sacred fountain. We've got enough wars on our hands already without getting mixed up in any holy ones. Incidentally, the train dispatching on this one-track line has been done until now over a single phone circuit from the Gulf up to Teheran. When the phone goes out, so does the train dispatching, which means that either the traffic can stop entirely until the phone goes on again or your trains can go right ahead and knock each other's brains out. Of course, the dispatching might be better if those Arabs in the desert didn't have such a passion for bright copper telephone wire and didn't keep snatching it off the poles. Well, it's the only railroad there is here and it will have to do. But, to exaggerate not very much, it's as though you suddenly had to serve all of Greater New York with the Coney Island scenic railway.

"Besides a few beat-up Krupp engines the old Shah bought from the Germans, the only locomotives available at present are some coal-burners the British turned over to us, and while there aren't any headlights or bells or cow-catchers on them, they'll have to do until our own locos get here. They were built during the last war for use on the flat country of France. The terrain between the Gulf and Teheran is different from the flat country of France. Once you've crossed the desert in the south, there are mountains you've got to climb that rise to over seven thousand feet. The four-wheeled Iranian freight cars that will have to be used until we can build some better ones aren't equipped with air brakes. With the huge loads our trains now have to carry, they are constantly snapping apart because their coupling is childish. The snapped-off parts roll backward down the mountains. Do you know what the Big Hook is? It's the name railroaders have for a wreck train. The Big Hook crews on this run are certainly going to earn their Spam. On this railroad there are two hundred and twenty tunnels. In one mountain section of a hundred and sixty-three miles there are a hundred and thirty-three tunnels—forty-seven miles of underground, if you spliced them. Every tunnel in the United States, according to law, has to have ventilation. There is no such law in Iran; none of the tunnels are ventilated. So the locos pack the longer tunnels with steam until the temperature sometimes reaches a hundred and eighty. It becomes so unbearable that the engineers and firemen have to throttle the trains down to a crawl, then climb to the ground and cling to their cabs' grab irons and stumble alongside them through the dark. 'Charging the ratholes' is what the boys call working this tunnel section.

"We've been setting up a truck route to supplement the railroad. In the first place, it should take good deal of strain off the railroad; in the second place, we need it as insurance. It's entirely possible that this railroad will be bombed out of action from time to time. The Italians from Eritrea bombed the oil wells on Bahrein Island, down in the Gulf, and there is still plenty of *Luftwaffe* on Rhodes, up in the Mediterranean. We had hardly landed here before the Axis radio was saying, 'Haha, the Americans are building up the port of Khorramshahr for us to take over.' The Germans have got to Mozdok in the Caucasus, which is within bomber distance of here, and if they stay there, and this command becomes as important to the Russians as we have every intention of making it, we're bound to have trouble. Anyhow, if the truck route turns out the way we hope it will, we'll be running one of the biggest trucking operations in the world.

"There's a few bugs that will have to be attended to, though, before we get squared away on the trucking. Between Khorramshahr and Andimeshk, the last town before you go into the mountains, there's a one-hundred-and-eighty-mile stretch of very nasty desert that will have to have a real, sure-enough road built over it. Truck drivers have been getting lost there, particularly at night, and the other day I heard one say, 'That ain't a road; it's a mirage.' "The rest of the way to Kazvin, mostly through the mountains, we have to use an ancient caravan route started by King Darius, the one who jumped the Greeks and got licked at Marathon. There's a town in these mountains called Khorramabad, where the Iranian Army hangs bandits when it can catch any, and outside it is a big stone marker that says Darius cut the ribbon across this road in five hundred-and-something B.C. and opened it up to commerce. Then, around about the time the Mayflower was landing, a shah named Abbas the Great built a chain of fortified red stone caravanserais all along this road. A caravanserai served as a kind of combination camel motel and pillbox. You can still see their ruins. You don't have to be the president of M.I.T., either, to see that nothing much has been done for this road since. In fact, this whole road in its present shape is just about as bad for our purposes as a road could be. The desert sand and the dust storms are chewing our truck parts away, and through the mountain section the holes in the road are so deep and there are so many of them that the most frequent equipment casualty we're getting is the jounced-off gas tank: the bumps simply tear them out by the roots. A good truck tire at home lasts eighty thousand miles; here they're lasting four thousand. We've got a trucking outfit, white and colored mixed, working the road now, and so far it's done a good job, but the men have been taking quite a beating. They crash their heads against the cab roofs and rub the skin off the small of their backs and they swallow a bushel of dust apiece every day. Down on the desert they sweat like wrestlers, and in the mountains they must be thinking they took a wrong fork and landed up in Alaska. In Aveh Pass there's still a pile of camel bones where a native caravan foundered in the snow last winter and froze to death. When the bandits in this country get hungry enough, they'll open fire on a truck or even a train. The road is very dangerous in places. On one hundred-and-thirty-five-mile stretch there are more than a thousand curves of greater than thirty degrees, and in plenty of parts it's so narrow and steep-sided a driver will get pitched over if he isn't careful.

"The Russians are desperate for trucks and planes, so we must turn them out for them as fast as we can in the little assembly plants that General Motors and the Douglas people put up for us here. Then, for all the huge amount of gear we'll be using ourselves, we'll be having to build some mighty large depots and shops and the Ordnance boys will have to keep them going around the clock. The Signal Corps has got quite a chore ahead putting in a decent communications system. We'll not only have to feed and clothe and house our own people but we'll have to hire and train and victual probably double their number in native labor, and we'll have to work everybody in a climate which in summer is the worst in the world. Down in the ports it's a hundred and forty in the holds at midnight sometimes, and all over the desert it's at least a hundred and thirty-five in the sun. Everybody will have to work stretches that would make an American labor leader scream. We'll have to battle malaria, dysentery, smallpox, typhus, sandfly fever, and venereals. There's a whole lot more things we'll have to do, but those I've mentioned will give you a rough idea of our problem."

It may as well be said at this point that the Persian Gulf Command licked this problem.[4]

The Great Offensive: Leningrad

With new armies and new equipment the Russians could seize and hold the offensive. And indeed the westward movement of the Red Army that started before Stalingrad and in the Caucasus at the end of 1942 never stopped until the Red banner was planted in the ruins of Berlin. All through 1943 and 1944 the Russians drove relentlessly forward in the greatest counter-offensive in the history of land warfare. One after another vast areas that the Germans had occupied and gutted were rewon: the Caucasus, the Donbas, Ukraine, White Russia, the Crimea. In one great battle after another those famous cities that the Germans had conquered and ravaged were reconquered: Rostov, Kharkov, Orel, Smolensk, Krivoi-Rog, Kiev, Vyazma, Velikie Luki, Kerch, Melitopol, Sevastopol, Odessa—and on into Poland and the Baltic States. The siege of Leningrad was finally lifted; the Finns were drive from the north and the Murmansk route completely freed; the Rumanians were sent hurtling out of Bessarabia—and out of the war.

It is impossible to present this vast and complex series of campaigns for the liberation of Russian. All we can do is select some scenes from the great drama, scenes either intrinsically important or typical.

As the Russians were annihilating the Sixth Army before Stalingrad, one thousand miles to the north the long siege of Leningrad was drawing to a close. The first blow in the counter-offensive that was to liberate Russia's former capital was struck from Oranienbaum—"the Tobruk of the Leningrad front." The main attack came on the morning of January 12, and within a few hours the Russians had crossed the ice, stormed formidable defenses, and established themselves on the left bank of the Neva River.

The German defenses did not give way at once: Germans had to be rooted out of each pillbox and fortification.

Not for fully a year were the Germans to be driven away from the Leningrad region. During that year there was continuous fighting, usually on a small scale. Now that access to Leningrad was easier, the striking power of the Russian army there could be reinforced. Armies to the south of the city, too, hammered ceaselessly at the Germans. Alexander Poliakov tells of one episode in that seesaw fighting—a tank attack across Lake Ilmen:

The commander of the unit to which our tank battalion belonged explained to us the importance of Lake Ilmen. Five rivers flow into it from the south. Ranging in width from seventy-five meters to half a kilometer, these rivers absorb dozens of tributaries. The lake itself and the river mouths afford the best natural protection for troops on the defensive, and ever since autumn the Germans had been holding this excellent line. It had been their main support for the blockade of Leningrad. During the

winter, they had strengthened it by erecting a large number of fortifications: strong points, trenches and barbed-wire entanglements. They had
laid mine fields, and set up batteries of trench mortars and heavy guns.
The entire area for hundreds of kilometers south of the lake was converted into a powerfully fortified district.

"That is why I have asked you to part for one day from your beloved
caterpillars, comrade tankmen, and take to your skis for a deep reconnaissance operation," the commander concluded.

Within twenty-four hours our tankmen on skis, under the command of
Major Maximov, covered about forty kilometers. Dressed in white hoods,
the scouts penetrated far into the frosty forest and on to the lake itself.
With infinite caution so as not to be heard by the Germans, they bored
holes in the ice to gauge its thickness.

After a day's rest, the tank battalion received the field orders for which
they had been so impatiently waiting. They were instructed to cross Lake
Ilmen and its tributaries during the night, penetrate thirty to forty kilometers behind the enemy's lines and launch a surprise attack on the flank
of his main forces in the Staraya Russa area. Their objective was to encircle
the 290th Infantry Division and the Skull-and-Bones SS Division of the
16th Army. As dusk fell, the engines began to hum and our battalion set
out from its temporary camp.

Our five KV's started off with a thunderous roar that shook the earth.
One could hear the rattle of the window panes in the peasant houses and
the dull thud of the tree trunks felled by our machines as they plunged
through the woods. A raging blizzard conveniently covered our approach
to the starting point of our offensive. On the outskirts of a small village we
halted for the last time before the decisive thrust, to have our tanks inspected. We had to reach the battle area in perfect order—a difficult
operation under the circumstances, for several water barriers separated us
from our objective. . . .

The tank column was accompanied by an infantry group which was to
form a landing party. The machines at the head carried sappers whose
assignment was to destroy the anti-tank mines. The infantrymen were
ordered to take their places on the tanks. The storm was so furious that the
order was scarcely audible as it passed along from tank to tank. . . .

A dash of about ten kilometers and Lake Ilmen was before us. Its waters
are not very deep, but they always teem with fish, especially since the war,
for all fishing has stopped, even at the height of the season. In winter, the
volume of water in the lake is greatly reduced; the severe frosts freeze it
almost to its floor.

The heavy tank on which I was riding together with a group of infantrymen cautiously lumbered forward across the ice. We were ordered to
jump off and walk alongside. Old Ilmen, as though annoyed by the sudden
disturbance of its nocturnal peace, creaked and groaned, as if shaken by a
storm. The fifty-ton machines—this meant a pressure of 300 pounds per
square centimeter of ice—caused the ice to crack with a strange tinkling
sound, and on places where the ice did not reach the bottom, its surface
could be seen palpably bending under their weight. The other heavy machines were not permitted to move along the tracks of the first ones, but
branched off to the right or left. Finally the lake was left behind.

We now had to cross the river near the Nazi lines. Because of the current, the ice on the river was much thinner, and had to be reinforced in order to support the weight of the heavy tanks. A few minutes before we came up, tankmen from another unit who had failed to take the necessary precautions met with a serious accident. In the middle of the river which was only a hundred meters wide, one of the heavy tanks crashed through the ice. The crew barely managed to save itself through the upper hatch.

Our engineers had prepared two thousand logs which they were supposed to spread over the ice and let freeze in. But we had arrived ahead of schedule, the Ilmen was already behind us, and the log-laying was still in progress. What was to be done? We could not afford to lose a minute. It was midnight. . . .

Every passing minute threatened our carefully planned operation with failure. But, once again, necessity proved the mother of invention. "Let's demolish the nearest village and use the timber from its houses to bridge the ice," suggested Major Maximov to our sappers. "But how will you get them here?" they asked. "We'll use our tanks, and then at least our advance can proceed."

No sooner said than done. An hour and a half later, our tanks brought a whole trainload of beams from the nearest village. Overjoyed at this unexpected solution to their problem, our sappers enthusiastically fell to work. . . .

Soon the small and medium tanks crossed the river one after another, followed by the cautiously crawling heavy KV's. We were now on the opposite bank, and the Germans had not yet noticed us. Four powerful machines took the tank that had been submerged in tow. At a given signal, thousands of units of horsepower yanked the fifty-ton machine out of the water throwing up heaps of ice as they dragged it to the shore. The river looked as though it had been split in two by a gigantic battering ram. . . .

Our column resumed its advance through woods and swamps. Day began to break when, still unnoticed by the enemy, we approached a second crossing. The sappers worked with gusto, carrying logs on their shoulders for several kilometers for the crossing, and soon a second bridge was laid for our tanks. . . .

Having crossed the river we outflanked the Nazis. Their confusion was indescribable; they had not imagined that our tanks could cross the frozen surface of Lake Ilmen and two rivers besides. The German guns had to make a ninety-degree turn to the left before opening fire. The first enemy shells burst on our bridge. "Shut the hatches! Watch the enemy!" Astakhov commanded. The infantry took cover behind the advancing machines. Although their ranges had been taken long ago, the Nazis were apparently too frightened to fire accurately. Our sappers who at first had scattered along both sides of the bridge, now ran back to it and resumed their work, helping to get the rest of the tanks to the opposite bank.

Astakhov had already crossed the river. Enemy shells and mines were coming dangerously close to our bridge. A few sappers were wounded, but none left his post. They bravely hammered back into place those logs that had been jerked out by the crossing tanks. But the German fire gradually grew more accurate. The crossing seemed doomed; a few more seconds, and two big shells tore up the logs, causing two enormous geysers of water mixed with ice. The whole bridge began to heave. Suddenly a new explosion came with a roar: but this time it was Astakhov's tank which had fired. Having located an enemy battery, he at once began to pound it. Two or three other tanks opened fire and the German battery was silenced. . . .

We had now been in action for twenty-four hours. No one had eaten anything or even thought of eating. We thought only of establishing ourselves firmly in our newly won positions. The Germans retreated, abandoning their blockhouses, guns, and dead. Our group commander ordered a small respite or, more accurately, a short period of preparation for a fierce new battle. The tankmen climbed out of their machines adjusting their sweaters and overalls. They were unrecognizable, their faces smeared with oil and blackened with soot. . . .

Their advance across the frozen rivers in heavy tanks was a great and unprecedented achievement. Our men felt that they had accomplished something significant although they knew that the big battles were still ahead.[5]

Orel and Kharkov

Some of the fiercest fighting of the entire war came in midsummer of 1943 in the Kursk-Orel region. Both armies had opened offensives in this area—the Germans to the south and east of Orel, the Russians to the north and west of Kursk. The Germans struck first with hundreds of massive tanks and self-propelled 70-ton tank destroyers, and during the second week in July a tremendous tank-artillery battle raged. No one could see the whole of this mighty battle, but a glimpse of it is given in the pamphlet *Orel*:

July 27, 1943—The third July of the war. The beginning of the month. As in previous years at this time, the German fascist troops again launched an offensive against the Red Army.

And again the dust of war rose over the fields of ripening corn, the broad meadows whose modest beauty outshines all the nurseries and luxuriant hothouses in the country, over the red burdock and cow-wheat, the yellow snapdragon, hart's clover and the bright pinks, over the lime trees sweetly blossoming on the outskirts of the villages, over the rivulets and the ponds overgrown with green slime and reeds, over the red brick cottages of the Orel villages and the whitewashed adobe huts of the Kursk and Belgorod countryside. . . .

For about three hundred hours a fierce battle raged in the Orel-Kursk and Belgorod-Kursk directions; a battle into which the Germans had hurled nearly forty divisions, scores of regiments of bomber and fighter planes, and vast masses of artillery.

Everything seemed to promise success. The area of operations was exceptionally limited. The stretch on which they had concentrated seventeen tank divisions could be covered in an automobile in a matter of forty or fifty minutes. Since the end of March columns of motor transports had been flowing in an unending stream to the point where, into the trap which they had prepared for our troops, they intended to hurl tens of thousands of tons of shells. By the date of the opening of the offensive they had accumulated from five to eight sets of ammunition equipment for every division, amounting, in the aggregate, to a weight of metal which even a geologist could not afford to ignore. . . .

The Germans failed to pass in the Belgorod-Kursk direction. They failed to pass in the Kursk-Orel direction. The most concentrated summer offensive the Germans ever launched was frustrated. . . .

Among the fields of ripening corn, across the broad sweet-smelling meadows, amidst the grey and yellow dust, under the threatening storm clouds in the July sky, amidst the rumbling of distant thunder and gusts of hot, stifling wind, our tanks, artillery, motorized infantry, and creaking baggage carts are moving. The radiators of the automobiles, the turrets of the heavy tanks and the muzzles of the guns are decorated with ears of corn and the bunches of pinks, cornflowers and daisies.

The Red Army is advancing.[6]

When the German tank attack failed, the Russians, under cover of the greatest artillery barrage of the war, drove forward from Kursk, out-flanked Orel and, just one month after the Nazis had launched their last great offensive, captured the city. Of this tremendous battle a Russian staff officer said:

It has perhaps escaped the notice of the average reader that the very first week of these battles surpassed by far in intensity even the climax of the fight for Stalingrad. At Stalingrad during the decisive weeks the German rate of loss is calculated to have stood at about 5,000 casualties per day. Yet during the first week of the Kursk-Byelgorod fighting this rate increased to over 8,000 casualties per day. In the Stalingrad struggle the German *Luftwaffe* intervened with about 1,200 sorties per day, whilst at the very opening of this summer's battle German aircraft are calculated to have made no less than 2,000 such daily sorties. Lastly the total of Hitler's tanks made available for this fighting in 1943 is infinitely greater than at Stalingrad.[7]

Equally damaging to German prestige, though not so costly in men, tanks, and planes, was the final capture of the great city of Kharkov which had changed hands so many times during the war. The capture was the climax of a campaign of encirclement similar to those which the Germans themselves had practiced so successfully in the past.

From the Caucasus to Sevastopol

Stalingrad really decided the fate of the German drive into the Caucasus, but the road back for the Russians was long and arduous. Most of the fighting in this region and in the Kuban was done by the famous Cossacks. Pyotr Pavlenko reports how the older men came from retirement to teach the trade of war as the Cossacks practice it.

I was their guest for a few days. They were holding a sort of training course in sabre fighting. Nikifor Natluck, a Cossack from the stanitsa (village) of Labinskoy, a patriarchal old man, whose sons are prominent Cossack Red Army commanders, proposed that young Cossacks should be taught the immortal sabre blow of the Zaporozhye Cossacks.

"The German must be slashed from the shoulder to the groin," he said. "Anyone can cut off a head or slice off an arm, but a Cossack must wield his sabre as his great-grandfathers did."

Another of the instructors was Trofim Njegoduyko, whose forefathers came with the first settlers from the mouth of the Dnieper in the time of Empress Catherine II. His great-grandfather knew Suvorov, who built forts on the shores of the Sea of Azov and formed the Kuban Corps.

Now, at 54 years of age, he is a senior sergeant, a volunteer in the Red Army. He fought near Moscow with the immortal Dovator, and later back home in the Kuban in Tseplyayev's motor brigade.

"I've known 16 generals in my time," he told me, "and honestly they all treated me like a brother."

"Why was that?"

He smoothed the flowing grey-black beard which spreads over his Circassian coat, and kept silent for some time, loving to keep our curiosity suspended in mid-air. Finally he said, "I do a Cossack's job well. What do they want from a Cossack? Fierceness. They expect him to deal heavy strokes. Well, I deal such strokes. A good stroke, boys, is never forgotten. It lives for ever."

Trofim's grandfather hewed through a Turkish horseman from shoulder to waist before Skobelev's face. All the papers were full of it at the time. In 1914, near Gumbinen, Trofim's father cut a German in six parts with two blows of his sword. It was the famous "criss-cross" blow, and the fame of it drew young officers to study with Alexander Njegoduyko. He showed them how to cut a calf in two, or a piece of cloth thrown up into the air.

Trofim Alexandrovich has upheld the honours of his family. Back in the days of the Civil War his comrades presented him with an old, silver-hilted sword with an Arabian inscription on the blade: "I serve the eagle-hearted." The silver hilt is now covered with 131 copper dots like freckles. That is Trofim's score of killed Germans. Trofim Alexandrovich says that eight dots are missing; they dropped off by accident.

Not all the 139 Germans were cut up: many of them tasted lead bullets, others were destroyed with the rifle-butt or crushed under Trofim's horse. With his sword he killed 43 Germans. One of his slashes he dedicated to his grandfather. "Even Grandfather Petro would have approved of it."

With one blow he cut a German officer near Rostov in three parts: head and shoulders, half the body and an arm, and the rest of the body.

Now he has been invited to show young Cossacks the art of sword play. Upright on his horse, he gallops spiritedly up to the clay figure of a German with out-spread arms. The young folks have been hacking away unsuccessfully at this "German" since the early morning. But their swords have got stuck in the moist clay at the level of the heart, or they have struck off only the head, which of course cannot be considered a decent stroke. Even a child can strike off a head.

So 54-year-old Trofim Njegoduyko, with set teeth, dashes up on his russet horse. The sword glitters brightly in his hand. He rises in his stirrups, raises the blade, and the clay German falls in two pieces.

The young folk shout "Hurrah!" Trofim, reining in his horse, explains: "The hardest thing, my lads, is to cut clay. I can feel no hatred for a clay figure, and therefore there is no heat in doing it. Why do I cut it? Only for the sake of your education.

"But my heart's not in it. I feel no anger. The conclusion to be drawn from this is that it is easier to strike at a German. In the first place, he usually turns tail. So if you stick a sword into him he'll run up it himself. He'll cut himself up. In the second place, you've got to apply pressure along the length of the blade, not downwards. It's not the same as chopping wood.

"Use your imagination. Pretend that the German is very broad and you're cutting him open like a cake. Don't hurry. Take it easy, and everything will turn out well.

"Of course, psychology plays a part too," adds Trofim mockingly. "But it's none of our business if a German yells. If the Germans don't like it they should have stayed at home in Germany. But once they've come on to our territory, friend, crying won't help. Run, damn you, run up the blade!"[8]

The fighting in the Kuban, the Kerch Peninsula and the Crimea, and along the north shore of the Sea of Azov was as tough as any in the great 1943–44 offensives. Not until October 1943 did the Germans finally retire from the Caucasus to the Crimea, and not until December were the Russians able to establish a beach-head on the Kerch peninsula.

Meantime the Russians were fighting their way, village by village and town by town, from Rostov to Melitopol and the Perekop Peninsula. In October Melitopol was cleared, street by street. Now, with control of the whole Sea of Azov, the Russians were ready for the campaign to reconquer the Crimea and its famous naval base. That campaign began early in April 1944, and was brought to a triumphant conclusion on May 10th.

The storming of Sevastopol, which had taken the Germans seven months, was accomplished in as many days. In the earlier assault the Russian Black Sea Fleet had made good its escape. Now it returned to participate in the recapture of the city and to prevent its defenders—chiefly Rumanians—from escaping. Altogether during the siege operations this fleet managed to sink 191 enemy vessels, including 69 transports.

The Liberation of Russia

Nineteen forty-four was the year when the soil of Russia was finally cleared of the invader who, three years earlier, had marched in with such arrogance. It was not an easy task. The Allies invaded in the west, but throughout the year the largest German forces fought on the Eastern front. This was the front of magnificent distances, of armies numbered by the millions, of great hammer strokes, of reverberating victories.

Something of these, and of the proud confidence which animated the Russians, can be gathered from Stalin's speech on the 27th anniversary of the USSR:

The decisive successes of the Red Army this year and the expulsion of the Germans from the confines of the Soviet Union was achieved by the series of crushing blows struck by our troops on the German troops. The blows were begun this year before Leningrad and Novgorod when the Red Army broke down the permanent defenses of the Germans and hurled them back to the Baltic area.

The result of this blow was the liberation of the Leningrad region. The second blow was struck in February and March of this year on the Bug River, when the Red Army routed the German troops and hurled them back beyond the Dnieper. The result of this blow was that the western Ukraine was liberated from the German fascist invaders.

The third blow was struck in April and May of this year in the Crimea area, when the German troops were thrown into the Black Sea. As a result of this blow the Crimea and Odessa were liberated from German oppression.

The fourth blow was struck in June of this year in Karelia, when the Red Army smashed the Finnish troops, liberated Viborg and Petrozavodsk and hurled the Finns back into the interior of Finland.

The result of this blow was the liberation of the major part of the Karelo-Finnish Soviet Republic.

The fifth blow was struck on the Germans in July of this year, when the Red Army ground down and smashed the German troops before Vitebsk, Bobruisk and Mogilev and accomplished its blow against the encircled German divisions in the Minsk area.

The result of this blow was that our troops completely liberated the Byelo-Russian Soviet Republic, reached the Vistula and liberated a considerable part of Poland allied to us; reached the Niemen and liberated the major part of the Lithuanian Soviet Republic; forced the Niemen and reached the frontiers of Germany.

The sixth blow was struck in July and August this year in the area of the western Ukraine when the Red Army smashed the German troops before Lvov and hurled them back beyond the San. The result of this blow was that the western Ukraine was liberated. Our troops crossed the Vistula and beyond the Vistula formed a powerful bridge-head west of Sandomierz.

The seventh blow was struck in August of this year in the area of Kishinev and Jassy when our troops utterly routed the German fascist troops and completed their blow by surrounding twenty-two German divisions before Kishinev, not counting the Romanian divisions.

The result of this blow was that the Moldavian Soviet Republic was liberated, that Romania, Germany's ally, was put out of commission and declared war on Germany and Hungary; that Bulgaria, Germany's ally, was put out of commission and also declared war on Germany; that the road was opened for our troops into Hungary, the last ally of Germany in Europe, and that the opportunity was presented for stretching out a hand in aid to our ally Yugoslavia against the German invaders.

The eighth blow was struck in September and October of this year in the Baltic Sea area when the Red Army smashed the German troops before Tallinn and Riga and drove them from the Baltic area.

The result of this blow was that the Estonian Soviet Republic was liberated, Germany's ally Finland was put out of commission and declared war on Germany. More than thirty German divisions found themselves cut off from Prussia, caught in pincers in the area between Tukums and Libau, and they are now being smashed by our troops.

In October of this year the ninth blow was launched by the movement of our troops between the Tisza and the Danube in Hungary which aims at bringing Hungary out of the war and turning her against Germany. The result of this blow, which has not yet reached its culmination, is that our troops have rendered direct aid to our ally Yugoslavia in the task of driving out the Germans and liberating Belgrade.

In October, too, our troops obtained the opportunity of advancing through the Carpathians and stretching out a hand of assistance to our ally Czechoslovakia, part of whose territory is already liberated from the German invaders.

Lastly, at the end of October of this year, a blow was dealt the German forces in north Finland when the German troops were knocked out of the area of Pechenga and our troops, pursuing the Germans, entered the territory of Norway, our ally.

By early summer of 1944 Russian armies were fighting in Poland, Finland, and Rumania. During June the Mannerheim Line was breached and Viborg captured. Other drives to the north of Lake Ladoga threatened to cut the hapless country in two. By September Finland had asked for an armistice, but though this was granted, she was not yet to know peace. German divisions here kept on fighting—as they did in Italy—and in the frozen north the war went on for some months. A correspondent with the Red Army describes the battle beyond the Arctic circle which resulted in the final capture of Petsamo:

Continuing to exploit their initial success, the Soviet troops captured Lucstari: here the Germans had their main northern air base, from which they raided Murmansk. Meanwhile an infantry formation under Col. Solovyev by-passed a number of strong points, making a 40-mile march into the enemy rear across tundra turned into mire by the autumn downpours. Ski troops plodding on foot carried arms and ammunition on their backs. Pack horses and reindeer drew the guns and mortars. This daring thrust cut the important road leading south-west. The enemy was left with only one escape route—the road north to Petsamo.

On the night of October 10 landings were made from the sea behind the enemy's positions. The sailors had a grim task at 4 degrees below zero in wicked weather with a snowstorm raging, to get a grip on steep cliffs bare of vegetation. There was no such thing as a sandy beach or a patch of level land. Thanks to the total unexpectedness of this operation, the enemy had no time to organise resistance, and the landing was effected without the loss of a single ship or man.

The main landing was aided by a decoy force which staged a landing further along the coast, distracting the enemy's attention. This auxiliary group met but weak opposition. As soon as the main force was safely ashore they returned to their boats and got back safely to base the following morning. Meanwhile the main force, moving against a strong gale, and drenched by the snow which melted as it fell, reached the road to Petsamo.

At this point the weather cleared a little, and formations of the Northern Fleet air arm were able to go hunting concentrations of enemy troops and vehicles.

In order to cut off the retreat by sea from Petsamovuono Bay and to speed up the rout of the Petsamo grouping, a naval force landed in Linahamari on the night of October 13 and seized the port in the face of furious resistance.

Pressed relentlessly from all directions and deprived of its main communications, the Lapland group of the German Army tossed about frantically, looking for a way out of the sack in which they had been trapped by the troops of the Karelian front and the seamen of the Northern Fleet. On October 15 the last German was driven from Petsamo—ancient Russian Pechenga.

That surprise sweep across the tundra to the Petsamo highway, behind the German lines, sounds like a tall story even to the men who did it. One of General Kononov's tankmen, still looking faintly astonished at his own achievement, said he would never have believed that tanks could move an inch in such country.

Easing huge stones out of their path, the KVs swayed, puffed and creaked, then ploughed on through the swampy moors. They descended slopes at an angle of 70 degrees, hurtled down 250 ft. heights. By the morning of October 14 the monsters had forced the tundra and reached the road. They raced triumphantly northward with their loads of tommy-gunners and sappers.

The Germans had three years to perfect their Arctic defences. They fortified the heights, they laid a wilderness of mines. This sector was held by the notorious 20th Lapland Army. The German Jaegers constituting its backbone were reckoned pretty tough. But they had some unpleasant memories to keep them company at night in the far north.

Back in the autumn of 1941, when the enemy was heading full speed for Moscow along the Smolensk road, the "Heroes of Narvik" were preparing to celebrate the conquest of the Soviet Arctic. General Ditl, then commander-in-chief of the 20th Lapland Army, announced in September, 1941, that his Jaegers would be in the main street of Murmansk before the winter set in.

They had a harsh awakening before the end of autumn on the banks of the Western Litsa, which they learned to call "the valley of death." There they lost nearly 12,000 men. After this defeat the 20th Lapland Army decided to sit tight. Every height was equipped for defence either as a link in a fortified chain, or independently. Outposts in the mountain spurs were to secure the Germans from any surprise. A complex system of

machine-gun and tommy-gun fire disposed step-like, vertically and hori-
zontally, on the slopes facing the Soviet positions was to serve them as an
invulnerable shield.

They counted on nature herself as an ally, on the tactical aid of cliffs
and swamps, roadless tundra, rain and snow. This theatre of war, we must
remember, is dozens of miles beyond the Arctic Circle.

It took three days for the Red Army men to carve out a lane through
the enemy's main defence zone shielding Petsamo from the land. The
tankmen's wild ride across the tundra, to which I have referred above,
settled the issue in the battle for the strong points. Sidling through the
hollows, they bypassed the enemy's centres of resistance on the crags, and
pounced in the rear.[9]

That summer, too, the Russians pushed steadily into pre-1939 Poland.
Vitebsk and Minsk had both fallen in June, and by July the Russians were
storming at Pinsk, Lwow, and Lublin. The fighting at Lublin was sharp.
Well might the Nazis fight bitterly to defend it, for near here was the
notorious Maidanek death camp—one of many which they had set up in
Poland.

In August, Rumania quit—and joined the Allies. Already the Russians
were driving on Bulgaria and Hungary. Bulgaria promptly followed Rumania's example and, for a brief moment, found herself spectacularly at
war with Germany, Russia, Britain, and the United States—an embarrassing position from which she hastened to extricate herself. Meantime the
British had landed in the Peloponnesus, and liberated Athens, as the Germans hastily tried to pull out what divisions they had in the Balkans—a
gesture which the Greeks and Yugoslavs would once have found most
gratifying but which they now tried their best to prevent.

By the end of the year the situation in the east had undergone a convulsive change. All Russia was free. The Nazis were extricating themselves
from the Balkans and of the Balkan countries only Hungary remained a
reluctant ally—and it was already fighting for its life. Finland was out of
the war against Russia and in the war against Germany. Half of Poland had
been liberated and the assault on Warsaw was about to begin. The Red
Army was already in East Prussia.

Into Germany

During 1945 the attention of Americans was fastened on the swift campaign across the Rhine and into Germany. The Russian campaigns in the
east seemed distant and confused. Yet these gigantic campaigns were on a
far larger scale than those in the west. Far more soldiers were engaged, far
more territory was involved, than in the fighting in any other theatre of the
war.

While the Red Army was storming ahead in the Balkans and in the far
north, the great armies along the center of the line were regrouping and
reorganizing for the final lunge. Then, at the beginning of the new year,
the grand strategy of this last series of campaigns unfolded. From the
south the armies of Tolbukhin and Malinovsky drove into Hungary and

Austria, seeking to flank Germany from the south in one of the greatest encircling operations in military history. To the north the armies of Konev and Zhukov leaped forward from their line along the Vistula in a spectacular race for the Oder. Still farther to the north other armies drove on Danzig, and Koenigsberg in East Prussia.

The speed of the new offensive caught the world by surprise. The drive from Warsaw to the west started on January 12; in three weeks the Reds were attacking Frankfurt on the Oder—275 miles away.

The capture of Warsaw was the climax to one of the most painful tragedies of the war. At the beginning of the previous August the patriot forces of that ruined city, believing that the current Russian offensive would carry across the Vistula, rose against their conquerors. But the Russians were stopped, and for 63 days the Poles waged an unequal conflict, fighting from street to street and house to house, enduring bombing and starvation and death. "Terrible damage," said Churchill, "has been inflicted upon that noble city, and its heroic population has undergone sufferings and privations unsurpassed even among the miseries of this war."

There was little left of the Warsaw that the Russians entered in January of the next year.

After the first great advance to the Oder there was another pause while the main Red armies regrouped and brought up supplies. But elsewhere on the thousand mile front almost every week brought some famous victory. Budapest fell on February 13 after a fight notable for its ferocity, and with it the Russians took over 100,000 prisoners. The great ports of Gdynia and Danzig gave in to assault the last week in March, and the Polish corridor—original excuse for the Nazi attack on Poland—was cleared. In East Prussia the Germans were being hemmed into an ever diminishing circle, and on April 9 the ancient fortress city of Koenigsberg, home of the Prussian Junkers, capitulated. That same memorable week saw the climax of the campaign in the far southwest as the Red Army entered Bratislava and Vienna, and pushed on towards the advancing U.S. Third and Seventh Armies.

A correspondent with General Chernyakhovsky's army describes the fighting in Koenigsberg:

I was present when the last Germans were cleared from the Koenigsberg Zoo, one of the hottest battle-zones on this front. The zoo was in a terrible state of chaos. The elephant, unfed for many days, trumpeted for food. The monkeys had escaped from their broken cages and ran after the Red Army men, who threw them bits of bread. The parrots and the humming birds died. They flew away from their heated cages, and perished in the frosty air. Blizzards swept Koenigsberg for nearly a fortnight. . . .

The inner defence zone at Koenigsberg is one of the toughest nuts that the Red Army men on this front have ever had to crack. I saw eight big concrete forts nearly on top of each other. They all had to be stormed by assault groups. Some of the suburbs are fortresses, in the fullest sense of the word.

Among the German prisoners shuffling along the roads are veterans who saw action at Moscow and Rostov, as well as members of the *Volkssturm* battalions, or "Wolki" (wolves) as the Russians call them. The enemy has sent the staffs of field post offices, slaughter houses and hospitals into action.

The grey winter sky over the Koenigsberg area is lurid—the Germans, as they retreat, are setting fire to stacks of unthreshed grain, dwellings and factories.

The ugly habits of the crafty enemy are everywhere in evidence. The water in a well near Berzhiven was found to be poisoned. The Germans have organised special squads whose job it is to poison stocks of food abandoned in warehouses. The Red Army men caught a complete platoon of these poisoners in Labiau.

The roads leading to Koenigsberg are strewn with overturned wagons. I saw pillows, mattresses, suitcases and bicycles lying about in the snow. The cows, sheep, pigs and calves have been left to their own devices on all the farms: the animals pace dejectedly through the yards. Many have wandered off into the forests.

The Prussian farmers were in such a hurry to get out that they left half-finished meals on the table—cutlets, potatoes, ersatz coffee, ersatz jam, ersatz honey. We have found in the barns tractors produced in the Stalingrad and Kharkov works, threshers and seeders from Rostov.

It seems that the slogan of the German exodus was "Save yourself if you can." In the frenzied rush even old mothers and fathers were abandoned by those whose legs were younger.[10]

Less spectacular, but more important economically, was the Red advance through southern Poland and into Silesia, second greatest industrial region in Germany.

Then came the last great offensive—the assault on Berlin. Zhukov struck from the center of the line, captured Frankfurt, and fought his way towards Berlin's flaming suburbs. Konev crossed the Neisse River, captured Kotbus, and pushed on to Potsdam.

Already the Americans and the Russians had made contact. The two great drives on Berlin, one of which started from the banks of the Volga, the other from the deserts of Egypt and the mountains of Tunisia, were about to join.

11

FROM D-DAY TO VE-DAY

The Great Invasion

FOR TWO YEARS the Russians had clamored for a second front. None knew better than Churchill and Roosevelt how hazardous such an operation would be, how prodigious were the efforts required to carry it out; none were more aware of its urgency; none more eager for its splendid rewards. Unable to mass the powerful forces necessary to assure success in 1943, these architects of victory planned instead for a third front in that year—the North African and Italian, and for the vigorous prosecution of the war against Japan and of the bombing of Germany and German-occupied Europe. Never for a moment did they abandon the plan for a second front, nor postpone it a day longer than was essential. But they were not to be hurried by propaganda or the outcries of amateur military critics into a premature assault that would cost countless lives and might endanger the success of the entire plan.

Churchill himself explained the genesis of the invasion:

In April, 1943, General Morgan, of the British Army, became the head of the British and American Planning Staff, which surveyed the whole project by the decision of the Combined Chiefs in Staff Committee. They made a plan, which I took with me last year to Quebec, where it was submitted to the President and the Combined British and American Chiefs of Staff. This plan selected the beaches for the attack and presented the outlines of the scheme, together with a mass of detail to support it. It received, in principle, complete agreement. It is rather remarkable that a secret of this character, which had to be entrusted from the beginning, to scores, very soon to hundreds and ultimately to thousands of people, never leaked out either in these Islands or the wide expanses of the United States.

At Teheran, we promised Marshal Stalin we would put this plan, or something like it, into operation at the end of May or the beginning of June, and he for his part promised that the whole of the Russian Armies

239

would be thrown, as indeed they have been, into general battle in the East. In January of this year, the commanders were appointed. The Mediterranean had a British commander, General Wilson, and General Eisenhower assumed the command of the Expeditionary Force gathered in Britain. No man has ever laboured more skilfully or intensely for the unification and goodwill of the great forces under his command than General Eisenhower. He has a genius for bringing all the Allies together, and is proud to consider himself an Allied as well as a United States Commander. . . .

I do not believe myself that this vast enterprise could have been executed earlier. We had not the experience. We had not the tackle. But, before we launched the attack in 1944 we had made five successful opposed landings in the Mediterranean, and a mass of wonderful craft of all kinds had been devised by our services and by our United States colleagues on the other side of the ocean. The bulk of these had to be constructed in the United States, although our yards were strained and gorged to the utmost. There are more than 60 variants of these landing craft and escort vessels, and they provide for the landing, not only of an Army, but of everything that an Army can need. . . .

An immense system of harbours, breakwaters and landing stages was also prepared which, as soon as the foothold was gained, could be disposed in their appropriate places to give large sheltered water space. In less than a month, harbours had been created compared with which Dover seems small. At these harbours, and on the beaches they protect, a very large Army, with the entire elaborate equipment of modern armies, which have about one vehicle for every four or five men, was landed, and by the end of June, in spite of the worst June gale for 40 years, a solid base had been created which gave us the certainty of being able to conduct an offensive campaign on the largest scale against any Forces which, according to our calculations, the enemy was likely to bring.

These operations were protected and supported by a considerable British Fleet, assisted by a strong detachment of the American Fleet, the whole under Admiral Ramsay. In spite of gales, in spite of mines, in spite of more than 100 German submarines waiting baffled in the Biscay Ports, and a swarm of E-boats and other marauders, ceaseless traffic has been maintained over the 100-miles stretch of channel, and General Eisenhower, with his lieutenant, General Montgomery, now stands at the head of a very large and powerful Army, equipped as no Army has ever been equipped before.

Overwhelming air power was, of course, as indispensable as sea power to the carrying out of such an operation. The strategic bombing by the combined British and American Bomber Forces, and the use of the medium bomber and fighter forces, was the essential prelude to our landing in Normandy. Preparations definitely began for the battle in April, and, not only at the point of attack, for that would have revealed much, but necessarily impartially all along the coast and far in the rear. Thus when our ships crossed the Channel, unseen and unmolested, half the guns that were to have blown them out of the water were already dismantled or silent, and when the counter-attack began on the land and under the sea, the Tactical and Coastal air forces held it back while our foothold on shore and our sea-lanes were being firmly established.[1]

After two years of vast invasion planning which massed over two million American and Empire troops in the British Isles and supplied them with 16 million tons of material—after giant rehearsal maneuvers in England and false "wet runs" in the Channel, D-Day in Europe, June 6, 1944, still was a tactical surprise. To the last moment the German High Command had expected the attack to come in the Pas de Calais area which had for so long been subjected to the heaviest kind of aerial bombardment. Equally surprising was the stupendous size, firepower, and organization of the striking force which the Supreme Commander, General Eisenhower, sent over the water in the first hours of D-Day. An armada of 4,000 boats and 11,000 planes backed up the invasion.

Only the weather surprised the Allies. Just before June 5th, the original D-Day, the worse June gale in 40 years struck suddenly along the treacherous Channel. The invasion boats that had started out were called back, the delicate timetable threatened. Twenty-four hours later the weather was clearing overhead and General Eisenhower took the responsibility of ordering the invasion to go ahead.

Early on June 6 the German news agency Transocean announced that the invasion had begun. In the past the Germans had often sent out—to achieve denial or confirmation or merely confusion—the first true reports of battles. But soon all doubt was dispelled. The army itself announced that: "Under the command of General Eisenhower, Allied naval forces, supported by strong air forces, began landing Allied armies this morning on the northern coast of France."

This was it. At last the long suspense was over; at last the dawn of liberation for the peoples of France and the Low Countries had come.

The Supreme Commander issued an order of the day to the troops under his command:

Soldiers, sailors and airmen of the Allied Expeditionary Force: You are about to embark on a great crusade, toward which we have striven these many months. The hopes and prayers of liberty-loving people everywhere go with you. In company with our brave Allies and brothers in arms on other fronts you will bring about the destruction of the German war machine, elimination of Nazi tyranny over the oppressed peoples of Europe, and security for ourselves in a free world.

Your task will not be an easy one. Your enemy is well trained, well-equipped and battle-hardened. He will fight, fight savagely. But in this year of 1944 much has happened since the Nazi triumphs of 1940 and 1941.

The United Nations have inflicted upon the Germans great defeats in open battle, man to man. Our air offensive has seriously reduced their strength in the air, and their capacity to wage war on the ground.

Our home fronts have given us an overwhelming superiority in weapons and munitions of war, and have placed at our disposal great reserves of trained fighting men.

The tide has turned. The free men of the world are marching together to victory. I have full confidence in your courage, devotion to duty and skill in battle. We will accept nothing less than full victory.

Good luck and let us all beseech the blessing of Almighty God upon this great and noble undertaking.

This order was distributed to assault elements. It was read by appropriate commands to all other troops in the Allied Expeditionary Force.

And the great leader who had from the beginning planned the invasion and whose faith in its inevitable success never faltered, broadcast a prayer for the Allied troops in France:

My Fellow-Americans:

Last night when I spoke with you about the fall of Rome I knew at that moment that troops of the United States and our Allies were crossing the Channel in another and greater operation. It has come to pass to success thus far.

And so in this poignant hour, I ask you to join with me in prayer:

Almighty God: Our sons, pride of our nation, this day have set upon a mighty endeavor, a struggle to preserve our Republic, our religion and our civilization, and to set free a suffering humanity.

Lead them straight and true; give strength to their arms, stoutness to their hearts, steadfastness in their faith.

They will need Thy blessings. Their road will be long and hard. For the enemy is strong. He may hurl back our forces. Success may not come with rushing speed, but we shall return again and again; and we know that by Thy grace, and by the righteousness of our cause, our sons will triumph.

They will be sore tried, by night and by day, without rest—until the victory is won. The darkness will be rent by noise and flame. Men's souls will be shaken with the violences of war.

For these men are lately drawn from the ways of peace. They fight not for the lust of conquest. They fight to end conquest. They fight to liberate. They fight to let justice arise, and tolerance and goodwill among all Thy people. They yearn but for the end of battle, for their return to the haven of home.

Some will never return. Embrace these, Father, and receive them, Thy heroic servants, into Thy kingdom.

And for us at home—fathers, mothers, children, wives, sisters and brothers of brave men overseas, whose thoughts and prayers are ever with them—help us, Almighty God, to rededicate ourselves to renewed faith in Thee in this hour of great sacrifice.

Many people have urged that I call the nation into a single day of special prayer. But because the road is long and the desire is great, I ask that our people devote themselves in a continuance of prayer. As we rise to each new day, and again when each day is spent, let words of prayer be on our lips, invoking Thy help to our efforts.

Give us strength, too—strength in our daily tasks, to redouble the contributions we make in the physical and the material support of our armed forces.

And let our hearts be stout, to wait out the long travail, to bear sorrows that may come, to impart our courage unto our sons wheresoever they may be.

And, O Lord, give us faith. Give us faith in Thee; faith in our sons; faith in each other; faith in our united crusade. Let not the keenness of our spirit ever be dulled. Let not the impacts of temporary events, of temporal matters of but fleeting moment—let not these deter us in our unconquerable purpose.

With Thy blessing, we shall prevail over the unholy forces of our enemy. Help us to conquer the apostles of greed and racial arrogances. Lead us to the saving of our country, and with our sister nations into a world unity that will spell a sure peace—a peace invulnerable to the schemings of unworthy men. And a peace that will let all men live in freedom, reaping the just rewards of their honest toil.

Thy will be done, Almighty God.

Amen.

The Landings

During the past years Hitler had built, along the French coast, a formidable network of defenses. "No power in the world," he said, "can drive us out of this region against our will." But he had not counted on the power that the Allies were able to mount, or on the marvellous thoroughness of the preparation. That preparation included patient collection of information on everything from the weather to Hitler's underwater beach defenses; equally patient practice in overcoming all obstacles; sweeping the Channel clear of German boats, and the "softening up" of the Normandy Coast. Everett Hollis tells of the aerial spearhead:

The preparatory bombing, all done in a pattern that could be understood only by the authors of this mighty attack, had been going on for three months. For every three bombs dropped around the still-secret target area, three more were dropped around Dieppe, and four around Pas de Calais, just to keep the Germans guessing. Then, twenty hours before H-hour, medium and heavy bombers by the hundreds began concentrating on the batteries, the command posts and the control stations of the Target Area itself. This attack reached its crescendo thirty minutes before H-hour when 2,000 tons of bombs were hurled upon the beaches, to blast open a path ashore. . . .

H-hour was at 6:30 A.M. in the clear early morning. But the invasion of Normandy really began at thirty minutes past midnight when swarms of Allied parachutists and airborne troops began descending on the base of the Cherbourg Peninsula. Theirs was one of the most perilous tasks of the whole undertaking, leaping in darkness into enemy territory, each group with its specific task—a bridge to be blown up, a railroad line to be cut, an enemy defense post to be dynamited, a landing field to be seized and held. Many were killed before they hit the ground, riddled with flak or machine-gun fire. Others were encircled the moment they landed and cut down by criss-crossing fire.

Behind the paratroopers came the gliders, towed by bombers. In the glare of bursting flak the tow-lines were cut and the gliders dove steeply down. Now and then one would be caught by the A-A fire and in an instant would be transformed into a plunging ball of flame. The crunch of breaking matchwood could be heard as gliders bounced on rocks and careened into trees. From those that landed safely there poured men, jeeps, guns and small tanks. One glider sat down on the thatched roof of a French house in the village of Sainte Mere Eglise. The house was a German sectional headquarters and the Germans inside were so flabbergasted that they surrendered immediately. This led to the surrender of the whole town, which was in Allied hands by 7 A.M., even before the invading troops had come ashore in that particular section.[2]

While paratroop landings were under way, the great armada of ships with its umbrella of planes was moving across the rough choppy waters of the Channel. C. S. Forester describes the naval bombardment that preceded the actual landings:

It was a blustery overcast night when the warships crossed the Channel and steamed on their appointed routes toward the rendezvous, navigators anxiously checking their position minute by minute. No German plane detected the monstrous force as it was on its way—the low clouds were a help in that respect—and they were hardly more than halfway across when they saw reflected against the clouds the bomb flashes and the antiaircraft fire which indicated that the final night air raid was in progress. . . .

Steady nerves were necessary as each ship edged up into her allotted position, finally checked by anxious navigators. Still, everything was quiet ashore, amazingly enough; to a despondent mind it might seem more likely that the wary Nazis had some tremendous surprise up their sleeves rather than that they had been taken completely by surprise. . . . As five o'clock approached, visibility increased until each ship could see her neighbor; at nine minutes past five, France was visible—as the staff had predicted—and at that second, as the orders had laid it down, the guns of the fleet opened fire, a sheet of flame from one end of the 100-mile-long line to the other, and 200 tons of shells every minute began to wing their way against the enemy.

The extraordinary thing was that the Germans were caught off their guard. Among the first prisoners brought in, later in the day, was a German noncommissioned officer of a coastal-defense unit who was actually blown out of his bed by the opening shells of the bombardment—clear proof that the garrison was not on the alert. . . .

Then the Germans began to hit back. Their fortress guns, 6 inch and upwards, opened fire on the ships, and to silence these weapons in their enormously powerful casemates and emplacements was the first duty of the big guns in the battleships.

Innumerable duels were fought out between batteries and battleships; it was kill or be killed—silence the batteries before the batteries sank the ships. In a few moments, there were great spouts of water leaping from the surface of the sea round the battleships to show how near the defending shells were falling. It was a supreme advantage for the ships to be able to move about; this disconcerted the German gun layers while it did not discommode the Allied gunnery control. A shore battery may be unsinkable, but it stays in one spot. . . .

The extraordinarily efficient technical training of the Allied navies made itself apparent at once. One cruiser, the U.S.S. *Quincy*, scored five direct hits in successive salvos on a heavy coastal battery, silencing it. . . .

With the bombardment at its height, three German destroyers came dashing out of the mouth of the Seine to see what was going on—another very definite proof that the Allies had achieved tactical surprise. They caught a single glimpse of the enormous fleet and fled immediately for shelter again. . . .

Under intense fighter protection and in the absence of any serious attempt by the *Luftwaffe* to interfere with them, the spotting planes were able to execute their orders in a way an artillerist dreams about. It was thanks to them that the indirect fire of the battleships, rumbling over the cliffs of the shore and the gentle slope of the back country, was guided to its mark. Some of the observers' recorded comments tell their own story:

"Got him. Finis. Next target please." And, after a "straddle," "That must be their headquarters. Generals running like billy-o. . . ."

Ten thousand tons of shells had been directed upon the known targets and upon those which had revealed themselves during the bombardment. The moment came for the plans to be put to the test, the crucial test, the moment of decision for the destiny of Europe.

Then the Allies struck their blow, at the moment that had been planned months before. The air-borne troops came hurtling in over the coast from their bases more than 100 miles away and the armies of the United Nations came sweeping ashore like a tidal wave. From observers in the air, from spotters in the ships, and soon from radio telephones carried by the troops struggling up the beaches, the reports began to pour in as the Germans revealed themselves. The dark rain squalls which swept over the battlefield, hampering though they might be to the landing craft, were useful at this vital moment. Darkening the sky, the squalls made it possible to see the stabbing pin points of fire which marked where machine guns opened up from villas and gorse patches. The fighting ships trained their guns round—already the paint on them was blistered and smoldering. . . .

The flow of signals from observers to guns was of a volume almost inconceivable; only the most carefully planned system could have dealt with 3500 gunnery signals. Seven signals a minute, each one demanding the attention of a specialist officer. In one case, a spotting aircraft complained that he was under fire from a four-gun AA battery which was interfering with his observation. He gave its position and proceeded to report the fall of the salvos.

The first salvo knocked out one gun. The second salvo knocked out another. The third salvo knocked out the remaining two and started a fire which blazed round the emplacement. "Thanks for the fun," signaled the observer. . . .

The strong points were knocked out one by one, enabling the infantry to push forward. . . . It was of the utmost importance to push with all possible speed. A broad belt of territory had to be secured, so wide that the landing beaches would be out of range of the field artillery which the Germans would hurry to the scene of action as fast as the Allied air forces would allow them. Up those beaches had to pour the enormous torrent of men and equipment needed to maintain hundreds of thousands of men in the field, and there is nothing so vulnerable, even to unobserved artillery fire shooting by the map, as an open beach crammed with combustibles and explosives. . . . It was the fire of the Allied ships that made this advance possible, and which enabled the gallant land forces to thrust forward and gain sufficient elbowroom for the landing. Success depended, of course, on innumerable other factors. . . .

But the solid, indisputable fact, evinced every moment of those anxious days, was that, at sea, America and England had an overwhelming artillery which could range deeper into the peninsula than any guns the Germans could bring up in a hurry, and that, furthermore, this artillery could be relied upon to hit its target accurately, hard and often. Military circles in Berlin, during the anxious days when the world awaited from hour to hour news regarding the progress of the invasion, commented bitterly about the "red line"—the line drawn on the map marking the distance inland that the naval guns could reach. The vital part which naval bombardment played in the invasion was a surprise to the world, just as it constituted a tactical surprise for the Nazis. . . .

So the military decision was taken—the landing was to be covered by an overwhelming artillery fire from a large naval force striking in by surprise.

Every one of 600 ships, from battleships to gunboats, had to be allotted her own particular targets; every observer, whether he was to be on board or in the air or on the land, had to be familiar with enough of the program to make sure he did not confuse the shots falling from one ship with those from another. Even in a battle at sea, with comparatively few units involved and with comparatively well-defined targets, the most elaborate arrangements are necessary to prevent this. Yet there could be no rigidity, no laying down of cast-iron firing tables to be adhered to through the period of the attack; on the other hand, there must be flexibility, so that fire could be switched from one target to another as the needs of the attack fluctuated.

Nor was it a question of pure gunnery; there was navigational problems to be met and solved at ever turn. . . . During the course of the bombardment, the assault was going to be launched, and there would be craft covering the whole surface of the sea. It would not be a time for elaborate maneuvers, and a single ship crossing the bows of a serried column of advancing craft might throw the whole into disorder. . . .

Under Sir Bertram Ramsay, commander in chief at sea, the attacking fleet was divided into two wings: a right wing of mainly American vessels under Adm. Alan Goodrich Kirk—whose flagship was the *Augusta*—covering the landing of mainly American troops; and a left wing under

Rear Adm. Sir Philip Vian, of mainly British ships covering the landings of mainly British troops. Vian's flagship was the *Scylla*. In both wings, the backbone of the force was composed of ships with a past as romantic as that of Nelson's *Victory*. The *Nevada* had been burned out to a mere hulk at Pearl Harbor, refloated, repaired and sent halfway round the world to take part in this battle. The old *Texas* and the *Arkansas* was there. The *Texas* had already had experience of service beside British ships—she had formed part of the Grand Fleet at Scapa Flow in 1918. The *Warspite* had fought at Jutland in 1916, where the fire of the German battle fleet had jammed her helm, causing her to circle twice under a tornado of fire from which she barely escaped; since that day she had fought in the Atlantic and the Mediterranean; bombed by the *Luftwaffe*, she had crossed the Pacific to be repaired at Bremerton, Washington, and then gone on to complete the circuit of the world and fight again in home waters.[3]

Then the troops waded ashore. The British Second Army, with the Canadian 3d Division, landed near Caen and pushed rapidly inland to capture Bayeux. In the face of the stiffest kind of resistance the Americans landed at Utah and Omaha Beaches, on either side the Vire River. "Only by guts, valor, and extreme bravery," said General Bradley, "we were able to make the landings a success." Charles Wertenbaker tells how guts, valor, and bravery won the day:

The western landing was evidently one which the enemy least expected. It was an unlikely spot, close to the marshes of the Carentan Estuary, far down the coast from Cherbourg, isolated from the interior by inundations behind the beaches. But it also had natural advantages to the attacker. Except for some dunes, there was no easily defended terrain between the beach and the flooded area: the long, yellow beach rose gently from the water's edge to a low ridge. Behind the ridge was the mile-wide moat, dead trees sticking out of the greenish water. Two narrow, paved causeways ran across the moat. It was here that the Germans counted on stopping us dead.

But across the moat we had bombed and strafed them well. Then the 101st Airborne Division, landed farther inland, advanced on them from the rear while the seaborne troops of the 4th Division swarmed up the beach. A dozen small, sharp skirmishes disposed of the machine-gun nests left on the beach, and tanks and ducks and lighter vehicles began to pour off the landing craft and cross the beach in the wake of the infantry. The enemy managed to blow one causeway bridge; shells hit a few vehicles and made a few shallow holes in the causeways; but engineers soon cleared the roads. Within three hours of landing, the VII Corps had strong forces across the moat and was spreading out into the sniper-peppered country between St. Martin and Ste. Marie du Mont.

On the British beaches, far to the east, the fight was harder, but the results almost as good. The British and Canadians also had parachutists to help, and Leonard Mosley, a British correspondent who jumped with them, lay on a hill overlooking the beach and watched the invasion fleet come in. It was 7:15. "There was an earth-shaking noise. Approaching the coast under cover of naval ships, the invasion barges were coming in, and coming in firing. It was a barrage that must have paralysed the defenses. Then ships began nudging toward the beaches, and we shook each other's hands in the knowledge that the invasion at long last had begun."

The waves were high, but most of the obstacles were above water, and the engineers blasted paths through them before the incoming tide could dash the landing craft against the steel rails. The boats shoved in, let out their cargo of infantry. . . .

On the second American beach, between VII Corps and the British, things were not going well. At 9:45 the first report from V Corps reached the *Acamar.*

Obstacles mined, progress slow on right. Amphibious tanks believed swamped. Landing on left more successful; nine waves landed by 7:35.
—GEROW

Two unpredictable things had combined to make the situation critical. One was the weather, which had raised waves four feet high to swamp the boats, conceal the obstacles, and make the infantry sick. The other was the stroke of intuition, information, or luck that caused the Germans to move their 352nd Division to the coast during the night of June 5–6. Many a German machine-gun crew set up its weapon on the bluff that morning, looked down, and beheld an invasion.

The landing went wrong from the beginning. The engineers' commanding officer and his second-in-command were killed a few minutes after they reached the beach. One engineer battalion lost 60 per cent of its men trying to clear a path ashore. While the army and navy demolition parties worked to clear the obstacles, the landing craft grew thicker behind them; they fouled one another, a few blew up on mines, and some others splintered against the steel hedgehogs. The enemy on the bluffs attacked them with mortars and machine guns. The enemy farther back attacked them with shells. From some parts of the beach the landing boats had to back away.

Where landings could be made, the paths through the obstacles were narrow; as the tide rose, wrecked boats floated in and blocked the paths. Infantry got ashore a boatload at a time, too few to storm the beach defenses. And so they lay there, flattened into shallow holes scooped out of the sand, or pitifully sheltered behind the obstacles, and waited for reinforcements. Some never reached the beach. They hid behind swamped tanks or bits of wreckage in the water, and there shells or bullets found them. . . . The deputy commander of the 1st Division went ashore late in the morning to try to save the situation. With him was . . . Don Whitehead of the Associated Press, who was one of two journalists to experience the terror of that beach on D-Day.

"As our boat was lowered from the transport it heaved and pitched, but it swung clear and we joined the other small craft bobbing about among the big transports stretching as far as I could see. . . . We could see the warships' guns flash and the explosions ashore. Gradually we moved toward shore. Some men leaned over the sides and vomited, seasick after only a few minutes in the boats.... A plane exploded in the air with a shower of sparks. Behind us came ducks wallowing through the swells. I didn't see how they could make it in such rough water, but I did not see a single one in trouble. Behind them followed the whole amphibious family of strange looking craft, loaded with troops and equipment. We patrolled offshore for a while, then headed for the beach....

"The enemy on the right flank was pouring direct fire on the beach. Hundreds of troops, pinned to the cover of the embankment, burrowed shallow trenches in the loose gravel. No one was moving forward. The congestion was growing dangerous as more troops piled in. Snipers and machine gunners were picking off our troops as they came ashore....

"Then the brigadier began working to get troops off the beach. It was jammed with men and vehicles. He sent a group to the right flank to help clean out the enemy firing directly on the beach. Quietly he talked to the men, suggesting next moves. He never raised his voice and he showed not the least excitement. Gradually the troops on the beach thinned out and we could see them moving over the ridge....

In the early afternoon the first waves got off the beach and began to spread out in the high ground beyond the bluffs. By then the beach was strewn with wreckage and it was hard to find a place to land. When the *Acamar* reached the transport area, a little after 2:30, most of the battleships and cruisers were moving east of the Carentan Estuary toward the beach that needed support....

It was a clear, sunny afternoon with a cool offshore breeze blowing. As we passed between the big warships and their objectives the jar of their distant broadsides kept the air a-tremble. In the two places where the landing parties had found exits from the beach destroyers standing in close to shore were pouring fire into the valleys beyond the exits. Smoke clung to the sides of the valleys, blowing up the slopes. On either side of the little Riquet Valley stood heavier ships, two cruisers to the west, two cruisers and a battleship to the east, and they crashed broadsides deep into the interior. Their guns spat orange flame into the clean air, and smoke from their guns and from a smoke-layer dodging around the battleship spread over the packed landing boats waiting to go in to shore. Enemy shellbursts still erupted from the beach, but gradually they grew fewer, and finally stopped, and one by one the big ships ceased firing.

The late afternoon sun brought out clearly the shape of the bluffs behind the beaches. In the late afternoon the first group of four wounded men was brought aboard the *Acamar*. By then we had heard that casualties had been light on the western beach, not so light on the other. The Navy had evacuated 400 of them during the day. In the late afternoon, too, came better reports from the beaches. VII Corps was still going well and General Collins had set up his command post ashore. V Corps had reached the Aure, three miles inland. It had a foothold, but it was a precarious one, unless the beach could be quickly cleared....

It was not over on the beaches, or in the restless waters off the beaches. Into the night destroyers stood inshore, firing intermittently. From the enemy also came intermittent shelling while the engineers on the beach worked to clear some of the wreckage....

At 11:30 the first enemy raiders came and the night lit with bomb bursts and with tracers firing into the clouds. . . . The firing came closer and enveloped us. An enemy plane dove to within 300 feet of the water and crossed the *Acamar*'s stern with our tracers on its tail. Another, off the starboard quarter, dropped a stick of bombs that made a row of bluish flashes in the water. . . . To the north two more raiders fell slowly flaming into the sea. By 12:15 it was quiet again offshore.

But inshore the firing went on against those stubborn batteries, and at intervals throughout the night the distant cruisers joined in. The trajectory of the shells was clearly traced against the blue-black night, those from the far ships making high arcs, those from the destroyers inshore almost a straight line. Now and then our ack-ack guns would spit at a raiding plane and the broken lines of tracers would melt into the clouds, but from three miles offshore it was impossible to tell whether the firing was from the destroyers or the beach. The night was very dark, with only a splash of lighter blue above the horizon, where the full moon was somewhere behind the clouds, to show which was sea and which was sky; there was no clear line of horizon. But toward 5 o'clock, after less than five hours of sheer night, the blue washed out of the east. The horizon appeared again, and by ones and twos and dozens and scores the great flotilla came into sight. . . . At 5:30 the first B-24s appeared. As the light grew, the obstacles on the beaches and the boats caught by last night's ebbing tide stood out sharply in the queer pre-dawn pink, which made dark things darker and sharper. From shore still came the sounds of shelling and of rifle and machine-gun fire; from the warships the distant beat of broadsides.

So ended the first 24 hours of the invasion. On the other beaches things were going well: British vehicles were in Bayeux; VII Corps was ashore and moving forward, with most of its D-Day craft unloaded on schedule; radio contact had been established with the 82nd Airborne. But on this beach, and on the heights beyond, there would be many more days' struggle to make the beachhead secure.[4]

Cherbourg and Caen

Within five days the Allies had landed 16 divisions in Normandy. By June 12 the two beach-heads had been joined at Carentan, captured by the 101st Airborne, and the Allies controlled 80 miles of the Normandy coast with a penetration, at Bayeux, of 20 miles. The next day General Eisenhower congratulated his troops on their performance:

One week ago this morning there was established through your coordinated efforts, our first foothold in northwestern Europe.

High as was my pre-invasion confidence in your courage, skill and effectiveness in working together as a unit, your accomplishments in the first seven days of this campaign have exceeded my brightest hopes.

You are truly a great Allied team, a team which in each part gains its greatest satisfaction in rendering maximum assistance to the entire body and in which each individual member is justifiably confident in all others.

No matter how prolonged or bitter the struggle that lies ahead you will

do your full part toward the restoration of Free France, the liberation of
all European nations under Axis domination and the destruction of the
Nazi military machine.

I truly congratulate you upon a brilliantly successful beginning to this
great undertaking. Liberty loving people everywhere would like to join me
in saying to you:

I am proud of you.

That same day came recognition from Premier Stalin who, with the
opening of the long-awaited second front saw some of the pressure relieved from his own veteran warriors. "The history of wars," he said, "does
not know any such undertaking so broad in conception, and so grandiose
in its scale and so masterly in execution."

The beach-heads having been consolidated, the next phase was the
conquest of the Cotentin Peninsula with its great port of Cherbourg. By a
miracle of inventive and engineering skill we have been able to construct
an artificial port off the Normandy beaches, putting up great prefabri-
cated piers and enormous artificial breakwaters of scuttled blockships,
steel floats anchored to concrete caissons, and vast rubber floats. But tides
and storms were treacherous things—one of the harbors was destroyed by
a storm—and the port of Cherbourg was needed.

By June 18 the Americans had swept across the Cotentin Peninsula,
establishing a corridor seven miles wide, and were prepared to advance on
Cherbourg. The Germans, rejecting an offer to capitulate because they
needed time to destroy the port facilities, withdrew into the town and
fought off American assaults for five days before surrendering.

"The fall of Cherbourg," said General Bradley, "ends the second phase
in our campaign of liberation." And to the people of France he announced:
"Here is your first large city to be returned to you."

Meantime the British Second Army was heavily engaged at Caen. That
important town was the pivot of the German Seventh Army in Normandy
and the Fifteenth along the Channel coast to the east. The Germans therefore put up the fiercest kind of resistance, and there followed the heaviest
tank battle since D-Day. Not until July 19 were the British able to clear
Caen and thereafter they were balked of a break-through. But the British
contribution was scarcely less important than the American for in the
ceaseless fighting here the Germans frittered away their armor and their
manpower.

With the Cotentin Peninsula cleared of the enemy, the campaign for
Normandy and Brittany began. As the fighting moved deeper into Normandy our troops met a new obstacle, the age-old hedgerows of the Normandy farms. An American officer from the Pacific told Ernie Pyle that
the man-to-man fighting in the hedges was the nearest thing to Guadalcanal that he had seen:

I want to describe to you what the weird hedgerow fighting in northwestern France was like. This type of fighting was always in small groups,
so let's take as an example one company of men. Let's say they were

working forward on both sides of a country lane, and the company was responsible for clearing the two fields on either side of the road as it advanced. That meant there was only about one platoon to a field, and with the company's understrength from casualties, there might be no more than twenty-five or thirty men.

The fields were usually not more than fifty yards across and a couple of hundred yards long. They might have grain in them, or apple trees, but mostly they were just pastures of green grass, full of beautiful cows. The fields were surrounded on all sides by the immense hedgerows—ancient earthen banks, waist high, all matted with roots, and out of which grew weeds, bushes, and trees up to twenty feet high. The Germans used these barriers well. They put snipers in the trees. They dug deep trenches behind the hedgerows and covered them with timber, so that it was almost impossible for artillery to get at them. Sometimes they propped up machine guns with strings attached so that they could fire over the hedge without getting out of their holes. They even cut out a section of the hedgerow and hid a big gun or a tank in it, covering it with bush. Also they tunneled under the hedgerows from the back and made the opening on the forward side just large enough to stick a machine gun through. But mostly the hedgerow pattern was this: a heavy machine gun hidden at each end of the field and infantrymen hidden all along the hedgerow with rifles and machine pistols.

We had to dig them out. It was a slow and cautious business, and there was nothing dashing about it. Our men didn't go across the open fields in dramatic charges such as you see in the movies. They did at first, but they learned better. They went in tiny groups, a squad or less, moving yards apart and sticking close to the hedgerows on either end of the field. They crept a few yards, squatted, waited, then crept again.

If you could have been right up there between the Germans and the Americans you wouldn't have seen many men at any one time—just a few here and there, always trying to keep hidden. But you would have heard an awful lot of noise. Our men were taught in training not to fire until they saw something to fire at. But the principle didn't work in that country, because there was very little to see. So the alternative was to keep shooting constantly at the hedgerows. That pinned the Germans to their holes while we sneaked up on them. The attacking squads sneaked up the sides of the hedgerows while the rest of the platoon stayed back in their own hedgerow and kept the forward hedge saturated with bullets. They shot rifle grenades too, and a mortar squad a little farther back kept lobbing mortar shells over onto the Germans. The little advance groups worked their way up to the far ends of the hedgerows at the corners of the field. They first tried to knock out the machine guns at each corner. They did this with hand grenades, rifle grenades and machine guns. . . .

Usually, when the pressure was on, the German defenders of the hedgerow started pulling back. They would take their heavier guns and most of the men back a couple of fields and start digging in for a new line. They left about two machine guns and a few riflemen scattered through the hedge to do a lot of shooting and hold up the Americans as long as they could. Our men would then sneak along the front side of the hedgerow, throwing grenades over onto the other side and spraying the hedges with their guns. The fighting was close—only a few yards apart. . . .

This hedgerow business was a series of little skirmishes like that clear across the front, thousands and thousands of little skirmishes. No single one of them was very big. Added up over the days and weeks, however, they made a man-sized war—with thousands on both sides getting killed. But that is only a general pattern of the hedgerow fighting. Actually each one was a little separate war, fought under different circumstances. For instance, the fight might be in a woods instead of an open field. The Germans would be dug in all over the woods, in little groups, and it was really tough to get them out. Often in cases like that we just went around the woods and kept going, and let later units take care of those surrounded and doomed fellows. Or we might go through a woods and clean it out, and another company, coming through a couple of hours later, would find it full of Germans again. In a war like this everything was in such confusion that I never could see how either side ever got anywhere. . . .

In a long drive an infantry company often went for a couple of days without letting up. Ammunition was carried up to it by hand, and occasionally by jeep. The soldiers sometimes ate only one K ration a day. They sometimes ran out of water. Their strength was gradually whittled down by wounds, exhaustion cases and straggling. Finally they would get an order to sit where they were and dig in. Then another company would pass through, or around them, and go on with the fighting. The relieved company might get to rest as much as a day or two. But in a big push such as the one that broke us out of the beachhead, a few hours' respite was about all they could expect.

The company I was with got its orders to rest about five o'clock one afternoon. They dug foxholes along the hedgerows, or commandeered German ones already dug. Regardless of how tired a man might be, he always dug in the first thing. Then they sent some men looking for water. They got more K rations up by jeep, and sat on the ground eating them. They hoped they would stay there all night, but they weren't counting on it too much. Shortly after supper a lieutenant came out of a farmhouse and told the sergeants to pass the word to be ready to move in ten minutes. They bundled on their packs and started just before dark. Within half an hour they had run into a new fight that lasted all night. They had had less than four hours' rest in three solid days of fighting. . . .

There in Normandy the Germans went in for sniping in a wholesale manner. There were snipers everywhere: in trees, in buildings, in piles of wreckage, in the grass. But mainly they were in the high, bushy hedgerows that form the fences of all the Norman fields and line every roadside and lane.

It was perfect sniping country. A man could hide himself in the thick fence-row shrubbery with several days' rations, and it was like hunting a needle in a haystack to find him. Every mile we advanced there were dozens of snipers left behind us. They picked off our soldiers one by one as they walked down the roads or across the fields. It wasn't safe to move into a new bivouac area until the snipers had been cleaned out. The first bivouac I moved into had shots ringing through it for a full day before all the hidden gunmen were rounded up. It gave me the same spooky feeling that I got on moving into a place I suspected of being sown with mines.[5]

But Normandy had its compensations. One of them was the ecstasy with which the French people greeted their liberators. Richard McMillan, who was with the British troops, tells how they were received:

I entered Bayeux with the first troops. It was a scene of rejoicing as the people went wild. The streets were blocked with cheering men and women and children. The Tricolor and Union Jacks were hung in the windows. Cafes threw open their doors and pianists began to play British and French patriotic tunes. Crowds danced and shouted, "Vive Tommy," "Vive l'Amerique."

It was a scene of mingled war and peace through which I passed as I drove a jeep into the interior along part of the front line. After a dusty dreary morning, the sun burst through and the skies cleared. It was a perfect summer day. Driving through the coastal defense belt, I saw the havoc wrought by the Allied naval and air bombardment which had wrecked some roads and many hamlets which the Germans had used as headquarters. . . .

In the fields peasants tended their sheep and cattle as if this day were no different from any other. The Allied war machine rolled past along the dusty highways, but the only sign the stolid peasants gave was a wave of the hand. It was the townspeople, like those of Bayeux, who really showed their appreciation, repeating again and again, *"C'est le jour de la liberation."*[6]

The Second Battle of Britain

On June 15 the Germans struck back, with a new weapon. The blow came not in Normandy, but against Britain. It was the V-1. The Battle of Britain, which the British had thought won, was renewed, and went on all through that summer, exacting casualties almost as heavy as during the dark days of the blitz.

For a long time British censorship about the new weapon was tight, for the War Office was determined to keep from the enemy all information about the results of the bombing. In November, however, after the problem of defense had largely been solved, an official story of the bomb, bomb damage, and counter-measures was released:

British Secret Service agents first reported that the Germans were contriving a new long-range bombardment weapon in April, 1943. . . .

For the first six months it was a battle of wits; the wits of a handful of British agents against those of the German nation; of R.A.F. reconnaissance and aerial photography against German camouflage.

Aerial photographs taken in May, 1943, showed a large experimental station at Peenemünde, on an island in the Baltic. This establishment was seen to possess some mysterious contrivances that the Intelligence Services were at that time quite unable to explain.

Peenemünde was photographed again and again. Eventually a photographic interpretation officer, Flight Officer Constance Babington-Smith, of the Women's Auxiliary Air Force, spotted a tiny blurred speck on one of the prints which, on enlargement, was found to be a miniature aeroplane sitting on a sloping ramp fitted with rails. A later photograph showed that the ground near the ramp was darkly streaked, as if seared by a very hot blast.

From these photographs and other evidence, it was concluded that the speck was a pilotless, jet-propelled aircraft; whether it was to be used as an offensive weapon or merely as a target plane could not then be decided. This was the secret V-1—the *Vergeltungswaffe*—the "Vengeance Weapon."

In August of 1943 a strong force of . . . the R.A.F. Bomber Command dropped over 1,500 tons of high explosives on Peenemünde. Thus the battle against the flying bomb began at the very source.

Germany's intentions soon became clear. In November it was found that she was building a chain of concrete launching sites like those at Peenemünde all along the French coast, from Calais to Cherbourg. They were pointed in the direction of London.

The Royal Air Force and the U. S. Army Air Forces began their vast bombing operations against the V-1 launching sites in December, 1943.

Continuous air reconnaissances, made in all weather throughout the winter, located each site as it sprang up. . . .

The bomber offensive dropped some 100,000 tons. It cost nearly 450 aircraft and 2,900 pilots and airmen.

But for these bombing operations, the flying-bomb attacks might have started in January instead of June. If they had come in January, winter weather would have caused many additional hazards to the defenses. . . .

Enough was known about the V-1 by this time to arrange for the defense of London.

Three lines of defense were established. First, a balloon barrage immediately surrounding the city. Next, an anti-aircraft gun belt, placed as near London as possible to shorten the length of the front and thus obtain the closest concentration of fire with the fewest guns. Then, outside that a fighter zone.

But preparations for the invasion of France were going on simultaneously, and every available gun and balloon was needed for the protection of embarkation ports. Since no one knew when the flying-bomb attack would start, these defenses had to be ready to switch, at a moment's notice, from the defense of the ports to the defense of London.

On D-Day plus six the long postponed attack at last began. The defenses were immediately moved in their prepared positions.

For the eighty days from June 12th until the end of August, an average of 100 flying bombs a day were launched against England—some 8,000 in all.

By day the small pilotless aircraft could be seen skimming the roof tops, or flying over the Kentish villages. At night their tails of flame lit up the blackout. London was a place of demonical noises—the sirens, the guns, the hideous roar as a flying bomb passed overhead, the sudden menacing silence when the bomb's motor cut off, and then the crash that meant more shattered limbs, more crushed bodies.

The bulk of the attack was aimed at London, where ninety-two per cent of the fatal casualties occurred. . . .

It was found that the flying bombs were immensely hard to shoot down; first, because they flew so fast—almost 400 miles an hour; and second, because their flying height of 2,300 feet or less was too low for the heavy guns and too high for the light guns.

They came in droves, often in cloudy weather, when the fighters' visibility was low.

Forty per cent of the number launched was destroyed during the first month, but even so the number of civilian casualties reached front-line proportions. . . .

Scientists went to work on the problem; one of them, Professor Sir Thomas Merton, produced a range-finder, so simple that the whole device costs little more than twenty cents, so ingenious that it answers the purpose completely. . . .

The percentage of bombs shot down by the guns soared up from 17% in the first week to 24% in the second, 27% in the third, 40% in the fourth, 55% in the fifth, and 74% in the sixth week. The total number of flying bombs destroyed by the guns had reached 1,560 by the end of August. Many of these were shot down into the sea.

Fighter pilots of the R.A.F. have shot down over 1,900 flying bombs since the beginning of the bombardment. Some pilots made individual scores of fifty bombs.

Their methods are unorthodox, and sometimes suicidal: but they are effective.

They were evolved out of trial and tragic error. . . . Hurling themselves at the bombs at 400 m.p.h. they shot them down from all angles and at all distances, until they discovered the minimum safety margin before the explosion.

The "nudging" method, discovered by a pilot who had ran out of ammunition, calls for split-second timing. The pilot flies alongside the robot, slips the wing tip of the plane beneath it, and, with a flick of the control column, sends it spinning to earth; at high speeds the air cushion formed between the two machines is powerful enough to deflect the bomb, without actually touching it.

"Slipstreaming" was discovered by accident, when a Mustang pilot power-diving down on to a bomb overshot it. Looking back he saw his target spiralling down into the Channel—the slipstream of his aircraft had thrown it out of control.

One R.A.F. pilot destroyed four bombs by three different methods in thirty minutes. He "slipstreamed" two, shot down one and, when his guns jammed, "nudged" a fourth, sending it crashing down onto the Germans in Boulogne.

Out of every 100 flying bombs launched by the enemy in the eighty days of the second Battle of London, forty-six were destroyed by the combined efforts of all three defenses; twenty-five were inaccurate and dived into the sea, or exploded in France, doing considerable damage among the Germans; twenty-nine got through to the London Region—that is, a total of some 2,300. . . .

Secret Service agents reported that tunnels and caves near Paris, formerly used for mushroom growing, had been turned into vast bomb storage depots. During July they were attacked three times by the R.A.F. Great 12,000-pounders crashed through into the caves. Everything inside was lost and many of the caves themselves were utterly destroyed. The enemy's communications were constantly strafed. . . .

Bombing greatly weakened the attacks, but the one completely effective way of stopping them was to capture the firing sites. The first of them were taken by the American troops in the Cherbourg area at the end of July, and the main concentration of them in the Pas de Calais were taken by Canadian troops early in September.

The flying-bomb launching sites in Northern France were captured in the ordinary course of military operations, the strategic objective of which was the defeat of the enemy. The sites were never an objective in themselves.

Bombs that have been hit but not exploded by gun fire have been known to turn in their tracks and make for home again.

More than 1,104,000 houses have been destroyed or damaged by flying bombs. This number does not include the 149 schools, 111 churches and ninety-eight hospitals. In Croydon, the worst bombed borough of London, three out of every four houses were hit.

Hampton Court Palace, St. Thomas's Hospital, the Royal Lodge, Windsor, and the Guards' Chapel, are among the many well-loved buildings that have been damaged.

Even now the attacks go on. A small number of flying bombs still reach Southern England from a due easterly direction.

These bombs are being launched, not from the ground, but from specially adapted German bombers flying over the North Sea. They were carrying the bombs pick-a-back—perhaps it would be more accurate to call them pick-a-belly as it has now been discovered that they are launched from under the fuselage.

R.A.F. Intruder squadrons are still always on watch, ready to intercept the pick-a-back bombers, and many have been shot down. . . . Nevertheless, pick-a-back attacks continue . . . and now *Vergeltungswaffe-II* has begun.[7]

"And now *Vergeltungswaffe-II* has begun." The British report on V-1 had closed with this bravely mild understatement of a new time of terror greater than the dangerous eighty days of the V-1.

V-2 was the German flying rocket. It was a stratosphere bomb, heavier than the V-1, and it traveled faster than sound. No public warning was possible. Defensive measures devised against the V-1 were useless against the new weapon.

When the Allied armies spread out through France and the Low Countries the barrage of the V bombs ceased, but the Germans continued to send the long-range V-2 rockets over London spasmodically until the very last days of the war.

Break-through

"I have a hunch," wrote Ernie Pyle, "that July 25 of the year 1944 will be one of the great historic pinnacles of this war." Like so many of Pyle's hunches, this was right. For that was the day of the great break-through that opened the road to Paris—and beyond to the Rhine.

When Cherbourg and the Cotetin Peninsula had been won, the American armies turned south, broke through the German left flank at Avranches, drove into Brittany, swung around and outflanked Paris from the South. Two weeks of savage fighting had won Saint Lo, on July 18, opening the way to a breach of the German lines. The break-through began with a tremendous bombardment by 3,000 planes and a sustained artillery bombardment west of Saint Lo. Ernie Pyle tells of that stupendous bombardment, and one of its tragic aspects:

Surely history will give a name to the battle that sent us boiling out of Normandy, some name comparable with Saint-Mihiel or Meuse-Argonne of the last war. But to us there on the spot at the time it was known simply as the "break-through. . . ." One evening Lieutenant General Omar Bradley, commanding all American troops in France, came to our camp and briefed us on the coming operation. It would start, he said, on the first day we had three hours of good flying weather in the forenoon. . . .

The general told us the attack would cover a segment of the German line west of Saint Lo, about five miles wide. In that narrow segment we would have three infantry divisions, side by side. Right behind them would be another infantry and two armored divisions. Once a hole was broken, the armored divisions would slam through several miles beyond, then turn right toward the sea behind the Germans in that sector in the hope of cutting them off and trapping them. The remainder of our line on both sides of the attack would keep the pressure on to hold the Germans in front of them so they couldn't send reinforcements against our main push.

The attack was to open with a gigantic two-hour air bombardment by 1,800 planes—the biggest ever attempted by air in direct support of ground troops. It would start with dive bombers, then great four-motored heavies would come, and then mediums, then dive bombers again, and then the ground troops would kick off, with air fighters continuing to work ahead of them. It was a thrilling plan to listen to. General Bradley didn't tell us that it was the big thing, but other officers gave us the word. They said, "This is no limited objective drive. This is it. This is the big break-through. . . ."

The attack was on. It was July 25.

If you don't have July 25 pasted in your hat I would advise you to put it there immediately. At least paste it in your mind. For I have a hunch that July 25 of the year 1944 will be one of the great historic pinnacles of this war. It was the day we began a mighty surge out of our confined Normandy spaces, the day we stopped calling our area the beachhead and knew we were fighting a war across the whole expanse of France. From that day onward all dread possibilities and fears for disaster to our invasion were behind us. No longer was there any possibility of our getting kicked off. No longer would it be possible for fate, or weather, or enemy to wound us fatally; from that day onward the future could hold nothing for us but growing strength and eventual victory. . . .

By field telephone, radio, and liaison men, word was passed down to the very smallest unit of troops that the attack was on. There was still an hour before the bombers, and three hours before the infantry were to move. There was nothing for the infantry to do but dig a little deeper and wait. A cessation of motion seemed to come over the countryside and all its brown-clad inhabitants, a sense of last-minute sitting in silence before the holocaust.

The first planes of the mass onslaught came over a little before 10 A.M. They were the fighters and dive bombers. The main road, running cross-wise in front of us, was their bomb line. They were to bomb only on the far side of that road. Our kickoff infantry had been pulled back a few hundred yards from the near side of the road. Everyone in the area had been given the strictest orders to be in foxholes, for high-level bombers can, and do quite excusably, make mistakes. . . .

Our front lines were marked by long strips of colored cloth laid on the ground, and with colored smoke to guide our airmen during the mass bombing. Dive bombers hit it just right. We stood and watched them barrel nearly straight down out of the sky. They were bombing about half a mile ahead of where we stood. They came in groups, diving from every direction, perfectly timed, one right after another. Everywhere we looked separate groups of planes were on the way down, or on the way back up, or slanting over for a dive, or circling, circling, circling over our heads, waiting for their turn.

The air was full of sharp and distinct sounds of cracking bombs and the heavy rips of the planes' machine guns and the splitting screams of diving wings. It was all fast and furious, yet distinct. And then a new sound gradually droned into our ears, a sound deep and all-encompassing with no notes in it—just a gigantic faraway surge of doomlike sound. It was the heavies. They came from directly behind us. At first they were the merest dots in the sky. We could see clots of them against the far heavens, too tiny to count individually. They came on with a terrible slowness. They came in flights of twelve, three flights to a group and in groups stretched out across the sky. They came in "families" of about seventy planes each. Maybe those gigantic waves were two miles apart, maybe they were ten miles, I don't know. But I do know they came in a constant procession and I thought it would never end. What the Germans must have thought is beyond comprehension.

The flight across the sky was slow and studied. I've never known a storm, or a machine, or any resolve of man that had about it the aura of such a ghastly relentlessness. I had the feeling that even had God appeared beseechingly before them in the sky, with palms outstretched to persuade them back, they would not have had within them the power to turn from their irresistible course. . . .

The Germans began to shoot heavy, high ack-ack. Great black puffs of it by the score speckled the sky until it was hard to distinguish smoke puffs from planes. And then someone shouted that one of the planes was smoking. Yes, we could all see it. A long faint line of black smoke stretched straight for a mile behind one of them. And as we watched there was a gigantic sweep of flame over the plane. From nose to tail it disappeared in flame, and it slanted slowly down and banked around the sky in great wide curves, this way and that way, as rhythmically and gracefully as in a slow-motion waltz. Then suddenly it seemed to change its mind and it swept upward, steeper and steeper and ever slower until finally it seemed poised motionless on its own black pillar of smoke. And then just as slowly it turned over and dived for the earth—a golden spearhead on the straight black shaft of its own creation—and disappeared behind the treetops. But before it was down there were more cries of, "There's another one smoking—and there's a third one now." Chutes came out of some of the planes. Out of some came no chutes at all. One of white silk caught on the tail of a plane. Men with binoculars could see him fighting to get loose until flames swept over him, and then a tiny black dot fell through space, all alone.

And all that time the great flat ceiling of the sky was roofed by all the other planes that didn't go down, plowing their way forward as if there were no turmoil in the world. Nothing deviated them by the slightest. They stalked on, slowly and with a dreadful pall of sound, as though they were seeing only something at a great distance and nothing existed between. God, how we admired those men up there and sickened for the ones who fell.

It is possible to become so enthralled by some of the spectacles of war that a man is momentarily captivated away from his own danger. That's what happened to our little group of soldiers as we stood watching the mighty bombing. But that benign state didn't last long. As we watched, there crept into our consciousness a realization that the windrows of exploding bombs were easing back toward us, flight by flight, instead of gradually forward, as the plan called for. Then we were horrified by the suspicion that those machines, high in the sky and completely detached from us, were aiming their bombs at the smoke line on the ground—and a gentle breeze was drifting the smoke line back over us! . . . And then all of an instant the universe became filled with a gigantic rattling as of huge ripe seeds in a mammoth dry gourd. I doubt that any of us had ever heard that sound before, but instinct told us what it was. It was bombs by the hundred, hurtling down through the air above us.

Many times I've heard bombs whistle or swish or rustle, but never before had I heard bombs rattle. I still don't know the explanation of it. But it is an awful sound. We dived. Some got into a dugout. Others made foxholes and ditches and some got behind a garden wall—although which side would be "behind" was anybody's guess. I was too late for the dugout. The nearest place was a wagon shed which formed one end of the stone house. The rattle was right down upon us. I remember hitting the ground flat, all spread out like the cartoons of people flattened by steam rollers, and then squirming like an eel to get under one of the heavy wagons in the shed.

An officer whom I didn't know was wriggling beside me. We stopped at the same time, simultaneously feeling it was hopeless to move farther. The bombs were already crashing around us. We lay with our heads slightly up—like two snakes—staring at each other. I know it was in both our minds and in our eyes, asking each other what to do. Neither of us knew.

We said nothing. We just lay sprawled, gaping at each other in a futile appeal, our faces about a foot apart, until it was over.

There is no description of the sound and fury of those bombs except to say it was chaos, and a waiting for darkness. The feeling of the blast was sensational. The air struck us in hundreds of continuing flutters. Our ears drummed and rang. We could feel quick little waves of concussion on the chest and in the eyes.

At last the sound died down and we looked at each other in disbelief. Gradually we left the foxholes and sprawling places and came out to see what the sky had in store for us. As far as we could see other waves were approaching from behind. When a wave would pass a little to the side of us we were garrulously grateful, for most of them flew directly overhead. Time and again the rattle came down over us. Bombs struck in the orchard to our left. They struck in orchards ahead of us. They struck as far as half a mile behind us. Everything about us was shaken, but our group came through unhurt. . . .

When we came out of our ignominious sprawling and stood up again to watch, we knew that the error had been caught and checked. The bombs again were falling where they were intended, a mile or so ahead. Even at a mile away a thousand bombs hitting within a few seconds can shake the earth and shatter the air. There was still a dread in our hearts, but it gradually eased as the tumult and destruction moved slowly forward.

Long before, the German ack-ack guns had gone out of existence. The ack-ack gunners either took to their holes or were annihilated. How many waves of heavy bombers we put over I have no idea. There were supposed to be 1,800 planes that day, and I believe it was announced later that there were more than 3,000. It seems incredible to me that any German could have come out of that bombardment with his sanity. When it was over I was grateful, in a chastened way that I had never before experienced, for just being alive.

I thought an attack by our troops was impossible then, for it is an unnerving thing to be bombed by your own planes. During the bad part a colonel I had known a long time was walking up and down behind the farmhouse, snapping his fingers and saying over and over to himself, "Goddammit, goddammit!" As he passed me once he stopped and stared and said, "Goddammit!"

And I said, "There can't be any attack now, can there?" and he said, "No," and began walking again, snapping his fingers and tossing his arm as though he were throwing rocks at the ground.

The leading company of our battalion was to spearhead the attack forty minutes after our heavy bombing ceased. The company had been hit directly by our bombs. Their casualties, including casualties in shock, were heavy. Men went to pieces and had to be sent back. The company was shattered and shaken. And yet Company B attacked—and on time, to the minute! They attacked, and within an hour they sent word back that they had advanced 800 yards through German territory and were still going. Around our farmhouse men with stars on their shoulders almost wept when the word came over the portable radio. The American soldier can be majestic when he needs to be.

I'm sure that back in England that night other men—bomber crews—

almost wept, and maybe they did really, in the awful knowledge that they
had killed our own American troops. But the chaos and the bitterness
there in the orchards and between the hedgerows that afternoon soon
passed. After the bitterness came the remembrance that the Air Force was
the strong right arm in front of us. Not only at the beginning, but ceaselessly and everlastingly, every moment of the faintest daylight, the Air
Force was up there banging away ahead of us.

Anybody makes mistakes. The enemy made them just the same as we
did. The smoke and confusion of battle bewildered us on the ground as
well as in the air. And in this case the percentage of error was really very
small compared with the colossal storm of bombs that fell upon the enemy.
The Air Force was wonderful throughout the invasion, and the men on
the ground appreciated it.[8]

During this aerial bombardment the Eighth Air Force dropped 3,400
tons of bombs in a single hour; the Ninth followed with another 1,000
tons. Then came a tremendous artillery barrage. When this lifted, the
infantry-tank attack was launched. Everett Hollis describes it:

They bounded over the hedgerows, pulled by bull-dozers, or they cut
straight through the hedgerows by means of a device invented by Sergeant
Curtis G. Colin of Cranford, N.J., who hit upon the idea of taking the
tetrahedrons of angle-iron which the Germans had installed on the Normandy beaches and transforming them into cutting blades. Four of these
blades, jutting out in front of a tank, were enough to cut through a good-
sized hedgerow. The tanks equipped with Colin's contrivance were known
as "rhino tanks," and came to be an accepted item of army ordnance.

Infantrymen rode into the attack atop the tanks, and behind them came
more trucks and half-tracks laden with more infantry. The whole idea was
to cram as many men and tanks as possible through the German "crust."
It worked, and the tanks, after breaking through into the open country,
fanned out in every direction—to the west toward Coutances to slam some
seven German divisions up against the western wall of the Normandy
peninsula, and to the south and east where a 20-mile bulge was driven into
the enemy positions. Over to the east, meanwhile, General Montgomery
sent his British crashing against the stout German defenses south and west
of Caen, mainly to the south toward Falaise. This was an important contribution to the grand success of Bradley's offensive, for it served to tie
down the major part of the Germans' strength, including six of the eight
Panzer divisions then on the Normandy front.

The Germans held on just outside Saint Lo for almost a week, wrecking
what was left of the town with their mortars and artillery, but the momentum of the Americans could not be broken and it finally carried across the
Saint Lo-Periers road and took a firm hold on the middle base of the
peninsula. On July 31 the Americans were at Avranches, leaving Normandy behind and entering Brittany.[9]

"We've really broken the bottleneck on the beachhead," said a commentator, and so it seemed. For, as Everett Hollis added:

The advance shot across French soil like a thunderbolt. This was the kind of an attack that destroys armies and wins wars, not just battles. From Avranches, the American tanks raced across the 100-mile base of the Brittany peninsula and down to the Bay of Biscay in less than a week and approached the port of Saint Nazaire. All of Brittany was sealed off, with its great ports of Brest, Lorient, Saint Malo, Nantes and their German garrisons. Some thirteen German divisions were either trapped or decimated, and, in the two weeks after Bradley's rocket shot out from Saint Lo, the *Wehrmacht* lost some 250,000 men, including prisoners.

Tank spearheads reached out toward Saint Nazaire and up through the middle of the Brittany peninsula toward Brest. They sent word back asking for instructions to their objectives.

"To hell with objectives, keep going!" was the answer that came from one American commander.

And while Bradley sent his tanks racing up into Brittany and down to the Loire River, another column cut eastward in a bold drive pointed directly at Paris. Le Mans was the immediate goal; an important railroad hub, its lines led straight to Paris 110 miles further on. The Germans were fighting to escape annihilation in a triangle that had as its base the line across Brittany, as its sides the Seine and the Loire, and its apex—Paris.

It was at this crucial point that General Eisenhower and General Bradley hit upon an idea that was sternly criticized on many sides at the time, but which turned out to be one of those bold and brilliant strokes that thrusts its authors into the ranks of the masters of warfare.

The Third Army had bumped up against stubborn German resistance around the Breton ports—this was not Nazi fanaticism but part of a shrewd German plan that was to give us plenty of trouble for months to come—and to overcome this resistance might require weeks of valuable time and large forces of men. The Germans defending the ports were hopelessly cut off and so Eisenhower, after talking it over with Bradley and Montgomery, decided to contain the ports with relatively small forces while he turned his main strength eastward to smash the already disorganized German Seventy Army and encircle Paris.

Not many generals would have given up the prospect of securing the big new ports, which the Allies needed so desperately at that moment for supplies, and chosen to gamble on a drive way across France with only the still crippled port of Cherbourg and the beaches to rely upon.[10]

The Germans, threatened with an unexpected attack from the south and—when the British broke through—ultimate encirclement, struck back. They tried to cut the American corridor to Avranches. They did succeed in penetrating it, but not in cutting it: even had they done so their position would not have been substantially improved. For four days German armor thrust at the American lines, while American planes and artillery subjected them to incessant bombardment. Then, even as this German counter-attack was going on, the British and Canadians broke through at Falaise to meet Americans coming up from Argentan and close a trap upon the German Seventh Army. In four days, August 19–23, the remnants of the Seventh Army were destroyed.

Now the road to Paris was open.

The Liberation of Paris

After the destruction of the German Seventh Army, Patton's forces swept forward on a broad front towards the Seine. By the 19th two columns had reached that river north of Paris; another column swung toward the great city from the south through Chartres in time to save the glorious cathedral there from irreparable damage; still another spearheaded to the south through Orléans and the Loire Valley. By the 20th American soldiers could see the beckoning spire of the Eiffel Tower.

With liberation so near, the Parisians rose:

Fragmentary broadcasts came out of Paris those first few days of hysteria, but none was more eloquent than one caught by the CBS short wave Listening Post at 6:03 P.M. EWT on August 24. You had to put on stethoscope headphones to hear it:

A voice on Radio France, inside the city, seems to announce the evening program. It blurs. Then you hear "We will use our last energies for the final struggle." Again a blur: then—"It is the duty of all Frenchmen to participate in the fight against the Germans."

Someone says something about one Georges Bidault, president of the French National Resistance Council . . . and he says: "Paris is liberated. It has liberated itself."

And suddenly over his voice you hear the machine guns. He resumes: "The Parisians have risen in irresistible spirit. The shame and treason are over. . . . I address, by radio, France, and the world." Then you hear the heavy guns.

At 6:20 the voice fades under a German voice—the Boche is jamming the wave-length. Presently another French voice says "the engineer is going to work." He apparently did, for at 6:38 Radio France is back on the air, saying "The street does not belong tonight to the joy of the people, but to the fighters . . . nearby barricades . . ." then *WHAM*—shooting, very nearby. Then: ". . . the morale is excellent, the people are confident, they have erected barricades. We will give you the news as soon as we get it." Then somebody quotes from a play about the French Revolution, the voice fades, and you hear music: *Malbrouk s'en va-t-en guerre,* and *Auprés de ma blonde.* The silence.[11]

Next day at 2 P.M. General Leclerc announced the surrender of the Germans in Paris in a scrubby baggage room at the Gare Montparnasse.

"Paris," said Larry Lesueur, "is certainly the happiest city in the world tonight." Unrestrained even by snipers' bullets, the celebrations continued for three days, reaching a delirious climax as General Eisenhower reviewed French, British, and American troops marching through the Arc de Triomphe. That joy was shared, too, by people everywhere in the world. Writing from London that shrewd observer, Raymond Daniell, interpreted the significance of the liberation:

Paris is . . . a token of a great nation freed and risen . . . but it is also a symbol of the resurgence in the minds of men in Europe of the spirit of liberty. Surrendered undefended to the Germans four years ago Paris was a warning of an impending defeat for freedom everywhere. Liberated now with the help of her own people, this French city on the Seine, where the dream of the dignity of man reached its first flowering, is a portent of Allied victory in the global war to free mankind from the new tyranny of authoritarianism.

The political, psychological and military value of Paris cannot be overestimated. But there is a liability as well. Having wrested the French capital from the Germans we must feed its more than 2,000,000 people hungry after weeks of siege. That, added to the task of keeping our fast-moving armies supplied with food, gasoline and ammunition, will not be an easy task. But it is one that must be done and done well if we are to retain the confidence of the French that we have today.

The exigencies of war and our strategy have been combined at present to give us credit for very gracious behavior. It suited our military ends to allow the French to assert themselves, and for that the people of France and all the little countries who were concerned about the motives of the big powers are grateful and relieved.

And it was a gesture that will not soon be forgotten in France that the first troops to go to the rescue of the underground forces who had tried to break the Germans hold on their beloved city were soldiers of France who had followed Brig. Gen. Jacques-Philippe Leclerc from Chadec in Africa to the final rescue of Paris.[12]

Invasion from the South

Even as the Germans were fighting desperately to extricate their battered armies from Normandy and trying to pull out of Paris, they were confronted with new difficulties. On August 15 a powerful Allied army landed on the coast of southern France and swept swiftly inland to effect a juncture with the armies of the north.

All through the first two weeks of August bombers from Italy and Corsica had hammered on the French coast, while another great fleet gathered in Mediterranean waters to escort an invasion army. Then on the night and early morning of August 15 came a tremendous air and naval bombardment.

The landing was "the war's worst kept secret" but opposition was slight. Paratroopers who had been dropped inland to seize roads and bridges and disorganize enemy counter-measures, found little to do.

Prime Minister Churchill, sitting on the bridge of the *Kimberley*, watched the invasion with satisfaction. Only two weak divisions were encountered by the Seventh Army, and these were promptly gobbled up. Leaving the reduction of the great ports of Marseilles and Toulon to the FFI, which here performed its most effective service, General Patch's men swept forward with spectacular speed. Within two weeks they had occupied the great industrial city of Lyon, and were pushing on to the Belfort Gap, gateway to southern Germany. As the FFI rose, the Germans were cleared out of all France south of the Loire except in some of the great ports like Bordeaux and St. Nazaire.

Into Germany

In the north the Allied armies had swept forward almost unopposed from the Seine to the Somme, the Marne and the Belgian border, through territory famous from the first World War. Third Army spearheads reached the historic Marne on August 28, drove through Chateau-Thierry, took Soissons and Rheims and the great fortress city of Verdun. To the north the First Army took Sedan at the Belgian border, and still farther north the British and Canadian armies of General Montgomery raced along the coast through Lille, into Belgium and to the Dutch border. The Battle for France was over; the Battle for Germany was about to begin.

On September 11, as Roosevelt and Churchill conferred in the ancient city where Montcalm and Wolfe had once fought, the American First Army freed Luxembourg and pushed into the "sacred soil" of Germany. The British advanced into the Netherlands. Just one hundred days after the landings on Normandy, Allied armies along a 250-mile line from Ostend to the Swiss border were poised for the invasion. To the German people General Eisenhower proclaimed:

We come as conquerors but not as oppressors. . . . We shall overthrow the Nazi rule, dissolve the Nazi party and abolish the cruel, oppressive and discriminatory laws and institutions which the party has created. We shall eradicate that German militarism which has so often disrupted the peace of the world.

There was hard fighting ahead before German militarism would be eradicated. In front of the Allied forces was the Siegfried Line, defended by an army probably as large, if not as well equipped, as Eisenhower's. A frontal assault would be bloody. The High Command decided to make a bold attempt to outflank the Siegfried Line, just as the Germans had outflanked the Maginot Line in 1940. On September 17 came the spectacular air-borne invasion of Holland—a gamble which, if successful, might end the war. In the greatest operation of its kind in history the U.S. 82nd and 101st Airborne and the British 1st Airborne Divisions flew from bases in Britain.

The 82nd and 101st Divisions captured Eindhoven and key bridges across the Meuse and the Waal Rivers, but the British 1st Division, landing

near Arnhem, were surrounded and overwhelmed. Everett Hollis tells of
the paratroop landings and the fighting that followed:

Lieutenant General Lewis H. Brereton's Anglo-American air army
was dropped on three principal objectives. The first was around Eindhoven where American and Polish sky troops seized the main communications and joined up with General Dempsey's force after diverting the
Germans' attention and enabling the Second Army to get across
the Dutch border. The second point of landing was at Nijmegen where
the Waal was broad and swift and spanned by a massive new steel and
concrete bridge that was needed for the Allied heavy tanks. When the
Americans landed on the south bank of the river, close by the tree-lined
Hunerpark, they found themselves fully exposed to the raking fire of
German anti-tank guns and snipers using the doors and windows of old
Fort Belvedere, a pile of stone left over from Charlemagne's reign. Assault on the fortress was impossible, so the Americans crouched behind
whatever cover they could find until three British tanks tore up the road
from Eindhoven, 20 miles to the south, and knocked out Belvedere's
guns. Then, in 26 rubber assault boats, they began crossing the river. By
this time, a few pieces of British artillery had arrived from Eindhoven up
through a perilously thin corridor under constant German fire, and began shelling the Germans on the north bank.

Each of the 26 rubber boats carried a dozen men, but after the first trip
only 13 boats returned for more paratroopers. Some of the men paddled,
others bailed with their canteen cups as German machine-gun bullets spat
into the boats. The second time eight boats returned, one with three dead
Americans and four wounded. After the third trip only five boats were
left; they kept going.

Finally the American flag appeared at the northern end of the bridge,
and the rest of the infantry stormed across, followed by tanks. There were
several awful minutes, as the first tanks rumbled across, while the men
waited to see whether German demolition charges would send tanks and
steel girders flying into the air. But a young Dutch lieutenant, parachuting
in with the first Americans, had telephoned to patriot friends inside Nijmegen (on a pay-station telephone). The patriots, who had waited
through four years of slavery for just such a chance, quickly removed the
detonators of the explosives strapped to the underspans.

Nijmegen went off like a dream, but at Arnhem on the Neder Rhine, 10
miles further north, the whole operation became a tragic nightmare.

The "Red Devils" of the First British Air-Borne division, carrying out
the toughest of the three assignments because they would have the longest
wait for the ground forces to catch up with them, came down just north of
Arnhem. There were eight thousand of them, in bright red berets, led by
Major General Robert Eliot Urquhart, a cheerful moustached Scot and at
42 one of the British army's youngest generals.

The job of the British was to hold a bridgehead there across the Neder
Rhine until the British Second Army came up overland. But the army
never got there in any strength. It was stopped two miles beyond Nijmegen
when the Germans, slashing in at the thin corridor from both sides, re-

peatedly cut General Dempsey's tenuous line of supply and communication. Only two regiments got through to the Neder Rhine, not enough to turn the battle.

Urquhart and his "Red Devils" ran into trouble before they could reach the bridge across the Neder Rhine. The Germans pressed them into a "little patch of hell," about nine miles by five miles, and turned a concentrated, murderous fire of artillery, mortars and machine guns upon them. A few were able to take shelter in the ruins of houses, but most of the British had nothing more than open slit trenches. Tiger tanks drove at them from all sides; German flame-throwers cremated living men.

It lasted for nine days and nights, and all the time the "Red Devils" were being cut up into smaller groups, in packed patches of screeching shells, fire-spouting tanks, strafing planes, sleepless nights, foodless days. The food allotment was cut to one-sixth. Ammunition was rationed. The men had almost nothing left with which to fight. Finally they were shooting their pistols at German tanks. . . .

The Allied command gave the "Red Devils" what reinforcement it could, but it was pitifully inadequate. After the third day some Polish air-borne troops arrived. Transport planes from England flew in food and ammunition, dropping the supplies by parachute. Sometimes the planes were set afire by German ack-ack fire, but they flew in anyway. Then the weather turned so bad that few planes could get through.

On Monday, September 25, Urquhart passed the word among the bedraggled, bloody remnants of his men to destroy their equipment. They would try to escape that night. When darkness came the survivors, including wounded who were barely able to walk but determined not to be left behind and be captured, tied strips of blanket around their shoes so their footsteps would be silent. They formed an Indian file, each man clutching the coat-tail of the man ahead, and shuffled past the Germans' guns still firing at the spot they had just left. Sometimes the tracer bullets almost scorched their ears. When they reached the river they lined up silently and waited their turns to cross in the few little assault boats sent over by the two second army battalions which had succeeded in reaching the southern shore of the Neder Rhine.

With their heads between their knees, ducking bullets, they rode across the river, gulped down some hot tea in a barn and walked all the rest of the night back to the stronger British positions outside Nijmegen. Several hundred of the men lined up along the north bank never got across. Daylight came, the Germans discovered what was going on and they were taken prisoners. One brigade lost its way to the river and was never heard from again. Another was macerated when it ran into a German column in the pitch-black night. All of the wounded who couldn't make it to the river afoot had to be left behind, to fall into the Germans' hands.

Eight thousand "Red Devils" came down at Arnhem; 2,000 of them came out alive. They had been through as much concentrated hell as any Allied soldier had had to face on the Western Front.[13]

General Montgomery paid tribute to the handful of survivors: "There can be few episodes more glorious than this epic. . . . In years to come it will be a great thing for a man to say, 'I fought at Arnhem.' "

As the effort to turn the Siegfried Line failed, it was necessary to storm it by frontal assault. The first major attack was on Aachen, which most Americans knew as Aix-la-Chapelle, where more than a thousand years ago Charlemagne had been crowned. The attack launched on October 2 encountered savage resistance, and it took three weeks of air and artillery pounding and street-by-street fighting to force the decimated German garrison to surrender. It was the first major German city to fall.

To the north General Montgomery opened an offensive designed to free the great port of Antwerp. Amphibious landings on Walcheren Island cleared the Scheldt estuary, and the supply lines were open, though from then on the city was subjected to ceaseless buzz-bomb attacks. Then from Arnhem to Metz the war settled down to a slugging match: at the great Roer River dams, before Duren, in the Hurtgen forest, at the approaches to Cologne, at Echternach, and in the Saar. And in the last weeks of November and early December the Allies built up for an advance that should carry them across the Rhine.

The Battle of the Bulge

The Allies were prepared for a major attack. So, too, were the Germans. On December 15 General von Rundstedt issued an order of the day: "Soldiers of the West Front, your great hour has struck. Everything is at stake." The next morning a tremendous artillery bombardment announced the most threatening German offensive of the war in the West.

The attack came through the rugged forests of the Ardennes. For von Rundstedt it was to be a repeat performance. Back in May, 1940, he had led his armored divisions through this country which the French had thought so unsuitable for armor that they left it practically defenseless. In three days he had reached the Meuse, crossed it, and broken through to the Channel coast. Now, again, German Intelligence found this area but lightly held. Three German armies were concentrated along the 90-mile front from Aachen to Echternach and all the planes the *Luftwaffe* could spare put at von Rundstedt's disposal. A break-through here offered dazzling possibilities: the capture of Sedan to the south, of Namur and Liége to the north; even the capture of Brussels and Antwerp, which would split the Allied armies, was not beyond hope.

In 1940, in a similar situation, the French had retired. The Americans, confronted with an offensive of comparable magnitude, stood their ground and fought back. The German operation had been skillfully conceived and planned: in "Operation Greif" German soldiers dressed as civilians, or in American army uniforms, dropped behind the American lines to carry out sabotage and to demoralize the defense. The saboteurs were rounded up, the defense was not demoralized.

The German offensive drove in three directions: the major attack was to the north through St. Vith to Liége and Antwerp; an attack on the center towards Bastogne, and an attack at the south from Enternach towards Sedan. The southern attack was stopped cold. To the north, in front of St. Vith, the Germans chewed up the green 106th Division, but were held up by a heroic defense of St. Vith. Progress in the center was most rapid. The 28th Division was sent reeling back on Bastogne and the Germans pushed confidently on toward the Meuse.

At Allied Headquarters the reaction was instantaneous. Reinforcements were rushed to the north, and the lines held. The famous 101st Airborne Division, then at a rest center behind the lines, was ordered to Bastogne to reinforce elements of the 9th and 10th Armored. General Patton swung his Third Army to the north, and sent the 4th Armored Division racing through Luxembourg and Arlon to Bastogne.

Bastogne, commanding a network of roads, was the key to the southern Ardennes. Without it the offensive in the center could not proceed. By December 19 the Germans had cut off the town from south and north, by the 22nd it was encircled. To a demand for surrender, Brigadier-General Anthony McAuliffe replied simply "nuts." Collie Small celebrates the epic of Bastogne:

The terrific momentum of Rundstedt's attack carried fourteen miles the first day. Out on the network of roads to the east of Bastogne, the gray-green avalanche rolled toward its key objective. Infantry and armor tried desperately to hold, but the German tidal wave flowed over them and around them. One regiment of the 28th Division was cut off five times in three days. One by one, isolated units disappeared in the maelstrom. From one company command post somewhere out in the snowy forests, a radio operator reported that an enemy half-track had moved up alongside his building. . . .

Combat Command B [of the 10th Armored Division] tanks entered Bastogne at dusk. The big Shermans lumbered through the empty cobblestone streets and, without even pausing in the city, turned east to meet three elite German spearhead divisions driving toward Bastogne. In fog and darkness at 5:45 A.M. Combat Command B smashed into the enemy. The battle began on the roads with furious tank duels, and then fanned out into the fields and forests. Trading lives for time, the men of the heroic task force fought for thirty-six hours along a slowly bending arc stretched over three main roads, while the 101st Division slipped into Bastogne from the west.

The battle for Bastogne, which began on the roads to the east, spread from spoke to spoke in the Bastogne wheel. Balked in his attempt to storm the city frontally, von Rundstedt sent columns to the north and south of the town in a pincers movement. A regimental combat team, first unit of the 101st to arrive in Bastogne, raced out from the city to help the 10th Armored screen, while the rest of the airborne division moved into the town. . . .

By afternoon, the entire 101st Division was in position in and around Bastogne, dictating anchor points in the battle line by frequent jabs that forced the enemy to stop and hold at those points.

Five miles north of Bastogne, in the dead village of Noville, the 506th

Regiment of the 101st closed with a platoon of tank destroyers and other armored units to hold the town. German artillery was slamming into Noville with terrible precision. . . .

The night in Noville was eerie. The town was burning, and the men inside the village moved stealthily through the gutted buildings because of silhouettes against the dancing flames. Enemy troops moved around the town on three sides, and the sounds of movement carried on the cold night air until the doughboys inside the town were almost completely unnerved by the suspense.

At dawn, the German tanks attacked. Three Mark IV's slipped into Noville through the fog. A Sherman completely out of armor-piercing shells stuck its snout out around the corner of a building and opened fire with high explosives. The Sherman rained shells on the hulls of the enemy tanks as fast as it could shoot, but each explosion on the thick German armor plate only served to knock the tank back a few feet. . . .

Like the curtain on a winter snow scene, the fog lifted with startling suddenness. There, deployed in an open field on the edge of Noville, sat six more German tanks. Three American tank destroyers opened fire. The enemy tanks tried to scoot over the brow of a near-by hill, but the unerring tank destroyers picked them off one by one, like ducks in a shooting gallery. . . .

Finally, the German ring around Bastogne was joined. The 101st, with elements of the 9th and 10th Armored Divisions and a small group of stragglers, was completely cut off.

The 101st had not fallen into a trap. General McAuliffe's mission was to defend Bastogne. The encirclement was simply an occupational hazard.[14]

A battering ram of tanks and infantry dispatched by General Patton broke through the encircling Germans. But the battle for the Ardennes was by no means over: indeed losses after Bastogne was relieved were heavier even than for the preceding ten days. The German advance was halted four miles east of the Meuse; during January the Germans were pushed steadily back, and by the end of the month all the ground lost in the offensive had been regained. The battle for the Ardennes, which had held out such promise for the *Wehrmacht*, was a costly failure. But it had done one thing: it had given Germany a breathing spell in which to reorganize her defenses.

Across the Rhine

"It is certain," said Prime Minister Churchill in an address to the Commons on June 20, 1944, "that the whole eastern and western fronts and the long front in Italy . . . will now be kept henceforward in constant flame until the final climax is reached." Already the Red Army was hammering on the Oder River front and flanking Germany from the south, and General Alexander's armies swarming into the Po Valley. The air offensive, calculated to reduce every German city to rubble, was stepped up: in a single week in February, 17,000 tons of bombs were dropped on Germany—

more than twice the total tonnage dropped by the *Luftwaffe* in the whole blitz on Britain.

While the armies, east, west, and south, were getting ready for the kill, Roosevelt, Churchill, and Stalin met at Yalta, in the Crimea, to draw up plans for the final offensive, reiterate demands for unconditional surrender, and formulate terms for the control of Germany. The communique said in part:

We have agreed on common policies and plans for enforcing the Unconditional Surrender terms which we will impose upon Germany. Those terms will not be made known until the final defeat of Germany has been accomplished. . . . The German people will only make the cost of their defeat heavier to themselves by attempting to continue a hopeless resistance. . . .

The forces of the three powers will each occupy a separate zone. Coordinated administration and control has been provided for . . . through a central control commission consisting of the supreme commanders of the three powers with headquarters in Berlin. . . . France will be invited by the three powers, if she should so desire, to take over a zone of occupation and to participate as a fourth member of the control commission.

By late February the pace of the Allied armies had quickened. On the 21st of that month the whole western transportation system of Germany was shattered by a gigantic bombing from no less than 7,000 planes. The next night the Allies crossed the Roer River, last water barrier before the Rhine. "The attacks we are seeing now," said General Eisenhower, "should mark the beginning of the destruction of the German forces west of the Rhine."

At midnight February 27 the assault on Cologne, already in ruins from repeated aerial poundings, began. On March 7 the city was in Allied hands. A task force of the 9th Armored Division moved up the left bank of the Rhine through the old university town of Bonn to the little town of Remagen—and found the bridge intact. Everett Hollis tells with what energy the Americans acted:

Lt. Col. Leonard Engemann of Minneapolis, in command of the reconnaissance party, was determined to save this bridge if it was at all possible. So, at 3:50 o'clock, a platoon led by Lieut. Emmett Burrows of New York City sped down slope to the bridge entrance. . . . Just as they stepped on the span, an explosion occurred three-quarters of the way down the bridge. The Germans were setting off demolition charges, and the men thought surely their chance was gone. But no, only slight damage was done. They raced on. . . . Soon the bridge was swarming with Americans, while Mitchell, joined now by other engineers, cut and jerked out wires leading to dynamite charges. Gingerly they detached detonators and lifted boxes of explosives from the piers.

Later, from prisoners, the Americans learned that the Germans had planned to blow up the span at precisely four o'clock. But the German officer assigned to the demolition job was drunk when the American tanks reached Remagen. This officer, a lieutenant, had gone into the town of Erpel as the Yanks approached and spread the word boastfully that "the bridge goes up at four o'clock this afternoon."

German soldiers and civilians, gathering from miles around, were sitting in "grandstand seats" at every vantage point on the east bank, waiting for the spectacular event to come off, when Burrows' patrol ran onto the bridge—ten minutes before the hour fixed for its destruction. The German lieutenant signalled the plunger down. Two small explosions occurred, but the bridge only shuddered and remained standing. Several of the fuses had been faulty.

The men of the Ninth Armored Division had forced a fantastic break in the fortunes of war. They had seized a Rhine bridge intact.[15]

The prompt exploitation of this opportunity was a tribute to the initiative as well as to the courage of the American soldier. Once across the Rhine, the First Army fanned out, seizing the superhighway running south to Munich, and threatening to drive north and take the Ruhr from the south and east. As the Germans hurried up reinforcements to plug the gap, they weakened their defenses elsewhere along the Rhine. Plans for a large-scale crossing of the Rhine further downstream were already completed, the landing barges that had seen service on D-Day in Normandy were ready. The big jump came on March 24 when four armies hurdled the Rhine and two paratroop divisions were dropped five miles inland at Wesel.

With six armies now across the Rhine, the crust of German resistance was broken. Now only 250 miles separated the Allied armies in the west from the Red Army in the east.

There was savage fighting ahead, but only one great battle—the battle of the Ruhr. This greatest industrial region in Europe, was the major prize of western Germany: with the Russians controlling Silesia and the Allies the Ruhr, Germany would be paralyzed. The campaign for the Ruhr was brilliantly conceived and executed. The whole area was encircled, then split in two, and the German armies systematically mopped up: over 300,000 prisoners fell into our hands. It was indeed, as General Eisenhower called it, a "victory offensive."

Thereafter the drive became a pursuit. Montgomery's armies liberated most of Holland and drove into Bremen and Hamburg. The U. S. First and Ninth Armies drove straight ahead towards the Elbe. The Third Army, with units of the French army, sped into Baden, Wuerttemberg, and Bavaria—towards Hitler's last "redoubt" in the Alps.

The news from Germany brought exultation to the peoples of the Allied countries: it brought, too, indignation and horror. For as the armies drove into the interior, they came on one prison camp after another, and what they reported confirmed all the atrocity stories that had come out of Russia and Poland. A Congressional Committee reported on conditions at Buchenwald, under whose beeches Goethe once had walked:

This camp was founded when the Nazi Party first came into power in 1933 and has been in continuous operation since that time, although its largest population dates from the beginning of the present war. . . .

The mission of these camps was an extermination factory and the means of extermination was starvation, beatings, tortures, incredibly crowded sleeping conditions, and sickness. The effectiveness of these measures was enhanced by the requirement that the prisoners work in an adjacent armament factory for the manufacture of machine guns, small arms, ammunition, and other matériel for the German Army. The factory operated 24 hours a day, using two 12-hour shifts of prisoners. . . .

The main elements of Buchenwald included the "Little Camp," the regular barracks and the hospital, the medical experimentation building, the body-disposal plant, and the ammunition factory.

The prisoners in this camp slept on triple-decked shelves, the clearance between the shelves being little more than 2 feet. They were so crowded into these shelves that the cubic content figured out to be about 35 cubic feet per man, as against the minimum for health of 600 cubic feet prescribed by United States Army Regulations. We were informed that after arriving new prisoners were initiated by spending at least 6 weeks here before being "graduated" to the regular barracks. During this initiation prisoners were expected to lose about 40 percent in weight. Jews, however, seldom, if ever, graduated to the regular barracks. Camp disciplinary measures included transferring recalcitrant prisoners back to the "Little Camp." As persons became too feeble to work, they were also sent back to the "Little Camp" or to the hospital. Rations were less than at the regular barracks and the death rate in the "Little Camp" was very high, recently about 50 per day. . . .

[The hospital] was a building where moribund persons were sent to die. No medicines were available, and, hence, no therapy was possible. Typhus and tuberculosis were rampant in the camp. About half of the wards of the hospital were about 15 feet deep and 5½ feet wide, with one window on the outside end. From 6 to 9 patients occupied each ward, lying crosswise on the floor shoulder to shoulder. The room was too narrow for most of them to extend their legs. The death rate in the hospital was from 5 to 20 persons per day.

Block No. 41 in the camp was used for medical experiments and vivisections with prisoners as guinea pigs. Medical scientists came from Berlin periodically to reinforce the experimental staff. In particular, new toxins and anti-toxins were tried out on prisoners. Few prisoners who entered this experimental building ever emerged alive. Prisoners were induced to volunteer for experimentation on the representation that living quarters provided there were far superior to those in the barracks and that their rations were far superior to those received by ordinary prisoners. . . .

The method of collecting bodies was as follows: . . . After roll call, a motor truck drove around the camp, picked up the bodies, and was driven to the front yard of the incinerator plant to await the next day's operation.

But this was not the only source of bodies. Emaciated prisoners who had been around too long, or who had committed infractions of discipline, or who knew too much, or who had refused to be broken in mind were arbitrarily condemned to death. For instance, in the little camp, where prisoners slept 16 to a shelf, an infraction of discipline—particularly an attempt to escape—not infrequently resulted in all 16 being condemned. Such persons were immediately marched on foot to a small door in the fence of the back yard at a point immediately adjacent to the incinerator building. This door opened inward until it hit a doorstop which held it in a position parallel to the building's wall, thus creating a corridor 4 feet wide and 3 feet deep. At the far end was an opening about 4 feet by 4 feet, flush with the ground, the head of a concrete shaft, about 13 feet deep, the bottom floor of which was a continuation of the concrete floor of the room at the front end of the basement. The condemned prisoners, on being hurried and pushed through the door in the fence, inevitably fell into this shaft and crashed 13 feet down to the cement cellar floor. This room, on the floor at one end of which they now found themselves, was the strangling room. As they hit the floor they were garrotted with a short double-end noose by S. S. guards and hung on hooks along the side walls, about 6½ feet above the floor, the row of hooks being 45 or 50 in number. At the time of our visit all of the hooks except 5 had been removed, but we could observe the holes where the other hooks had previously been. When a consignment had been hung up, any who were still struggling were stunned by a wooden mallet, which was exhibited to us in the chamber, still bearing stains of blood. The bodies were left on the hooks until called for by the incinerator crew. An electric elevator, with an estimated capacity for 18 bodies, ran up to the incinerator room, which was on the floor above the strangling room. The day's quota of approximately 200 bodies was made up of from 120 to 140 prisoners who had died (mostly in the "hospital," the medical experimental building, or the "Little Camp"), and from 60 to 80 were supplied by the strangulation room.

I Have Finished the Course . . .

As the war in Europe was drawing to its close, the civilized world was plunged into mourning by the news that its greatest leader was dead. Death came to Franklin Delano Roosevelt at 5:50 P.M., April 12, at Warm Springs, Georgia.

The next day newspapers carried this notice:

TODAY'S ARMY-NAVY CASUALTY LIST
    WASHINGTON, Apr. 13.—Following are the latest casualties in the military services, including next-of-kin.

ARMY-NAVY DEAD
    ROOSEVELT, Franklin D., Commander-in-Chief, wife, Mrs. Anna Eleanor Roosevelt, the White House.

Sorrow entered every home and every heart and even his bitterest political opponents stood abashed and humble. Americans of every creed and faith crowded into churches where memorial services were read for the lost leader. The funeral services on the estate at Hyde Park which he had loved were simple:

As President Truman looked on with a face frozen in grief, Franklin D. Roosevelt was committed today to the warm brown earth of his native soil.

Under a cloudless, spring sky, the body of the late Chief Executive was lowered solemnly into a grave in the flower garden of his family estate.

Watching with strained faces were members of the family, dignitaries of government and little sad-faced groups of plain people—the employees on the place and neighbors from the countryside.

A detail of gray-clad cadets from the U. S. Military Academy at West Point fired a volley of three farewell salutes. A bugler played "Taps," its sweet but still sad notes echoing through the wooden estate.

Soldiers, sailors and marines, who had held an American flag over the casket, folded it and handed it to Mrs. Roosevelt.

The garden where Mr. Roosevelt rests lies between the family home where he was born sixty-three years ago and the library which houses his state papers and the gifts of a world which recognized him as one of its pre-eminent leaders.

It was exactly 10 A.M. when the first gun of a presidential salute was fired from a battery in the library grounds to the east of the quarter-acre garden. They boomed at solemnly spaced intervals.

An honor guard lining the hemlock hedge around the garden stood at attention.

A few moments later, the distant melody of a bugle came to those within the garden. A flight of bombers and another of training planes droned overhead.

The beat of muffled drums in slow cadence rolled through the wooded hills above the Hudson. In the distance, gradually drawing nearer, a band played a funeral dirge.

Promptly at 10:30 A.M., the National Anthem sounded and, as the wheels of the caisson noisily ground the gravel of the roadway, the notes of "Nearer, My God, to Thee," were played softly. Through a passageway at one corner, the elderly, gray-bearded rector of the President's Episcopal Church at Hyde Park walked across the newly clipped grass toward the grave.

The Rev. George W. Anthony was wearing the black and white surplice and stole of the clergy. He removed a black velvet skull-cap and took his position at the head of the grave, toward the west.

"All that the father giveth me shall come to me," the Rev. Mr. Anthony said.

A lone plane circling above almost drowned his words as he declared that unto Almighty God "we commit his body to the ground; earth to earth, ashes to ashes, dust to dust."

There was a stirring in the crowd.

"Blessed are the dead who lie in the Lord," the rector intoned. "Lord, have mercy upon us. Christ, have mercy upon us. Lord, have mercy upon us."

The pastor repeated the words of the Lord's Prayer. Elliott's lips moved with him.

The services followed the ordinary Episcopal burial rites for the dead. There were no words of eulogy, only the word of God.

Near its conclusion the Rev. Mr. Anthony recited the poem written by John Ellerton in 1870: "Now the laborer's task is o'er; now the battle-day is past."

"Father, in Thy gracious keeping we now leave Thy servant sleeping," the rector continued.

The services were brief. They were over by 10:45. The flag which Mrs. Roosevelt clutched tightly was handed to Elliott, and the family filed out.[16]

Not only Americans grieved, but people everywhere in the world who had fought to make men free. In Britain, especially, the sorrow was universal and profound. Winston Churchill cabled to Mrs. Roosevelt:

I send my most profound sympathy in your grievous loss. It is also the loss of the British nation and the cause of freedom in every land. I feel so deeply for you all.

As for myself, I have lost a dear and cherished friendship which was forged in the fires of war. I trust you may find consolation in the glory of his name and the magnitude of his work.

And to a hushed House of Commons he said: "There died the greatest American friend we have ever known and the greatest champion of human freedom who has ever brought help and comfort from the New World to the Old."

The Memorial Service at St. Paul's Cathedral was typical of those held throughout the United Kingdom:

LONDON, Tuesday—In St. Paul's Cathedral, so miraculously preserved in the burnt and devastated City of London, Britain gave national expression to-day of her admiration and respect and her mourning for President Roosevelt by a memorial service attended by the King and Queen and Princess Elizabeth, the Prime Minister and Cabinet, Dominion leaders, and representatives of every section of our national life. Diplomatists of the Allied countries were there, including Mr. Winant, the American Ambassador, who from the reading-desk spoke the lesson from Revelation:

After this I beheld, and, lo, a great multitude, which no man could number, of all nations, and kindreds, and people, and tongues, stood before the throne . . . and palms in their hands.

We who represent the two great English-speaking peoples are specially bound to pray that through our co-operation one with another the great cause for which Franklin Delano Roosevelt laboured may be brought to fruition for the lasting benefit of all the nations of the world.

These words read by the Dean reverberated from the dome which was there when the two nations were one. The Prime Minister, sad and slumped in his seat, seemed far away in his thoughts.

The service began with the sentences "I am the Resurrection and the Life," followed by the Introduction.

> Brethren, we are gathered together in the presence of God to commemorate the life and work of Franklin Delano Roosevelt, thirty-second President of the United States of America, and to render thanks to Almighty God for the services which he gave to the welfare and peace not only of his own people but of all the peoples of the world.

The psalm was "The Lord is My Shepherd"; the lesson, read by Mr. Winant, followed, and the hymn "Fight the good fight with all thy might," in which the congregation joined. After the prayers "The Battle Hymn of the Republic," with the organ, choir, and congregation, was sung with a volume and intensity not usual in great ceremonies:

> *As He died to make men holy,*
> *Let us die to make men free,*
> *While God is marching on.*

Prayers followed, then "The Last Post" tore into the silence that followed, blown by the buglers of the Royal Marines standing in the gallery over the great west door. The bugle notes flew up the great dome to throb and echo there with their quick calls to our everyday world, and the long, enigmatic questioning at the end. Nowhere do the bugles call so searchingly as they do in the great dome of St. Paul's.

Then came "The Star Spangled Banner," reminding us of battles long ago between Britain and America; but to-day the line in that anthem that hung in our mind was "And the rockets' red glare, the bombs bursting in the air." The National Anthem ended the service, and again at a high moment in St. Paul's history the captains and the kings departed.[17]

The wisest of American publicists interpreted the significance of Roosevelt:

Roosevelt lived to see the nation make the crucial decisions upon which its future depends: to face evil and to rise up and destroy it, to know that America must find throughout the world allies who will be its friends, to understand that the nation is too strong, too rich in resources and in skill, ever to accept again as irremediable the wastage of men who cannot find work and of the means of wealth which lie idle and cannot be used. Under his leadership, the debate on these fundamental purposes has been concluded, and the decision has been rendered, and the argument is not over the ends to be sought but only over the ways and means by which they can be achieved.

Thus he led the nation not only out of mortal danger from abroad but out of the bewilderment over unsettled purposes which could have rent it apart from within. When he died, the issues which confront us are difficult. But they are not deep and they are not irreconcilable. Neither in our relations with other peoples nor among ourselves are there divisions within us that cannot be managed with common sense.

The genius of a good leader is to leave behind him a situation which common sense, without the grace of genius, can deal with successfully. Here lay the political genius of Franklin Roosevelt: that in his own time he knew what were the questions that had to be answered, even though he himself did not always find the full answer. It was to this that our people and the world responded, preferring him instinctively to those who did not know what the real questions were.[18]

He left his country strong and righteous, and the great combination of democracies, which he had done so much to contrive, victorious. But to everyone who contemplated his life and the drama of its final act there came the lines, he—

should have died hereafter.
There would have been a time for such a word.

12

THE SETTING SUN

Guadalcanal

THE FIRST PHASE of the battle for the Pacific ended with Midway. The second, the offensive phase, began with Guadalcanal. This is, to be sure, too pat a division. For one thing, MacArthur's offensive in New Guinea was already under way. For another, Guadalcanal might well be regarded as primarily defensive in character—an attack designed rather to protect American supply lines between New Caledonia and Australia than to push the Japanese out of the great island barrier. But whatever its original strategic purpose, it was, in fact, the first of a long series of offensives that finally paralyzed Japanese power in the South Pacific and opened the way to the recovery of the Philippines.

The Japanese, it will be remembered, had occupied the Solomons in the spring of 1942, and during that summer they built up strength at Tulagi and began the construction of an airfield on Guadalcanal. Their strategy was clear. From the Solomons they could strike at New Hebrides and New Caledonia and, controlling these, threaten the American supply line to Australia. The Battle of the Coral Seas was the first serious check to this grandiose plan; MacArthur's offensive in New Guinea the second; the rapid development of air and naval bases in New Caledonia and New Zealand the third; the destruction of a large part of the Japanese fleet at Midway the fourth. Yet the Japanese still had air and, probably, naval supremacy in the South Pacific.

It was the Americans, however, who seized the initiative. On August 7 the 1st Marine and elements of the 2nd Marine Division, protected by a task force under Vice-Admiral Robert L. Ghormeley, landed on Florida, Tulagi, and Guadalcanal. Opposition on Florida and Tulagi was fierce, but the Guadalcanal landings were almost unopposed. The Japanese reaction was, however, swift. On August 8, air and naval forces caught elements of the American fleet off Savo Island and sank four cruisers. Thereafter the battle for Guadalcanal was a seesaw affair—a series of naval engagements, a long-drawn-out and peculiarly bitter land campaign.

Except in the mountains and jungles of New Guinea, Americans have

never waged war under harder conditions than those which the Marines—
and later the American infantry—encountered in Guadalcanal. Their
problem was to hold the island—and above all the airstrip quickly converted into Henderson field—until supplies and reinforcements could be
brought in. The task laid upon the men and ships of the navy was equally
difficult. A thousand miles from their nearest base, they were exposed to
attack not only from powerful Japanese warships but from nearby air
bases at Rabaul and Bougainville. The first battle, off Savo Island, had
been a sharp defeat. Thereafter came a series of engagements—in the
fighting of August 23–25 our naval forces damaged an enemy carrier,
cruiser, and several destroyers; in mid-September we lost the carrier *Wasp*
and five destroyers. On October 11 an American flotilla intercepted the
"Tokyo Express" making one of its runs from Bougainville to Guadalcanal
and sank or damaged several enemy cruisers and destroyers. Towards the
end of October, planes from the *Enterprise* and the *Hornet* swooped down
on a Japanese force off Santa Cruz Island, sinking two destroyers and
heavily damaging two carriers, two battleships, and several cruisers.

In this process of attrition Japanese losses were heavier than American,
but the naval fighting was inconclusive. The decisive battle—the Fifth Battle of the Solomons—came in mid-November. Ira Wolfert gives us the
story:

The land forces had girded themselves for a repetition of the October
13 bombardment. Men huddled in foxholes, and asked each other silently
with their embittered faces, "Where's our Navy?" and wondered what
would be left to stop the Jap transports.

Those seven hours of darkness, with each moment as silent as held
breath, were the blackest our troops have faced since Bataan, but at the
end of them our Navy was there, incredibly, like a Tom Mix of old, like the
hero of some antique melodrama. It turned the tide of the whole battle by
throwing its steel and flesh into the breach against what may be the heaviest Jap force yet engaged by surface ships in this war.

Again the beach had a front-row seat for the devastating action. Admiral Callaghan's force steaming in line dove headlong into a vastly more
powerful Jap fleet which was swinging around tiny Savo Island with guns
set for point-blank blasting of Guadalcanal, and loaded with high-explosive
shells instead of armor-piercing shells. Matching cruisers and destroyers
against battleships is like putting a good bantamweight against a good
heavyweight, but the Japs unquestionably were caught with their kimonos
down around their ankles. They could have stayed out of range and
knocked out our ships with impunity, and then finished us on the ground
at their leisure.

We opened fire first. The Jap ships, steaming full speed, were on us,
over us, and all around us in the first minute. Torpedoes need several
hundred feet in order to arm themselves with their propellers. Our destroyers discharged torpedoes from such close range that they could not
wind up enough to explode. The range was so close that the Japs could not
depress their guns enough to fire at the waterline, which is why so many
hits landed on the bridge and two of our admirals were killed.

The action was illuminated in brief, blinding flashes by Jap searchlights which were shot out as soon as they were turned on, by muzzle flashes from big guns, by fantastic streams of tracers, and by huge orange-colored explosions as two Jap destroyers and one of our destroyers blew up within seconds of one another. Two Jap planes, which were overhead intending to drop flares on the target, were caught and blown to bits.

In the glare of three exploding ships, the two naval forces could be seen laboring and wallowing in their recoils, throwing up waves in the ordinarily lakelike harbor which hit like rocks against the beach. The sands of the beach were shuddering so much from gunfire that they made the men standing there quiver and tingle from head to foot.

From the beach it resembled a door to hell opening and closing, opening and closing, over and over. The unholy show took place in the area immediately this side of Savo Island. Our ships, in a line of about three thousand yards, steamed into a circle of Jap ships which opened at the eastern end like a mouth gaping with surprise. They ran, dodged, and reversed their field, twisted, lurched, and lunged, but progressed generally along the inside of the lip of the Japs.

Since the Jap circle was much bigger than our line, the Jap ships, first at one end and then the other, fired across the empty space into one another. It took about thirty minutes for our ships to complete the tour of the circle and by the end of the tour the Jap ships had ceased to exist as an effective force.

The whole thing was like a huge ring around a thin finger with the finger trying to burst through the ring and the ring trying to break every bone in the finger. Then the battling ring and the embattled finger seemed to crawl slowly toward us, still locked in a deathlike embrace and swayed, thundering and shuddering backward and forward.

After thirty minutes the Japs crawled out of the harbor without having dropped a single shell on Guadalcanal, but in the morning twenty new Jap landing boats were seen on their portion of the beach, so a landing must have been made under the cover of the battle.

The exact composition of the Jap force probably will remain unknown until we break open Tokyo's archives after the war. From the beach twenty-six Jap silhouettes were counted, but they were shifting shapes illuminated fitfully and duplication in counting was possible. Our force was composed of eight destroyers, two heavy cruisers, and three light cruisers, but there's not a man living who could remain a statistician before so gruesome and incalculably costly a spectacle.

The Japs had at least one battleship of the Kongo class. That is certain, for it figured all the next day in one of the most fantastic episodes of this war—"the episode of the unsinkable battleship." There likely was another battleship sunk. Several of our destroyers' survivors recall seeing the whole bridge of a battleship leap into the air, but when daylight came, the "unsinkable battleship" was seen to have its bridge undamaged.

Also, flames from one of our burning destroyers illuminated a ship which was upside down with only the hull showing above water. The hull was huge, but the Navy refuses to concede it was a battleship unless concrete evidence is produced, which is impossible in the deep water where the ship sank. It is certain that few Japs ships could remain unhit in that avalanche of fire, or they would not have broken off action against a force stripped down to the bone, and with that bone broken in several places. . . .

Four of our destroyers and at least two Jap destroyers and this "whatzit," which most of us call a battleship, but which the Navy called "heavy cruiser or battleship," sank within thirty minutes. One of our mortally hit light cruisers remained on the scene with a crippled heavy cruiser fumbling and floundering for such Jap ships as were unable to withdraw. They found one cruiser at dawn, and the heavy cruiser shot it to its death, turning it bottom-side up with the first salvo.[1]

Thereafter ultimate victory in the Solomons was no longer in doubt. There was still fierce fighting ahead—not until February were the last Japanese cleared out of Guadalcanal—and the fight for New Georgia, Choiseul, and Bougainville in the northern Solomons continued through most of next year. But the naval losses which the enemy had suffered in this prolonged campaign constituted a disaster only second to that of Midway. Official Navy communiques list Japanese losses from August 7, 1942 to February 10, 1943 as:

	SUNK OR PROBABLY SUNK	DAMAGED
Battleships	2	7
Carriers	1	4
Cruisers (light & heavy)	11	31
Destroyers	22	51
Transports	24	13
Oilers	0	2
Seaplane tenders	0	2
Cargo vessels	5	15
Miscellaneous craft	4	1
	69	113

Personnel losses, although not accurately known, were estimated at fully 50,000, and airplane losses placed at 797.

The nature and significance of the Guadalcanal campaign is summed up by Lieutenant General A. A. Vandegrift of the Marine Corps:

The planning for the Tulagi-Guadalcanal operation was hurried. When the enemy was discovered building airfields in the lower Solomons, the decision to undertake a land offensive came much earlier than those who were to carry it out had anticipated. Our preparations were made with what we had, not what we had expected to get. Marine aerial reconnaissance consisted of one flight over the future theatre of operation by two officers in a B-17. Above Guadalcanal they were attacked by three Zeros, but escaped.

There was no appreciable softening up of the objective prior to D-day. For three hours on that morning our surface task force and Army and Navy planes bombarded Guadalcanal and its satellite islands, and then we went ashore. While resistance was being overcome on Tulagi and Gavutu Islands, our main force on Guadalcanal moved across the beach unopposed. The landing went so smoothly that we felt we could handle any opposition that might arise, and the enemy's garrison troops watching from distant hills obviously agreed.

However, it was to be expected that the Japanese reaction at sea and in the air would be violent. It was, and, because the enemy was able to bring heavy air and naval concentration to bear in the area, our own air and surface support was forced to act with utmost caution.

In the early days ashore we had no coastal artillery and Henderson Field was bereft of planes. Supplies could not be brought in often enough to meet the needs. Our weapons were equal to, and usually better than, comparable weapons used by the Japanese, but attrition left us with serious shortages.

In mid-October, after some planes had joined us, our aviation gasoline reserves fell desperately low. Ammunition became pure gold. Food problems forced us to settle for two meals a day. Just before a major enemy attack broke, heroic efforts by naval supply forces brought sufficient relief to see us through.

The ability of the Japanese to bring in reinforcements and to pound our positions at the airfield from both air and sea resulted in recurring crises ashore. During the first four months fighting rose each month to a climactic struggle in which a fresh and determined enemy force strove to push our ground troops into the sea. Slashed and repulsed, the enemy withdrew each time to gird for another try with replenished manpower and supplies.

Meanwhile, we were unable to undertake a full-scale offensive of our own because we lacked sufficient combat troops to drive inland in strength and hold positions guarding the airfield at the same time.

Despite all these original handicaps, the final triumph of American arms at Guadalcanal was decisive and complete. Our years of prior Navy-Marine Corps study in amphibious warfare and jungle fighting, and the fact that we possessed specially trained troops, if not too many of them, did much to get us ashore and keep us there when the going was toughest. But it remained for the ultimate teamwork of our sea, air and land forces to prove to be the key to amphibious mastery.

This teamwork developed as the campaign progressed. Steadily the interaction of these three forces whittled down the odds against us. Guadalcanal, in effect, became a trap into which not only crack units of the Japanese Army but highly prized warships, transports and planes were drawn to their destruction.

American seamen and airmen, outnumbered and outgunned, gained the upper hand with superior skill, courage and equipment. In time, able to hold off enemy interference, they could pour fresh ground troops and supplies into the island at will. The Japanese had to count off Guadalcanal as a lost cause.

The victory marked a turn much more decisive than generally had been foreseen Only once since—at Leyte—have the Japanese attempted a counter-landing in strength. Not for eighteen months, until our invasion of Saipan, did the Japanese Navy make any serious effort to intercede during an Allied amphibious operation. Not until the battle for Okinawa, at Japan's front door, did Japanese land-based air power seek to break up a land operation with something of the same energy it once showed at Guadalcanal.[2]

The Aleutians

While the Japanese were pushing westward into Burma and eastward along the great island barrier towards the Solomons and New Zealand, there was a third and potentially serious thrust in the far north. That neglected prophet, Homer Lea, had predicted a Japanese invasion of the United States through the long chain of the Aleutians, stretching some nine hundred miles out into the Bering Sea and forming a bridge between Asia and the American continent. On June 3, 1942, as the great battle of Midway was about to begin, a Japanese flotilla approached and bombed Dutch Harbor at the eastern end of the Aleutians. Whether this and the subsequent seizure of Attu, Kiska, and Agattu were actually preliminary to an invasion of Alaska or whether the whole campaign was merely diversionary, cannot now be determined.

Dutch Harbor withstood assault, but the occupation of the Aleutian chain was strategically effective. As Gilbert Cant points out:

By occupying Kiska, they made it impossible for our Navy to proceed with its plans to develop the fine harbor there as an advance base for operations in the northwest Pacific and the Bering Sea. They made it impossible for us to develop airfields there from which reconnaissance could be maintained over the northernmost Japanese islands (southern Sakhalin and the Kurile group).They made it impossible for us to develop bases from which Tokyo could be brought under direct bombing attack, which might have been feasible if we had been willing to make the effort to blast runways out of the forbiddingly rocky terrain of Kiska. They made it impossible for us to guarantee the security of ships moving to ports on the eastern coast of Siberia, such as Petropavlovsk in Kamchatka, and extremely difficult for us to move securely in the Bering Sea toward more northerly Siberian ports. They imperilled our fur sealing and salmon fishing in the Bering Sea. They imperilled the mainland of northwestern Alaska. Most important of all, they put us on the defensive in an area from which we had expected to be able to take the offensive toward Japan, eventually if not immediately.[3]

Appropriately enough, on July 4 American submarines nosed their way into Kiska harbor and hit three Japanese destroyers; within a month five more destroyers were sunk. In September Americans landed at the centrally located island of Adak, built an airfield, and proceeded to bomb the enemy at Kiska.

It was not until May, 1943, however, that a real offensive could be mounted. There was an estimated 10,000 troops on Attu and Kiska, and against them we sent our largest invasion force since Guadalcanal, a whole army division, two battleships, and an escort carrier. The plan of attack was for one battalion to land at Holtz Bay and a larger force to hit the southern shore at Massacre Bay. These two groups were to merge, trapping the garrison in the eastern half of the island. Neither landing met with initial resistance, for the enemy had entrenched himself in the high central ridges, from which he poured deadly artillery fire upon the invaders. Howard Handleman tells the story of the fight:

It was a slow advance. The men were deployed widely, in little groups. The chief opposition was machine-gun fire from the high ground on the other side of the valley; so it was dangerous to bunch up together.

The advance was tedious. Every foxhole, trench and dugout had to be examined, pried into with bayonets ready. The men had to watch for wires. The Japs may have left booby traps and land mines. Gunfire was sporadic, and most of it came from the Japs. The American troops made good targets as they moved across the relatively flat valley. The Japs, hidden in prepared positions, couldn't be seen. Later we learned Jap snipers wore a hula-skirt of tundra grass which they pulled over their heads for concealment.

There were no Japs on the floor of the valley. Apparently they had pulled out, retreated into the east arm. . . .

Part of the Jap encampment was behind a bluff, protected from gunfire from the Japs on the high ground to the east. Soldiers congregated there, around the only two tents in the Jap camp area. This was their first chance to dig into Jap stores for souvenirs, and they took time out from their advance to do a little digging.

Not much, of course, but enough to grab a few Jap postcards or a Jap gun or a pair of chopsticks. A uniform doesn't take the tourist out of an American.

Each new group of soldiers made the stop at the Jap tents before it moved up the bluff to continue the advance. There was no urgency up there, not much gunfire; so the tired soldiers adopted this place as a good spot to rest. Nobody would complain if they used their rest period to grab a few trinkets to take home after Attu.

Occasionally on the flat land above the bluff there was a flurry of movement, localized excitement in which a few soldiers, a half dozen or so, saw something or heard something which sent them scurrying for cover or after a Jap in a foxhole. There were few wounded Japs on the flat land, left in foxholes by their retreating fellows.

The wounded Japs had to be killed. They wouldn't surrender, wouldn't come out when they were called. Our soldiers threw grenades in the holes, rather than risk needless death by crawling into the darkness to pull out the Japs.

This was a strange adventure, moving through an abandoned Jap camp area. It was good, too, to be some place where people had lived before after spending four nights in the cold, treeless wilderness of the mountains. It was good, even though the Jap camp had an offensive, fishy odor. There were tents and dugouts and wooden shacks and warehouses and trails where men had lived and worked and walked. The island lost some of its strange mystery, even if this was a ghost camp now, left by people who were foreign and unfathomable.

It was so good to move into a place where people had lived that Sgt. Emil Polansky, a farmer of Belleville, Kans., sat down for ten minutes in one of the wooden shacks and played dice with some buddies. Polansky didn't like the shacks, though.

"I used to raise hogs in Kansas," he said, "and I never made them live in places as dirty as those Japs lived in."

The fog lifted in the early evening and the sun came out. There, on the towering mountain between the east arm of Holtz Valley and the Chichagof Harbor, hundreds of Japs struggled up a zigzag trail in the snow, up a mountain so steep they couldn't climb straight up but had to make sharp turns, almost right-angle turns, to climb gradually.

The Jap was evacuating his main base, leaving without making a stand with his main forces. He was retreating to Chichagof, to unite with the smaller forces stationed there.

It was estimated 400 Japs went up that zigzag trail. How many reached the top was never known. Capt. Jim Simons turned his cannon on them, plunking shells right in their midst. And the clearing weather brought air support, Lightning fighters from Amchitka. The Lightnings came over in a formation of eight. They judged the situation quickly and went to work. They cut their motors almost out and glided in over the Japs. The heavy machine guns in the wings of the Lightnings spat fire and lead and death. The Japs scattered. Americans in the front lines, 1,500 yards from the retreating Japs, heard their screams as they scattered to escape the hail of bullets.

The "ah-ah-ah" of the machine guns in the planes filled the evening. All forward movement stopped on the zigzag trail. Dead Japs lay in the snow. It was the biggest killing so far, the worst blow to Jap manpower on the island.

The Lightnings kept coming, cutting down their speed as they glided over the trail so they would have longer to shoot at the Japs. From a mountain the Japs sent up AA, trying to cover the retreaters, but the AA was wild, wilder than any the Japs had fired before.[4]

Japanese resistance ceased on May 30 with a series of suicidal attacks on American artillery positions. The desperate character of the fighting is suggested by the fact that we buried 2,100 Japs, took 11 prisoners.

In capturing Attu, Kiska had been by-passed. During June and July the navy and air force turned their attention to Kiska. The landings came on August 15, and proved a not unwelcome anti-climax. There were no Japanese there.

Kiska fell without a shot. Under cover of fog the Japanese had evacuated the island. Now all the Aleutians were back in American hands, and from newly constructed air bases our planes were soon bombing the Japanese islands in the Kuriles, notably the great naval base of Paramushiro.

New Guinea

While this campaign of fog and ice was being fought to a victorious conclusion, General MacArthur was on the first lap of his long journey back to Luzon. We have already seen how in midsummer 1942 he had established an advanced base at Port Moresby and built an airstrip at Milne Bay. The Japanese, who were firmly established at Lae, Salamaua, and Buna, drove down from the north to throw the Americans and Australians back into the sea. In September the Japanese advance was halted, just 32 miles from Port Moresby, and the Allied advance on Buna, Gona, and Salamaua began. George H. Johnston describes the road back over the Owen Stanley mountains:

I may be wrong, for I am no soothsayer, but I have an idea that the name of the "Kokoda Trail" is going to live in the minds of Australians for generations, just as another name, Gallipoli, lives on as freshly today, twenty-seven years after it first gained significance in Australian minds. For thousands of Australians who have walked the weary, sodden miles of this dreadful footpath—and these Australians are the fathers of the next generation—it will be the one memory more unforgettable than any other that life will give them.

Five days ago the Japanese began their resistance again—on the wide shallow plateau of the Gap, the pass through the forbidding spurs of the main range. The weather is bad, the terrain unbelievably terrible, and the enemy is resisting with a stubborn fury that is costing us many men and much time. Against the machine gun nests and mortar pits established on the ragged spurs and steep limestone ridges our advance each day now is measured in yards. Our troops are fighting in the cold mists of an altitude of 6700 feet, fighting viciously because they have only a mile or two to go before they reach the peak of the pass and will be able to attack downhill—down the *north* flank of the Owen Stanley's. That means a lot to troops who have climbed every inch of that agonizing track, who have buried so many of their cobbers and who have seen so many more going back, weak with sickness or mauled by the mortar bombs and the bullets and grenades of the enemy, men gone from their ranks simply to win back a few more hundred yards of this wild, unfriendly, and utterly untamed mountain. Tiny villages which were under Japanese domination a few weeks ago are back in our hands—Ioribaiwa, Nauro Creek, Menari, Efogi, Kagi, Myola—and we are fighting now for Templeton's Crossing.

Fresh troops are going up the track, behind on the slimy trail from which the tide of war has ebbed and in ebbing has scattered the debris of death and destruction all the way along the green walls that flank the snaking ribbon of rotten mud. The men are bearded to the eyes. Their uniforms are hotch-potches of anything that fits or is warm or affords some protection from the insects. I remember years ago how we used to laugh at newsreels showing the motley troops of China when they were fighting the Japanese in the days when the men of Tokyo could do no wrong in the eyes of the western world. These men on the Kokoda track look more unkempt, more ragged, than any of the Chinese of those old film shots. . . .

There are many Japanese graves, some crude, some elaborate, all marked with the piece of sapling bearing Japanese ideographs. There are many crudely penciled signs stuck in the bushes or nailed to the trees: "Bodies two Australians—'th Battalion, 25 yards into Bush." "Twelve Jap Bodies 50 yards northwest." "Unknown Australian Body, 150 yards down slope." In the green half-light, amid the stink of rotten mud and rotting corpses, with the long lines of green-clad Australians climbing wearily along the tunnel of the track, you have a noisome, unforgettable picture of the awful horror of this jungle war.

There are the bodies, too, of native carriers, tossed aside by the Japs to die, discarded callously and left unburied in the jungle. These natives were recruited in Rabaul, sent to Buna, roped together in the stinking holds of Japanese freighters, and then thrown into the enemy's carrier lines. They received little food, no medical attention and payment with worthless, newly printed Japanese one shilling notes of their invasion currency. They died in the hundreds of overwork, malnutrition and sickness.

Since then the Japs have made their stand in the toughest area of the pass through the Owen Stanley's—a terrible terrain of thick mountain timber, great rocks drenched in rain, terrifying precipices and chasms. Often the troops have to make painfully slow progress by clawing with hands and feet at slippery rock faces overlooking sheer drops into the jungle. The almost constant rain or mist adds to the perils of sharp limestone ridges, narrow ledges flanked by chasms, slimy rocks, and masses of slow moving mud.

In this territory the Japanese are fighting, with a stubborn tenacity that is almost unbelievable, from an elaborate system of prepared positions along every ridge and spur. Churned up by the troops of both armies, the track itself is now knee deep in thick, black mud. For the last ten days no man's clothing has been dry and they have slept—when sleep was possible—in pouring rain under sodden blankets. Each man carries all his personal equipment, firearms, ammunition supply and five days' rations. Every hour is a nightmare.

General Allen, who has fought in the last war and who has been leading these Australians in the attack on the Kokoda Trail, says without hesitation: "This is the toughest campaign of the A.I.F. in this or any other war. . . ."

The Australians have re-conquered the Owen Stanley Range. Today, on November 2, they marched into Kokoda unopposed, through lines of excited natives who brought them great baskets of fruit and decked them with flowers. They marched back to the little plateau where Colonel Owen had died so many weary weeks before. They marched downhill through Isurava and Deniki, where many of them had fought the bloody rearguard

action of August. The Japs had fled. Patrols cautiously went ahead to
scout, squirmed their way through the rubber trees to test out Kokoda's
defenses. But Kokoda was empty. There was no sound but the droning of
insects and the noise of the rain pattering through the trees, Kokoda, "key
to the Owen Stanley's," had been abandoned by the Japanese without a
fight. Their defense of Kokoda had been the pass through the range, and
they had failed to hold that defense line.[5]

Pat Robinson recorded the push to Buna and Gona:

The rainy season was now on in earnest and the daily downpours made
life miserable for everybody, turned streams into raging torrents, wiped
out bridges, transformed swamps into lakes and make the few existing
roads impassable. Most of the boys were unshaven, and it was not long
before they all became hollow-eyed. They had cold bully beef and biscuits
to eat and wet mud for a bed.

The Japs were trapped with their backs to the sea in a triangular area
that stretched from Cape Endaiadere, three miles below Buna, to a point
beyond Gona, fourteen miles above Buna, and inland for distances that
varied from mere yards to a mile or more. Americans formed the spearhead of the thrust against Buna, while Australians concentrated on knocking out the Japs entrenched at Gona.

It was difficult to distinguish our own and the Japs' positions at any time
because there was no such thing as a front line. But there were pockets of
resistance everywhere. Sometimes the enemy were in foxholes or machine-
gun pits only ten yards from us. For instance, around Sanananda Point the
Japs were along the shore. Farther inland there was a strong force of
Australians. Still farther inland was still another force of Japs, who in turn
were sandwiched in between two groups of Americans. . . .

The main body of our forces, laying direct siege to Buna itself, encountered a heavy barrage of enemy artillery and mortar fire. Our own 75 mm.
guns replied in kind. Jap barrages often appeared pointless, but they were
effective nevertheless. They would try to knock out our artillery, of course,
but they also seemed to fire aimlessly all over the landscape. And enemy
planes, taking advantage of the thick weather which held our own airmen
on the other side of the mountains, swooped down on our positions in
strafing attacks. At one point seven Zeros raked our positions with
machine-gun fire. There is nothing more trying than to face a plane traveling more than 300 miles an hour only twenty feet over your head with all
its guns spraying the earth with bullets.

The enemy troops were as quick to take advantage of weather conditions as were their brothers in the Jap Air Corps, and they repeatedly
sought to infiltrate our positions with small guerrilla bands. Once along the
Giriwu River near Saputs they tried to slip in under cover of a fog to wipe
out an Australian company in a surprise attack, but the Australians had
long since become wise to every Jap trick; they met the Japs this time with
a withering blast of rifle fire. . . .

By December 3rd the Australians and Yanks had cut off Gona and had infiltrated into the defenses around Buna. The end was in sight for the Japs, but they never stopped trying to land reinforcements. They made their fifth attempt on December 9th, when six destroyers tried to send troops ashore on barges. Our bombers and pursuit planes suddenly swooped down on them, sank all the barges and routed the destroyers.

The Japs were being trapped in an ever-narrowing beachhead and they made repeated attempts to break through the encircling ring of steel. Near Sanananda Point a large force of Australians surrounded ninety-five Japs and called on them to surrender. It was a case of surrender or die. These Japs, all tough Marines, chose death. They not only would not surrender but they wouldn't even dig in. They attacked, and every one of them was killed. . . .

Gona fell to the Australians on December 10th, and the next day the Japs were hemmed in on a thin fringe of beach and coastal jungle around Buna. Every foot of that defense line bristled with guns.

Then the torrential rains came. The fighting almost ceased for a day or two, and we took advantage of the weather-enforced truce to bury 638 Japs. These dead men had been lying outside Jap positions for days and the enemy had had no chance to bury them under the constant avalanche of mortar, machine-gun and artillery fire from our side, to say nothing of a steady downpour of bombs and bullets from our airmen. The stench was unbearable, and we wondered how the live Japs had borne it until we discovered they were wearing gas masks as protection against their own dead.[6]

With control of the Solomons passing to the Americans, the Japanese could not afford to lose New Guinea. Their great naval and air base at Rabaul, in New Britain, enabled them to harass Allied lines of supply and push in reinforcements to stem the Allied advance. On March 1 reconnaissance planes sighted a great Japanese convoy in the Bismarck Sea. Fortresses and Liberators streamed to the attack, and in three days sank an estimated 22 ships with 15,000 troops and destroyed over 100 planes. In June MacArthur landed on the Woodlark and Trobriand islands; in September he occupied Salamaua and Lae, and from airfields there and in the Solomons, Rabaul was subjected to relentless bombardment: one great attack, in October, was reported to have sunk or damaged 123 ships and destroyed 177 planes. With the partial neutralization of Rabaul, the Allies were able to land on New Britain itself, and from December 1943 to February 1944 units of the U.S. Sixth Army and the 1st Marine Division completed the conquest of western New Britain. Meantime the Admiralties had been occupied and Rabaul encircled. Beginning in the spring of 1944 MacArthur's forces started that series of leaps along the New Guinea coast—Wewak, Hollandia, Biak—that eventually brought them within striking distance of Halmahera and the Philippines.

Tarawa to Saipan

New Guinea and the Moluccas opened one road to the Philippines and Japan. It was the infantry which would have to travel this road—supported, of course, by the air force and the navy—fighting from one large island to another. Another road to Japan was through the central Pacific—the Gilbert, Marshall, Marianas, Bonin, and Ryukyu islands. Clearing and safeguarding this road was largely a task for the navy—supported by air force and army. Two years after Pearl Harbor our military and naval strength had grown to such prodigious proportions that—not withstanding our North African and European campaigns—we were able to take both roads. As MacArthur pushed up from New Guinea, the navy began that process of island-hopping that ended with the conquest of Iwo Jima and Okinawa and the bombardment of the home islands of Japan.

The basis for the naval advance on Japan was the spectacular growth of the American navy and naval air arm to the point where it was not only the largest and most powerful in the world, but larger than the combined navies of all the warring powers. By the beginning of 1944 the navy totalled 4,167 ships, including 613 warships, and 80,000 landing craft. Seven great new battleships, including the 45,000-ton *Missouri*, *Illinois*, and *Kentucky*, had joined the fleet. Even more significant was the astonishing growth of the navy's air arm. By 1944 the Pacific fleets alone had about 100 carriers with thousands of planes—the giant Mars, the Grumman Wildcat and Hellcat, the Curtis Helldiver, the Douglas Dauntless, the Chance-Vought Corsair, and others as formidable as their names. Task Force 58, controlling a large part of the carriers, was alone more powerful than the entire Japanese navy.

Task Force 58 is really something new under the sun. It is so big that one captured Jap pilot said he knew they'd lost the war when he got his first bird's-eye view of its hundreds of ships, from destroyers to huge carriers and 45,000-ton battlewagons, spread over 40 square miles of ocean. It is so fast that no pre-Pearl Harbor battleship could keep pace with it. And it is relentless, because it never has to go home. "When you go to sea with Mitscher, by God, you stay at sea!"

The secret of Mitscher's staying power is the Navy's fabulous Pacific "supply train"—hundreds of ships carrying food, fuel, ammunition, spare parts, repair facilities, replacement planes and pilots, mail and even a floating hospital. Meeting TF 58 at a secret rendezvous this train reprovisions the force completely. It is protected by its own carriers, cruisers and destroyers.

Thus fortified, TF 58 shapes up much like a crack varsity football team. Battleships, cruisers and destroyers screen the play and run interference. Flat-tops carry the ball and pack the scoring wallop. Calling the signals for this two-billion-dollar aggregation is Pete Mitscher, who hasn't missed a trick yet.[7]

Now this vast navy was ready to strike a series of prodigious blows. The first of these was aimed at Tarawa atoll in the Gilberts, 2,500 miles southwest of Hawaii, 1,200 miles northeast of Guadalcanal. The landing here was significant both strategically and tactically, strategically because it inaugurated the great ocean-borne offensive, tactically because it taught unforgettable lessons in island-landing.

The coral island of Betio, in Tarawa atoll, a tiny speck in the vast Pacific, about as large as New York's Central Park, was garrisoned by some 3,000 Japanese marines protected by the most elaborate system of defenses that Americans had as yet encountered. The authors of *Betio Beachhead* tell how:

The Japanese over a period of fifteen months did a very sound job in perfecting their defenses for the Gilberts, and the heart of their efforts was little Betio. They transformed its flat insignificance into one solid islet fortress which they felt, with considerable justification, would prove impregnable.

For its beaches and the reef were lined with obstacles—concrete pyramid-shaped obstructions designed to stop landing boats, tactical wire in long fences, coconut-log barricades, mines, and large piles of coral rocks.

And for its beach defense there were numerous weapons—grenades, mortars, rifles, light and heavy machine guns, 13-mm. dual-purpose machine guns, 37-mm. guns, 70-mm. infantry guns, 75-mm. mountain guns, 75-mm. dual-purpose guns, 80-mm. antiboat guns, 127-mm. twin-mount, dual-purpose guns, 140-mm. coast-defense guns, and 8-inch coast-defense guns.

The emplacements for these weapons were often seven feet thick of solid concrete, reinforced by steel, coral sand, and coconut logs.

The pillboxes for the automatic weapons, and even the riflemen's pits, were scientifically constructed to withstand heavy bombardment. Around a concrete floor in a three- to five-foot excavation was built a twelve-inch reinforced concrete wall. Over this were alternate layers of coral sand, coconut logs, and sandbags. The roof was made in the same way with coral sand covering the entire outside, then tapering off gradually to prevent the casting of shadows which would show in aerial photographs.

In places the blockhouses were of concrete with a roof thickness of five feet, on top of which were palm-tree trunks with a diameter of eighteen inches, and a final layer of angle irons made of railroad steel.

Guarded by these defenses was a landing field: the long, dusty airstrip that gave the Japanese a position of strategic importance in the Central Pacific because it was their nearest point to our travel routes from San Francisco to Hawaii to Australia, because it was our first major obstruction on the road to Tokyo.

In addition to these Japanese-made defenses there were the barriers and hazards of nature. There was the reef. There were the tides.

The Japanese who manned this islet fortress of Betio were not of the ordinary run. They were all volunteers. They possessed a finer physique and training than any other group in the Emperor's forces. They were men of the Imperial Japanese landing forces, and there were four thousand of them. Their rear admiral in command at the atoll is known to have stated that the invading Americans faced certain annihilation, for "a million men could not take Tarawa."

The Admiral's confidence was based on realism. . . .

Our operations at Tarawa were entirely offensive in nature. Once this bastion fell, we were on our way to Tokyo. The road would be cleared for attack upon the highly strategic Marshalls, conquest of the Marianas, victory at Palau. With this open ocean flank secure, General MacArthur was then in position to mount his now historical blow at the Philippines.

Guadalcanal was a gamble. A gamble which had to be made. For America was faced with the greatest challenge confronting a nation at war—the challenge of amphibious warfare on a huge scale. . . .

We were not underequipped for Tarawa. Offshore stood the mightiest fleet ever assembled up to that time in the Pacific. In the two years since Guadalcanal, an amazing variety of special landing craft had been developed to meet the needs of transporting men and material for massive sea-borne invasions.

Yet Tarawa, too, was a gamble. For the first time in martial history a sea-borne assault upon a heavily defended coral atoll was to be launched. As General Julian Smith told his troops on the eve of D-Day: "We are the first American troops to attack a defended atoll. What we do here will set a standard for all future operations in the Central Pacific area."

The operation against Tarawa was brilliantly conceived and magnificently executed. It did become, as General Smith predicted, a standard for all future operations. The strategy and tactics devised for Tarawa do not differ qualitatively from subsequent assaults. The differences are quantitative alone. The severity of the bombardment, the weight of the artillery, the number of tanks and amphibian tractors in the later operations have varied with the size of the job.[8]

Before the invasion of November 20. Tarawa was softened up by a terrific air and naval bombardment which, however, failed to destroy the blockhouses and pillboxes with which the island was covered. The first waves of Marines landed at high tide and were held by murderous machine gun fire on the beaches; supporting forces, grounded on reefs offshore, were forced to wade in.

The water was full of landing craft being held back of the Line of Departure while waiting for the order to go in. Some of the boats from earlier waves were still trying to get in and the shore guns took their toll on these.

The men who were held up aboard these boats suffered the enraging frustration of knowing that the men ashore could see them. One veteran of Guadalcanal clenched his knuckles and shouted the prayer: "For Christ's sake, let us in! What can those people be thinking in there, seeing these boats in the water, needing our help, and us sitting here like we was back home?"

But General Smith knew that it was useless to send in these boats loaded with reserves, supplies of ammunition, food, and water until a more secure beachhead had been established.

There are times when fighting men cry, when they shed tears of frustration and rage, and there were tears and curses off the beaches of Betio, in the Tarawa Atoll, on November 20, 1943.

So the eyes of some Marines were wet with a fierce, bitter passion. They were tears bred of impatience, of the tenseness of the moment, of the knowledge that they were needed in the fight and could not get in. . . .

4:45 P.M.—The Sixth Marine Regiment, listed as Corps Reserves for use either at Tarawa or Makin, was released to the control of the Second Marine Division. With the Sixth Marines in the fight the men on Betio would have all that was left of their available manpower. The bolt was shot.

The men ashore, when they got the news, were cheered. The boys of the Sixth were veterans of Guadalcanal. They had been the first troops to land in Iceland, and on the "Canal" they had fought with distinction.

Aboard the transports gloom had been thick among men of the Sixth. They had watched the bombardment unfold, and had swallowed their disappointment.

Announcement over the ship's speaker that they were to go in to help out brought a spontaneous cheer from the ranks. Disappointed gave way to feverish preparation. Grins replaced frowns. They knew what it meant to go in, but few would have traded their positions for anything else life had to offer.

5:20 P.M.—General Smith received from Colonel Shoup his first few fragmentary casualty reports. They were bad.

10:00 P.M.—Colonel Shoup summed up D-Day in this message to General Smith:

"Have dug in to hold limited beachhead. . . ."

You can perhaps think of this "limited beachhead" more graphically as having been a little chunk of ground about three hundred yards in width and of thirty to fifty yards in average depth around the head of the pier, while on Red Beach 2 it extended on a shallow front about one hundred and fifty yards.

This was the small foothold which the men had secured during the first afternoon and which they had held against every effort that the Japs could muster to dislodge them. In this crowded atom of space they had lain or huddled close on the open sands and pressed against the sea wall for shelter against Jap fire. From such unbelievably awkward and exposed positions they had returned the fire in the best fashion that they could. And they had held.[9]

That night reinforcements, including tanks, were landed on the island, and the next day destroyers and dive bombers went into action against the flaming pillboxes. After four days of the most savage fighting, the last Japanese were killed or committed suicide. Tarawa was ours. And at the same time a task force of the 27th Infantry Division had seized Makin, a seaplane base one hundred miles to the north.

Two months later the navy was ready to move on the Marshalls, hundreds of miles to the north and about 1,000 miles from the massive naval base of Truk. Kwajalein atoll, its airfields garrisoned by some 8,000 troops, was picked for the invasion. The way was prepared by an overwhelming naval bombardment. Then, at dawn January 31, the 7th Infantry landed on perimetral islands of the atoll. The next day one end of Kwajalein had been overrun. The defenses were as formidable as on Tarawa and the enemy as fanatical, but by the third day more than three-quarters of the island was in our hands.

After three days of fighting Kwajalein was in our hands; the Japanese had lost over 8,000 killed, our casualties were 286 killed and 1,230 wounded.

Control of the Gilberts and Marshalls and, shortly after, of the Admiralties to the south, enabled the fleet to strike a series of devastating blows at the Japanese air and naval bases. In mid-February, carrier planes destroyed 201 planes and 23 ships at the major naval base of Truk. A week later Spruance's fleet raided Saipan in the Marianas with results almost as good. At the end of a three-week excursion in the central Pacific the fleet could give this accounting:

Combat sorties	5,456
Bombs dropped, in tons (and pin-pointed!)	2,026
Enemy aircraft destroyed (including 12 by ships' AA)	484
U.S. Navy aircraft lost in combat (all causes)	45
Ships sunk (including 3 by ships' gunfire at Truk)	32
Ships damaged	18
U.S. Navy ships sunk	0

With the neutralization of Truk our navy was able to steam, almost with impunity into the waters of the Marianas, only 1,500 miles from Tokyo. Chief of these islands was Saipan, which had been converted into a powerful air base, and Guam. June, 1944, saw the beginning of the Marianas campaign. The approach of Admiral Spruance's task force to what were practically home waters was a challenge the Japanese could not ignore. Their carrier fleet put out to meet us, and in the ensuing battle of the Philippine Sea, June 19–20, we destroyed over 400 Japanese planes at a cost of 27, and sunk or damaged four carriers, 3 cruisers, 3 destroyers, 2 tankers and a battleship. This notable victory made possible the subsequent conquest of the Marianas.

The first landings came on June 15. The fighting on Saipan was concluded on July 9. Its conquest, paving the way to B-29 attacks on the Japanese homeland, brought about the fall of the Japanese cabinet and the reorganization of army and navy high commands. Two weeks later the little island of Tinian was overrun. Less important strategically but far more gratifying to the American public was the reconquest of Guam which was completed by August 10.

The conquest of the Gilberts, Marshalls, and Marianas in the central Pacific, and of all the northern coast of New Guinea, Biak, Palau, and Morotai islands in the southern Pacific, the neutralization of Truk and other enemy air and naval bases, and the smashing of the Japanese fleet, opened the way to direct assault upon the Philippines.

The Return

It came sooner than was expected, sooner even than planned, and this because our air and naval power had all but driven the Japanese from the Philippine seas and paralyzed the normal striking power of their air force. This background of the invasion is delineated by Lieutenant Oliver Jensen:

The line at which the Japanese finally decided to stand ran along their innermost defenses, from Japan on the north down the Ryukyu Islands, Formosa and the Philippines. Against that line, however, combined forces of the Central and Southwest Pacific commands now pitted a new one of their own, and the resulting advantages of strategy were not on the enemy side. The U. S. had established a line of departure, as the Navy calls it, for the amphibious assault on the Philippines. It was drawn almost straight from Guam southwest through Ulithi and Palau to Morotai, just off the northern tip of Halmahera, first big island south of the Philippines. Ulithi had been occupied without resistance on September 20, thus neutralizing the nearby Japanese base on Yap. MacArthur's troops had just overrun Morotai under air cover furnished by carriers commanded by Vice Admiral John S. McCain.

The taking of southern Palau in mid-September, in itself a major and bloody operation, filled in the new line and deprived the enemy of his last naval base in the open Pacific. It completed the isolation of all the other enemy bases to the east and south—Truk, Rabaul, Kavieng, many others. It was necessary to capture only the southern Palaus in order to nail down the rest of the group and admit their garrisons to the by-pass club.

But a principal result of the September operations was to limit severely the area in which the Japanese fleet could safely operate. It now had to base entirely behind the Philippines, in the China and South China Seas. The passage south of the Philippines between Mindanao and Halmahera was closed by General Kenney's Army fliers. In order to repel a U.S. attack on the Philippines, enemy ships could approach only from the north or through the two narrow passages in the central Philippines, the Surigao and San Bernardino straits. Many of the areas still open to them were under long-range surveillance from the air, and in the others no Japanese admiral could feel entirely sure that someone was not staring at him through a periscope and measuring him for size.

At the same time the Japanese now had to reckon with a new, strong U.S. fleet at large in the Pacific. This was the Third Fleet, which had demonstrated its strength in taking Palau. Its commander, who had arrived on August 24, was no stranger to the Pacific. Thousands of plain men at a Central Pacific base thrilled when Admiral William F. Halsey, sixty-two years old now but shaggy, tough and witty as ever, rolled up a wooden gangplank to assume command. . . .

The Third Fleet was as large as, if not larger than, the Fifth Fleet, with which Admiral Spruance had brought the campaign to its present peak of success. For the time being this new fleet was to carry on where Spruance had left off. Like the Fifth, the Third could be when necessary a self-contained amphibious force, with Army and Marine units, landing craft and older surface ships. But its core of strength was the fast carrier force. . . .

The Third Fleet was soon where Admiral Mitscher says his ships belong—at sea. During the month of September it suddenly raided Mindanao and the central Philippines. The main objective was to flatten Japanese airfields in that vicinity, but Mitscher's fliers came back with an interesting discovery—that the much-vaunted Japanese Army air force in that area was weaker than anyone thought.

On September 21, while Radio Manila was playing "Music for Your Morning Mood," Mitscher's fliers began to peel off over Manila harbor, Cavite and Nichols Field. The harbor was jammed with cargo ships and tankers. One fighter pilot who was part Filipino reported that Manila didn't seem greatly changed. Cavite was rebuilt, part of Dewey Boulevard was blocked off as an airstrip, there was a big concentration camp at Las Pinas village, shell-scarred Corregidor looked green again. . . . A man-made tornado sent many of the ships to the bottom. An ammunition dump blew up. Later in the day mist closed in and spared a few enemy planes, and some of them attempted unsuccessfully to hit Halsey's carriers next day. But Japanese air power failed here as dismally as elsewhere.

Convinced we should take immediate advantage of the demonstrated weakness, Admiral Halsey himself at once flew down to confer with MacArthur, and the plans of both parties were integrated for the Philippine landing. To Halsey fell the task of softening up the enemy yet at the same time keeping him wondering where the next big blow would land. Here was just the kind of job Halsey liked best. It was arranged that a U.S. surface force would bombard Marcus on October 9. At the same time, thousands of miles from that lonely atoll, Halsey and Mitscher set out on a week-long series of raids deep in Japanese waters.

The day after the bombardment of Marcus, to the intense surprise of the enemy, carrier planes suddenly raided Okinawa in the Ryukyu Islands. Twenty-four hours later, while the Japs were still groggy, Halsey's planes appeared hundreds of miles to the south over Luzon. Then, beginning on the twelfth, they worked for three days on Formosa, long a major enemy stronghold. They gave it such a pasting that the Japanese may well have suspected it was the next invasion target.[10]

The punishment inflicted by Admiral Halsey's Third Fleet between September 9th, when Mindanao was attacked, and the attack on Marcus just a month later totalled 957 planes destroyed, 313 ships damaged or sunk. During the next ten days this mighty armada, ranging from the Ryukyus to Luzon, added 1,200 planes to their kill and at least another 150 ships.

This destruction of Japanese air power and disruption of supply lines, plus reports from Filipino guerrillas that Leyte was weakly held, induced General MacArthur to make a swift change of plans. Instead of landing on Mindanao, he would tackle Leyte in the heart of the Philippines; instead of waiting two months he would move at once. The plan was submitted to the Joint Chiefs of Staff. Royal Arch Gunnison takes up the story from there:

It was accepted as sound, with only one "if." That was: If General MacArthur and Admiral Kinkaid of the Seventh Fleet felt they could speed up their preparations and be ready to go.

Admiral Daniel E. Barbey, one of the original American amphibious warfare experts who helped plan the North African invasion and who, up to the Philippines invasion, had pulled off fifteen successful landings in the Southwest Pacific, was called back from his Morotai operation by destroyer and plane. Could he stage this invasion based on guerrilla and naval air information? And if he felt it could be staged now, quickly, how many rehearsals would the men need?

Uncle Dan is as aggressive as Bull Halsey and a man with long-range vision who said: "The Navy can land any body of troops and their supplies anywhere in the Pacific today and get them ashore—and that goes for Japan. From there on, it's the timing and the G.I.'s fighting ability that will determine whether he stays ashore."

Kinkaid, Barbey, Lieutenant General Walter Krueger, commanding the Sixth Army, and General MacArthur were bothered by only one thing: air support for so great an undertaking. To jump 1,500 miles to the central Philippines now meant they'd have to go without General Kenney's Fifth and Thirteenth air support until they were able to get sufficient air strips to handle the long-range fighters and bombers. Until then, the invasion fleet and force would be at the mercy of Jap land-based planes from Formosa, Borneo and Hainan, unless the Navy could put in enough large and small carriers to keep the Jap back for nearly twenty-five days. Well, hadn't Secretary of the Navy Forrestal said we have over one hundred carriers in the Pacific? That should be enough to hold the Jap counterattack back for ten days before the invasion, seven days after the first landings, after which some of the air strips should be ready, and another eight or ten days following until land-based day and night fighters plus medium and heavy bombers could pick up the offensive from the carrier pilots.

This strategy was viewed in naval headquarters as the most daring maneuver in the history of naval and amphibious warfare, but Nimitz and Halsey felt they could pull it off. MacArthur had full confidence that, once ashore, his G.I.s would handle themselves so expertly they'd have the landing strips ready on schedule. In other words, MacArthur and Halsey put themselves out on the end of a 1,500-mile limb, and the Japs had a fifty-fifty or better chance of cutting them off. . . .

If the MacArthur-Nimitz-Kinkaid force got away with this, it was admitted, in the close circle of planners, that the war colleges would be rewriting their tactical courses.

Admiral Nimitz supplied Halsey with the heaviest U. S. Fleet force, including carriers, that ever sailed any ocean. He gave Kinkaid the largest number of CVEs ever put in one spot to cover the actual invasion and to do the first ten days' air-cover job. A rough estimate shows that at the height of the invasion fighting, the United States had some 1,500 carrier-borne planes fighting and available for action. Halsey's job was to keep the Imperial Jap fleet north of Luzon and to ground and wreck Jap planes and shipping beginning ten days before MacArthur hit the beach.[11]

On October 20, 1944, came the dawn of liberation for the Filipinos who for three years had fought a guerrilla war against the conqueror.

Six hundred vessels brought the Sixth Army to Leyte. From one of these vessels General MacArthur stepped ashore, two and one half years after he had quit Bataan, and made a simple announcement:

People of the Philippines: I have returned. By the grace of Almighty God our forces stand again on Philippine soil—soil consecrated in the blood of our two peoples. . . . Rally to me. Let the indomitable spirit of Bataan and Corregidor lead on.

More men went ashore on the first day of the Leyte invasion than landed in Normandy on D-Day. Perhaps 225,000 troops swept inland. The late President Sergio Osmena called upon his people to assist the invading forces. Within two days Tacloban, capital of the island, was captured. Here a vital airfield was taken and immediately bulldozers went to work preparing two airstrips, one long enough to land the medium bombers and long range fighters so sorely needed from Kenney's air force. But before this airstrip could be prepared, events ushered in a new phase of the battle for the Philippines. The date was October 23, 1944.

Three separate Japanese groups of naval forces approached the Philippines. One moved east through the Sulu Sea for Surigao Strait and the second circled north through the Sibuyan Sea for San Bernardino Strait, the third attacked from Formosa with carriers. The Japanese fleet was first sighted on October 23rd by two submarines. The submarines attacked, scoring twelve direct hits, but did not stop the force. Word spread through American forces that "The Jap fleet is coming out." This was the moment Halsey, Mitscher, and Nimitz had been waiting for.

On October 24th Vice-Admiral Mitscher's pilots struck at five Japanese battleships screened by eight cruisers and thirteen destroyers in the strait south of Mindoro Island. Four battleships were hit badly, 150 planes shot down, and almost every other ship in the force hit by at least one bomb. A strong Japanese air attack on our carriers resulted in the sinking of the light carrier *Princeton*. Then came one of the most skillful operations in our naval history.

Admiral Kinkaid's Seventh Fleet was smaller and less powerful than the great force under Halsey. But he built with it a trap in which the ships were teeth so placed that each could do the utmost damage to the enemy entering the jaws.

As darkness fell, his flotillas of PT boats took station in the Mindanao Sea, just outside Surigao Strait. The destroyers lined the 35 miles of the Strait itself. At the end of the narrow passage, within sight of Leyte Gulf, were placed the battleships. Five of them had been sunk or damaged at

Pearl Harbor, repaired, modernized, and sent to avenge themselves. The cruisers were with them.

About midnight, a PT boat signaled that the Japanese were approaching the Strait. In the darkness, the PTs got two hits but the Japanese steamed on, in double column, tearing through the passage at 20 knots. The destroyers held their fire; battleships and cruisers were silent, hidden by the dark.

About 3 A.M. Admiral Olendorf ordered "Commence firing!" The destroyers sped toward the enemy ships, turned to launched their torpedoes. Surigao Strait was lit by incandescent flashes as the torpedoes struck home. The cruisers, ranged on opposite sides of the trap, opened fire on the Japanese caught between them. Colored recognition lights flashed as the confused enemy, thinking they were attacked by their own ships, tried to stop the hail of steel. The lights gave our cruisers beautiful targets—until both the Japanese ships and our destroyers laid down smoke screens. The one destroyer crippled by Japanese fire lurched in the smoke, while the others withdrew and opened fire with their five-inch batteries.

Confusion did not alter Japanese determination: the ships plunged on through the strait, firing wildly and inaccurately. Their star shells fell in front of the American ships instead of beyond them, so they were not silhouetted. Soon the Japanese stubbornness gave Admiral Olendorf an opportunity granted to few naval commanders. He "crossed the T"—an action so called because one fleet advancing in column forms, as it were, the vertical bar and thus can fire only its forward-pointing guns, while the attackers form the horizontal bar and thus bring their broadsides to bear.

One after another the Japanese ships reached a narrow part of the strait and turned, presenting perfect targets. The six American battleships, only 12 miles away, did not even have to shift the range. Ship after Japanese ship became a torch in the night. Not one escaped. The cruisers and destroyers sank the remainder as they fled.

The Japanese lost fifteen ships in this action—one a battleship. Admiral Olendorf said: "I sent planes out to get pictures of that one, but the damn thing sank before they could get there."

The carrier force from the Formosa Sea had been spotted on the afternoon of the 24th. Seventeen warships paraded in formation. When Mitscher's airmen finished with them one carrier, two cruisers, and two destroyers were seen to sink. Four other ships were dead in the water.

The battle at this stage totalled seven Japanese warships sunk, two battleships badly damaged. At this juncture a frantic message was received from Rear Admiral Thomas A. Sprague, in command of a comparatively helpless group of escort carriers guarding MacArthur's men ashore on Leyte. Halsey, in sending the main portion of the Third Fleet north to meet the carrier threat coming from the direction of Formosa, had left Sprague's Seventh Fleet exposed to heavy surface attack. He counted confidently on Kinkaid stopping the Japanese at Surigao Strait and he believed that Mitscher had rendered the Japanese force in the Sibuyan Sea, above San Bernardino Strait, helpless. So why not move all free forces north to meet the Japanese carrier threat?

At 6:50 A.M. on October 25th, 1944, Admiral Sprague's Fleet suddenly sighted the tops of giant Japanese battleships coming over the horizon.

Apparently the central Japanese force, turned back by an all-day air attack at San Bernardino Strait on the 24th, had reversed course during the night and came on to strike at the Leyte beachhead. Sprague's small CVEs were no match for the four battleships and seven cruisers that hove into view. The Japanese fleet steamed straight on, paying little attention to the four destroyer escorts and three destroyers that laid down smoke screens, darting in and out, matching their guns with the massive rifles of the battleships. Heavy Japanese cruisers sank one American escort carrier and hit others, while battleships sank two destroyers and one destroyer escort. The ships under Admiral Olendorf hurried up to take part in the fight, but it could not match the firepower of the enemy ships. The Japanese were in a position to enter Leyte Gulf, sink the carriers, cargo ships, and transports, and accomplish a substantial part of their original mission. Why they turned and retired toward San Bernardino Strait has not been satisfactorily explained.

One theory is that Admiral Halsey, after severely mauling the Japanese carrier fleet, broke off the action and hurried back. His vanguard arrived at 1:30 P.M.—"like the hero in a horse opera"—and his planes joined those of the Seventh Fleet in harrying the fleeing enemy. One more giant carrier was sent down, and on the evening of the 25th a submarine made a final kill—a heavy cruiser. The official score stood: four carriers, two battleships, six heavy cruisers, three light cruisers, and about six destroyers sunk; at least 35 other vessels probably sunk or damaged. A Navy communique declared that "this might turn out to be among the decisive battles of modern times."

On Leyte MacArthur's troops made rapid progress. The Japanese, aware that this was the real battle for the Philippines, pushed in reinforcements from neighboring islands, but these could not stem the American advance. By December the enemy gave up the attempt to bring in additional reinforcements—an admission of defeat. Two months and a day after the first landings, the battle for Leyte was, for all practical purposes, over. Total Japanese casualties were estimated at 90,000; remnants of Japanese forces, lurking in the hills and jungles, fought on viciously but hopelessly.

Already MacArthur had turned to other Philippine islands. Samar was overrun and landings were made on Mindoro. First landings on Luzon were made at Lingayen Gulf on January 9th. Under cover of an immense array of sea and air power, a force of 100,000 men swarmed ashore. Opposing them but scattered widely on Luzon were an estimated 150,000 Japanese. The first big battle carried the Allies across the Agno River, over low hills paralleling the Gulf, and out onto the great plain leading to Manila 110 miles southeast of Lingayen. There Allied tanks could make free use of the open terrain and fine roads.

On January 30th, a brave band of Rangers made a daring raid deep into Japanese-held territory to a war prison at Cabanatuan. With the aid of Filipino guerrillas 513 prisoners were set free, 532 Japanese killed, at a cost of 27 dead Allies.

By early February new landings had been made at Subic Bay on the west and at Nasugbu on the south. At both points Allied forces were moving quickly inland. By February 4th, two American columns were within 15 miles of Manila itself. Heretofore the Japanese had fought mostly a delaying action: now from the buildings and streets of the capital they put up the same kind of stiff resistance that Americans had encountered from New Guinea to Saipan. The Americans drove in from three sides—the First Cavalry Division from the east, the 37th Division from the north, and units of the Eighth Army from the south.

In the fierce fighting that ranged for a week Manila was ruined. As the *New York Times* said:

The first two forces had to fight their way from house to house, in the face of fires and demolitions and through mined streets, to the north bank of the Pasig River which cuts the city in two. After they crossed the stream in a fleet of amphibious trucks and moved into southern Manila, they were met with steady machine-gun and mortar fire from upper floors and from concrete pill-boxes placed at important intersections by the Japanese, who were still clinging to "Intramuros," the old walled section of the city on the Pasig's lower bank.

Among the prime objectives of the vanguard was the liberation of Allied prisoners held by the Japanese in north Manila. Immediately on their entrance into the capital, a flying squadron of cavalrymen sped to the gates of the Santo Tomas internment center where 3,700 persons, mostly women and children, were being detained. The troopers pushed through machine-gun nests and sniper fire up to the camp grounds and then fought from room to room to clean out the Japanese. Other forces, meanwhile, moved against burning Bilibid Prison where 1,100 war prisoners and civilian internees were saved from flames.[12]

Following the fall of Manila, MacArthur sent parachute troops to capture the tunnelled rock fortress of Corregidor, where the last valiant stand had been made by Wainwright during the dark days of April, 1942. On the 2nd of March MacArthur himself stood on this island and told his men: "Hoist the colors and let no enemy ever haul them down."

The Japanese continued to resist violently on Luzon. South of Manila, the strong Shimbu Line was shattered on March 17th, trapping the Japanese in caves or forcing them to retire into the remote Sierra Madre chain of mountains—a malaria infested region, much of it never thoroughly explored by white men. In the north of Luzon troops moved on Baguio. Although sporadic fighting was to continue throughout the Philippines, the essential parts were now firmly in our hands. On Mindanao an amphibious landing on the Zamboanga coast on March 10 had been exploited. On April 8th the *New York Times* pointed the possibilities of the reconquest of the Philippines:

The campaign in the Philippines last week was moving into its closing phase—one which heralded great new drives to the south. From Zamboanga on Mindanao, in the southwestern corner of the islands, veteran infantrymen of the Forty-first Division made a 200-mile amphibious leap to the Sulu Archipelago, where they seized the small islands of Bongao, Sanga Sanga and Tawi Tawi, less than thirty miles from oil-rich Borneo and springboards for invasion of the Netherlands East Indies.

Elsewhere, mopping up operations were being speeded. On Luzon, Sixth Army troops, after an intensive naval bombardment, landed at Legaspi on the island's long southeastern peninsula and quickly secured the city and near-by airfields. Just south of Legaspi, other American units invaded Masbate, in the central Philippines and the eleventh largest island in the group, meeting little opposition. In the six months since American troops first went ashore on Leyte last October, most of the larger islands—Mindoro, Luzon, Mindanao, Panay, Cebu—have been liberated. The end of formal Japanese resistance is near. The final collapse would mean that the Allies could: (1) accelerate their build-up of Luzon, their largest land mass in the western Pacific, into a staging area for further large-scale amphibious moves; (2) release an estimated 250,000 seasoned troops, with their naval support and all their equipment, for other operations. Whether these would be directed north, against Japan proper, northwest, against the China coast, or south, toward the Indies, the enemy would have to wait and see.[13]

Iwo Jima

Even as General MacArthur was pushing ahead in the Philippines, the next great—and costly—step forward was taken. The date was February 19, 1945.

The battle for Iwo opened with prolonged air bombardment. For 54 consecutive days the Pacific Strategic Air Force bombed the tiny isle. On the 55th day reconnaissance showed that at least 16 new big guns had been brought up by the Japanese and set in strategic positions. The daily bombing was resumed for another 20 days. At intervals, units of the fleet shelled the island and staged carrier-based bombing attacks.

On January 24th, a task force under Rear Admiral Oscar C. Badger attacked Iwo with particular severity, destroying three enemy ships. On February 1st, the army assigned "every available aircraft in the Pacific" to the Iwo mission. From February 16 to 19 a task force of six battleships and supporting cruisers and destroyers circled the island, pounding every sector with thousands of tons of giant shells.

At dawn on D-Day, from below the horizon, appeared a great fleet of hundreds of ships to join the naval vessels bombarding Iwo. They drew up in a semi-circle seven miles out and inside the arc was a great array of landing craft. On this fleet were three divisions of Marines under command of Major-General Harry Schmidt. John P. Marquand describes it:

The amphibious vehicles, churning up the sea into foaming circles, organized themselves in lines, each line following its leader. Then the leaders moved out to the floating flags, around which they gathered in circling groups, waiting for their signal to move ashore. The gray landing craft with the Marines had left the transports some time before for their own fixed areas and they also were circling, like runners testing their muscles before the race. The barrage which had been working over the beach area had lifted, and the beach, with the smoldering terraces above it, was visible again. It was time for the first wave to be starting.

It was hard to pick the first wave out in that sea of milling craft, but suddenly a group of the barges broke loose from its circle, following its leader in a dash toward shore. Close to land the leader turned parallel to the beach, and kept on until the whole line was parallel. Then the boats turned individually and made a dash for it. The Navy had landed the first wave on Iwo Jima—at nine o'clock on the dot—or, at least, not more than a few seconds after nine.[14]

Ashore, Japanese General Kuribayashi had 23,000 men under his command. He had literally thousands of pillboxes, cleverly camouflaged underground defenses, mines, bunkers—governing every square foot of the beaches. Inland he had thousands more of the same. Fighting against such crafty defenses is described by five Marine Corps combat correspondents:

When the 24th Marine Regiment's 2d Battalion reached the scene, they called it "the Wilderness," and there they spent four days on the line, with no respite from the song of death sung by mortars among those desolate crevices and gouged shell holes. The Wilderness covered about a square mile inland from Blue Beach 2, on the approaches to Airfield No. 2, and there was no cover. Here and there stood a blasted dwarf tree; here and there a stubby rock ledge in a maze of volcanic crevices.

The 2d Battalion attacked with flame throwers, demolition charges, 37-millimeter guns, riflemen. A tank advancing in support was knocked out by a mortar shell. After every Japanese volley, Corsair fighter planes streamed down on the mortar positions, ripping their charges of bombs into the Wilderness. But after every dive was ended, the mortars started their ghastly song again.

Cracks in the earth run along the open field to the left of the Wilderness, and hot smoke seeped up through the cracks. Gains were counted in terms of 100 or 200 yards for a day, in terms of three or four bunkers knocked out. Losses were counted in terms of three or four men suddenly turned to bloody rags after the howl of a mortar shell, in terms of a flame-thrower man hit by a grenade as he poured his flame into a bunker. The assault platoon of flame throwers and demolitionists, spearheading the regiment's push through the Wilderness, lost two assistant squad leaders killed.

The Japs were hard to kill. Cube-shaped concrete blockhouses had to be blasted again and again before the men inside were silenced. Often the stunned and wounded Japs continued to struggle among the ruins, still trying to fire back. A sergeant fired 21 shots at a semiconcealed Jap before the latter was killed. Another Marine assaulting a pillbox found a seriously wounded Jap trying to get a heavy machine gun into action. He emptied his clip at him but the Jap kept reaching. Finally, out of ammunition, the Marine used his knife to kill him.

Forty-eight hours after the attack began, one element of the Third Division moved into the line under orders to advance at all costs.

Behind a rolling artillery barrage and with fixed bayonets, the unit leaped forward in an old-fashioned hell-bent-for-leather charge and advanced to the very mouths of the fixed Jap defenses. Before scores of pillboxes the men flung themselves at the tiny flaming holes, throwing grenades and jabbing with bayonets. Comrades went past, hurdled the defenses and rushed across Airfield No. 2. In three minutes one unit lost four officers. Men died at every step. That was how we broke their line.

Across the field we attacked a ridge. The enemy rose up out of holes to hurl our assault back. The squads reformed and went up again. At the crest they plunged on the Japs with bayonets. One of our men, slashing his way from side to side, fell dead from a pistol shot. His comrade drove his bayonet into the Jap who had killed him. The Japs on the ridge were annihilated.

And now behind those proud and weary men, our whole previously stalled attack poured through. Tanks, bazookas and demolition men smashed and burned the by-passed fortifications. In an area 1,000 yards long and 200 deep, more than 800 enemy pillboxes were counted.

The survivors of this bold charge covered 800 yards in an hour and a half. Brave men had done what naval shelling, aerial bombardment, artillery and tanks had not been able to do in two days of constant pounding. What was perhaps the most intensively fortified small area ever encountered in battle had been broken.[15]

Newsweek tells how the flag went up:

When the Marines first hit the black, cindery beaches on the morning of Feb. 19, the Japs let them come on for a few hundred yards, probably suspecting that the first landing was a feint. Then, as it became evident that the Americans were going to cut across the narrow tail of the pork-chop-shaped island, the waiting enemy let them have it.

Artillery and mortar shells walked up and down the beach. From pillboxes built to withstand anything less than a direct hit of a 1,000-pound bomb or a 14-inch shell came streams of fire which did not slacken even when American planes and ships laid down thunderous barrages.

It looked as if the Marines on the beach and the invasion of Iwo Jima were equally doomed. Tanks could hardly operate in the loose, volcanic soil. The wreckage of boats, vehicles, supplies, and equipment littered the beach for 2 miles. Ammunition dumps blew up in sheets of flame. The congestion was so great men stepped on each other. The Japs had the Americans zeroed in from Mount Suribachi, the extinct volcano on the island's southern tip, and from the hills north of the beachhead. Anywhere they put a shell it hit something.

But later in the day the Marines discovered a soft spot near Mount Suribachi and, swiftly exploiting the opportunity, lunged in to open up the beachhead. One regiment swung across the island to isolate the volcano. Another unit bored ahead to Suribachi airfield, directly in front of the beach. Simultaneously, the Fourth Division in the north forged westward foot by terrible foot. The airfield fell 27 hours after the first landing—30 hours before schedule. Then the Fifth reached the western shore and cut the island in half. The two divisions turned north to push up the island.

The key position of Iwo, however, was Mount Suribachi itself. Defensively and offensively, it was probably the most formidable spot the Americans had yet tackled in the Pacific. From the sea the ships battered Suribachi at point-blank range. Bombers and rocket planes raked it again and again. But the enemy positions had been planned to withstand such bombardment.

At 10:35 on the morning of Feb. 23 a small patrol reached the summit and ran up the flag.

Though Suribachi was secured, Japanese artillery still ranged over the island's 5-mile length. Its severely limited area gave no space for maneuver, and the Marines had to make costly frontal assaults on pillboxes, bunkers, and caves.

Assessing the action, Lt. Gen. Holland M. Smith, commander of the Pacific Fleet Marine Forces, said Iwo was the toughest battle in the history of the Marine Corps. On Tarawa . . . the Second Division sustained 3,603 losses in 76 hours, and Saipan . . . cost 16,525. On Iwo, 3,650 Marines fell in the first 48 hours (most of them wounded). The figure climbed to 5,372 in 58 hours, or three for every two minutes of action.[16]

For twenty-six days the fighting on Iwo raged with unparalleled intensity. By D-Day plus 14 many of the Japanese cross-island defenses had been smashed. On the high ground in the center of the island, Marines of the Third Division had driven a wedge into the northern third of the island still held by the Japanese. This wedge was exploited in fighting through what has been called a "jungle of stone"—wild lava ledges, smoking sulphur pits, chasms, cliffs, caves, boulders—and on D-Day plus 18 the break-through to the sea was accomplished and the Japanese force split. Turning southward the eastern pocket was cleaned out, and it was on the northern tip of the island, at Kitano Point, that the final Japanese rally was staged. It wasn't really a rally, but it was there that General Kuribayashi was killed in one of the innumerable caves that studded the island.

On March 16, 1945, it was announced that the central airfield on Iwo was in operation.

Okinawa

Iwo Jima lies 750 miles south of Tokyo; 825 miles to Iwo's west lies Okinawa, in the Ryukyu island group, destined to be the scene of the final major land attack of the war. Landings were made there on April 1st. On April 8th the *New York Times* wrote:

An integral part of the Japanese homeland, some 362 miles southwest of the main island of Kyushu, Okinawa's capture would bring immediate, manifold gains. The island sits astride Japan's sea lanes to riches of the

East Indies—lanes already endangered by the American occupation of the Philippines. In American hands Okinawa would deprive the Japanese of a very extensive string of air and naval bases. As an American outpost, the island would: (1) provide bases from which to wage air war against Japan— Okinawa is large enough to handle hundreds of bombers and close enough to Kyushu to make possible the use of medium bombers and fighters against Japan's industries and ports; (2) open the way for American surface fleets to the China and Yellow Seas and provide access to the coasts of China and Korea; (3) provide an advanced staging area for an amphibious approach to Japan, either directly or by way of the China coast.

Last week's landing, which followed by six days earlier invasions of the Kerama Islands, west of Okinawa, was preceded by nine days of bombardment by the guns and planes of the United States Fifth Fleet— consisting of more than 1,400 ships of all types—and those of a powerful British squadron. Okinawa was believed to have been garrisoned by 50,000 to 80,000 Japanese troops. It is some sixty-seven miles long and three to ten miles wide; landing operations, therefore, did not have to be limited to one or two heavily defended beaches as at Iwo. Terrain was expected to aid the enemy in making an effective defense and in prolonging resistance.

Considering the size of the Japanese garrison and the island's defensive advantages, the initial resistance was surprisingly light. Landing beaches were made secure in the face of only sporadic mortar, artillery and small-arms fire. While the unloading of supplies was begun, infantry and marine veterans pushed up steep slopes into the interior. By the second day they had penetrated three miles inland along an eight-mile front and had captured two important airfields. Later they reached the east coast at several points, cutting the island in two, and began driving north and south. To the south, where the main Japanese forces are believed concentrated, resistance stiffened; in drives to the north, the American forces continued to score gains of as much as five miles a day.[17]

On April 6th, the Japanese sent large air formations over Okinawa, evidently in an attempt to destroy American ships and shore-held installations. This attack sank three American destroyers and damaged others, but the Japanese lost 391 aircraft. Later, fleet search planes spotted enemy surface forces leaving the protection of their Inland Sea. Fast American carriers steamed north to meet the threat. Their planes caught the Japanese some fifty miles southeast of Kyushu and sank six warships—the 45,000 ton *Yamato*, largest remaining Japanese warship, two light cruisers, and three destroyers.

Ashore on Okinawa the fighting was prolonged and heavy. Both army and Marine units took part in it, cleaning a tenacious foe from fortified ridge after fortified ridge.

Above Naha, Okinawa's capital, a strong Japanese line held up the advance for weeks. Yet the eventual outcome was never in doubt. By May the Japanese had been reduced to some 15,000 fanatical defenders still holding out in hills and caves. Already we were making ready airstrips from which to bomb the home islands. It had been a costly victory—the most costly in terms of casualties of any Pacific battle—but it was clearly worth the price.

As American forces were advancing on Okinawa and with Iwo won, it was evident that the Japanese either had to sink Allied naval power or lose the war. They could not prevent losing their island outposts even when garrisons numbered as many as 80,000 troops. So they invented a "secret" weapon, the Kamikazes.

The Kamikazes were a weapon born of desperation. One type, the so-called Baka bomb, was a 20-foot, two-ton airplane launched from a conventional bomber. The nose was simply a ton of TNT. It was powered by three rockets and could dive on a vessel with a speed up to 600 m.p.h. It had no landing gear. The pilot had no chance of escape. A more common type was any kind of airplane rigged with a tremendous explosive charge set to go off on contact. Most of the attacks were made in daylight, and almost invariably they were launched against capital ships, since smaller vessels were not worth the sacrifice. Hanson Baldwin, writing after Japan's surrender, tells of the damage done by the Kamikazes:

Japanese suicide weapons in the last months of the war sank at least twenty naval vessels and damaged at least thirty and possibly scores of other. The Kamikazes caused more loss, damage and personnel casualties to the American Navy in the period between the Leyte invasion last October and the present than in any previous period in its history.

During the Okinawa campaign, when our ship damages were at their peak, West Coast shipyards were glutted with ship repairs and some of the worst-damaged vessels were sent to East Coast yards.

Japanese suicide attacks probably were experienced by some ships one or two years ago. But they were not undertaken on a large scale and were unimportant in results achieved until the Leyte invasion. The Japanese Naval Air Force then commenced what it called "body-ramming" tactics with the "special attack" units of the Kamikaze, or "Divine Wind" squadrons, so named for the "divine wind" (typhoon) which, according to Japanese legend, broke up the fleet of Kublai Khan in 1281. The Japanese Army Air Force then undertook the organization of suicide squadrons, and the semi-fanatical, though carefully inspired and organized, cult spread until a number of other suicide weapons were developed.

The Okinawa campaign witnessed the peak of the suicide attacks. That campaign has been much reported as a great land struggle, but few Americans have realized that it also was the greatest sea-air battle ever fought, a decisive three-month day and night action, sometimes continuous for hour after hour, in which the Navy suffered more casualties in ships and in personnel than in any previous war. But as the magnificent picture of the Okinawa campaign just released by the Navy—"The Fleet That Came to Stay"—shows, it was a battle won by the Navy, despite the Kamikazes. But the cost was high.[18]

The Kamikazes scored a hit on one of the great American ships of the war—the carrier *Enterprise*, which had fought through every major battle of the Pacific except Coral Seas, and had rolled up a record of 911 Japanese airplanes downed and 71 enemy ships destroyed. It happened on May 14, 1945. As reported by Stanley Woodward:

Our force attacked the Kyushu airfields without much interference from the special attack corps in the daylight hours of May 13. After dark the Japanese became active and kept us at quarters all night by dropping flares and firing torpedoes. The next morning, after our carriers had launched the dawn strike, the Kamikazes attacked in force. After a few preliminary passes twenty-two "Banzais" came at once out of the southwest.

Our force was spread over miles of ocean and the *Enterprise*, as seen from the bridge of the *Hornet*, was virtually on the horizon. The action began in the "Big E's" sector. We saw great gunflashes, then a plume of white smoke and fire shot up from the flight deck of the *Enterprise*. It was followed by a cloud of black smoke, but she kept her place in the formation without diminution of speed.

A minute later we heard over the inter-ship radio the voice of her captain, Grover B. H. Hall, "I have suffered a hit abaft the forward elevator," he said. "I am inoperative."

Then we ourselves were attacked and forgot the *Enterprise* in the wild commotion of battle. This reporter, standing on the starboard wing of the *Hornet*'s bridge, was knocked flat by the muzzle blast of the upper forward five-inch turret. After three Kamikazes had been splashed around us we had time to look at the "Big E" again. She was still plowing serenely on as if nothing had happened.

The rest of the story we got the next day after being transferred by two breeches buoys and the destroyer *Taussig* to the *Enterprise*.

She was still smoldering in the forward area. The Japanese plane had crashed through her flight deck six feet aft of the No. 1 elevator and had carried into the well, where the bomb exploded. Apparently the plane, which was a Zeke single-engined fighter, had been armed with a 250-kilogram bomb (about 600 pounds). The explosion blew the elevator, which weighed thirty tons, 400 feet into the air. The blast penetrated three decks downward, killing six men in the pump-room below. Eight others were killed on the hangar deck. One who took cover by lying flat on the starboard quarterdeck sponson had his skull crushed when the blast blew in a steel door. If he had been four inches forward, behind the solid bulkhead, he would still be alive.

Shrapnel made a sieve of the forward elevator bulkheads, and many of the men in the outboard alley-way, bunkrooms and forward officers quarters were wounded. One hangar-deck sailor complained after three days that his back hurt. A ship's surgeon investigated and took out a jagged half-pound piece of steel.

Gasoline from the Japanese plane started a raging fire in the elevator well, but the damage-control section under Lieutenant Commander John U. Monro, Andover, Mass., extinguished it in seventeen minutes. Lieutenant Dud Murphy, forty-five-year-old New Yorker, and Lieutenants Bud

Wilkinson, of Minneapolis, and Rip Whalen, of Chicago, former Western Conference football players, performed prodigies and were cited with Lieutenant Commander Monro for bringing the fire under control.

Admiral Mitscher was about to take his flag to another ship, by way of a breeches buoy, when this reporter came aboard. Standing with him on the scarred quarterdeck was Byron "Whizzer" White, staff member and former all-American football player from Colorado. The admiral gave the ship a "well done," saying he had never seen faster damage control. He was wearing his habitual baseball cap and seemed composed despite having had two flagships shot from under him in four days.

Lieutenant (j.g.) Jerry Flynn, of Rochester and Notre Dame University, gunnery-control officer stationed in the main top, had the best view of the attack. According to him, the Japanese had been ducking in and out of the spotty, low cloud cover for some time before he dove. The *Enterprise* had fired at him without result. He waited his chance, then came hurtling out of a cloud on the port quarter, apparently aiming for the carrier's island.

He dove steeply, but with his plane in control, screaming through the fire of all guns that would bear on him. Halfway through his dive, Lieutenant Flynn says, it seemed as if he would miss the ship, but he corrected his overshot by flipping the plane on its back. He was upside down when he crashed through the beam center of the flight deck.

The ship's loud-speaker system had warned the crew to take cover when the Japanese started his dive and the small loss of life may be attributed at least in part to the warning. Admiral Mitscher, standing on the flag-bridge, probably was the most completely exposed man aboard.[19]

Burma

Nineteen forty-two had been a year of disaster in Burma. During most of 1943 the Italian offensive and the creation of an invasion base in Britain precluded a major counter-offensive in this theatre. At the Quebec Conference in August of that year, however, Roosevelt, Churchill, and the Chinese representative, T. V. Soong, decided that the time was propitious for a counter-offensive. Supreme command in southeast Asia was given to Lord Louis Mountbatten; Brigadier-General Albert C. Wedemeyer was made his deputy and command of Chinese and American ground forces left to General Stilwell.

The most urgent task was to reopen a supply line to China. General Stilwell had already established an air transport ferry over the Himalayas and by the end of 1943 this service was flying more supplies into China than had ever gone over the hair-pin turns and gorges of the Burma Road. It was, said Churchill, "an incredible feat of transportation. Certainly no more prodigious example of strength, science, and organization in this class of work has ever been seen or dreamed of."

Late in 1943 American engineers and native labor undertook the construction of a new road to connect Ledo with that part of the Burma Road still in Chinese hands. First, however, it was necessary to clear out the enemy in northern Burma. Major-General Wingate, and his famous raid-

ers, had already begun this operation. Here is Charles Rolo's story of
Wingate and his Raiders:

Led by 39-year-old Brigadier Orde Charles Wingate, eight British columns secretly crossed from India through the Japanese lines into Burma
recently and for three months spread confusion and panic. The Japanese
buzzed about like bees out of an overturned hive, but never caught up with
the raiders. Wingate's expedition wiped out Jap outposts, exploded ammunition dumps, wrecked airfields, put highways out of commission, blew
up bridges and dynamited the railway.

The raiders—Wingate named them the Chindits, after the dragons
which guard Burmese temples—penetrated 300 miles into Japanese-held
territory, then made a heroic march back to India. Casualties were fewer
than anyone had dared predict. It is one of the great romantic tales of this
war.

The expedition accomplished important aims. It relieved pressure on
the Chinese; it gathered information which enabled the RAF to make
devastating raids; it tied up the Japs and probably staved off an invasion of
India. Above all, it set a pattern of training and tactics for the reconquest
of Burma. Gurkhas, Burmese and a regiment of city-bred Englishmen
showed the Jap he no longer was master of the jungle.

Wingate's British Chindits were second-line troops—nearly all of them
married men from the North of England, aged 28 to 35. Wingate told
them: "We have to imitate Tarzan." For six sweltering months in the
Indian jungles he trained them in river crossing, infiltration tactics and
long forced marches with heavy packs, until they were the toughest of
shock troops. On returning from the raid one private remarked: "The
whole job was a piece of cake compared to the training. . . ."

The half-mile-wide Chindwin River, boundary between British- and
Jap-held territory, was the first critical lap in the advance. Reconnaissance
parties reported no enemy patrols for some miles. Heavy equipment was
ferried over in sampans, rubber boats and canoes; officers and men
stripped and swam the swift current. The crossing continued all night,
through the next day, and far into that night. Wingate tossed his helmet
into the last canoe, peeled off his clothes and plunged into the swirling
water.

The Chindits pushed through dense jungle, over razorback mountains,
along narrow paths flanked by precipices, then down into valleys where
the elephant grass grows taller than a man. Skeletons marked the tracks
over which the Allies had retreated the summer before.

Wingate mostly kept clear of beaten trails, hacking his own path
through the jungle. He sent out "deception groups" to lay false trails but
mainly relied on speed of movement. Jap patrols were often so close that
scouts would bump into each other in the jungle. Skirmishing was almost
continuous, and the Chindits killed more than 1000 Japs. But the enemy
never caught up with them in force.

Frequently the Chindits covered 30 miles a day in a temperature of 105
in the shade. Wingate saw to it that not a moment was wasted. He forbade
shaving because it would mean ten minutes less sleep. He had a theory that

sickness could be kept down by constant marching—and it is a fact that there was hardly a case of malaria.

At the head of each column trotted scouting dogs, trained to recognize the scent of the Japanese. The eight prongs of the expedition kept in constant touch with one another by radio, messenger dogs, carrier pigeons and strange birdcalls. Elephants, ridden by little Burmese mahouts, plodded ahead with the mortars, Bren guns, folding boats and wireless sets. Next came the horses and men; then the mules. In the rear were oxen and bullocks drawing carts loaded with machine guns, tommy guns, grenades, rifles and ammunition. Each column was a mile long. "Looks like Noah's Ark," said one Tommy as the weird assortment of animals clambered up the banks of a river. Strangely enough, the columns could not be heard 200 yards away, for the jungle deadens sound.

The Chindits had rubber-soled hockey shoes, Australian-type slouch hats, antimosquito veils and machetes. Each man entered Burma with six days' paratroop rations on his back and thereafter was supplied from the air. All told, the expedition received 500,000 pounds of air-borne supplies.

An RAF flying officer marched with each column to select sites for dropping the supplies—rice fields, dried-up river beds, tracts of flattened elephant grass. Code messages notified the air base in Assam of the exact time and place for the next delivery. Smoke fires guided the aircraft in daytime, flares at night. The big planes would swoop as low as 150 feet to release their loads of arms, ammunition, dynamite, and ration cans containing bully beef, biscuits, dates, raisins, tea, sugar, salt and Vitamin-C tablets. The only breakage was one bottle of rum.

The base officer in charge of supplies was a Captain Lord. One day Wingate radioed: "Oh, Lord, send us bread!" and got the prompt reply: "The Lord hath heard thy prayer." A few hours later 60 loaves—manna from heaven—were dropped.

A Chindit raiding party came upon the headquarters of a Jap unit, deserted except for servants busily preparing dinner. The Burmese obligingly waited on Wingate's men, who polished off every scrap of food in the camp.

The expedition penetrated within 120 miles of the Burma Road, then was ordered to return. When the columns got back to the Irrawaddy—it was a bitterly cold night with a brilliant moon—the Japs opened up with mortars and machine guns. Wingate could have forced a crossing, but it would have meant heavy losses. Standing on a sandbank in the Irrawaddy, looking like some minor prophet with his huge beard and a blanket wrapped around his shoulders, he made a split-second decision. He ordered the Chindits to break up into groups of 40 and play hide-and-seek in the jungle until they had given the Japs the slip. Within 48 hours every party had managed to cross the river safely. Then they buried their wireless sets, smashed their heavy equipment and set off on the 300-mile trek to India.

Without radios, no more air-borne supplies were possible. The Chindits first ate their bullocks and mules, and after that lived on rice, snakes, vultures, banana palms, jungle roots and grass soup. Hunted every yard of the way, they were forced to avoid the main drinking places and sometimes went for days with only a few mouthfuls of water drained out of hollow bamboos. Knowing that their security lay in speed, Wingate drove his men without mercy.[20]

Wingate's success so impressed General Arnold that he ordered the formation of the First Air Commando Force of the AAF—a force which operated effectively throughout 1944 in support of bands of raiders behind the Japanese lines. A typical operation—Operation Thursday— reveals the co-ordination of air and ground forces:

On the night of March 5, 1944, fifty-four gliders full of heavily armed desperadoes in green battle dress took off for a 150-mile flight over 7,000-foot mountains to a destination far inside the enemy lines, designated simply as "Broadway."

The fly-in was the work of a special U. S. Air Command. The ground troops were the vanguard of Wingate's famous Chindits of the 3rd Indian Division. "Broadway" was merely a clearing in the forest. The landings were made without lights, and there were some desperate moments. But within thirteen hours the engineers had built a landing strip and the troop transports were coming down in a steady procession. Within five days 12,000 men and 1,200 mules had been flown in to this and a second landing strip, and the first columns, under Lentaigne, "Mad Mike" Calvert, and other veteran jungle leaders, had already disappeared into the hinterland to start work on the communication lines of an enemy who did not yet know they were there. It was Wingate's finest exploit, and his last, for he was killed on March 24th flying back from a tour of his forward positions. Brigadier Lentaigne succeeded his old chief.

This daring and highly organized operation (known by its code name of "Operation Thursday") was no mere harassing raid like those of 1943. It was an essential part of Admiral Mountbatten's over-all plan, being designed to support General Stilwell's operations in the Mogaung-Myitkyina-Ledo area by cutting off the enemy divisions opposing him from their bases in the plain.

The Japanese, under steady pressure from General Stilwell in the north, reacted furiously to these fatal incisions in their supply lines, and a series of bloody engagements followed. Their sites are marked on no maps, but their military labels, "Aberdeen," "White City," "Blackpool," and a dozen more, will live in the annals of Gurkha and Kachin and West African regiments, of the South Staffordshires and the Lancashire Fusiliers, of the Cameronians and the King's Own Royal Regiment. The air forces ranged overhead and, in addition to maintaining supplies, contributed not a little to the systematic throttling of the Jap communications.

Before their task was completed and the "Long Range Penetration Groups" made their way back to join the Allied forces to the north, Calvert's men had stormed Mogaung, the enemy's main base in North Burma; and another of Lentaigne's columns joined (from the southwest) in the long siege of Myitkyina.[21]

As Wingate's Raiders and their American prototype, Merrill's Marauders, harried the enemy in north Burma and General Stilwell fought down from China to protect the construction of the Ledo—later named the Stilwell—Road, the Japanese prepared to attack across the Indian border at Chittagong and Imphal, main base of the 14th Imperial Army. The offensive got under way in March 1944:

Imphal was encircled, almost surrounded, for two and one-half months. But two entire divisions were flown in to reinforce the defense (one being transported straight from the Arakan front); and with steady air supply (at first insufficient, later, under Air Marshal Sir John Baldwin, stepped up to a classic regularity and profusion) its defenders held the Japs expensively at bay. Kohima was completely surrounded for eighteen days, and none of those who fought in the "box"—the Royal West Kents, some base troops, the sick and wounded from the hospital—would thank the historian who minimized the critical character of their predicament. But the garrison, fighting day and night under terrific pressure, had this great satisfaction: they realized that if the Jap had simply bypassed the embattled town he could have done in forty-eight hours what its capture was a mere preliminary to—he could have cut the railroad. But the methodical plan in Tokyo said, "First take Kohima, then cut the railroad," so the methodical Japanese Army ignored the final objective until it could check off the preparatory one.

The Japs never took Kohima, although they set 20,000 men to the job. They never got into Imphal. And as the weeks of bitter fighting passed their losses mounted, their supplies dwindled and the monsoon approached. It was at this point that the Commander of the Japanese 15th Army ordered his crack 33rd Division, recently reinforced, to carry out a last desperate assault on Imphal. "The fate of the Empire," he said in an Order of the Day, "depends on the result of this battle. Imphal will be taken at all costs." The Division's Commander added his own footnote to this: "You will take Imphal," he said, "but the Division will be annihilated." With its accustomed fanaticism, the 33rd delivered a series of attacks which, after bloody fighting, were repulsed. It was, for all practical purposes, annihilated. But it did not take Imphal.

The tide turned, and General Slim passed over to the attack. He threw the Lushai Brigade (Burmese hillmen) and other formations across the Jap lines of retreat, supplying them by air. The 14th Army swept the now exhausted enemy southwards. And in the area Palel-Tamu-Uhkrul there was consummated such a killing of Japanese as had not been known in history. Of the 80,000 picked troops who had started out so bravely, and on so skillful a plan, to invade India, over 50,000 were counted corpses. The remainder, riddled with disease and wounds, emaciated with hunger, attempted to escape southwards in disorganized parties; abandoning their heavy equipment, a prey to revengeful Burmese hillmen and with small chance of ever fighting again.

These victories had been costly, as are all victories against the Japanese. The 14th Army alone had suffered 40,000 battle casualties. But when

General Slim reached Kalewa, he had beaten the Japanese 15th Army. It was here, in the dark days of the 1942 retreat, that he had burned his last tanks and buried his last guns. It was here in 1944 that he dug up those same guns and put them to chasing the Jap back down the road he came up—the road to Mandalay, to Rangoon, to Tokyo.[22]

In August 1944 Merrill's Marauders wiped out all Japanese resistance around Myitkyina in August 1944. In the closing months of the year Stilwell's army, now commanded by General Wedemeyer, cleared the way for the opening of the Stilwell Road. On January 28, 1945, the first convoy crossed the Chinese frontier. The next four months saw the great Allied offensive. Three armies converged on the Japanese in Burma: the American-trained Chinese from the north, General Slim's 14th Imperial Army from the center, and three divisions of Indian and African troops from the south. Before these overwhelming forces Mandalay fell on March 20, Rangoon on May 3. Except for mopping up operations the campaign was over.

Over Clouds and below Seas

The air offensive against Japan started as a stunt intended to shock the Japanese and give a fillip to American morale. This first blow was the famous Doolittle raid of April 18th, 1942. The new carrier *Hornet* was the base for Lieutenant-Colonel James H. Doolittle's sixteen medium bombers. In April the great ship steamed out into the Pacific. Few on board knew that Tokyo itself was the target. As the *Hornet* neared Japanese shores the small force ran across a Japanese patrol craft. It was promptly sunk, but there was the possibility that it had already radioed the presence of the force. Doolittle's men took off immediately, still too far from China's airfields to hope to make safe landings. Six of Japan's greatest cities were hit in this token raid—Tokyo, Yokohama, Kobe, Nagoya, Kenegawa, and Osaka. Captain Ted W. Lawson tells what happened at Tokyo:

We skimmed along. We went over the rooftops of a few small villages, and I began to worry. Twenty minutes was what it was supposed to take to reach Tokyo from the point where we came in. Now we had been over land for nearly thirty minutes, and no sign of the city. I saw one fairly large town off to the left, however, and I said to myself that if worst same to worst and we couldn't find Tokyo, I'd come back here and do at least some damage.

But just then we came up over a hill, dusting the top of another temple, and there before us, as smooth as glass, lay Tokyo Bay.

It was brilliant in the mid-day sun and looked as limitless as an ocean. I came down to within about fifteen feet, while McClure checked our course. I kept the same slow speed, gas-saving but nerve-racking when I thought occasionally of the 400 mph plus diving speed of the Zeros.

We were about two minutes out over the bay when all of us seemed to look to the right at the same time and there sat the biggest, fattest-looking aircraft carrier we had ever seen. It was a couple of miles away, anchored, and there did not seem to be a man in sight. It was an awful temptation not to change course and drop one on it. But we had been so drilled in what to do with our four bombs, and Tokyo was now so close, that I decided to go on.

There were no enemy planes in sight. Ahead, I could see what must have been Davey Jones climbing fast and hard and running into innocent-looking black clouds that appeared around his plane.

It took about five minutes to get across our arm of the bay, and, while still over the water, I could see the barrage balloons strung between Tokyo and Yokohama, across the river from Tokyo. . . .

In days and nights of dreaming about Tokyo and thinking of the eight millions who live there, I got the impression that it would be crammed together, concentrated, like San Francisco. Instead it spreads all over creation, like Los Angeles. There is an aggressively modern sameness to much of it and now, as we came in very low over it, I had a bad feeling that we wouldn't find our targets. I had to stay low and thus could see only a short distance ahead and to the sides. I couldn't go up to take a good look without drawing anti-aircraft fire, which I figured would be very accurate by now because the planes that had come in ahead of me all had bombed from 1,500 feet. The buildings grew taller. I couldn't see people.

I was almost on the first of our objectives before I saw it. I gave the engines full throttle as Davenport adjusted the prop pitch to get a better grip on the air. We climbed as quickly as possible to 1,500 feet in the manner which we had practiced for a month and had discussed for three additional weeks.

There was just time to get up there, level off, attend to the routine of opening the bomb bay, make a short run and let fly with the first bomb. The red light blinked on my instrument board, and I knew the first 500-pounder had gone.

Our speed was picking up. The red light blinked again, and I knew Clever had let the second bomb go. Just as the light blinked, a black cloud appeared about 100 yards or so in front of us and rushed past at great speed. Two more appeared ahead of us, on about the line of our wingtips, and they too swept past. They had our altitude perfectly, but they were leading us too much.[23]

Fifteen planes crashed from lack of fuel, one was safe in Siberia. Sixty-four of the fliers escaped through the valiant efforts of the Chinese underground. Eight were captured by the Japanese. In addition to giving a lift to Allied morale, the Doolittle raid perhaps persuaded the Japanese to keep a certain number of fighter planes in the home islands that otherwise would have gone south. But the raid did very little military damage. Asked from what base the planes had flown, President Roosevelt whimsically replied "Shangri-la."

The building up of a real air offensive against Japan was a long and arduous process. It was more than two years after the Doolittle raid that the first raid of military importance was made.

In the early stages of the B-29 campaign against Japan the giant airships flew from bases in the far Marianas and in China. Using bombs of a new petroleum jelly, fleets of planes would fly up over the home Japanese islands, strike their appointed targets, and return to their bases—a round trip taking 18 or more hours. At first no fighter protection could be given and a crippled ship had little chance of completing the long journey back to the Marianas. With the capture of Iwo Jima in mid-March, 1945, fighter protection became available. During the first three months after its capture Iwo provided haven for more than 850 B-29s.

Bombing tactics were to select specific targets in a relatively small area and bomb that intensely. Thus, as a typical example, on March 17th a force of 300 B-29s dropped 2,500 tons of bombs on Kobe, setting 12 square miles afire. City after city was systematically destroyed.

Late in March the B-29s undertook a new mission—that of sowing mines throughout Japanese waters. The mining was so effective that communication lines with the Asian land mass were practically cut off.

By late July Lieutenant-General Carl Spaatz, in command of the B-29 fleets, could boldly warn Japanese cities of impending raids, affording civilians a chance to seek safety elsewhere. Raids of 600 bombers became frequent and resistance increasingly slight. The tremendous effect of the B-29 air offensive is summarized in a report from W. H. Lawrence:

Gen. Carl A. Spaatz, commanding general of the United States Army Strategic Air Forces, reported . . . that Superfortresses operating from the Marianas, India and China flew 32,612 sorties against the Japanese and dropped 169,421 tons of bombs in their fourteen months of war operations. The B-29's destroyed the major portion of the industrial productive capacity of fifty-nine Japanese cities, laid 12,049 mines in enemy waters and destroyed or damaged 2,285 Japanese planes.

Total combat losses to the American forces amounted to 437 B-29's, of which the crew members—usually eleven to a plane—of 297 bombers were not rescued. About 600 airmen from downed B-29s were saved.

The "Superforts" flew more than 100,000,000 miles to accomplish their goal, which was to knock Japan out of the war before it was necessary to invade the home islands.

In a communiqué summing up the operation of the B-29's with their carrying capacity of ten tons of bombs each, General Spaatz said their attacks on specific Japanese industrial targets had reduced enemy aircraft production by 60 per cent and steel production by 15 per cent and had almost completely destroyed Japan's major oil refining capacity.

He said a total of 581 important enemy factories engaged in the production of war materials had been either totally destroyed or severely damaged.

The B-29 mining missions, which began last March 28, resulted in an almost complete blockade of every Japanese shipping lane.

General Spaatz's figures made it clear that never in the history of warfare has so much been accomplished by one arm of a fighting force at so small a price.

General Spaatz reported also on the activities of the long-range Army planes based on Iwo that have operated with his forces, either to escort

Superfortresses or to run interference for them by neutralizing strikes against Japanese airfields.

These P-51 Mustangs and P-47 Thunderbolts flew 8,012 sorties totaling more than 38,000 hours, in which they destroyed or damaged 1,047 enemy aircraft. We lost 106 fighters.[24]

Air power was engaged primarily in destroying the industrial productivity of Japan. A very different kind of war was waged on the lines of supply, and that was the war of the "silent service"—the submarine fleet. Their work was done in lonely waters, in constant proximity to the enemy. They struck and vanished—or sometimes were struck and vanished. They took an important part in naval battles, shelled enemy strongholds, reported enemy fleet movements; their main contribution, however, was in whittling down enemy shipping. Even early in the war submarines were operating within sight of Japan. Robert Casey reported one episode from such a mission:

"Off Japan I spotted a large blot in the darkness—so big that it looked like an island. The chart showed some islands in that direction but they were about fifty miles away and I was puzzled. I called the captain's attention to the blot and he looked at it awhile. Then he said:

" 'If that's an island, it's moving. Clear the bridge!'

"We moved over and pretty soon the detail began to come out of the darkness. The island was a big tanker. She was loaded and low in the water, and she seemed to be all by herself.

"We fired a torpedo, but whether it was a defective torpedo or we'd miscalculated, it went past the bow. We were getting all set for another when we discovered that we'd made one principal error. She'd been masking an escort destroyer, and the destroyer was coming across her bows toward us at better than thirty knots.

"We dived in a hurry and the clunks began to come down. We sat there expecting the worst for a while and then we noticed the bombs weren't getting any closer. We'd made considerable progress underwater during the dive and apparently we'd stepped out of the ash-can barrage.

" 'Take her up!' ordered the captain. And I began to blow tanks.

"One officer who was pretty disturbed wanted to know if the captain hadn't heard the depth charges.

" 'Certainly,' Brockman said. 'Of course I heard them. But they're all back there and while the can is dropping them he'll be doing us no harm.'

"So we came up and had another look around and Captain Brockman's judgment turned out to be perfect. The destroyer was still over there dropping charges into the hole where we'd gone down.

" 'Pay no attention to him,' said the captain. 'Stand by to fire torpedoes. . . . Fire Two! Fire Three!'

"Both torpedoes hit. The tanker buckled up and there was fire all over the Pacific. We dived again and the can came over to work on us some more.

"We stayed down that time counting the bombs until no more came down. Then we figured that the destroyer had just about run out of material . . . or rather Brockman did. And he came up again.

"By the time we got the periscope up the destroyer was moving around the edge of the fire, probably picking up survivors if there were any. We moved into range and fired a fish at him. He saw it coming and dodged. But apparently it was enough for him. Instead of rushing at us he swung about and headed for home. We watched the rest of the tanker burn up.

"The next morning we came in a little closer. The day was clear and the water calm as it sometimes gets in that region. We were hardly moving in the water when we saw a destroyer coming out. A spit of land or something had screened him and he was almost on top of us before we knew about it. But it was obvious that he hadn't sighted us. He was moving in a straight course at an angle. We turned about a little, and when he crossed our bows we let him have it. We blew him in two.

"I suppose he'd been sent out to look for us but he never got any chance to make a report. So we kept on moving toward the harbor. We got in and sat down.

"When we got a look at what was going on, we saw plenty of activity. A couple of transports and a tanker were on their way out with a cruiser escort. One of the transports we recognized right away. She was a liner which used to run between Yokohama and the Pacific ports.

"We didn't waste any time about it. We let a cruiser go by and put a couple of fish into the liner. She went down almost as fast as we did.

"There was unshirted hell in the bay for the next few minutes. The place was cluttered up with destroyers and patrol boats and they were all dropping depth charges. The first one almost got us. It rolled us over sidewise and knocked men clear across the boat. I sat there in front of the diving wheels expecting the depth gauges and all the diving controls to come right into my lap. But the next ones weren't so close. We'd done our job and we moved away fast—once we found out that the boat was going to hold together. We got into the channel and the current was with us. We were doing about seven knots all the way out.

"We went out to sea and tried to patch up the damage the bombs had done to us. Nothing very important had happened.

"However, we did the best we could and went back toward the bay still wondering what course we ought to take. While Captain Brockman was mulling over this problem a freighter came sailing by, all alone.

"We moved in and knocked her off. It was the easiest target we'd had since we'd gone into business. Captain Brockman waited until it was all under and then he waved his hand over his head.

" 'And that will be about enough,' he said. 'Let's go back to Honolulu.' "

Comsubpac was surprised when the boat opened up her transmitter and announced that she was coming home. The Japs had reported her sunk, and with some logic.[25]

Before the end of the war statistics showed that American submarines had accounted for more Japanese shipping than all other arms of the services put together.

At the start of the war the Japanese merchant marine was estimated at

7,000,000 tons. At its conclusion only 1,000,000 to 1,500,000 tons remained, counting even small ships. This decline in shipping made it impossible for the enemy to reinforce disputed areas effectively, and almost impossible for them to maintain distant outposts. The submarine fleet was largely responsible for this achievement. Vice-Admiral Charles A. Lockwood, Jr., commander of the Pacific Fleet submarine task force, on August 30, 1945, gave out figures that put the total "killings" of submarines in the Pacific at:

JAPANESE COMBATANT SHIPS SUNK

Aircraft carriers	4
Cruisers	18
Destroyers	55
Submarines	2
Tenders	3
Other combatant ships	85
Total	167

JAPANESE NON-COMBATANT SHIPS SUNK

Tankers	116
Transports	167
Cargo and supply ships	704
Miscellaneous merchant ships	102
Total	1,089

This makes a grand total of 1,256 Japanese ships seen to go down. An additional 300 ships should be added as "probably sunk" or "damaged."

The combined air and submarine attacks so seriously crippled Japanese production and supplies that by summer of 1945—even before the Russian entry and the atomic bomb—it was doubtful whether Japan could long continue the war. Her army was still almost intact, but with her shipping gone, with overseas supplies cut off, with factories and cities in ruins, she faced certain defeat.

13

VICTORY

The End in Italy

THROUGH THE WINTER months the line in northern Italy had remained static. Patrols were active, but neither side had launched any major offensive. In January and February, 1945, there were rumors that the Germans were withdrawing. Lieutenant-General Ira C. Eaker, the Allied air commander, however, refused to admit that his reconnaissance planes and bombers saw more than the usual troop and supply movements between the German front lines and the Brenner Pass.

Then, in April, General Clark announced an Allied "Spring Offensive." The Allied line still ran south of Bologna. The attack, launched in mid-April, pressed the Germans back on both flanks and exerted strong pressure in the middle. By April 18th, 1945, Vergato and Toscanella were captured. On the 21st the key city of Bologna fell, and Fifth and Eighth Army units dashed forward in pursuit of the Germans fleeing across the Po Valley. The Germans evidently feared encirclement by the Eighth Army along the Adriatic, and retreated to the towering mountains across the Po Valley, harried by Allied planes.

The end came soon. Winston Burdett gives an eyewitness account of how the Italian phase of the war ended, on April 29th, 1945:

German forces in Italy have surrendered unconditionally to the Supreme Allied Commander. The instrument of surrender—the first formal surrender by a German Army or armies since Allied troops first stormed the shores of Europe, nearly 20 months ago—was signed at 2:14 Italy time on Sunday afternoon, April 29th. The surrender became effective at 2:00 P.M., Italy time, today. All German and Italian forces under General Heinrich von Bietinghof (?), successor to Marshal Kesselring as Commander-in-Chief of the German Southwest Command, formally laid down their arms just four and a half hours ago. The war in Italy is over, and this is probably the first announcement to the listening world. . . .

The negotiations that culminated in this scene at Caserta were short and swift. A few days before the signing, the German Command in northern Italy got word through to us that it was ready to sue for surrender. On Saturday afternoon, April 28th, an Army transport plane bore south through a driving rainstorm and landed at the Caserta airfield at 4:00 o'clock. There were two civilian passengers. One was tall, blond, blue-eyed, square-jawed and terribly tense. The other was sleek, small, dark, and apparently unmoved. The tall German, a Lieutenant Colonel, had papers authorizing him to negotiate on behalf of General von Bietinghof. That meant the German 10th and 14th Armies and the Italian Ligurian Army, an enemy force that totalled perhaps 600,000 men. The dark and unperturbed German was a Major. He represented General Karl Wolffe, Supreme Commander of SS and security troops in northern Italy and western Austria. That meant perhaps another two hundred and fifty or three hundred thousand enemy troops.

There were many reasons, of course, for secrecy. There were particular reasons for the civilian clothes. The German generals were acting on their own. As far as is known, they negotiated this separate surrender without consulting their higher command. They were prepared on their own to carry out the surrender terms without instructions from above. Negotiations at Caserta began late Saturday afternoon. Lt. Gen. Morgan, Chief of Staff of Field Marshal Sir Harold Alexander, led them on the Allied side. By Sunday morning he had convinced the German delegates that surrender must be unconditional or not at all.

In the small chamber at the Royal Palace, eight spotlights were trained on a long table behind which hung a big operational map of the Po Valley. The table was bare except for a pen-and-inkwell at either end. The walls were bare except for the Po Valley map and another map of Vienna. The ceiling bore the coat of arms of various Italian provinces and one souvenir of another era, the sign of the Fascists. It was two o'clock and staff officers were buzzing importantly in and out, arranging the formality involved in the supreme military act of surrender. At five minutes after two, the door to the right opened and the Allied officers filed in. Among them were American and British Generals, . . . Rear Admirals and an Air Vice Marshal. General Morgan came last. As he stood at his end of the table, he seemed the embodiment of all you think of a British Army General . . . red-faced, impeccable, and utterly calm. An Englishman next to me remarked: "He looks like General Haig. It's extraordinary!"

The door to the left of the long table opened. The two Germans stepped in and halted awkwardly before the waiting inkwell. The tall Lieutenant Colonel stared a moment defiantly at the spotlights. His blue eyes burned as they rapidly took in the assembly. His throat muscles were taut and his hands were clenched fiercely behind his back. But he stood firm and erect, like a soldier, as General Morgan glanced down at him the length of the table. The little German, the dark Major, stood to one side, unruffled. . . .

General Morgan began. In a calm, unemotional voice that was cutting in its firmness, he addressed the Germans:

"I understand that you, Lieut. Colonel X, are prepared to sign terms of surrender on behalf of General von Bietinghof, and you, Major X, are prepared to sign on behalf of General Vogt(?). Is this correct?" The tall German's throat muscles quivered, and he replied in a hoarse voice "Ja!"

And the little German said "Jawohl," when the question was translated to him.

General Morgan continued:

"I have been empowered by Field Marshal Alexander to sign on his behalf. The terms of the instrument of surrender will take effect at 12:00 noon, British Mean Time, on the 2nd of May, 1945. I now ask you to sign the documents, and I will sign after you."

The German Colonel's tension had mounted as General Morgan spoke. It was as though the enormity of defeat and the finality of his present act of total surrender had now hit him with a cold shock. Perhaps the spotlights angered him, too. But whatever he felt, he did not lose his self-control. He asked to repeat a statement he had made at previous meetings. In a husky voice he said, for the record, that he had received limited powers from his Commander-in-Chief, that he had been forced to overstep those limits, that he assumed his commander would approve his action, but that he could not be absolutely sure.

General Morgan replied casually: "We accept those conditions."

The Germans sat and signed five copies of the surrender document. General Morgan signed last. . . . The Germans went swiftly out. It was 17 minutes after 2:00. The ceremony was over. . . .

The front-line troops involved in this surrender are those we've been fighting here ever since we landed at Salerno. . . . It's impossible to estimate their number today, but at the start of our offensive in northern Italy the twenty-two divisions were believed well up to strength. Their total at the time of the surrender, an AFHQ Staff officer estimates, was 600,000. . . .

The surrender which two Germans in sports clothes signed last Sunday means more than the end of the war in Italy.

It carries us automatically across the Alps.[1]

The End in Germany

Throughout the first weeks of April the people of Berlin, living among the rubble of Allied air bombings, waited in terror for the end. "Why are the Americans not advancing faster to protect us from the Russians?" the Berliners asked. They, too, remembered Stalingrad!

Vivid glimpses of the final push on the doomed city are given by two Russian correspondents who were part of the surging, triumphant army.

None of us will ever forget that night. Twenty-three bridges had been thrown across the swollen Oder. Engines roared in unison. Pillars of heavy dust hung in the air.

The glow on the western horizon grew bigger and bigger as our parachute flares exposed every nook and cranny of the German lines. Shellbursts lit up the sky. The earth trembled, and over the German positions rose an immense fountain of smoke, earth and rocks. . . .

The Guards advanced over the level plain, tanks and self-propelled guns spitting fire ahead of them and leaving a dense trail of dust behind.

Flails, or "trawler tanks" as the Red Army men call them, cut lanes through the minefields. . . .

By seven in the morning it was fully light. Dust and smoke lay over us like a blanket, getting thicker every moment. Ahead of us a red flag waved from a hilltop, planted by Senior Lieutenant Nikolai Derevenko. . . .

I have never seen anything to equal the density of the German trench system on the Berlin approaches. Each village, each railway station squats inside a closely meshed web of trenches. Single buildings are elaborately girdled with them. . . .

The Germans are floundering in dust and smoke as Soviet guns burn them out of their nests. The sun is hot. The great toilers of war, the sappers, pass by us. They blow up everything the Germans can build, even their trickiest fortifications, lying underground to a depth of two hundred feet, like those in the Oder zone of the Berlin fortified area.

There is a cloud of dust over the Berlin autobahn. Russia, the Ukraine, Byelorussia, Georgia, Armenia, Azerbaidjan, Uzbekistan, Kazakhstan, Kirghizia, Lithuania, Latvia and Esthonia are marching on Berlin. . . .

Dust, dust, dust. . . . Nothing to drink, everything dried up, burnt out. But nothing matters. We are going on to Berlin with lips black and parched. The distant grows less and less on the signposts. The heavy guns go by on their way to fire their first salvos into Berlin.[2]

Another Russian picks up the story:

On the walls of the houses we saw Goebbels' appeals, hurriedly scrawled in white paint: "Every German will defend his capital. We shall stop the Red hordes at the walls of our Berlin." Just try and stop them!

Steel pillboxes, barricades, mines, traps, suicide squads with grenades clutched in their hands—all are swept aside before the tidal wave.

Drizzling rain began to fall. Near Bisdorf I saw batteries preparing to open fire.

"What are the targets?" I asked the battery commander.

"Centre of Berlin, Spree bridges, and the northern and Stettin railway stations," he answered.

Then came the tremendous words of command: "Open fire at the capital of Fascist Germany."

I noted the time. It was exactly 8:30 A.M. on April 22. Ninety-six shells fell in the centre of Berlin in the course of a few minutes.[3]

At this time the mighty Allied armies were at the banks of the Elbe, almost within earshot of the death rattle of Berlin. On April 27, Richard C. Hottelet reported one of the war's most dramatic and significant events:

The American and Russian Armies have met! We made contact at 1:32 Wednesday afternoon, on the bank of the Elbe River northwest of Dresden. There were no brass bands, no sign of the titanic strength of both these armies. The Americans who met the Red Army were a couple of dust-covered young lieutenants and a handful of enlisted men in their jeeps on reconnaissance. For days we had known that the Russians were near, but did not know where. More than a week before, General Bradley had ordered our First Army to stop. He did not want both armies to meet head-on. There might be mistakes and tragic incidents. So our divisions stood along the Fulde River and waited for the Russians to climb over the nearest hills. But the Russian commander seemed to have had the same idea. He ordered his troops to stop on the line of the Elbe River. Between our forces was a twenty-mile gap of unknown territory. On Tuesday, we sent jeep patrols probing deep out ahead of us; over dusty country roads they drove through crowds of German civilians fleeing westward from the Russians and through groups of German soldiers who kept their rifles and machine-guns in their hands and did nothing.

In the town of Kiese, a 69th Division patrol spotted the Russians. And that was it! Some hours later, another lieutenant got to Torgau on the Elbe and crawled out to the middle of a wrecked bridge, brought back some Russian officers to Division Headquarters, which made it official.

That's just the way it was . . . as simple and untheatrical as that . . . just some men meeting, shaking hands, glad to see each other. Since then the Division and Corps commanders have met, but it was fitting that the front-line troops made the first contact, men of our own 69th Division and Marshal Konev's men of the Russian 173d Regiment of the Guards. These were the sort of men who for two and a half years have fought their way halfway around the world to reach this moment, to meet and to complete the destruction of the enemy.[4]

Even as Berlin was being overwhelmed by the Red Army the two wicked men who had been responsible for the holocaust of the Western world met their death. On April 27 Italian partisans caught Benito Mussolini as he attempted to flee across the Alps, shot him, and hung him up to the jeers and taunts of crowds. On April 30 Radio Hamburg made a "grave and important announcement":

It is reported from the Fuehrer's headquarters that our Fuehrer, Adolf Hitler, fighting to the last breath against Bolshevism, fell for Germany this afternoon in his operational headquarters in the Reich Chancellory.

Hitler's body was not found, and doubts about his death persisted. Those who contemplated the fate of Germany, however, felt that the worst punishment which could come to him would be to live on and see the ruin and the agony of Germany.

Two days later Berlin finally fell to the exultant Red Army.

Now the end had come and even the most fanatical knew that further resistance was hopeless. On the same May 2 the whole Alpine redoubt, where the Nazis had threatened to hide out, collapsed. In the following four days two million troops on the northern and eastern fronts gave up. The formal surrender came the next day.

On May 7, 1945—at a little red schoolhouse which was General Eisenhower's headquarters at Rheims, France—the enemy signed an instrument of unconditional surrender.

A correspondent for *The Times* (London) described "freedom's finest hour" and the men who took part:

The end of the journey came in Rheims where at General Eisenhower's advanced headquarters in the early hours of to-day emissaries of Admiral Dönitz accepted the unconditional surrender of Germany's stricken military forces wherever they may still be fighting in the scattered pockets of Europe.

One minute after midnight to-morrow the last shot of the war should have been fired. . . .

After the enemy's collapse in the North and South of Germany and the scores of thousands of prisoners it has involved there was relatively little left to surrender, though the present issue of the conflict has saved needless bloodshed in Norway, in the remaining pockets in Czechoslovakia, and on the French Atlantic coast. It is a strange reflection of the amazing course the conflict has taken that the end should come with German garrisons still in possession in the Channel Islands and at Dunkirk, where, nearly five years ago, the flame of the most glorious British Army of all time leapt forth from disaster.

There is an eloquent comparison between that day and this in the final words of the chief German delegate in Rheims, General Gustaf Jodl, the author of the ten-point programme for annihilation of Britain and America, who recently succeeded Guderian as Chief of Staff.

Rising at the conclusion of the signing and addressing the assembled Allied chiefs, he said: "I want to say a word," and, proceeding in German: "With this signature the German people and German armed forces are, for better or worse, delivered into the victors' hands. In this war, which has lasted more than five years, both have achieved and suffered more than, perhaps, any other people in the world. In this hour I can only express the hope that the victor will treat them with generosity." There was no reply.

Already negotiations had been in progress for two days, but a last message had been sent to Dönitz and a signature was confidently expected for eleven o'clock on Sunday night. But as the hours went by with little sign of life but the shuffling of military police mounted at the main entrance it seemed that another hitch had occurred and that an end could not be made until late Monday morning. All the delegates, however, were remaining on the alert and about 2 A.M. the staff cars began to arrive.

First came General Bedell Smith, the Allied Chief of Staff, who has borne the main brunt of the negotiations, closely followed by General Carl Spaatz, Chief of the American Air Forces in Europe, and by Admiral Sir Harold Burrough, Allied Naval Commander-in-Chief, with Lieutenant General Sir Frederick Morgan, who was now to see the fulfillment of his masterly planning for D-Day.

Then came a little group of Russian officers in their dark-blue and gold—Major General Ivan Suslapatoff, chief of the Russian Mission to France, with special powers from the Soviet Government; Colonel Ivan Zenkovitch, and their interpreter. Major General S. Sevez, representing the French Chief of Staff, arrived next, followed by the Germans in two cars, with their escorting Allied officers. They wore neat Service uniform and were frigidly correct, and with Jodl was Admiral von Friedeberg, now Commander-in-Chief of the German Navy in succession to Dönitz.[5]

Here is the surrender document:

1. We the undersigned, acting on behalf of the German Supreme Command, agree to unconditional surrender of all our armed forces on land, on sea and in the air, as well as all forces which at present are under German command, to the Supreme Command of the Red Army, and simultaneously to the Supreme Command of the Allied Expeditionary Forces.
2. The German Supreme Command will immediately issue orders to all German commanders of land, naval and air forces and to all forces under German command to cease hostilities at 23 hours 1 minute (Central European time) on May 8, 1945, to remain at the places where they are at that time, and completely disarm themselves, handing over all their arms and war equipment to local allied commanders or officers designated by representatives of the Allied Supreme Command, not to destroy or cause any damage to steamships, vessels and aircraft, their engines, hulls and equipment, as well as machines, arms, apparatus, and in general to all military technical means of war.
3. The German Supreme Command will immediately appoint appropriate commanders and will ensure the fulfillment of all subsequent orders issued by the Supreme Command of the Red Army and the Supreme Command of the Allied Expeditionary Forces.
4. The present act will not serve as an obstacle to its supersession by another general document on surrender concluded by the United Nations or on their behalf, applicable to Germany and the German armed forces as a whole.
5. In the event of the German Supreme Command or any armed forces under its command failing to act in conformity with the present act of surrender, the Supreme Command of the Red Army as well as the Supreme Command of the Allied Expeditionary Forces will take such punitive measures or other action as they deem necessary.
6. The present act is drawn up in the Russian, English and German languages. Only the Russian and English texts are authentic.

Signed on May 8, 1945, in Berlin.

In Moscow Marshal Stalin once more set the victory guns thundering—

ORDER OF THE DAY No. 369

On May 8, 1945, in Berlin, representatives of the German High Command signed the Instrument of unconditional surrender of the German armed forces.

The Great Patriotic War which the Soviet people waged against the German-Fascist invaders is victoriously concluded. Germany is utterly routed.

Comrades Red Army men, Red Navy men, Sergeants, Petty Officers, Officers of the Army and Navy, Generals, Admirals and Marshals, I congratulate you upon the victorious termination of the Great Patriotic War.

To mark complete victory over Germany, to-day, May 9, the day of victory, at 22.00 hours (Moscow time), the capital of our Motherland, Moscow, on behalf of the Motherland, shall salute the gallant troops of the Red Army, the ships and units of the Navy, which have won this brilliant victory, by firing thirty artillery salvos from one thousand guns.

Eternal glory to the heroes who fell in the fighting for the freedom and independence of our Motherland!

Long live the victorious Red Army and Navy!

STALIN, Marshal of the Soviet Union,

Supreme Commander-in-Chief

May 9, 1945

King George VI sent this message to General Eisenhower and the American Armed Forces:

Eleven months ago you led the Allied Expeditionary Force across the English Channel, carrying with you the hopes and prayers of millions of men and women of many nations.

To it was entrusted the task of annihilating the German armies in Western Europe, and of thus liberating the peoples whom they had enslaved.

All the world now knows that, after fierce and continuous warfare, this force has accomplished its mission with a finality achieved by no other such expedition in history.

On behalf of all my peoples I ask that you, its Supreme Commander, will tell its members how deeply grateful we are to them, and how unbounded is our admiration for the courage and determination which, under wise leadership, have brought them to their goal of complete and crushing victory.

I would ask you also to convey a special message of congratulation to my own forces now under your command. Throughout the campaign they have acquitted themselves in all services with a valour and distinction for which their fellow-countrymen will for ever hold them in honour.

And from a London balcony Prime Minister Churchill addressed cheering crowds:

"We must begin the task of re-building our hearths and homes and do our utmost to make this country a land in which all have a chance and in which all have a duty, and there we must turn ourselves to fulfill our duty to our own countrymen, to our gallant allies the United States, who were so foully and treacherously attacked by Japan. We will go hand in hand with them, and even if it is a hard struggle we shall not be the ones who will fail.

"This is not the victory of a party or of any class or large section in the country; it is a victory of the great British nation as a whole.

"We were the first to draw the sword against tyranny. After a while we were left alone against the most tremendous military power that has been seen. We were all alone for a whole year.

"There we stood alone. Did anybody want to give in?"

The crowd roared back a terrific "No."

"Were we downhearted?" asked the Premier.

"No," came back the answer.

Mr. Churchill: "The lights went out——." There was a great burst of laughter at this, because the floodlighting of the balcony from which he was speaking had been turned off shortly before his appearance.

"And the bombs came down. But every man, woman, and child had no thought of quitting the struggle.

"London can take it. So we came back after long months from the jaws of death, out of the mouth of hell, while all the world wondered.

"I say that in the long years to come, not only the people of this island but of the world, wherever the bird of freedom chirps in human hearts, will look back to what we have done and they will say 'Do not despair. Do not yield to violence and tyranny, march straight forward and die—if need be—unconquered.' "[6]

From the White House President Harry S. Truman issued his official proclamation announcing the Allied victory:

The Allied armies, through sacrifice and devotion and with God's help, have won from Germany a final and unconditional surrender. The Western World has been freed of the evil forces which for five years and longer have imprisoned the bodies and broken the lives of millions upon millions of free-born men. They have violated their churches, destroyed their homes, corrupted their children and murdered their loved ones. Our armies of liberation have restored freedom to these suffering peoples, whose spirit and will the oppressors could never enslave.

Much remains to be done. The victory in the West must now be won in the East. . . . I do hereby appoint Sunday, May 13, to be a day of prayer. . . .

Done at the City of Washington this eighth day of May, in the Year of Our Lord 1945, and of the Independence of the United States of America the 169th.

The End in Japan

During the later months of 1944, the Japanese Army launched an offensive in southern China and captured Liuchow and several other advanced bases from which fliers of the Fourteenth U.S. Air Force had been raiding shipping and harassing ground troops. But this was a dying flurry, quickly countered by a Chinese offensive which began soon after the surrender of Germany.

By the summer of 1945, Japan was reeling. Tokyo was a charred wasteland where the skeletons of concrete buildings stood up as ghostly relics. Her chief industrial cities were in nearly as bad—and in some cases in worse—condition. The people of many remaining cities, including Hiroshima and Nagasaki, had been warned to evacuate or be obliterated along with the buildings for the series of fire raids by B-29s had mounted steadily since February in fury and intensity.

Admiral Halsey's Third Fleet cruised at will up and down the Japanese home islands; navy planes ranged over harbors sinking the remnants of the enemy's shipping and the few war vessels left afloat; they ripped up airfields and burned planes on the ground. B-29s had strewn the water with mines and blasted railways and roads; transportation to the islands and from place to place within them had almost ceased. The officers of the Japanese Cabinet, shuffled and reshuffled many times as the situation grew worse, trotted back and forth between the Imperial Palace and the Diet and gave forth cries of despairful defiance.

On the 17th of July, a British fleet moved up to join Admiral Halsey in a pitiless shelling of the Japanese coast. On the 22nd the first American troops from Europe reached the Philippines. And on the 26th the Allied leaders, meeting in Potsdam, gave the last warning.

The Potsdam Declaration, stripped to its essentials, reads as follows:

We—the President of the United States, the President of the National Government of the Republic of China, and the Prime Minister of Great Britain, representing the hundreds of millions of our countrymen—have conferred and agreed that Japan shall be given an opportunity to end this war. . . .

The time has come for Japan to decide whether she will continue to be controlled by those self-willed militaristic advisers whose unintelligent calculations have brought the empire of Japan to the threshold of annihilation, or whether she will follow the path of reason.

Following are our terms. We will not deviate from them. There are no alternatives. We shall brook no delay.

There must be eliminated for all time the authority and influence of those who have deceived and misled the people of Japan into embarking on a world conquest. We insist that a new order of peace, security and justice will be impossible until irresponsible militarism is driven from the world.

Until such a new order is established and until there is convincing proof that Japan's war-making power is destroyed, points in Japanese territory to be designated by the Allies shall be occupied to secure the achievement of the basic objectives we are here setting forth.

The terms of the Cairo declaration shall be carried out and Japanese sovereignty shall be limited to the islands of Honshu, Hokkaido, Kyushu, Shikoku and such minor islands as we determine.

The Japanese military forces, after being completely disarmed, shall be permitted to return to their homes with the opportunity to lead peaceful and productive lives.

We do not intend that the Japanese shall be enslaved as a race or destroyed as a nation, but stern justice shall be meted out to all war criminals, including those who have visited cruelties upon our prisoners. The Japanese Government shall remove all obstacles to the revival and strengthening of democratic tendencies among the Japanese people. Freedom of speech, of religion and of thought, as well as respect for the fundamental human rights, shall be established.

Japan shall be permitted to maintain such industries as will sustain her economy and permit the exaction of just reparations in kind, but not those which would enable her to rearm for war. To this end, access to, as distinguished from control of, raw materials shall be permitted. Eventual Japanese participation in world trade relations shall be permitted.

The occupying forces of the Allies shall be withdrawn from Japan as soon as these objectives have been accomplished and there has been established, in accordance with the freely expressed will of the Japanese people, a peacefully inclined and responsible Government.

We call upon the Government of Japan to proclaim now the unconditional surrender of all Japanese armed forces, and to provide proper and adequate assurances of their good faith in such action. The alternative for Japan is prompt and utter destruction.

Although the Japanese had already attempted peace overtures through Russia, they publicly announced that they would "ignore" the Potsdam Declaration. Therefore, on the 6th of August, a lone B-29 flew over Hiroshima, a city of 343,000 and dropped a small bomb packed with the destructive force of 20,000 tons of TNT.

From 1940 onward Nazi scientists in Germany and Norway, and Allied scientists working principally in the United States, had been engaged in a secret race to develop a weapon which would utilize man's newly-discovered ability to split atoms and turn loose the infinite energy locked in their cores. The Allies produced the weapon first. This was it. Hiroshima was instantly obscured by a great rolling cloud of dust and smoke. When it settled, sixty percent of the city was gone. To the stunned Japanese, President Truman gave a new surrender ultimatum. This, too, was ignored and on the 8th a second, improved, atomic bomb was released on Nagasaki. William E. Laurence, consultant to the War Department, went on the flight which dropped the bomb.

We flew southward down the channel and at 11:33 crossed the coastline and headed straight for Nagasaki about 100 miles to the west. Here again we circled until we found an opening in the clouds. It was 12:01 and the goal of our mission had arrived.

We heard the prearranged signal on our radio, put on our arc-welder's glasses and watched tensely the maneuverings of the strike ship about half a mile in front of us.

"There she goes!" someone said.

Out of the belly of *The Great Artiste* what looked like a black object went downward.

Captain Bock swung around to get out of range; but even though we were turning away in the opposite direction, and despite the fact that it was broad daylight in our cabin, all of us became aware of a giant flash that broke through the dark barrier of our arc-welder's lenses and flooded our cabin with intense light.

We removed our glasses after the first flash, but the light still lingered on, a bluish-green light that illuminated the entire sky all around. A tremendous blast wave struck our ship and made it tremble from nose to tail. This was followed by four more blasts in rapid succession, each resounding like the boom of cannon fire hitting our plane from all directions.

Observers in the tail of our ship saw a giant ball of fire rise as though from the bowels of the earth, belching forth enormous white smoke-rings. Next they saw a giant pillar of purple fire, 10,000 feet high, shooting skyward with enormous speed.

By the time our ship had made another turn in the direction of the atomic explosion, the pillar of purple fire had reached the level of our altitude. Only about forty-five seconds had passed. Awestruck, we watched it shoot upward like a meteor coming from the earth instead of from outer space, becoming ever more alive as it climbed skyward through the white clouds. It was no longer smoke, or dust, or even a cloud of fire. It was a living thing, a new species of being born before our incredulous eyes.

At one stage of its evolution, covering millions of years in terms of seconds, the entity assumed the form of a giant square totem pole, with its base about three miles long, tapering off to about a mile at the top. Its bottom was brown, its center was amber, its top white. But it was a living totem pole, carved with many grotesque masks grimacing at the earth.

Then, just when it appeared as if the thing had settled down into a state of permanence, there came shooting out of the top a giant mushroom that increased the height of the pillar to a total of 45,000 feet. The mushroom top was even more alive than the pillar, seething and boiling in a white fury of creamy foam, sizzling upward and then descending earthward, a thousand Old Faithful geysers rolled into one.

It kept struggling in an elemental fury, like a creature in the act of breaking the bonds that held it down. In a few seconds it had freed itself from its gigantic stem and floated upward with tremendous speed, its momentum carrying into the stratosphere to a height of about 60,000 feet.

But no sooner did this happen than another mushroom, smaller in size than the first one, began emerging out of the pillar. It was as though the decapitated monster were growing a new head.

As the first mushroom floated off into the blue, it changed its shape into a flower-like form, its giant petal curving downward, creamy white outside, rose-colored inside. It still retained that shape when we last gazed at it from a distance of about 200 miles.[7]

On the same day the armies of Russia, who had come into the war on August 8, drove hard across the Manchurian border of Japan's stolen empire. This blow Japan had greatly feared and now the impact was increased manyfold because it came on the heels of devastation such as the world had never known. Marcus Duffield, of the *New York Herald Tribune*, summarized the results at Hiroshima:

Although the fighting ended a month ago, Japanese still were dying from the effects of the atomic bomb; the Japanese estimate in Hiroshima was that about one hundred persons were dying every day. So far 126,000 persons had lost their lives from the bomb and 10,000 missing were presumed to be dead. There was little hope for thousands more of the wounded.

Physicians were baffled by the fact that persons with wounds which seemed trivial suddenly would sicken and die. The white corpuscles in their blood were consumed as though by a virulent infection. . . . American experts were on their way to study the bomb's effects.

American newspaper men who went to Hiroshima found the destruction incomparably greater than any they had seen in the worst-bombed cities of Europe. In places hit by ordinary bombs the shells of buildings remained. In Hiroshima an area at least three miles square was completely leveled except for an occasional reinforced concrete wall. Reporters could tell when they passed what used to be a block of small shops because office safes lay at regular intervals.

The 10,000 who had been killed in the original blast in Hiroshima never knew what hit them. The population had feared large-scale raids, but paid no attention to the lone B-29 that flew five miles above the city on that morning of Aug. 6. The bomb descended by parachute and exploded before it landed, so there was no crater.[8]

On August 10th President Truman told the enemy that more atomic bombs would be dropped unless surrender was immediate. The Japanese agreed to accept the Potsdam terms provided that the Emperor retained his sovereignty. To this the Allies consented, with the stipulation that he would submit to the authority of the Supreme Allied Commander in Japan, and that his future would depend on free election by the Japanese. On August 14th the Japanese announced the acceptance of these terms. The Emperor's messengers hurried to isolated armies scattered throughout Asia and the Pacific. Emissaries went out to arrange details of a bloodless occupation with Admiral Nimitz and General MacArthur. The most powerful fleet the world had ever known moved up into Tokyo Bay, and under a cloud of warplanes, paratroopers and Marines set foot upon the soil of Japan, which had known no invader in more than a thousand years. The surrender document was signed aboard the battleship *Missouri* on September 2nd.

On September 9th an American flag which had flown over the capitol in Washington when Pearl Harbor was bombed and which had subsequently waved over Algiers, Rome, and Berlin, was raised over Tokyo. Escorted by the Second Squadron, of a famous Cavalry Regiment which

fought under Custer on the Little Bighorn, General MacArthur proceeded
to the United States Embassy.

Standing alone before Lieut. Gen. Robert L. Eichelberger, commander
of the Eighth Army, which will garrison Tokyo, General MacArthur said:

"General Eichelberger, have our country's flag unfurled and in Tokyo's
sun let it wave in its full glory as a symbol of hope for the oppressed and
as a harbinger of victory for the right."[9]

And so the most devastating of all wars came to an end. It ended,
fittingly enough, in such a holocaust as made clear to every man and
woman that humanity could not survive another war. Civilized men everywhere had hoped that World War I would be the war to end all wars.
In this hope they were tragically disappointed. After twenty troubled years
evil and ambitious men had ventured once more to gain their ends through
violence and terror. They had almost succeeded. The details of their failure will intrigue students of strategy and tactics for generations to come.
But the fundamental reason for their failure is clear enough. They failed
because they repudiated human values and human faith, and from that
repudiation flowed all the consequences that led to final defeat. In the end
it was those who had faith in the virtues and dignity of man who tri-
umphed. Against wickedness and terror and hatred, the free peoples of
the world fought back. Their courage was a match for the force of the
enemy, their ingenuity for his cunning, their free industry for his slavery,
their faith for his cynicism.

These qualities, that brought victory in the end, were not exhausted by
the agony of war. The free peoples of the world emerged from that conflict strong in the consciousness that they had fought the good fight, fought
it as decently as any war can be fought, fought it for ends that were not
ignoble. Victory brought not exultation, but a recollection of the objective
which that great architect of victory, Franklin Roosevelt, had proclaimed:

The true goal we seek is far above and beyond the ugly field of battle.
When we resort to force, as now we must, we are determined that this
force shall be directed toward ultimate good as well as against immediate
evil.

Now the necessity of maintaining a lasting peace was inescapably clear.
The nature of that peace, too, had been stated by President Roosevelt:

Today we seek a moral basis for peace. It cannot be a real peace if it fails
to recognize brotherhood. It cannot be a lasting peace if the fruit of it is
oppression or starvation, or cruelty, or human life dominated by armed
camps. It cannot be a sound peace if small nations must live in fear of

powerful neighbors. It cannot be a moral peace if freedom from invasion is sold for tribute. It cannot be an intelligent peace if it denies free passage to that knowledge of those ideals which permit men to find common ground. It cannot be a righteous peace if worship of God is denied.

It is for this generation to make sure that a moral peace, a lasting peace, and a righteous peace is achieved.

Acknowledgments and References

Chapter 1

1. Chapter 1 is based on *The Growth of the American Republic* (Vol. 2) by S. E. Morison and H. S. Commager, Oxford University Press, New York 1942.

Chapter 2

1. Grove Haines and Ross Hoffman, *Origins and Background of the Second World War.* Oxford University Press, New York 1943.

2. Otto D. Tolischus, *They Wanted War.* Reynal and Hitchcock, New York 1940.

3. Kazimierz Wierzynski, *The Forgotten Battlefield.* Roy Publishers, New York 1944.

4. Virginia Cowles, *Looking for Trouble.* Harper & Brothers, New York 1941.

5. Strategicus, *The War for World Power.* Faber and Faber Ltd., London 1940.

6. Edmond Taylor, *The Strategy of Terror* (1942 revised ed.). Houghton Mifflin Co., Boston 1940, and Ann Watkins, Inc.

7. William L. Shirer, *Berlin Diary.* Alfred A. Knopf, New York 1941.

8. A. D. Divine, *Navies in Exile.* E. P. Dutton & Co., New York 1944, and Ann Watkins, Inc.

9. Theodore Draper, *The Six Weeks' War.* Viking, New York 1944.

10. Theodore Draper, *The Six Weeks' War.* Viking, New York 1944.

11. A. D. Divine, "Miracle at Dunkirk," *Reader's Digest* Dec. 1940. Copyright, The Reader's Digest Association, Inc., Pleasantville 1940.

12. Herbert L. Matthews, *The Fruits of Fascism.* Harcourt, Brace and Co., New York 1943.

13. Virginia Cowles, *Looking for Trouble.* Harper & Bros., New York 1941.

14. William L. Shirer, *Berlin Diary.* Alfred A. Knopf, New York 1941.

Chapter 3

1. Winston S. Churchill, *Blood, Sweat, and Tears.* G. P. Putnam's Sons, New York 1941.

2. Winston S. Churchill, *Blood, Sweat, and Tears.* G. P. Putnam's Sons, New York 1941.

3. *The Battle of Britain.* His Majesty's Stationery Office, London 1941.

4. Allan A. Michie and Walter Graebner, *Their Finest Hour.* Harcourt, Brace and Co., New York 1941.

5. *The Battle of Britain.* H. M. S. O., London 1941.

6. Ernie Pyle, *Ernie Pyle in England.* Robert M. McBride & Co., New York 1941.

7. Winston S. Churchill, *Blood, Sweat, and Tears.* G. P. Putnam's Sons, New York 1941.

8. Mollie Panter-Downes, *Letter from England.* Little, Brown & Co. and Atlantic Monthly Press, Boston 1940, and Ann Watkins, Inc.

9. F. Tennyson Jesse, *The Saga of San Demetrio.* H. M. S. O., London 1942.

10. C. S. Forester, "How the British Sank the *Scharnhorst,*"*Reader's Digest* May 1944. Copyright, The Curtis Publishing Co., Philadelphia 1944 (*The Saturday Evening Post,* March 25, 1944). Harold Matson.

11. *His Majesty's Minesweepers.* H. M. S. O., London 1943.

12. Cmdr. Griffith B. Coale, *North Atlantic Patrol.* Farrar & Rinehart, New York 1942.

13. Winston S. Churchill, *Blood, Sweat, and Tears.* G. P. Putnam's Sons, New York 1941.

14. Edward Stettinius, *Lend-Lease, Weapon for Victory.* The Macmillan Co., New York 1944.

Chapter 4

1. Winston S. Churchill, *Blood, Sweat, and Tears.* G. P. Putnam's Sons, New York 1941.

2. Bartimeus, *East of Malta, West of Suez.* Little, Brown & Co. and Atlantic Monthly Press, Boston 1944.

3. *The Abyssinian Campaigns.* H. M. S. O., London 1942.

4. Robert St. John, *The Land of the Silent People.* Doubleday, Doran & Co., New York 1942.

5. Robert St. John, *The Land of the Silent People.* Doubleday, Doran & Co., New York 1942.

6. Donald Cowie, *The Campaigns of Wavell.* Chapman & Hall Ltd., London 1942, and Donald Cowie.

7. Alexander G. Clifford, *The Conquest of North Africa: 1940–1943.* Little, Brown & Co., Boston 1943.

8. Alexander G. Clifford, *The Conquest of North Africa: 1940–1943.* Little, Brown & Co., Boston 1943.

9. John Gunther, *D Day.* Harper & Bros., New York 1944.

10. Alan Moorehead, *The End in Africa.* Harper & Bros., New York 1943.

11. Philip Guedalla, *Middle East, 1940–1942.* Hodder and Stoughton Ltd., and A. P. Watt, London 1944.

12. Alexander G. Clifford, *The Conquest of North Africa: 1940–1943.* Little, Brown & Co., Boston 1943.

Chapter 5

1. Grove Haines and Ross Hoffman, *Origins and Background of the Second World War.* Oxford University Press, New York 1943.

2. Frederick C. Oechsner, *This Is the Enemy.* Little, Brown & Co., Boston 1942.

3. Frederick C. Oechsner, "Bloodiest Front in History," *The Saturday Evening Post* September 19, 1942. Copyright, The Curtis Publishing Co., Philadelphia 1942.

4. Colonel G. N. Filonov, "Escape from Encirclement," *Infantry Journal*, Dec. 1942. Copyright, Infantry Journal, Inc., Washington 1942.

5. C. L. Sulzberger, "The Russian Battlefront." *Reader's Digest* Sept. 1942. Copyright, Time, Inc., New York 1942 (*Life*, July 20, 1942).

6. Henry C. Cassidy, *Moscow Dateline*. Houghton Mifflin Co., Boston 1943.

7. Walter Kerr, *The Russian Army*. Alfred A. Knopf, New York 1944.

8. Frederick C. Oechsner, *This Is the Enemy*. Little, Brown & Co., Boston 1942.

9. Hugo Speck, "The Scorched Earth," *Collier's* Dec. 6, 1941. Copyright, Crowell-Collier Publishing Co., New York 1941, and King Features Syndicate, Inc.

10. "Batya," *Soviet War News Weekly* Aug. 20, 1942.

11. Harrison Salisbury, "Russia Beckons Big Business," *Collier's* Sept. 2, 1944. Copyright, Crowell-Collier Publishing Co., New York 1944.

12. William Mandel, "Leningrad Under Siege," *Soviet Russia Today* Feb. 1943, and Mary Leonard Pritchett.

13. Alexander Werth, *Moscow War Diary*. Alfred A. Knopf, New York 1942.

14. Boris Voyetekhov, "Last Days of Sevastopol," *Reader's Digest* Aug. 1943 (Copyright Alfred A. Knopf, New York 1943).

15. Major Velichko, "The 62nd Army," *Soviet War News Weekly* Feb. 11, 1943.

16. Edgar Snow, *People on Our Side*. Random House, New York 1944.

17. Albert Parry, *Russian Cavalcade*. Ives Washburn, New York 1944.

Chapter 6

1. Gordon Carroll, ed., *History in the Writing*. Duell, Sloan and Pearce, New York 1945.

2. Forrest Davis and Ernest K. Lindley, *How War Came*. Simon and Schuster, New York 1942.

3. O. D. Gallagher, *Action in the East*. Doubleday, Doran and Co., New York 1942.

4. Winston S. Churchill, *The Unrelenting Struggle*. Little, Brown & Co., Boston 1942.

5. Frazier Hunt, *MacArthur and the War Against Japan*. Charles Scribner's Sons, New York 1944.

6. John Hersey, *Men on Bataan*. Alfred A. Knopf, New York 1942.

7. Gilbert Cant, *America's Navy in World War II* (revised ed.). The John Day Co., New York 1943.

8. Winston S. Churchill, *The End of the Beginning*. Little, Brown and Co., Boston 1943.

9. Fletcher Pratt, *The Navy's War*. Harper and Bros. New York 1944.

10. Gilbert Cant, *America's Navy in World War II* (revised ed.). The John Day Co., New York 1943.

11. Gilbert Cant, *America's Navy in World War II* (revised ed.). The John Day Co., New York 1943.

12. Fletcher Pratt, *The Navy's War*. Harper & Bros., New York 1944.

13. Robert B. Hotz, *With General Chennault*. Coward-McCann, New York 1943.

14. Jack Belden, *Retreat with Stilwell*. Alfred A. Knopf, New York 1943.

Chapter 7

1. Stephen Spender, "I Think Continually of Those Who Were Truly Great," *Ruins and Visions*. Random House, New York 1942.

2. Hilton H. Railey (Stevens Rayleigh), "Wasps of War," *The Saturday Evening Post* Ap. 25, 1942. Copyright, The Curtis Publishing Co., Philadelphia 1942, and Willis K. Wing.

3. Xavier Pruszynski, *Poland Fights Back*. Roy Publishers, New York 1944.

4. Walter Taub, "Norway Out from Under," *Collier's* July 14, 1945. Copyright, Crowell-Collier Publishing Co., New York 1945, and Mark Hanna.

5. John Kobler, "Needle in the Nazis," *The Saturday Evening Post* Jan 16, 1943. Copyright, The Curtis Publishing Co., Philadelphia 1943, and Curtis Brown, Ltd.

6. André Girard (as told to George Kent), "The French Underground Fights," *Reader's Digest* May 1944. Copyright, Tricolor, New York 1944 (*Tricolor* May 1944).

7. J. Kessel, "Patriot's Notebook," *The Nation* Jan. 22, 1944. Copyright, The Nation, New York 1944.

8. C. L. Sulzberger, *The New York Times* Dec. 21, 1943.

Chapter 8

1. Daedalus, "The Role of the Luftwaffe in 1943," *Infantry Journal* Aug. 1943. Copyright, Infantry Journal, Inc., Washington 1943.

2. W. B. Courtney, "Air Power—Today and Tomorrow," *Collier's* Sept. 15, 1945. Copyright, Crowell-Collier Publishing Co., New York 1945.

3. W. B. Courtney, "Air Power—Today and Tomorrow," *Collier's* Sept. 15 1945. Copyright, Crowell-Collier Publishing Co., New York 1945.

4. Hector Hawton, *Night Bombing*. Thomas Nelson & Sons, London 1944.

5. Hector Hawton, *Night Bombing*. Thomas Nelson & Sons, London 1944.

6. "Air War Over Europe," British Information Service, 1944.

7. Captain Don Gentile, as told to Ira Wolfert, *One-Man Air Force*. L. B. Fischer, New York 1944.

8. Allan A. Michie, "Germany Was Bombed to Defeat," *Reader's Digest* Aug. 1945. Copyright Henry Publishing Co., New York 1945. (*Skyways*, Aug. 1945).

Chapter 9

1. Edgar McInnis, *The War: Fourth Year*. Oxford University Press, New York 1944.

2. Winston S. Churchill, *Onwards to Victory*. Little, Brown & Co., Boston 1944.

3. John Steinbeck, "It Was Dark as Hell," *The New York Herald-Tribune* Oct. 4, 1943, and McIntosh & Otis.

4. Herbert L. Matthews, *The New York Times* Oct 12, 1943.

5. Herbert L. Matthews, "Road to Mud, Fatigue—and Glory," *The New York Times* Dec. 26, 1943.

6. Ernie Pyle, *Brave Men*. Henry Holt, New York 1944. Pp. 97–100.

7. Ernie Pyle, *Brave Men*. Henry Holt, New York 1944. Pp. 159–162.

8. W. F. Shadel, "Street Fighting in Cassino, *Infantry Journal* June 1944. Copyright, Infantry Journal, Inc., Washington 1944.

9. Eric Sevareid, "Velletri," *The American Legion Magazine* Oct. 1944. Copyright, The American Legion, New York 1944, and Harold Matson.

10. Martha Gellhorn, "Cracking the Gothic Line," *Collier's* Oct. 28, 1944. Copyright, Crowell-Collier Publishing Co., New York 1944.

11. *The New York Times*, Review of the Week, Oct. 8, 1944.

Chapter 10

1. Wendell L. Willkie, *One World*. Simon and Schuster, New York 1943.

2. Lt. Col. Paul W. Thompson, "The Portrait of the Red Soldier," *Infantry Journal* June 1943. Copyright, Infantry Journal, Inc., Washington 1943.

3. Robert Carse, *There Go the Ships*. William Morrow & Co., New York 1942.

4. Joel Sayre, "Persian Gulf Command," *The New Yorker* Jan. 13, 1945. Copyright, F-R Publishing Corp., New York 1945.

5. Alexander Poliakov, *White Mammoths*. E. P. Dutton, New York 1943.

6. *Orel*. Foreign Languages Publishing House, Moscow 1943.

7. Philip Graves, *The Sixteenth Quarter*. Hutchinson & Co., London 1943.

8. Pyotr Pavlenko, "Cossacks of the Kuban," *Soviet War News Weekly* Sept. 23, 1943.

9. "Battle Beyond the Arctic Circle," *Soviet War News Weekly* Oct. 19, 1944.

10. "Smoking out the Koenigsberg Rats," *Soviet War News Weekly* Feb. 15, 1945.

Chapter 11

1. Winston S. Churchill, *The Dawn of Liberation*. Little, Brown & Co., Boston 1945.

2. Everett Hollis, *Unconditional Surrender*. Howell-Soskin, New York 1945.

3. C. S. Forester, "History's Biggest Gamble," *The Saturday Evening Post* Aug. 12, 1944. Copyright, The Curtis Publishing Co., Philadelphia 1944, and Harold Matson.

4. Charles C. Wertenbaker, *Invasion*. Appleton-Century Co., New York 1944.

5. Ernie Pyle, *Brave Men*. Henry Holt, New York 1944. P. 302 f.

6. W. W. Chaplin, *The Fifty-Two Days*. Bobbs-Merrill, Indianapolis 1944.

7. "The Flying Bomb," British Information Services, Nov. 1944.

8. Ernie Pyle, *Brave Men*. Henry Holt, New York 1944. P. 295 f.

9. Everett Hollis, *Unconditional Surrender*. Howell-Soskin, New York 1945.

10. Everett Hollis, *Unconditional Surrender*. Howell-Soskin, New York 1945.

11. *From D-Day Through Victory in Europe*. Columbia Broadcasting System, New York 1945.

12. Raymond Daniell, *The New York Times* Aug. 27, 1944.

13. Everett Hollis, *Unconditional Surrender*. Howell-Soskin, New York 1945.

14. Collie Small, "Bastogne: American Epic," *The Saturday Evening Post* Feb. 17, 1945. Copyright, The Curtis Publishing Co., Philadelphia 1945.

15. Everett Hollis, *Unconditional Surrender*. Howell-Soskin, New York 1945.

16. Douglas B. Cornell, "The Burial," Associated Press, New York 1945.

17. "The Service at St. Paul's," *The Times* (London), Ap. 20, 1945.

18. Walter Lippmann, "Roosevelt is Gone," *The New York Herald-Tribune* 1945.

Chapter 12

1. Ira Wolfert, *Battle for the Solomons.* Houghton Mifflin Co., Boston 1943.

2. Gen. A. A. Vandegrift, "Guadalcanal to the Shores of Japan," *The New York Times* August 5, 1945.

3. Gilbert Cant, *America's Navy in World War II* (revised ed.). The John Day Co., New York 1943.

4. Howard Handleman, *Bridge to Victory.* Random House, New York 1943.

5. George H. Johnston, *The Toughest Fighting in the World.* Duell, Sloan and Pearce, New York 1943.

6. Pat Robinson, *The Fight for New Guinea.* Random House, New York 1943.

7. Paul W. Kearney and Blake Clark, " 'Pete' Mitscher, Boss of Task Force 58," *Reader's Digest* July 1945. Copyright, The American Legion, New York 1945 (*The American Legion Magazine* July 1945).

8. U. S. Marine Corps Correspondents, *Betio Beachhead.* G. P. Putnam's Sons, New York 1945.

9. U. S. Marine Corps Correspondents, *Betio Beachhead.* G. P. Putnam's Sons, New York 1945.

10. Lt. Oliver Jensen, *Carrier War.* Pocket Books, Inc., New York 1945.

11. Royal Arch Gunnison, "Close Call at Leyte," *Collier's* Dec. 9, 1944. Copyright, Crowell-Collier Publishing Co., New York 1944, and Gertrude Algase.

12. *The New York Times,* Review of the Week, Feb. 11, 1945.

13. *The New York Times,* Review of the Week, Apr. 8, 1945.

14. John P. Marquand, "Iwo Jima Before H-Hour," *Harper's Magazine* May 1945. Copyright, Harper & Bros., New York 1945, and Brandt and Brandt.

15. U. S. Marine Corps Correspondents, "Iwo: Red-hot Rock," *Collier's* April 4, 1945. Copyright, Crowell-Collier Publishing Co., New York 1945.

16. John Lardner and William Hipple, "This Is Iwo," *Newsweek* March 5, 1945. Copyright, Weekly Publications, Inc., New York 1945.

17. *The New York Times,* Review of the Week, Apr. 8, 1945.

18. Hanson W. Baldwin, *The New York Times* Aug. 12, 1945.

19. Stanley Woodward, *The New York Herald Tribune* Aug. 28, 1945.

20. Charles J. Rolo, "Wingate's Circus," *Reader's Digest* Oct. 1943. Copyright, The Atlantic Monthly Co., Boston 1943 (*The Atlantic Monthly,* Oct. 1943).

21. *Victory in Burma,* British Information Services, July 1945.

22. *Victory in Burma.* British Information Services, July 1945.

23. Captain Ted W. Lawson, *Thirty Seconds Over Tokyo.* Random House, New York 1943.

24. W. H. Lawrence, *The New York Times* Aug. 18, 1945.

25. Robert Casey, *Battle Below.* Bobbs-Merrill, Indianapolis, 1945.

Chapter 13

1. Winston Burdett (report from Rome), *From D-Day Through Victory in Europe.* Columbia Broadcasting System, New York 1945.

2. V. Vishnevsky and I. Zolin, "Stalingrad Banners on Berlin Hills," *Soviet War News* Apr. 26, 1945.

3. Roman Karmen, *Soviet War News* Apr. 26, 1945.

4. Richard C. Hottelet (report from First Army headquarters), *From D-Day Through Victory in Europe*. Columbia Broadcasting System, New York 1945.

5. *The Times* (London), May 7, 1945.

6. Winston S. Churchill, *The Manchester Guardian Weekly* May 8, 1945.

7. *The New York Times*, Sept. 9, 1945.

8. Marcus Duffield, *The New York Herald Tribune* Sept. 9, 1945.

9. *The New York Times*, Sept. 8, 1945.

Index of Authors

Index of Books and Articles